Rulemaking

Rulemaking

HOW GOVERNMENT AGENCIES
WRITE LAW AND MAKE POLICY

Cornelius M. Kerwin
The American University

PRESS

A Division of Congressional Quarterly Inc.
Washington, D.C.

Printed in the United States of America

Cover design: Ben Santora, New York, New York

Second Printing

Library of Congress Cataloging-in-Publication Data

Kerwin, C. M. (Cornelius M.)
  Rulemaking : how government agencies write law and make policy / Cornelius M. Kerwin.
    p. cm.
    Includes index.
    ISBN 0-87187-993-X (cloth) -- ISBN 0-87187-673-6 (pbk.)
    1. Administrative procedure -- United States.   2. Administrative regula-
tion drafting -- United States.   I. Title
KF5411.K47   1994
342.73′066 -- dc20   93-46944
[347.30266]   CIP

To Ann Kerwin and Mary Kerwin
women I love and admire

and

to Michael Kerwin, Alex Kerwin, and Paul Kerwin
men I love and admire.

Contents

Tables and Figures   *ix*

Preface   *xi*

Chapter 1 THE SUBSTANCE OF RULES AND THE
             REASONS FOR RULEMAKING   1

   The Definition of Rulemaking   3
   The History of Rulemaking   7
   Categories of Rules   20
   The Reasons for Rulemaking: What It Has to Offer   27

Chapter 2 THE PROCESS OF RULEMAKING   39

   Process and Substance   43
   The Core Elements of Rulemaking:
     Information, Participation, Accountability   52
   Information: Increased Legal Requirements   57
   Participation: Expanded Opportunities
     Mandated by Law   65
   Mechanisms of Accountability   70
   How the APA Model Has Changed   71
   Exceptions, Exemptions, and Evasions   72
   The Stages of Rulemaking   75

Chapter 3 ISSUES AND CONTRADICTIONS   89

   The Volume of Rulemaking   90
   Quality in Rulemaking   96
   Timeliness   105

Participation   114
Bureaucratic Discretion   117
Inseparable Issues   117

Chapter 4 THE MANAGEMENT OF RULEMAKING   121

Presidential Management   122
Management on the Agency Level   127
Managing Individual Rules   146

Chapter 5 PARTICIPATION IN RULEMAKING   161

The Purposes of Participation   162
The Origins and History of Participation   163
Actual Patterns of Participation   191
Does Participation Matter?   205

Chapter 6 OVERSIGHT OF RULEMAKING   215

Accountability and the Congress   216
Accountability to the President   229
Accountability to the Courts   250

Chapter 7 RULEMAKING: THEORIES AND REFORM
             PROPOSALS   271

The Value of Theory   271
The Elements of Rulemaking Theory   272
The Reform of Rulemaking   293

Appendix A Titles and Chapters in the *Code
            of Federal Regulations*   299

Appendix B Agency Documents Consulted   303

Appendix C Agencies Surveyed   305

Appendix D Questions Asked in Survey of Agencies   307

Index   309

Tables and Figures

TABLES

1-1   Final Rule Documents Published in the *Federal Register,*
1982-1989   18

1-2   *Code of Federal Regulations* Page Count by Selected Title
and Year   19

2-1   An Outline of Rulemaking Activity   76

5-1   Number of Rules, Rules with Notices, and Rules with
Comments, January-June 1991   193

5-2   Comparative Importance to Interest Groups of
Involvement in Rulemaking   194

5-3   Interest Groups Reporting Participation in Rulemaking
Activities, by Type of Organization   196

5-4   Budget and Staff Time Dedicated to Rulemaking,
by Type of Organization   197

5-5   Concerns of Interest Groups When Participating in a
Rulemaking, by Frequency Reported   198

5-6   Devices Employed by Interest Groups to Monitor
Rulemaking, by Frequency of Use   201

5-7   Devices Employed by Interest Groups to Influence
Rules, by Frequency of Use   202

5-8   Ratings by Interest Groups of the Effectiveness of
Techniques   203

5-9   Agency-Initiated Contacts Reported by Interest Groups,
by Frequency   204

5-10   Reasons Given by Interest Groups for Contact by
Agency, by Frequency of Reason   205

5-11   Success in Influencing Rulemaking Reported by
Interest Groups   209

5-12   Frequency of Changes by Agencies to Rulemakings
        Based on Participation by Interest Groups, by Type
        of Organization   210
6-1   Frequency of Use of Oversight Techniques, Ninety-fifth
        Congress   223
6-2   Effectiveness of Oversight Techniques, Ninety-fifth
        Congress   224
6-3   Legislative Vetoes Passed by Congress, by Decade   226
6-4   Extent of the Legislative Veto, 1983   227
6-5   Types of Actions Taken by the OMB on Agency Rules
        during 1988   232
6-6   Types of Actions Taken by the OMB on Agency Rules
        during 1988, by Percentage   234
6-7   Types of Actions Taken by the OMB on Agency Rules
        during 1989   235
6-8   Types of Actions Taken by the OMB on Agency Rules
        during 1989, by Percentage   237
6-9   Types of Actions Taken by the OMB on Agency Rules,
        1981-1989   238
6-10   Regulations Returned to Agencies by the OMB for
        Reconsideration during 1989   240
6-11   Average Review Time by the OMB of Rules under
        Executive Order 12291   243

FIGURES

1-1   Comparison of Rules Reviewed during 1981-1989   17
2-1   Sample of the Hazardous Materials Regulations in
        the *Federal Register*   41
4-1   Abbreviated Sample Schedule of the Rulemaking
        Process at the Federal Aviation Administration   134
6-1   Oversight Days and Pages in the *Federal Register*,
        1961-1983   225

Preface

Rulemaking is the single most important function performed by agencies of government. Some readers may find this a surprising, if not outrageous, assertion. But consider the breadth and depth of influence that rulemaking has on our lives.

Rulemaking refines, and in some instances defines, the mission of every government agency. In so doing it provides direction and content for budgeting, program implementation, procurement, personnel management, dispute resolution, and other important government activities. Rules provide specific, authoritative statements of the obligations the government has assumed and the benefits it must provide. It is to rules, not statutes or other containers of the law, that we turn most often for an understanding of what is expected of us and what we can expect from government. As a result, intense political activity surrounds the contemporary rulemaking process, and effective political action in America is no longer possible without serious attention to rulemaking.

The centrality of rulemaking in our public policy system has placed it under considerable stress. The demand for rules created by hundreds of new government programs and the intense scrutiny of the process by which they are developed gives rise to persistent questions from the business and academic communities about the quantity of rules, their quality, and the time it takes to write them. Whether the problems the questions address are real or perceived, the questions themselves raise doubts in the public's mind about the ability of rulemaking to play its vital role. These doubts—and the failures they sometimes reflect—often reduce the effectiveness of public programs and reverberate throughout the political system.

This book is the first general text on rulemaking intended for students and practitioners of public administration, political science, and public policy. In an effort to give the reader a broad understanding of this crucial government function, I have included elements of rulemaking that have not previously been treated together in a single source. Familiar topics, such as basic rulemaking procedure and judicial consideration of rules, are reviewed, but also considered are the history of rulemaking, public participation in the development of rules, the management of rulemaking, and the constant struggle between the White House, Congress, and the courts for control of rulemaking. The problems that beset rulemaking, and the prospects for solving them, are given extensive attention.

It is important that the academic and practitioner communities consider rulemaking a discrete government function worthy of their focused, energetic attention. Practitioners may be considerably ahead of their academic counterparts in this regard. Various handbooks and encyclopedias of public administration and management published during the past decade give scant attention to rulemaking. Invariably, it is subsumed in a section devoted to administrative law, legal issues, or regulation. It is time for social scientists to match the effort and insights of legal scholars and to advance an understanding of other critical elements of rulemaking. Such research will contribute to the work of rulemaking practitioners. This book is a small step toward that larger goal.

Although this book is distinctive in the breadth and mix of issues considered, it is hardly unique in its focus on the general topic. James O'Reilly's *Administrative Rulemaking* and Arthur Bonfield's *State Administrative Rule Making* are legal treatises on rulemaking. Virtually every text on administrative law includes a chapter or section devoted to rulemaking. In *Bureaucratic Discretion*, Gary Bryner examines rulemaking in many agencies to determine the extent of freedom agency officials enjoy when making policy decisions. Wesley Magat and his colleagues stand virtually alone in their attempt in *Rules in the Making* to apply rigorous empirical analysis to explain the outcomes of rulemaking in a single regulatory program. In his classic *Smoking and Politics*, Lee Fritschler uses rulemaking to explore the dynamics of subsystem politics. William West, in *Administrative Rulemaking: Politics and Processes*, examines the topic in the context of the Federal Trade Commission. In *Setting Safety Standards*, Ross Cheit explores the differences between public institutions and private organizations in establishing a certain type of rule. I have drawn on the findings and considerable wisdom contained in each of these books.

I would like to thank many people for their help on this project. My colleagues in the School of Public Affairs have been enormously helpful and patient, discussing various elements of this book at much greater length than I am sure they would have preferred. Laura

Langbein, Bernard Ross, David Rosenbloom, David Koehler, Murray Comarow, and James Thurber absorbed the bulk of my queries and pleas for advice. Student research assistants provided invaluable help and ideas. I am especially obligated to Scott Furlong, now on the faculty of the University of Wisconsin at Green Bay; John Visser, who now works at the National Aeronautics and Space Administration; and Joe Williams and Adrienne Woodward, my talented undergraduate research assistants. My administrative assistant, Cynthia Lindstrom, demonstrated uncommon grace, tact, and forbearance during the seemingly endless stream of drafts and revisions.

Colleagues at other institutions helped as well. I am especially indebted to Phillip Cooper, at the University of Kansas, Rosemary O'Leary at Syracuse University, and Gary Bryner at Brigham Young University, who reviewed the draft manuscript for CQ Press. Their extensive comments, insights, and suggestions improved the book greatly. I would be remiss if I did not thank Brenda Carter of CQ Press. She acquired the manuscript and encouraged me throughout the writing process. Finally, Joanne S. Ainsworth did a skillful job editing the manuscript, enhancing the presentation without damaging the meaning.

I would dearly love to blame the remaining mistakes, lapses in judgment, and shortcomings on some or all of those listed above. Fortunately, the unwritten code for authors prevents me from acting on my worst instincts. Any remaining errors are all mine.

Cornelius M. Kerwin
Washington, D.C.

CHAPTER 1

The Substance of Rules and the Reasons for Rulemaking

On June 13, 1990, the *Washington Post* carried a story about the effect of the proposed Clean Air Act on small businesses. The article was about dry cleaners who use a chemical called perchloroethylene, or "perc," which is suspected of being a carcinogen. Perc is one of nearly two hundred chemicals whose emissions were to be controlled under the provisions of the bill then under consideration by Congress. Of particular concern to the dry cleaning establishments, one of the few "mom and pop" businesses left in the United States, was the type of equipment owners would have to install in order to meet new legal restrictions on perchloroethylene.

By the time the *Post* article was published, the new Clean Air Act had been in the making for thirteen years. Numerous congressional committees had labored long and hard to hammer out provisions in what promised to be the most broad-ranging and detailed environmental statutes ever written. Yet, despite all this effort, operators of dry cleaning establishments could not get the information they needed to make a sound business decision from the legislation. Whether what was commonly in use in most shops—filters and protective equipment— would be adequate or new, higher technology dry cleaning machines, costing more than $50,000 per unit, would be required could not be determined from the language of the new law. Rather, as the article stated:

> In fact, neither the environmentalists nor the business advocates know what the Clean Air Act will cost small businesses. . . . *The final emissions guidelines that will affect small businesses will not be written by the Environmental Protection Agency until after the bill becomes law.* (Emphasis added.)

No piece of legislation in recent memory, save perhaps our annual budget ordeals, occupied more of Congress's attention than the revision of the Clean Air Act. Still, with all this time and talent dedicated to the alteration of a single statute, those affected by its provisions were unable to plan for or predict the impact of the new statute until rulemaking specified what their prerogatives and obligations would be. When Congress finished its work with the Clean Air Act of 1990 the work of the Environmental Protection Agency (EPA) had just begun. Every major provision of the act required subsequent rules to clarify and refine it. By its own count the new legislation needed, at minimum, several hundred new regulations before the statutory provisions could become operational. Some would not be written for several years. The number of rules and level of effort were remarkable, but the basic process at work here is not exceptional.

Reliance on rulemaking to provide the essential details of our law is commonplace and has been for some time. It is instructive that the Clean Air Act of 1990 followed the same model of the original Clean Air Act of 1970. At the time of its passage the 1970 law was also commonly described as the most complex regulatory statute ever devised. But with all its complexity and technical detail it could not be implemented as written. It too required massive amounts of subsequent rulemaking to establish the working details of what became a singularly important regulatory program. During the twenty years between these two landmarks in environmental law, much was learned of the threats posed by air pollution. Still, we depended on rulemaking to transform the promises of an ambitious new statute into the specific requirements and procedures of ˜new programs to clean the air.

Our experience in pursuit of cleaner air is but one example of a much broader and profoundly important development in our contemporary political system. Rulemaking is a ubiquitous presence in virtually all governmental programs. For a variety of reasons Congress is unwilling or unable to write laws specific enough to be implemented by government agencies and complied with by private citizens. Between Congress and the people it represents and the goals we seek to achieve when a law is written stands a crucial intermediate process. We have come to rely on rulemaking to an increasing degree to define the substance of public programs. It determines, to a very large extent, the specific legal obligations we bear as a society. Rulemaking gives specific form to the benefits we enjoy under a wide range of statutes. In the process it fixes the actual costs we incur to meet the ambitious objectives of our many public programs.

Rulemaking is important for many reasons. The best place to begin a discussion of these reasons is with a definition of rulemaking and an explanation of why it is crucial to our system of government.

THE DEFINITION OF RULEMAKING

Colin Diver, the dean of the University of Pennsylvania Law School and one of the most thoughtful observers of rules and rulemaking, has stated, in a paraphrase of the great jurist Oliver Wendell Holmes, that a "rule is the skin of a living policy . . . it hardens an inchoate normative judgement into the frozen form of words. . . . Its issuance marks the transformation of policy from the private wish to public expectation. . . . the framing of a rule is the climactic act of the policy making process." [1] This definition underscores the pivotal role that rules play in our system of government, but more light must be shed on their key characteristics.

Nearly fifty years after its enactment into law, the best definition of the term *rule* can still be found in the Administrative Procedure Act of 1946 (referred to henceforth as the APA). The act was written by Congress to bring regularity and predictability to the decision-making processes of government agencies, which by the mid-1940s were already having a profound influence on life in this country. Rules and rulemaking were already important parts of the administrative process in 1946. Both, however, required careful definition so that the procedural requirements established in the act would be applied to the types of actions Congress intended to affect.

The APA states: "rule means the whole or part of an agency statement of general or particular applicability and future effect designed to implement, interpret, or prescribe law or policy." [2] At first reading this statement does not appear to reveal much. On closer examination, however, it is a definition with several elements, each crucial to understanding contemporary rulemaking. Not the first element mentioned but a good place to start is a single word— agency—because it identifies the source of rules.

THE SOURCE OF RULES: AGENCIES

We learn first from this definition that rules do not come from the major institutions created by the Constitution. They are not products of Congress, or some other legislature. Rules are by-products of the deliberations and votes of our elected representatives, but they are not themselves legislation. Congress does have its own institutional rules, but they apply only to its members and committees. Under the APA definition, rules do not originate with the president, or some other chief executive. As we will see subsequently, the actions of the president of the United States and chief executives at the various levels of government certainly have a profound effect on the rulemaking process. These people do employ executive orders and directives of various sorts in the course of their management responsibilities, but rarely, if ever, do they write rules of the type considered in this book.[3]

Various and sundry courts may have reason to consider rules. Their actions may result in rules being changed or eliminated. But judges do not write rules in the first instance either, except, like Congress, to establish procedures for their colleagues and the operation of the courts over which they preside.

Rules are products of the bureaucratic institutions to which we entrust the implementation, management, and administration of our law and public policy. We usually view bureaucracies as inferior in status to the "constitutional" branches of government—Congress, the president, and the judiciary. We do so because the authority of these agencies is derivative, patterned after and drawn from the three main branches. In one important respect, however, agencies are the equal of these institutions. The rules issued by departments, agencies, or commissions are law; they carry the same weight as congressional legislation, presidential executive orders, and judicial decisions. An important and controversial feature of our system of government is that bureaucratic institutions are vested with all three governmental powers established in the Constitution. Through a device called delegation of authority government agencies perform legislative, executive, and judicial functions. Rulemaking occurs when agencies use the legislative authority granted them by Congress.

It is significant that agencies are the sources of rules, because it means rulemaking is subjected to the external and internal influences that have been found to affect decision making in our public bureaucracies. Agencies behave differently from the constitutional branches of government. Their decisions cannot be explained simply by reference to the admittedly strong pressures they continually feel from Congress, the White House, the courts, interest groups, and the public at large. As one group of scholars put it, "Public agencies are major political actors in all phases of the policy process." [4] The organization, division of labor, culture, professional orientation, and work routines of bureaucracies affect the way they make decisions. So too do the motives of individual bureaucrats. These themes will be developed further in the final chapter. We must expect the law and policy embodied in rules written by agencies to be different from what would be developed by Congress, the president, or the courts. So the very source of rules makes them immediately distinctive for other instruments of law and public policy.

Agency can mean any one of a number of organizational arrangements used to carry out law and policy. Public bureaucracies have many names. We have departments, such as the Department of Transportation. There are commissions, such as the Federal Trade

Commission (FTC); administrations, such as the Federal Aviation Administration (FAA); and agencies, such as the Environmental Protection Agency. However organized or named, most of these bodies have the authority to issue rules and use a rulemaking process to carry it out.

THE SUBJECT MATTER OF RULES: LAW AND POLICY

Having specifically identified the source of rules, the APA definition, interestingly, does not refer to subject matter other than "law" and "policy." In this respect, the definition could not be written more broadly. No area of public policy is excluded. This was not intended by the drafters of the APA as an invitation or authorization to engage in rulemaking in any area that a given agency found interesting or attractive. On the contrary, authority to issue rules can derive only from the statutes that establish the mission of agencies and set their goals and objectives. The definition simply acknowledges that rules can be developed in any area in which Congress adopts a valid statute that is signed by the president.[5] Our experience since the time this definition was framed makes it plain that the decision to put no substantive limits on the potential reach of rules was wise. Rules covered a large range of topics in 1946; in 1990 the scope is virtually limitless.

THE RANGE OF INFLUENCE OF RULES OVER LAW AND POLICY: IMPLEMENT, INTERPRET, PRESCRIBE

The definition clearly establishes an expansive relationship between rules, law, and public policy. The terms *implement, interpret,* and *prescribe* describe the fullest range of influence that a rule could have. Rules merely *implement* when law or policy has been fully developed in a statute enacted by Congress, an executive order of the president, or a judicial decision. Hence, rules need provide no additional substantive elaboration. In these cases rules give instructions to administering officials and the public in the form of procedures and interpretation of statutory provisions but add nothing else of substance to the direction already provided by Congress.

Rules *interpret* when law and policy are well established but confront unanticipated or changing circumstances. Statutory terms, clear and precise when written, may require adaptation when new business practices or technologies appear. Legislation administered by the Federal Trade Commission, for example, seeks to eliminate improper restraints on competition. This creates tasks in the present time that are very different from those created in the era of the robber barons and the trusts. Similarly, statutes mandating air or water quality clearly require agencies to be attentive and respond to industry structure and production processes that may, in turn, alter the sources and types of pollution to be regulated.

Rules *prescribe* when Congress establishes the goals of law or policy in statutes but provides few details as to how they are to be put into operation or how they are actually to be achieved. The Occupational Safety and Health Act stated its ambitious goals in this way: "to assure so far as possible every working man and woman in the Nation safe and healthy work conditions." [6] While it provided some additional guidance, it left to the administering agency, the Occupational Safety and Health Administration (OSHA), the job of defining through rules key legal terms such as *so far as possible*, *safe*, and *healthy*. And once these terms were given an authoritative, legal meaning the huge task of finding the ways that health and safety could be protected was left to the agency as well. Similarly, it was not uncommon for statutes dealing with economic regulation to set agencies off in search of "the public interest" as the criterion for their actions.[7] The APA definition allows agency rulemaking to fill whatever vacuum has been left by Congress, the president, and the courts in the formation of public policy or law. The greater the demands on these institutions, the more likely that the role of rules will expand.

THE RANGE OF CIRCUMSTANCES AFFECTED BY RULES: GENERAL AND PARTICULAR APPLICABILITY

Rules affect persons or activities in the widest possible range of circumstances. The phrase "general or particular applicability" in the APA allows rules to range from those that affect large segments of the population and economy to those that produce changes in a single individual, group, firm, or governmental unit. Some may find this element of the definition confusing, even troubling. We tend to think of legislative action as being concerned with general issues and problems that affect groups of people and activities. The judicial process is generally thought to be better designed for dealing with individual circumstances.[8] So, should not a reduction in number of activities or persons affected by a government action cause an agency to shift from a quasi-legislative process to a quasi-judicial mode of decision making? Should an agency not use other delegated authority to act in a judicial capacity? The short answer is that, although the number of persons affected might influence the specific procedures used to make a decision, this characteristic alone does not determine whether an action that is contemplated is best classified as a rule. The underlying purpose of the action is a key element in this regard and it is addressed directly in the APA definition.

The Importance of Future Effect

Rules, like legislation, attempt to structure the future. By creating new conditions, eliminating existing ones, or preventing others from coming into being, rules implement legislation that seeks to improve the quality of life. The term *future effect* is thus a crucial element in the definition of rules because it allows a clear contrast to situations in which agencies issue decisions, acting in their judicial capacity.[9] Often, agencies are primarily concerned with determining the legal implications of current or past events and conditions. This occurs when an individual challenges an adverse regulatory decision, such as a denial of her petition for a benefit provided by some government program, or applies for a license. In these instances the government is being asked to issue an *order*, the term used when agencies are acting in a judicial capacity. An order applies existing rules to past or existing circumstances. Although an order may have a future effect, such as granting benefits to an individual or permission to operate a particular type of business, its primary purpose is not the creation of policy or law to create new conditions. Again, while the type of *procedures* an agency uses to issue rules may at times resemble those used by courts, the *purpose* of rules is more clearly distinct from other forms of administrative actions.

The key features of rules, then, are that they originate in agencies, articulate law and policy limited only by authorizing legislation, and have either a broad or a narrow scope but are always concerned with shaping future conditions. This tells us what rules are. Now we must examine the growth of rulemaking through time to determine why it has come to play so central a role in our system of government.

THE HISTORY OF RULEMAKING

Rulemaking is a direct consequence of the demands the American people make on government. It would be hard to argue that there is enthusiastic, explicit, or even conscious public support for rulemaking. It is not altogether clear whether people appreciate or are willing to acknowledge that their efforts to persuade elected officials to improve health care, clean the environment, or protect them from deceptive business practices leads inexorably to rules issued through the rulemaking process. There is no Association of American Rulemakers hard at work making emotional appeals for more rules in more areas or for better treatment of those who write them. Instead, the support for rulemaking is implicit in the public's seemingly insatiable appetite for new public initiatives and programs. Virtually all new laws enacted by Congress to deal with real or perceived problems bring with them the need for additional rulemaking. It has been this way since the dawn of the Republic, so the American people have had ample time to learn about this unavoidable relationship.[10]

The evolution of rulemaking is best conceived as a by-product of the historical development of American statute law. The symbiotic relationship between legislation and rulemaking was established in the earliest days of the very first Congress. Put simply, statutes and rules depend on one another. Statutes provide the legal authority for rules and the various processes by which they are made. Rules provide the technical detail so often missing in statutes, and rulemaking brings a capacity for adaptation to changing circumstances that the letter of the law alone would lack. These two vital elements of American public policy and law have been growing and diversifying throughout our history.

THE EARLY SESSIONS OF CONGRESS

In its very first sessions, Congress enacted laws that delegated to the president of the United States the authority to issue rules that would govern those who traded with Indian tribes.[11] The law had scant content, relying instead on the president's rules to provide the substance.[12] Subsequent Congresses continued to delegate the power to write rules to officials of the executive branch. For the most part, these powers were confined to matters of trade and commerce.[13] In 1796, for example, the president was given the authority to develop regulations that set duties on foreign goods. Twenty years later, these powers were expanded considerably when Congress granted sweeping rulemaking powers to the secretary of the treasury to regulate the importation of goods into the United States. This particular statute is notable because it recognizes a subordinate official of the executive branch—a cabinet officer—as the authority to whom rulemaking power is delegated. This is the norm in contemporary legislation. The vague and sweeping language used in the legislation—"to establish regulations suitable and necessary for carrying this law into effect; which regulations shall be binding"—has also become common in many modern statutes.[14] The reasons that Congress would decide not to provide important details in the legislation such as this will be explained shortly.

THE LATE NINETEENTH AND EARLY TWENTIETH CENTURIES: AN EXPANDING NATIONAL GOVERNMENT

During the twentieth century the government of the United States has experienced two periods of extraordinary growth. Each was a response to a crisis, real or perceived. The New Deal was an effort to plan and regulate the economy out of depression during the 1930s; the 1960s saw much broader and deeper efforts to eliminate poverty, pollution, injury, and inequity. These were indeed pivotal periods in our political and legal history. Their legacies with regard to rulemaking are extremely important. But a careful examination of legislative activity demonstrates that, although these were extraordinary periods of expansion, government and rulemaking have been growing steadily since the late nineteenth century.

In the earliest days of the Republic, rulemaking was limited. The reach of federal government powers for much of the nineteenth century was comparatively modest. This began to change in the late nineteenth century, however, when Congress turned its attention to domestic issues and problems and sought solutions. The 1880s, for example, saw the creation of the Interstate Commerce Commission (ICC), which would serve as a model for serial interventions by the federal government into many other sectors of the economy.[15] Programs to protect American agriculture and livestock production from contamination were authorized by legislation. Statutes designed to protect wildlife were passed in this same decade, as well. These laws required varying numbers of rules to be issued by the responsible agencies to implement important provisions. By the beginning of the second decade of the twentieth century, rulemaking had become prominent enough to attract the first serious academic attention in the form of studies by legal scholars of what one termed "delegated legislation."[16] These early works did not suffer any illusions about what rulemaking was: it was, and is, lawmaking by unrelated administrative officials.

From roughly 1900 to the onset of the Great Depression, Congress created public programs that affected a wide variety of previously private activities.[17] Many were designed to protect consumers from dangerous or unfair practices. The creation of the FTC, passage of the Clayton Act to extend its jurisdiction, legislation to ensure the quality of food and the efficacy of drugs, the creation of a federal program to inspect meat, and the establishment of the Federal Reserve System all occurred during this period. Agriculture was also a frequent target for new legislation during this time. Included among the many statutes were laws designed to ensure the purity of milk and the quality of grain, to extend existing powers of quarantine, and to regulate the operation of stockyards and packing houses. Congress ventured into the energy arena by passing the Federal Water Power Act and increased the powers of the ICC with the Hepburn Act. The nation's natural resources got considerable legislative attention as well through statutes that emphasized the importance of conserving and protecting wildlife and migratory birds and managing public lands effectively.

The congressional actions undertaken during these thirty years resulted in a broader and deeper federal role in the affairs of the American people. The authority of existing laws was amended and usually extended into new areas, and wholly new types of commitments were made.

THE NEW DEAL: NEW ROLES FOR GOVERNMENT AND NEW REPOSITORIES FOR RULEMAKING

The most casual student of this country's political history knows that the election of Franklin Delano Roosevelt and the coming of the New Deal brought an outpouring of legislation unprecedented in its volume and implications for the role of government. In response to an economic crisis and aggressive presidential agenda, Congress enacted laws that greatly increased the powers and responsibilities of the federal government. The centerpiece of the New Deal was the National Industrial Recovery Act (NIRA), enacted in 1933. The act authorized the president to create bodies of rules, called "codes," that would establish fair competition in many sectors of the economy.[18] The legislation was breathtaking in its scope—very few significant industries or economic activities were unaffected. The reliance the NIRA placed on rulemaking and other forms of administrative action was near total. Although it fell to a constitutional challenge in 1935 and was subsequently amended extensively by later Congresses, it stands as an important milestone in the history of rulemaking.

The New Deal is properly thought of as a period of intense economic regulation, but many forms of new public policy appeared during the period. Agriculture, labor relations and employment conditions, assistance for the aged and disadvantaged, housing and home ownership, transportation, banking, securities, consumer protection, rural electrification, natural resources, wildlife, energy, and transportation were all profoundly affected by the statutes of the New Deal.[19]

If we assume a direct relation between statutes and the rules needed to implement them, the legislation that had accumulated by the time the New Deal was at its height would suggest that by the late 1930s rulemaking was a major governmental function. But there was no way accurately to assess the volume and significance of rulemaking done by agencies. Until 1934 there was, for example, no single authoritative way to publish and make available the rules and related decisions made by federal agencies. This situation was corrected by the creation of the *Federal Register*. With the *Register* came the *Code of Federal Regulations* (CFR), which was organized functionally by agency and program and will be considered in more detail later. The ability to state unequivocally that rulemaking was a pervasive and important activity is due to a remarkable study done by a committee appointed by the attorney general at that time, Robert Jackson. Among other things, the committee inventoried rulemaking by the federal government. Completed during the closing days of the New Deal, the study reveals that all agencies were actively engaged in rulemaking but that there was considerable variation in both substance and volume.

THE STATE OF RULEMAKING AT THE CLOSE OF THE NEW DEAL

The magnitude of delegated authority granted to agencies during the New Deal and the manner in which certain agencies used these new powers caused a great deal of concern. It was perceived that these administrative processes were not only growing at an alarming rate but were operating in violation of basic legal principles. As described by the Brownlow Committee, a group empowered by Franklin Delano Roosevelt to examine governmental management, they were a "headless fourth branch of government." [20] In response to mounting criticisms and calls for change, President Roosevelt created a committee to study administrative practices currently in force in the main agencies of the federal government. It was intended to be FDR's answer to the Brownlow Committee.[21] Called the Attorney General's Committee on Administrative Procedure, it conducted a series of case studies that today provides us an invaluable historical record on the status of rulemaking more than fifty years ago. It demonstrates conclusively that frequent and highly significant rulemaking was occurring in most agencies and that it was often the result of legislation that predated the New Deal. The following examples from the committee's research, published in 1941, will help put contemporary rulemaking into the proper historical perspective.

The committee found that nearly thirty administrative entities were empowered to issue rules that had significant effects on the public. Some of these agencies were delegated rulemaking authority under multiple statutes. Of all the agencies studied by the committee the one with the greatest accumulation and annual production of rules was the Department of the Interior. The committee wrote that other agency functions were "obscured" by the "momentousness" of rulemaking at the Interior Department. It was estimated that at the time of the study there were several thousand rules in effect with several hundred new rules issued each year. The rules dealt largely with the department's responsibilities for the protection of fish, wildlife, and birds and its stewardship of the many uses of public lands. But wildlife and public lands were not the sole concern of the rulemakers. The program that regulated the coal industry had a rulemaking task that was described as "monumental." The making of one rule alone involved the participation of 387 people, including more than 200 lawyers, and generated more than 700 supporting documents.[22]

The volume of rules issued by the Department of the Interior was rivaled by the various agencies that at different times were responsible for veterans' affairs. The program had been in operation in some form since the late 1700s, so it is not surprising that a large body of rules had accumulated. In fact, rules affecting veterans filled several thousand pages, and the matters they covered ranged from minor administrative details to policies of considerable substance. The study group found them so comprehensive and specific that they left little discretion for agency administrators.[23]

The ICC was also heavily engaged in rulemaking under the Motor Carrier Act. It prepared "a dozen sets" of rules from one five-year period following passage of the act. In another area of its statutory responsibilities, the ICC was involved in constant rulemaking from 1908 to 1940, issuing seven full revisions of rules governing the transport of explosive materials.[24] Apparently as active in a related area was the Bureau of Marine Inspection and Navigation, an agency performing functions that had been conducted under one administrative arrangement or another since the earliest days of the Republic. The bureau's rules were described as "voluminous" and covered all aspects of vessel constitution and operation to ensure safety.[25]

Rulemaking, although clearly established as a crucial government function in the late 1930s, was not undertaken uniformly in all major policy areas. In some instances rulemaking was avoided; in others the agencies wrote rules but added little to what Congress had provided in legislation. Notable among the agencies that did not undertake large programs of rulemaking were the FTC and the National Labor Relations Board (NLRB). Both agencies chose to proceed largely in a quasi-judicial manner, dealing with individual cases brought to them by individuals or groups with complaints. Their policies and law evolved through the accumulation of individual decisions.

The legislative history of the statutes of the FTC indicates that Congress intended it to be a vigorous rulemaker. But this role had not developed by the late 1930s, and indeed it was not until the 1970s that political forces and significant legislative reforms forced the FTC to undertake rulemaking.[26] The NLRB continued to eschew rulemaking, and it does so to this very day, despite frequent entreaties from those who believe more rules are badly needed.[27]

The Social Security Administration (SSA), then called the Social Security Board, undertook a considerable amount of rulemaking after passage of amendments to the Social Security Act in 1939, but little of it was legislative, or substantive, in nature. Instead, the SSA adopted the practice of issuing interpretive rules based almost entirely on congressional hearings that preceded passage of the act.[28] In this instance, the agency adopted rulemaking but chose to exercise little or no discretion in the process. This would change as the programs administered by the agency grew and diversified.

By the time the *Code of Federal Regulations* began publication, in 1938, the legislative phase of the New Deal was winding down. Organized in fifty titles, which correspond to different areas of law and public policy, the CFR of 1938 provides a summary, albeit incomplete, of the results of rulemaking up to that time. Several titles were reserved for Congress, the judiciary, the president, the *Federal Register*, and "government accounts." A substantial portion of the CFR was devoted to national defense and the conduct of foreign relations. Other elements of the 1938 CFR contain material that has since been superseded or subsumed by more recent legislative activity. Some programs are notable by their absence. The "Public Welfare" title contained chapters devoted to an office of education in the Department of the Interior, the Civilian Conservation Corps, the Works Progress Administration, and the National Youth Administration. There was no mention of Social Security; in 1938 the regulations mentioned earlier were still being developed. As one would expect from the previous discussion of statutory developments, there were titles devoted to agriculture and meat production, labor, banking, commerce, transportation, housing, public health, pure food and drugs, telecommunications, public lands, public resources, and wildlife. Some constituted larger bodies of rules, others were small. The rules pertaining to agriculture filled eight chapters and nearly 1,200 pages, whereas those devoted to labor could be contained in just 39 pages.

FROM THE END OF WORLD WAR II TO THE MID-1960S

From the end of World War II to the mid-1960s combined effects of legislation and rulemaking continued to expand the reach of the federal government. As in the past we see the amendment of existing statutes as well as the creation of new programs. The CFR grew and was periodically reorganized to reflect these changes. Consisting of 50 titles and 121 chapters in 1938, the CFR expanded to 138 chapters in 1949, and new titles for highways and atomic energy appeared. By 1959 the number of chapters had increased to 152; in 1969 the number stood at 221. What began as a publication of fifteen volumes in 1938 filled forty-seven volumes in 1949.

In the 1950s and 1960s, legislative attention focused heavily on ways to provide basic rights, benefits, and services to the American people.[29] Statutes established national standards for unemployment insurance, aid to veterans, health care for the elderly and indigent, food stamps, support for urban mass transit systems, and programs to protect consumers from dangerous products, ineffective vaccines, food additives, and unscrupulous lenders. Laws were passed to prevent or punish discrimination based on age, race, and sex. Existing statutes to protect fisheries were extended, and new programs to preserve wilderness areas, scenic trails, and wild rivers were created. The 1950s saw the first tentative incursions by the federal government into the areas of air and water quality; and the close of the 1960s brought the landmark National Environmental Policy Act that required rulemaking in every agency whose actions directly or indirectly disturbed the ecology.

THE DECADE OF THE 1970S: RULEMAKING ASCENDANT

By 1969 the crucial importance of rulemaking in our system of government was unmistakable. Rulemaking had developed into a major force in our legal, political, and economic lives. The volume of rules was formidable, and the range of areas covered by the rules was enormous. Why, then, is it the decade of the 1970s that is frequently characterized as the "era of rulemaking"?[30] Although such characterizations tend to underestimate the importance of earlier periods, there are good reasons why the 1970s deserve their special reputation.

In the 1970s the content of congressional delegations of authority, and the general political environment in which they occurred, brought fundamental changes to rulemaking. The number of statutes that established major programs requiring extensive rulemaking was unprecedented. By one count, 130 laws establishing new programs of social regulation were enacted during this one decade.[31] Proposals dealing with virtually all types of environmental problems, health and safety hazards in virtually all workplaces, and comprehensive consumer protection became law. Congress also enacted broad-ranging reforms in worker pensions. The rulemaking tasks created by legislation like this differed from those that accompanied earlier statutes in a number of ways.

To be sure, agencies operating under earlier statutes often faced formidable obstacles when writing rules. Rarely, however, did their delegations of rulemaking authority sweep so broadly across the economy in the manner that became commonplace in the regulatory legislation of the 1970s. Environmental legislation, taken as a whole, required rulemakers to identify, locate, prevent, control, or mitigate virtually every form of harmful pollutant or dangerous substance in the air, water, and ground. The health and safety of the majority of American workers, regardless of industry or occupation, and the safety of most consumer products were similarly entrusted to newly created programs and agencies.

For the most part, the rulemaking authority granted to agencies prior to the 1970s was more narrowly confined, affecting specific industries and activities.[32] As noted above, those agencies granted broadly based powers, such as the National Labor Relations Board and the Federal Trade Commission, used the rulemaking authority granted to them quite parsimoniously. Furthermore, industry-specific programs of regulation had grown incrementally through time, giving the agencies an extended period of time to develop working relationships with those they regulated or served. Even when dealing with multiple constituencies, as in the areas of natural resources and employment conditions, the agencies could trade on long-term relationships and work at a pace that they largely dictated. More will be said about the relationships between such agencies and the private entities they regulated in a subsequent chapter devoted to public participation in rulemaking.

The rulemaking of the 1970s afforded the affected agencies none of the luxuries seen earlier. The authorizing legislation often represented sudden and radical shifts in the federal role, creating agencies from whole cloth or through the consolidation of programs from numerous departments. These new agencies could neither avoid nor delay rulemaking; the authorizing statutes frequently mandated that rules be developed in specified areas.[33] Often the same laws contained mandatory deadlines by which rules were to be completed. The relationships between the rulemakers and affected parties were given no time to mature. Instead, the rulemaking agencies were immediately positioned between well-organized, aggressive environmental, labor, and consumer groups on one side and threatened, equally aggressive business interests with plentiful resources on the other.

To the volume of work, accelerated pace, and inevitable conflict contained in their delegations of rulemaking authority, the statutes of the 1970s added several layers of substantive and procedural complexity. Environmental and workplace safety programs are good examples of statutes that sent rulemaking routinely to the edge of human knowledge and technical capabilities and beyond. Agencies were expected to create information, such as that which would establish "safe" levels of various chemicals and substances, like benzene and asbestos, in the workplace, while simultaneously incorporating that information into a rule that could be implemented, complied with, and enforced. Further, as we will see in the next chapter, Congress became increasingly concerned with the process by which rules were being written by agencies. It is sufficient to say that the rulemaking provisions of new statutes created more complex and difficult processes for rulemakers to use.

The breadth of the new legislation brought about the potential for conflict between new rules and those of more established programs. The responsibilities of OSHA with regard to all American workers appeared to overlap considerably with those of agencies having jurisdiction over specific industries, such as transportation, food and drug production, and even nuclear power plants. Conflict could occur within a single agency as well. Actions taken as a result of the rules put forth by one office of the EPA to protect the air could result in pollution of the water, which was the responsibility of another office. The need for coordination between agencies of the federal government was dwarfed by intergovernmental issues created by these new statutes. Many laws created partnerships between federal and state governments in which standards were set in Washington but supplemented and enforced in the fifty states.[34] The federal legislation of the 1970s set off considerable rulemaking activity in the states as well.[35]

The rulemaking of the 1970s was also more important than that which had come before. If we assume Congress had properly identified real threats in the wave of protective legislation that occurred in the 1970s, then to a remarkable extent the health, safety, financial well-being, and general quality of life of Americans would hinge on the success of rulemaking by agencies. These rules would also impose unprecedented costs, transfer huge amounts of wealth across our society, and affect our capacity to vie in increasingly competitive world markets.

THE REAGAN/BUSH ADMINISTRATION: THE RETREAT THAT FAILED

As a period in the history of rulemaking, the 1980s are more difficult to characterize. On the one hand, much of the massive agenda for rulemaking established in legislation of the 1970s remained to be completed in the 1980s. Exacerbating this backlog of work were important amendments to existing environmental, workplace safety and health, and consumer statutes that added even more responsibilities and caused the revision of rules already in existence. In the face of these formidable pressures, however, powerful political forces were at work to eliminate some rules, to prevent some others from being made, and to impose new decision-making criteria on those that remained.

The administration of Ronald Reagan introduced the most significant changes since the basic process for rulemaking was established in the Administrative Procedure Act of 1946. These changes will be discussed at length in two subsequent chapters. One of Reagan's reforms was the institution of a review of rules by the president's Office of Management and Budget (OMB) prior to their publication in the *Federal Register*. According to some evidence, the combined effect of this and other reforms was a slowing of the pace of rulemaking for at

Figure 1-1   Comparison of Rules Reviewed during 1981-1989

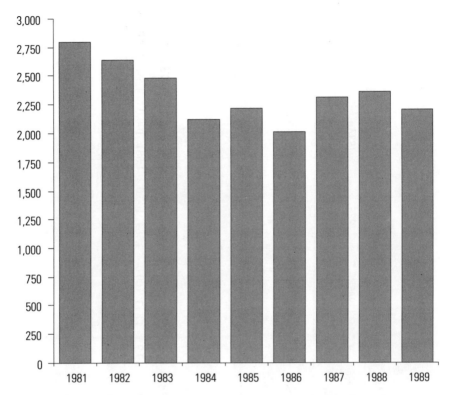

Source: Executive Office of the President, *Regulatory Program of the United States Government* (Washington, D.C., 1991).

least part of the 1980s. Figure 1-1 summarizes the number of rules reviewed by the OMB as part of President Reagan's reform program. Since these figures are drawn exclusively from the rules reviewed by the OMB, they do not include rules exempt from review requirements. In some instances the categories of exemptions contain large numbers of rules, so the actual effect of the political reaction of the 1980s is difficult to determine from this information alone.

Fortunately, other measures are available. Table 1-1 contains information on the numbers of rulemaking documents published in the *Federal Register* during the 1980s. There is considerable variation from year to year, but we can see a marked decline from 1982 through 1984, a slowing of the decline in 1985, and then the beginning of a slow reversal of direction in 1988. The type of rule documents published also varies as a proportion of the total. It is interesting to note that throughout the period the number of new rules is small

TABLE 1-1　Final Rule Documents Published in the *Federal Register*, 1982-1989

	1982		1983		1984		1985		1986		1987		1988		1989	
	No.	%	No.	%	No.	%	No.	%	No.	%	No.	%	No.	%	No.	%
New requirement	294	4.7	248	4.1	260	5.0	358	7.4	366	7.6	451	9.8	395	8.4	367	7.8
Revision to existing requirements	1,530	24.3	1,430	23.6	1,350	26.2	1,255	25.9	1,267	24.2	1,241	27.1	1,250	26.6	1,175	24.9
Elimination of existing requirements	299	4.8	217	3.6	162	3.1	177	3.7	142	3.3	85	1.9	74	1.6	51	1.1
All other	4,165	66.2	4,154	68.7	3,383	65.6	3,053	63.0	2,814	64.9	2,804	61.2	2,978	63.4	3,118	66.2
Total	6,288	100.0	6,049	100.0	5,155	99.9 [a]	4,843	100.0	4,589	100.0	4,581	100.0	4,697	100.0	4,711	100.0

Source: Executive Office of the President, *Regulatory Program of the United States Government* (Washington, D.C., 1991).

[a] Less than 100 percent due to rounding.

TABLE 1-2   *Code of Federal Regulations* Page Count
by Selected Title and Year

Title	1938	1989
Agriculture	1,174	10,613
Labor	39	5,721
Environment	0	8,250

when compared with revisions of existing rules. Deletions of rules decline in number in virtually every year. It is also notable that agencies were issuing more new rules by 1989 than they were at the beginning of the decade. This could not be encouraging to those who sought to reduce the influence of regulations on the conduct of affairs in the United States.

Although these data are reasonable indicators of rulemaking activity, the cumulative effect also needs to be understood as well. This can be observed in the growth of the *Code of Federal Regulations*. In 1938 the CFR was made up of 121 chapters; in 1949, 138; in 1959, 131; in 1969, 221; in 1979, 284; and in 1989, 313. Chapters generally correspond to the programs for which rules are written. Table 1-2 shows the growth from 1938 to 1989 in the number of pages in the CFR devoted to selected areas of law and public policy.

The growth in CFR pages follows no set pattern; there are considerable variations by policy area. "Protection of the Environment," which did not exist in 1969, had swelled to more than 4,000 pages by the end of the decade and nearly doubled in the next ten years. Most of the growth in "Agriculture" occurred in the 1950s and 1960s, and the growth in "Labor" has been consistent since the 1950s. Taken together, as we entered the 1990s these three areas alone accounted for nearly 25,000 pages of rules.

TOWARD THE YEAR 2000

What will the 1990s bring? Early evidence suggests more of the same. It appears that the first twelve months of the new decade constituted a banner year for new rules. Congress was at work creating legislation that would keep rulemakers in a raft of agencies busy for years to come. One statute alone is instructive. As noted earlier, the new Clean Air Act was some thirteen years in the making. One might expect legislation so long under consideration to deal with a large number of issues and problems. When the act was passed by Congress, the Environmental Protection Agency estimated that its implementation would require between 300 and 400 rules. This estimate did not include the subsequent rulemaking that would occur in the states. It appears from this evidence that the pattern of the 1970s and 1980s persists in the early 1990s. There is, however, an alternative view.

Some have argued that rulemaking, despite the numbers, is actually in decline as a method for making law and policy. In the next chapter we will explore the process of rulemaking and how it has developed through time. It will be evident that for some rules, especially those with the greatest potential effects on the economy and society, the rulemaking process can be complex, expensive, time-consuming, and risky. Several prominent scholars have concluded that these and other factors have led agencies away from rulemaking to other mechanisms for implementing programs.[36] Clearly the data on the volume of rules may be somewhat misleading in that it cannot convey the types of issues being handled through rulemaking and those diverted to less onerous and visible administrative devices. Rulemaking will certainly not disappear, but the avoidance of it by agencies is a serious issue that will be covered at length in both Chapter 3 and the concluding sections of this book.

This brief review of the historical growth in rulemaking demonstrates rather clearly that rulemaking is a direct, if not always desired, consequence of legislation. More to the point, rulemaking, as a mechanism for refining law and policy, has been essential to the government's effort to assume responsibility for the range of activities demanded by the voters. It was and remains an inevitable and indispensable by-product of any significant legislative activity. As long as the American people demand new or altered public policies, and as long as Congress responds to these demands, rulemaking will remain a basic and determining element of our political and legal systems.

CATEGORIES OF RULES

If nothing else is evident from this brief history of rulemaking it should be apparent that defining or categorizing the substance of rule-making is very difficult. All topics, issues, and activities touched by public policy are or will be the subject of a rule. Still, there are ways to categorize rules that capture certain key characteristics, if not their full richness.

POLICY AREA AND AGENCY OF ORIGIN

The *Code of Federal Regulations* organizes rules in fifty distinct categories called titles and chapters, which correspond to distinct public programs, policies, or agencies. For example, the rules for banks and banking can be found in Title 12; those for protection of the environment, in Title 40; and the rules governing acquisition of goods and services by the federal government, in several dozen chapters of Title 48. The subject matter of rules contained in the fifty titles of the CFR is vast; any attempt at classification based on substance is not likely to improve on the categories found in it. The current index of the CFR's titles and chapters is included in Appendix A.

FUNCTIONS PERFORMED BY RULES

There are alternative ways to look at the total body of rules that convey other important dimensions of their status, purpose, and effect on our society. The oldest method for classifying rules is suggested in the APA definition cited earlier. The first and most important category consists of "legislative" or "substantive" rules. These are instances when, by congressional mandate or authorization, agencies write what amounts to new law. These rules bind the agency and the public and must be developed in accordance with mandatory procedures that will be discussed in the next chapter.[37] In the terms of the APA definition, legislative rules "prescribe" law and policy.

A second category consists of "interpretive" rules. These occur when agencies are compelled to explain to the public how it interprets existing law and policy. Although these may entail stretching law, or rules, to fit new or unanticipated circumstances, they do not in themselves impose new legal obligations.[38] A good example of this type of rule are the "Uniform Guidelines on Employee Selection" issued by the Equal Employment Opportunity Commission in conjunction with other agencies that have responsibilities for enforcing Title VII of the 1972 Civil Rights Act.[39] Like all interpretive rules, these were intended to advise the public how the agencies interpreted their legal obligations under the act and assorted court cases that it had stimulated. The agencies issued interpretive rules in this case because civil rights was one of the very few areas of statutory development in the 1960s and 1970s in which Congress failed to grant authority to write legislative rules. Because they are advisory in nature, interpretive rules can be developed in any way the agency sees fit, but they are generally published in the *Federal Register*.

The third category consists of procedural rules that define the organization and processes of agencies. Although they are often regarded as little more than bureaucratic housekeeping, they do deal with matters of importance to the public. Among other things, they inform the public how they can participate in a range of agency decision making, including rulemaking. As we will see in the next chapter, external forces have taken much of the initiative in the rulemaking process away from agencies. Nevertheless, procedural rules provide essential road maps for those attempting to find their way around the decision-making pathways of our massive and complex bureaucracies.

This way of classifying rules actually predates the APA by many years. Studies of administrative processes in federal agencies conducted in the 1930s refer repeatedly to these different types of rules and suggest that the distinctions had been commonly understood for some time.[40] The distinctions are still important. Many agencies, for example, still use variations on interpretive rules to supplement legislative rules. These come in a variety of forms—guidelines, policy statements, technical manuals—as we noted above, and some suspect that agencies use them to avoid the procedural rigors of legislative rulemaking.[41] We will return to this controversy in a later chapter.

WHAT AND WHOM RULES AFFECT

Another way to consider the body of rules is to classify them by the segment of our society they influence and direct. There are rules that deal with private behavior. There are others that guide those individuals, groups, or firms that are approaching the government to obtain a payment, a service, or permission to engage in some activity. Finally, there are rules that deal with the way the government conducts its business. Most, if not all rules, can be placed in one of these three categories.

RULES FOR PRIVATE BEHAVIOR.   One good way to appreciate the scope of rules directed at the private sector is to consider how they might affect a business.[42] Quite literally, rules govern American businesses from their very beginning to beyond their demise. Virtually every business decision of any substance is affected by rules written in government agencies. Rules can have a determining effect on the decision to go into business in the first place. Before one enters certain businesses or occupations a license is required. The granting of a license, the qualifications needed to obtain one, and the conditions that are attached to it are determined by rules. Money is needed to start most businesses, and banks are often the providers. Banking rules determine in large part the availability of funds and the manner in which financial institutions make business loans. Assuming the owners of the business are prudent, they will want to protect their business from claims of damage arising from negligence or faulty products. Insurance regulations will determine whether they can get coverage and what it will cost.

Where a business is located is not a decision that can be made without reference to rules. Environmental and zoning rules have a significant influence on where businesses are established. Companies whose operations involve substantial amounts of air or water pollution may find it difficult to locate in areas where rules set tight limits on new sources of pollution. The zoning authorities of local areas use rules to implement land-use plans that restrict, sometimes severely, where new businesses can locate.

Once the decision to go into business is made and a location is selected, rules may affect who is employed and how they are treated by the new concern. If the firm expects to do business with the federal government, it will be required, under a variety of rules, to have an affirmative action program. Those doing no government business must still take care not to discriminate in hiring. The Uniform Guidelines on Employee Selection, mentioned above, provide direction to employers in this area. These guidelines affect virtually all employment decisions, from initial interviewing of candidates to termination of those who fail to meet expectations.

What a new business produces and how that product is made are governed by a multiplicity of rules, some designed to protect workers, others to protect consumers, and still others to protect the environment. Industrial operations are constrained by rules that are designed to ensure safety in the workplace and to prevent or minimize pollution of the air, water, and land. These rules frequently specify the types of equipment that can and cannot be used and how the machinery is to be designed or operated. The service sector is similarly affected by rules that govern how it will operate. The energy, banking, insurance, securities, transportation, and even education sectors are governed by industry-specific rules that dictate finances, employee qualifications, service quality, and even internal management.

Once the business has a product to sell, rules may determine how it will be sold, how it will get to consumers, the price that is charged for the good or service, and the company's obligations after it has been bought. The potential consumers of goods and services are protected by rules intended to prevent deceptive advertising. Other rules require that information be provided, on labels or packaging inserts, informing the public about the content, purpose, and potential hazards of consumer products. Recently, the nation was treated to an intense conflict between the Department of Agriculture and the Department of Health and Human Services about the content of food labels. Rules written to regulate airlines, railroads, trucks, telecommunications, pipelines, and electricity transmission facilities profoundly affect how and at what cost goods and services get in the hands of consumers. Some commodities and services are still affected by rate making done by agencies. Agricultural commodities and energy transmission are two major areas of the economy where rules directly or indirectly set the price that consumers will pay. Once a good is sold, rules establish the producer's obligations. Rules can require that products, such as automobiles, be recalled by the manufacturer if defects are found that threaten safety or environmental quality. Similarly, rules outline the types of information consumers should have regarding warranties provided by the manufacturer or vendor of products should the product or service they purchase fail to provide what was promised.

Rules determine under what conditions a firm can go out of business. Here two types of rules are notable. One governs the ongoing obligations that firms and businesses have to their retirees. Under the Employee Retirement Income Security Act (ERISA), rules have been developed to secure the pension rights of retirees even when a firm decides to go out of business. The rules written under laws governing the disposal of hazardous waste also carry obligations for companies to clean up the mess they might otherwise leave behind, and try to forget, after they cease operations.

HOW RULES AFFECT PRIVATE BEHAVIOR.   When considering rules that affect private parties it is also useful to think of the kinds of requirements they contain. Although the scope of government activity is virtually limitless, the instruments at the disposal of agencies to accomplish these varied tasks are not. We can observe a number of common instruments in rules of agencies with profoundly different missions, clienteles, and resources.

A relatively infrequent but nonetheless significant instrument is outright prohibition of certain substances, products, or activities. The number of rules that include unconditional prohibitions is comparatively small, but they attract considerable attention because of the consequences to affected parties and society at large. Recall the hue and cry that accompanied the ban on cyclamates, which had been used to sweeten soft drinks, and other actions that took suspected carcinogens off the market. Agencies with responsibilities to protect the traveling public impose prohibitions on key personnel working for airlines, railroads, and interstate buses. A recent and rather frightening reminder of the need for these types of rules was provided by the criminal prosecution of two Northwest Airlines pilots charged with violating the Federal Aviation Administration's ban on alcohol consumption during the twenty-four-hour period prior to takeoff.[43] There are rules prohibiting certain types of advertising, such as the ban on television ads for cigarettes and hard liquor. Other rules proscribe activities on wild and scenic rivers, national parks, and wilderness areas. Rules governing benefit programs prohibit recipients from engaging in certain types of activities. Various types of political action is off limits to the recipients of some federal grants and contracts.

More common than outright prohibitions are rules that place limitations on substances, products, and activities. Most of us have heard of, and have probably been revolted by, the rather disgusting forms of foreign matter that can find their way into processed meats. Hundreds of environmental regulations impose limits on the production of and exposures to toxic substances of various kinds and uses. The Occupational Safety and Health Administration has struggled since its creation to set limits on the amounts of certain types of chemicals that are potentially harmful to workers. The ordeal of setting standards for occupational exposure to the chemical benzene spanned more than a decade. The recent crisis in the savings and loan industry and the shakiness of banks have focused attention on rules of various agencies that limit the high-risk investments these types of institutions can make. The Federal Aviation Administration places limits on the number of hours airplane pilots and attendants can work. The few agencies that still set prices and rates limit what can be charged for certain types of products and services, and agricultural marketing rules place close restrictions on the amounts of certain commodities that can be shipped and sold during specified time periods. Perhaps the most common form of rule is the one that sets standards for products and activities. Limits and standards are different versions of the same instrument of government control. They allow the private sector to do what it wants, but only within certain boundaries.

A common form of rule that serves as an adjunct to rules that prohibit, impose limits, or set standards is the one that establishes information requirements. It is increasingly common for rules to contain requirements that private individuals, groups, and firms collect, analyze, retain, and report information about their activities. Information rules provide agencies an unparalleled mechanism for monitoring the behavior of persons who fall under their programs. In some instances, programs could not be managed and requirements could not be enforced if agencies were required to develop these data on their own. Labels, package inserts, requirements to conduct tests of various sorts and report the results, and rules requiring recipients of various types of government assistance or licensees to report periodically are all forms of information rules on which the integrity and success of many governmental programs depend.

RULES FOR THOSE WHO APPROACH THE GOVERNMENT.   Private individuals, groups, or firms approach the government for many reasons but usually to obtain a payment or service or to gain permission to conduct an activity that requires official sanctioning of some sort. The types of rules that apply in such circumstances establish the criteria for eligibility to receive the assistance or benefit offered under a government program. Social security programs of various sorts, welfare, medical care, educational assistance, housing benefits, and a host of other public programs operate on the basis of these eligibility rules.

A substantial number of activities conducted by private individuals, groups, or firms require various forms of governmental permission. Licenses and permits are required for a wide variety of activities, ranging from the operation of nuclear power plants to the flying of an airplane. When requesting licenses or permits, individuals must meet the standards set in rules. For example, the applicant for a license to operate a hydroelectric power plant must demonstrate that he or she can meet financial, engineering, and environmental standards established by the responsible agency, in this case the Federal Energy Regulatory Commission.[44]

RULES FOR GOVERNMENT. Purely governmental activities are guided by rules as well. These are—broadly defined—the procedural rules mentioned earlier. The *Code of Federal Regulations* has titles devoted to the management of government accounts, administrative personnel, administration of the judicial branch, public contracts and property management, and the acquisition of goods and services. In addition, the other titles of the CFR contain procedural rules that apply to the operation of individual programs. These detail, among other things, how the agency intends to comply with laws governing public and private information, how agency hearings and other proceedings involving the public will be conducted, and who within the agency has authority to make various types of decisions.

Two statutes, the Freedom of Information Act and the Privacy Act, require agencies to issue regulations about how and why information is being used. Under the Freedom of Information Act, the agency must explain to members of the public how they can obtain information. The Privacy Act requires the agency to describe personal information it has collected and is holding, how people can get access to records that agencies maintain on them, and how personal information is being protected from unwarranted disclosure.

We see, then, that the targets of rules include the private and public sectors. Whether regulated entities or potential beneficiaries of the federal government's largesse, individuals, groups, firms, states, and local governments must look to rules for refinements of their rights and obligations and for procedures by which the programs with which they are concerned will operate. The vast range and diversity of subject matter that rules now touch has been mentioned. It is also important to note the remarkable variations in the complexity of rules, the numbers of persons or activities they affect, and the duration of their effects.

DIFFERENCES IN SCOPE AND IMPORTANCE.   Most rules published in the *Federal Register* are brief and deal with a very narrow range of activities. They may be based on complex technical or scientific information, such as regulations issued by the Federal Communications Commission to allocate radio frequency bands to individual stations and the Federal Aviation Administration rules dealing with flight paths at airports. Other rules, fewer in number, are enormously long and complex and cover vast areas. But it is important to note that the length of the rule is not always an accurate indicator of the rule's effects. An "air-worthiness directive," the type of rule the FAA issues to correct potential safety problems on aircraft, will affect every person that flies on the affected planes. Similarly, an "agricultural marketing order" that limits the amount of a commodity that can be shipped to sellers will affect every consumer who buys the affected vegetable or fruit. Both types of rules usually take up no more than a single page in the *Federal Register*.

Rules, then, vary greatly in their purpose and significance, but why do we rely on them for so much law and policy?

THE REASONS FOR RULEMAKING: WHAT IT HAS TO OFFER

However they are categorized and classified it is apparent that we rely on rules to accomplish most of the ambitious goals we set for ourselves as a society. Up to now we have discussed rulemaking as a constant force in our political and legal history and as an inescapable contemporary reality. But this history inevitably requires further explanation. Rulemaking has the place it does in our government system for many reasons.

The number and diversity of rules written in this country are evidence that rulemaking is, at least, a common form of government decision making. We have not yet fully explored why it has come to occupy so central a position in the policy process. In general, it has achieved its prominence because of the contributions it makes to the conduct of government and the benefits it provides, as described in the next sections. But, it has disadvantages also.

THE CAPACITY OF BUREAUCRACY
AND THE LIMITS OF THE LEGISLATURE

If we examine the body of laws enacted by Congress it is immediately apparent that they touch virtually every aspect of human life. Consequently, every known professional discipline must be drawn upon for the knowledge needed to achieve their ambitious goals. This range and depth of expertise has never been present among members of Congress or the staff that supports legislative operations. Congressional staffs are large and diverse but still limited. Many are concerned with matters other than the crafting of new legislation. Substantial numbers of representatives' personal staffs are engaged in the constituency-related work that is so close to the hearts of elected officials. Committee staffs and those in the General Accounting Office are preoccupied with oversight, the importance of which is magnified by the way Congress writes law. More about this in a moment.

Since the Progressive Era, there has been faith—much diminished in recent years—in the neutral competence of a professionalized bureaucracy. The public has confidently expected bureaucrats to carry out the will of the people efficiently and effectively.[45] This confidence, combined with the principle of separation of powers, has provided considerable justification for Congress to rely on rulemaking to supplement legislation rather than attempt to enact laws that answer all questions and anticipate all circumstances associated with a new program. In one view, since it is the task of the executive branch in our constitutional system to see that the law is carried out, bureaucracies, as instrumentalities of the executive branch, can be expected to clarify what the law means and take the steps necessary to ensure that its goals are achieved. Our laws require the constant application of knowledge and expertise to varied conditions and circumstances, so it makes sense to concentrate specialists in the administrative agencies that execute them rather than in the legislature.

This view, of course, begs the fundamental constitutional question of who will write the law. We saw that under the APA definition the term *rule* can have many different meanings. Each has different implications for lawmaking. When a rule merely "implements" a law there is no constitutional dilemma, because it will restate, perhaps in more functional language, what the Congress has already enacted. When a rule "interprets" legislation the rulemaking activity may be more substantial, bordering on lawmaking. But here there is no pretension of making new law. Rather, the agency is answering questions that have arisen about the law's reach and meaning in particular instances. It is when a rule "prescribes" law that conflict between the constitutional roles of the executive and the legislature is most evident.

The depth of concern about rulemaking hinges to a considerable extent on whether agencies are agents of the legislature or the executive branch. If bureaucracies are merely extensions of Congress, then we should be no more alarmed by rulemaking than we are by reports that congressional staff members play a vital role in the drafting of statutes. If, however, these agencies are properly viewed as extensions of the president, then their exercise of substantial rulemaking powers threatens the constitutional design. But the question of who runs the bureaucracy is by no means settled; the Congress and president have long struggled to gain the hearts and minds of bureaucrats.[46] Both have formidable powers at their disposal when attempting to influence the course of bureaucratic decision making. The president prepares budgets, appoints senior officials, and issues executive orders that have profound impact on how agencies manage their work. Congress is the ultimate decision maker on budgets and appointments, conducts oversight and investigations, and engages in casework on behalf of constituents. In the battle for influence over the bureaucracy, congressional powers are at least as substantial. Congressional power to define an agency's mission and fix its budget is more determinative than the transitory and fragmented sources of presidential influence. Therefore, when delegating the power to interpret and prescribe law, Congress does it in the secure knowledge that it retains sufficient power and opportunity to redirect rulemakings that go astray. We will examine control of rulemaking through oversight in Chapter 6.

Expertise situated in a constitutionally acceptable relationship to Congress is not the sole reason why rulemaking by agencies is beneficial. It is the ability to respond in a timely manner to unanticipated and changed conditions, and most especially emergencies, that is one of the great advantages of rulemaking based in agencies. Agency officials who administer and enforce programs are the first to learn that an existing program is flawed in some way. They are also the first to observe that conditions affecting the program, or conditions that programs intend to affect, have changed significantly. They are most likely to be the first government body to learn that an emergency situation exists. As James Landis wrote in 1938, "The Administrative [process] is always in session." [47]

A good illustration of this capacity is evident in the rulemaking of the Federal Aviation Administration. Through its inspection and regulatory enforcement programs, the FAA regularly discovers problems in the design, operation, or maintenance of airplanes. Some of these problems are trivial; others pose serious threats to the flying public. The organization of the FAA allows for swift communication from the field staff to those in the Washington headquarters that a new rule is required. For example, should a review of maintenance records or a series of inspections reveal excessive corrosion in the fan blades of a particular type of jet engine, the FAA technical staff can decide how serious the problem is, the steps that must be taken to correct the problem without endangering passengers and crew, and how quickly these actions should be taken. The rule in this case is the "airworthiness directive" mentioned above, hundreds of which the FAA issues each year.

Consider the same situation without rulemaking. To establish the new obligations borne by manufacturers or carriers for their jet engines, an amendment to the existing statute would be required. For such an amendment to come to pass, the information would have to work its way up the FAA organization and be communicated to the appropriate House and Senate subcommittees; legislation would have to be drafted; hearings would have to be held; votes would have to be taken in subcommittee, full committee, and the floors of both houses; possibly conference committee deliberations and another round of votes would be required; and then the president would have to sign the legislation. If real danger existed, a tragedy could occur long before action of this sort was completed. Those of us who are averse to risk are especially so when we step through the doors of an aircraft being readied for a takeoff. Rulemaking to flyers like me is a godsend.

Rulemaking supplements the legislative process in another significant way. In subsequent chapters I will demonstrate that the revolution in public participation that has swept through public administration since the 1960s has affected rulemaking profoundly. It is not surprising that the proponents of increased public involvement in the decisions of agencies would focus on a function as crucial as the development of rules. Rulemaking adds opportunities for and dimensions to public participation that are rarely present in the deliberations of Congress or other legislatures. As the quote from the *Washington Post* in the introductory section of this chapter suggests, it is often difficult for interested parties to determine exactly what a bill under consideration means to them. The more vague the proposed provisions, the more difficult it is for the public to decide whether participation is worth the effort and, if so, what position to take.

In rulemaking the decisions regarding participation become much clearer because the issues are better defined, the actions the government is contemplating are more specific, the implications for affected parties are much easier to predict. Positions are thus easier to formulate and articulate. And there are many ways for the public to get involved in rulemaking and to influence the content of rules that are developed. The cost of effective participation in rulemaking may be lower, as we will see in a later chapter, and the chances of success in rulemaking greater than those that confront the public during legislative deliberations.

A MEANS OF CONTAINING ADMINISTRATIVE DISCRETION

However contradictory it may at first appear, rulemaking is an important tool in limiting the power and discretion of bureaucrats.

During the past fifty years the growing power of bureaucracy has been viewed by many with considerable alarm. Armed with vast but poorly defined authority delegated to them by Congress, bureaucrats are seen as able to exercise discretionary powers that threaten the rights and security of individuals.[48] Many critics have claimed that administrative officials with the power to deny or rescind benefits and licenses, impose regulatory requirements and sanctions, and force the reporting of all types of information do so without adequate standards to guide them and to protect the public. But rulemaking is a potential remedy for the abuse of bureaucratic discretion, at least in the opinion of some respected scholars.

While acknowledging that some discretion is essential if the administrative process is to operate effectively, efficiently, and fairly, Kenneth Culp Davis, in his highly influential book *Discretionary Justice*, concluded "our . . . systems are saturated with excessive discretionary power which needs to be confined, structured and checked."[49] He argued, however, that the answer to the problem was not the then common prescription that Congress and other legislative bodies work harder to specify limits in legislation. "Legislative bodies do about as much as they reasonably can do in specifying the limits on delegated power," he stated. And he was quite specific about the tool in which he placed the most faith: "Altogether, the chief hope for confining discretionary power does not lie in statutory enactments but in much more extensive administrative rulemaking, and legislative bodies need to do more than they have been doing to prod the administrators."[50]

Whether Congress heard this plea is unclear, but it certainly acted as if it had. Professor Davis was writing on the verge of the 1970s, a period, as we have noted, that has been called the "era of rulemaking." The statutes of the 1970s, 1980s, and early 1990s expressed a clear preference for rulemaking as a device for administering the programs they created. Many mandated rulemaking and more than a few imposed deadlines on agencies for completing this work. While they are often viewed from the perspective of the private citizen or firm whose behavior is constrained, rules control agencies and bureaucrats as well. Rules set limits on the authority of public officials in all areas of their work, identifying what they can know, how they can learn it, when they must act, what they must do, when they must do it, and actions they can take against those who fail to comply. A violation of rules puts the bureaucrat no less at risk than the private scofflaw. Fears of unfettered discretion in the hands of willful or ignorant bureaucrats are largely unfounded in a system in which citizens can trust that rulemaking will occur subsequent to any legislative enactment and set effective and reasonable limits on the use of otherwise discretionary power. Again, this is not to say that rulemaking is the font of wisdom and success for public programs. It, like most governmental functions, is beset with problems. We will consider these in depth. But it clearly provides advantages over the legislative process, which is overloaded with demands for action but impeded by shortages of time and expertise. There are reasons other than these institutional considerations why rulemaking is so prominent and has assumed a position of such importance in our governmental system. It serves the interests of the most powerful players in our public policy process.

RULEMAKING AND SELF-INTEREST

In all matters determined by politics the self-interest of the major participants must be scrutinized and understood. Rulemaking is certainly no exception. Its other advantages notwithstanding, rulemaking occurs to the extent it does because of the clear benefits it delivers to the main actors in our political system. Consider what rulemaking provides Congress, the president, the judiciary, interest groups, and the bureaucracy itself.

CONGRESS. By resorting to widespread delegation of legislative power to the rulemaking process, Congress both frees and indemnifies itself. Rather than spending all their available time in drafting, debating, and refining statutes, members of Congress are free to engage in other activities, like getting reelected. Of course, rulemaking promotes reelection in more ways than just generating free time. If we examine the statutes of the 1970s, 1980s, and the record to date in the 1990s, it is clear that members of Congress are routinely faced with the legislative equivalent of a Catch-22. Squeezed by powerful and contending interests— environmentalists and industry, workers and management, program beneficiaries and taxpayers—members of Congress realize that their votes on very specific legislative proposals that clearly identify winners and losers can erode support or foster outright opposition. As others have noted, this provides powerful incentives for Congress to remain vague, leaving the specific, painful, and politically dangerous decisions to the agencies.

Congressional self-interest is served by rulemaking for reasons other than the "responsibility avoidance" that accompanies delegations of authority.[51] Congress remains free to intervene in ongoing rulemakings and to review completed rules using a variety of devices that will be discussed presently. Some of these devices allow members to perform services to individual constituents, an always-popular reelection activity.

PRESIDENTS. It took a long time for presidents to learn how to make the most of it, but rulemaking provides extraordinary opportunities to influence the direction and content of American public policy. President Reagan instituted changes that gave the White House power to review and influence all rules written by federal agencies. Viewed from one perspective, this reform gave the president a new weapon in the ongoing struggle with Congress to define public policy. In a period of divided government, presidential management of the rulemaking process is especially significant. Because it is based in the White House it avoids some of the perennial problems presidents have had in gaining control of their own executive machinery in departments and agencies. With the power of review, even presidents who take a dim view of big government and regulation should favor expanded use of rulemaking, since it allows them to influence the full range of public policy in a manner that does not directly entail negotiations with Congress.

JUDGES. Although it is less common to think of the judiciary as dominated by self-interest, there is no question some judges relish an active role in the public policy process and most hold strong views on the proper scope and channels for governmental action. As an opportunity for the exercise of authority and power by the courts, rulemaking makes it much easier for judges to supervise and impose their will on the operations of bureaucracies. This is true whether judges seek to impose their personal beliefs about law and policy or are simply attempting to meet the obligations of their branch in the political system.

Clearly articulated rules offer judges an efficient way to review and determine agencies' stewardship of the law and public policy. When lawsuits challenge the results of rulemaking, judges are able to evaluate the content of a rule to determine whether it is consistent with the statutes from which they derive their sole claim to authority and legitimacy. Further, judges can review the process by which rules were developed to determine if the obligations to allow for meaningful participation and to conduct required analyses were met. Judges have developed a number of devices to correct deficiencies in the substance or process of the rules they review. Many of these vest in the judges themselves the equivalent of supervisory power over rulemaking, giving them the potential for great influence over the ultimate content of laws and policies. Other forms of administrative action, notably case-by-case decision making, are theoretically as susceptible to judicial review but are labor-intensive in the extreme. Given the limited resources of the judiciary, review of rules is by far the more cost-effective path for judges to pursue personal power and institutional influence or merely to fulfill their constitutional responsibilities.

INTEREST GROUPS.   Interest groups could find few modes of government decision making better suited to their particular strengths than rulemaking. Here and throughout the book, *interest group* will refer to organizations of any sort, including individual companies, that attempt to influence the decisions of government. Their size, longevity, and issues of interest are not important. Because rulemaking is specialized it allows these groups to focus their attention and use their resources to influence decisions they know will effect their members. As we have already noted, rulemaking often requires a considerable amount of substantive, often technical, information. Agencies are rarely in possession of all the information or insights they require to write sound, defensible rules. Frequently, interest groups and the individuals or firms they represent have ready access to the information that agencies need. This gives such groups a considerable amount of leverage in the development of rules. Unlike legislative deliberations, in which political considerations frequently overwhelm or obscure operational issues and technical details, the outcome of rulemaking often hinges on the amount and quality of information available, which is a stock-in-trade for interest groups.

STATE AND LOCAL GOVERNMENTS.   The explosion of rulemaking that began in the late 1960s and has continued since was of great consequence to state and local governments. Not only were they affected directly, becoming, in effect, regulated parties under environmental, workplace safety, equal employment, and other programs, they also became more active rulemakers in their own right. Many of these statutes also allowed states to be the primary rulemaker as long as their rules were at least as strict as those developed by the federal agency with primary jurisdiction for the program. Thus, state and local government could not avoid federal rulemaking and they would have to await its results before exercising their own. Because of these powers, state and local governments could expect to have considerable influence over the federal rulemaking process simply by virtue of what they might do subsequently. Even when states and localities did not write rules, they were often responsible for enforcing the federal ones. By successfully influencing the content of federal rules, state and local governments could ease the burdens of subsequent implementation.

BUREAUCRATS.   An equivocal position on rulemaking by bureaucrats would not be surprising. For many agencies rulemaking represents a daunting workload that curtails their discretion and exposes them to scrutiny and pressure from Congress, the president, courts, and interest groups. Such a situation would seem sufficiently unattractive to put off even the most mildly self-interested bureaucrat. Still, although some may consider it nothing more than an unavoidable chore, rulemaking does bring certain benefits to at least some bureaucrats. Those "zealots" identified two decades ago by Anthony Downs have in rulemaking the possibility of putting their indelible mark on public policy and law. His "climbers" find rulemaking presents an excellent opportunity to advance careers in and out of the agency. The author of a major rule gets considerable visibility in an agency and may become marketable on the outside. Even Downs's "conserver," who avoids risk in favor of a more predictable existence, sees in rules the opportunity to stabilize and regularize the working environment.[52]

In short, rulemaking has something for every key institution and actor in our political system. For this reason alone we should expect it to be a permanent feature of the way we govern ourselves.

The objective of this first chapter was to convince the reader that rulemaking is a significant government function that has, since the start of the Republic, come to play an increasingly pivotal role in the definition of American public policy and law. In the hope that this case has been made, the next task is to explain how rules are written. The process of rulemaking has been evolving since the enactment of the first statute that delegated the authority to develop rules to the first president. Today it can be highly complex. The way it is conducted has important implications for the nation's well-being and the functioning of our democracy. It is to the process of rulemaking we turn next.

NOTES

1. Colin Diver, "Regulatory Precision," in *Making Regulatory Policy*, ed. Keith Hawkins and John Thomas (Pittsburgh: University of Pittsburgh Press, 1989), p. 199.
2. 5 U.S.C. 551 (4).
3. For discussion of these instruments of presidential power, see Phillip Cooper, "Power Tools for an Effective and Responsible Presidency," Department of Public Administration, University of Kansas, 1993.
4. Charles Levine, B. Guy Peters, and Frank Thompson, *Public Administration Challenges, Choices, Consequences* (Glenview, Ill.: Scott Foresman/Little Brown, 1990), p. 99.
5. One scholar would argue that this broad definition is just an example of the APA's rulemaking provisions in which "Congress' delegation of vast lawmaking power was acknowledged and legitimated" (Martin Shapiro, "APA: Past, Present, Future," *Virginia Law Review* 72 [1986]: 453).
6. 29 U.S.C. 553, 651-678.
7. Florence Heffron and Neil McFeeley, *The Administrative Regulatory Process* (New York: Longman, 1983), p. 152.
8. Stephen Breyer and Richard Stewart, *Administrative Law and Regulatory*

Policy, 2d ed. (Boston: Little, Brown, 1985), pp. 466-467.

9. Ibid. The relation between rules and future effects has been accepted in the literature for a long time. See Ralph Fuchs, "Procedures in Administrative Rulemaking," *Harvard Law Review* 52 (1938): 261.

10. As James O'Reilly puts it, "Rules are as old as the republic" (*Administrative Rulemaking* [Colorado Springs, Colo.: Shepard's/McGraw-Hill, 1983], p. 4).

11. Gary Bryner, *Bureaucratic Discretion: Law and Policy in Federal Regulatory Agencies* (New York: Pergamon, 1987), p. 10.

12. Attorney General's Committee on Administrative Procedure, *Administrative Procedure in Government Agencies*, S. Doc. 8, 77th Cong., 1st sess., 1941, p. 97 (hereafter cited as Attorney General's Committee).

13. Ibid.

14. Ibid.

15. David Rosenbloom, "Public Law and Regulation," in *Handbook of Public Administration*, ed. Jack Rubin, Bartley Hildreth, and Gerald Miller (New York: Marcel Dekker, 1989), pp. 544-545.

16. See Attorney General's Committee, p. 98, at n. 17.

17. At this point it is important to note that a large number of sources deal with the historical development of public policy in the areas mentioned in the text. Various authors consider successive "eras" of growth and diversification in public policy, regulation, and rulemaking. An accessible list of major statutes that established programs and authorities for a wide variety of agencies that issue rules can be found in the *Federal Regulatory Directory*, 6th ed. (Washington, D.C.: CQ Press, 1990).

18. Ernest Gelhorn and Barry Boyer, *Administrative Law and Process in a Nutshell*, 2d ed. (St. Paul, Minn.: West Publishing, 1982), p. 17.

19. Rosenbloom, "Public Law and Regulation," pp. 553-555.

20. Phillip Cooper, *Public Law and Public Administration* (Palo Alto, Calif.: Mayfield, 1983), p. 75. In a subsequent chapter we will review Supreme Court decisions that invalidated much of the legislative basis for the New Deal. While these cases hinged on perceived defects in the NIRA, the way agencies conducted rulemaking and other program functions were prominent elements in the Court's opinions.

21. Ibid.

22. Attorney General's Committee, part 7, Department of the Interior, p. 57, and part 10, Bituminous Coal Division, Department of the Interior, pp. 12-13.

23. Ibid., part 19, Veterans Affairs.

24. Ibid., part 11, Interstate Commerce Commission, p. 67.

25. Ibid., p. 99.

26. William West, "The Politics of Administrative Rulemaking," *Public Administration Review*, September/October 1982, pp. 421-423.

27. Susan Estreicher, "Policy Oscillation at the Labor Board: A Plea for Rulemaking," *Administrative Law Review* 37 (1985): 163.

28. Attorney General's Committee, part 3, Social Security Board, p. 23.

29. This summary of legislation draws on material found in Rosenbloom, "Evolution of the Administrative State," pp. 563-564, and the *Federal Regulatory Directory*.

30. Antonin Scalia, "Making Law without Making Rules," *Regulation*, July/August 1982, p. 25.

31. Theodore Lowi, "Two Roads to Serfdom: Liberalism, Conservatism and Administrative Power," *American University Law Review* 36 (1987): 298.

32. A. Lee Fritschler, "The Changing Face of Government Regulation," in *Federal Administrative Agencies*, ed. Howard Ball (Englewood Cliffs, N.J.: Prentice Hall, 1984); Bryner, "Bureaucratic Discretion," p. 13.

33. Bryner, "Bureaucratic Discretion," p. 13.

34. See, for example, Harvey Lieber, *Federalism and Clean Waters* (Boston: Lexington Books, 1974).

35. Arthur Bonfield, *State Administrative Rule Making* (Boston: Little, Brown, 1986), pp. 19-20.

36. Jerry Mashaw, "Improving the Environment of Agency Rulemaking: An Essay on Management, Games and Legal and Political Accountability" (Report to the Administrative Conference of the United States, August 1992); Thomas McGarrity, "Some Thoughts on Deossifying the Rulemaking Process," *Duke Law Journal* 41 (1992): 1385-1462; Robert Anthony, "Interpretive Rules, Policy Statements, Guidances, Manuals, and the Like—Should Agencies Use Them to Bind the Public," *Duke Law Journal* 41 (1992): 1311-1384.

37. Anthony, "Interpretive Rules," pp. 15-21, 25.

38. Ibid., pp. 18-19.

39. 29 CFR, part 1607.

40. Attorney General's Committee, p. 100.

41. Anthony, "Interpretive Rules."

42. The effects of government rules and regulations on American business are summarized in a large number of texts and reports. See, for example, Murray Weidenbaum, *Business, Government and the Public*, 4th ed. (New York: Prentice Hall, 1990).

43. "Northwest Pilots Are Found Guilty of Drunken Flying," *New York Times*, August 21, 1990.

44. Cornelius Kerwin, "Transforming Regulation," *Public Administration Review*, January/February 1990.

45. See Marvin Bernstein, *Regulating Business by Independent Commission* (Princeton, N.J.: Princeton University Press, 1955).

46. There are many treatments of the struggle between the White House and Capitol Hill for control of the bureaucracy. See, for example, Louis Fisher, *The Politics of Shared Power*, 3d ed. (Washington, D.C.: CQ Press, 1993), chap. 4.

47. James Landis, *The Administrative Process* (New Haven: Yale University Press, 1938), p. 69.

48. Lowi, "Two Roads to Serfdom."

49. Kenneth Culp Davis, *Discretionary Justice: A Preliminary Inquiry* (Urbana: University of Illinois Press, 1969), p. 27.

50. Ibid., p. 55.

51. Morris Fiorina, "Legislative Choice of Regulatory Forms: Legal Process or Administrative Process," *Public Choice* 39, no. 1 (1982): 46-47.

52. Anthony Downs, *Inside Bureaucracy* (Boston: Little, Brown, 1967), chap. 9.

CHAPTER 2

The Process of Rulemaking

Return with me now to one of those countless times you have found yourself driving behind a large truck. A sign on its rear with a familiar diamond shape and markings triggers the recognition that you are sharing the roadway with something dangerous. As you strain to make out the message of the sign, you goose the accelerator to get a bit closer. You are attracted to those hurtling explosives, corrosives, or combustibles like a moth to a flame. Finally you can read the dire warning and it says, "Drive Gently: Have a Nice Day."

Empty tanker trucks with their banal messages notwithstanding, the amount of hazardous cargo transported on the road, rails, and water and in the air and the dangers they pose are no joke. The volume is impossible to estimate, but we know that the government has established more than twenty different classes of dangerous cargo. The substances that fill these various categories number in the thousands. And we are routinely treated to the depressing sight of overturned tractor-trailers, punctured railroad cars, or tankers with gaping holes surrounded by emergency response personnel outfitted like something out of a low-budget science fiction film. The threat is real, and for nearly a century government has been attempting to deal with it.

With passage of the Explosives and Combustibles Act of 1908 the federal government assumed regulatory authority over dangerous substances and material moving through interstate commerce. The rules written to implement this legislation and the amendments to it that followed have grown in number until they now fill 1,400 pages in the *Code of Federal Regulations*. Known collectively as the Hazardous Materials Regulations (HMR), these rules have developed over a long period of time. By the government's own admission their evolution has been incremental and disjointed; by the 1970s they were being roundly criticized for being too long, too complex, too difficult to use, and too hard to enforce.

The work of revising the HMR began sometime in 1981, and in April 1982 the first public notice that the Department of Transportation (DOT) was developing new regulations appeared in the *Federal Register*. The notice invited the public to comment on the new rules. Many supplemental public notices were issued during the development process, and members of the public took full advantage of each of these opportunities to influence the rulemaking. It is estimated that the last notice before the new regulations became official generated more than 2,200 written comments from interested parties. Controversy, sometimes intense, occurred often. There were disagreements in the department, disagreements between the DOT and other agencies, and opposition from those affected by the rules. During the more than ten years it took to develop the new regulations, dozens, if not hundreds, of DOT personnel were involved in some way in their writing. In the final two and one-half years of intensive work, more than twenty employees were engaged in a "core workgroup," concentrating on completing the regulations. Dozens of individual analyses and studies were conducted. The agency did evaluations of the effect of the new rules on the environment, small business, federalism, paperwork, and the economy in general. Countless individual decisions were made, some large, some small, that determined the final content of the rules. The Office of Management and Budget, a staff organization serving the president, reviewed all these analyses. The rules were cleared by the OMB before they were published in both draft and final form. On December 21, 1991, the Department of Transportation announced its comprehensive revision of the HMR, dealing with packaging, classification, communication, and handling. While the specific contents of these rules are important to all of us, of interest to us here is the process of their development.

It would be misleading to suggest that this long, complex, and resource-intensive process by which the new HMR was developed is typical of contemporary rulemaking. Still, it is by no means unique. In fact, the Department of Transportation concluded that the rule, which filled 327 triple-columned, double-spaced pages in the *Federal Register*, was a "significant" regulation but not a "major" one (Figure 2-1).[1] We can point to rules that took longer to write, generated more interest and conflict, involved more studies and negotiations, and occupied the time and talent of more agency personnel, but the HMR and similar rules have much to tell us about rulemaking. The process by which rules are written is a critical element in our legal and political system. The contemporary rulemaking process is the evolutionary product of forces that have been at work for many decades, and the attention it has attracted through the years confirms its status as a prime element of governmental decision making.

Figure 2-1   Sample of the Hazardous Materials Regulations in the *Federal Register*

52402   Federal Register / Vol. 55, No. 246 / Friday, December 21, 1990 / Rules and Regulations

---

DEPARTMENT OF TRANSPORTATION

Research and Special Programs Administration

49 CFR Parts 107, 171, 172, 173, 174, 175, 176, 177, 178, and 179

[Docket Nos. HM–181, HM–181A, HM–181B, HM–181C, HM–181D and HM–204; Amdt. Nos. 107–23, 171–111, 172–123, 173–224, 174–68, 175–47, 176–30, 177–78, 178–97, and 179–45]

RIN 2137–AA01, 2137–AB87, 2137–AB88, 2137–AA10, and 2137–AB90

Performance-Oriented Packaging Standards; Changes to Classification, Hazard Communication, Packaging and Handling Requirements Based on UN Standards and Agency Initiative

AGENCY: Research and Special Programs Administration (RSPA), DOT.

ACTION: Final rule.

SUMMARY: This final rule comprehensively revises the Hazardous Materials Regulations (HMR; 49 CFR parts 171–180) with respect to hazard communication, classification and packaging requirements. The changes are based on the United Nations Recommendations on the Transport of Dangerous Goods (U.N. Recommendations) and RSPA's own initiative. They are made because the existing HMR are: (1) Difficult to use because of their length and complexity; (2) relatively inflexible and outdated with regard to non-bulk packaging technology; (3) deficient in terms of safety with regard to the classification and packaging of certain categories of hazardous materials; and, (4) generally not in alignment with international regulations based on the U.N. Recommendations. This action will: (1) Simplify and reduce the volume of the HMR; (2) enhance safety through better classification and packaging; (3) promote flexibility and technological innovation in packaging; (4) reduce the need for exemptions from the HMR; and (5) facilitate international commerce.

DATES: Effective October 1, 1991. However, compliance with the regulations as amended herein is authorized on and after January 1, 1991. The incorporation by reference of certain publications listed in these amendments is approved by the Director of the Federal Register as of October 1, 1991.

Petitions for reconsideration must be received on or before March 21, 1991.

ADDRESSES: Address comments and petitions for reconsideration to the Dockets Unit, Research and Special

Programs Administration, Department of Transportation, Washington, DC 20590–0001. Comments should identify the docket and be submitted in five copies. If confirmation of receipt is desired, include a self-addressed stamped postcard showing the docket number (i.e., Docket HM–181). The Dockets Unit is located in room 8421 of the Nassif Building, 400 Seventh Street SW., Washington, DC 20590–0001. Public dockets may be reviewed between the hours of 8:30 a.m. and 5 p.m., Monday through Friday, except holidays.

FOR FURTHER INFORMATION CONTACT: Delmer Billings, telephone (202) 366–4488, Office of Hazardous Materials Standards, or Charles Hochman, telephone (202) 366–4545, Office of Hazardous Materials Technology, U.S. Department of Transportation, 400 Seventh Street SW., Washington, DC 20590–0001.

SUPPLEMENTARY INFORMATION:

Special Notices

The amendments presented in this document entail changes, both editorial and substantive, to substantial portions of the existing HMR. In a rulemaking project of this magnitude it is inevitable that errors and omissions will come to light subsequent to publication. Comments addressed to such errors and omissions are requested, so that they may be corrected in future rulemaking action under this docket.

For this final rule, the 30-day limitation for the receipt of petitions for reconsideration (49 CFR 106.35) is hereby waived and 90 days is provided in consideration thereof.

Preamble Outline

I. Overview of the HMR
II. Problems with the HMR
III. The International System
IV. History of HM–181 Proposals
V. Related Rulemakings
VI. Major Features of the Final Rule
VII. Shipper/Manufacturer Responsibility
VIII. Transition Period
IX. Impact on Exemptions
X. Enforcement of Performance-oriented Packaging Standards
XI. Public Input to International Standards-Issuing Entities
XII. Section-by-section Review
    A. Part 107
    B. Part 171
    C. Part 172
    D. Part 173
    E. Part 174
    F. Part 175
    G. Part 176
    H. Part 177
    I. Part 178
    J. Part 179
XIII. Administrative Notices
    A. Executive Order 12291
    B. Executive Order 12612
    C. Impact on Small Entities

    D. Paperwork Reduction Act

I. Overview of the HMR

The Hazardous Materials Regulations (HMR) apply to the interstate (and in some cases intrastate) transportation of hazardous materials in commerce. They have their origins in the Explosives and Combustibles Act of 1908, originally administered by the Interstate Commerce Commission. The HMR are currently issued pursuant to the Hazardous Materials Transportation Act (HMTA) of 1974, administered by DOT, and are found in the Code of Federal Regulations (CFR), title 49, subtitle B, chapter 1, subchapter C, parts 171 through 180.

The HMR govern the safety aspects of transportation. They include requirements for classification of materials, packaging (including manufacture, continuing qualification and maintenance), hazard communication (i.e., package marking, labeling, placarding, and shipping documentation), transportation and handling, and incident reporting.

Subchapter C occupies approximately fourteen hundred pages of the CFR. The largest parts, part 173, entitled "Shippers—General Requirements for Shipments and Packagings," and part 178, entitled "Shipping Container Specifications, occupy about three hundred and fifty and four hundred and fifty pages, respectively.

Part 171 of the HMR includes definitions, reporting requirements, a listing of matter incorporated by reference, and procedural requirements, including provisions which permit use of other regulations, such as the ICAO Technical Instructions and the IMDG Code. Part 172 of the HMR contains a listing of hazardous materials in the Hazardous Materials Table (§ 172.101) and various communications requirements for shipping paper descriptions, marking and labeling of packages, placarding of vehicles and bulk packagings, and emergency response communication.

Part 173 contains various hazard class definitions for classifying materials, lists the DOT packagings authorized for specific materials and references the appropriate sections of part 178 when DOT specification packagings are required. Parts 174 through 177 contain requirements applicable to specific transport modes: Part 174 for transport by rail car, part 175 for transport by aircraft, part 176 for transport by vessel, and part 177 for transport by motor vehicle. Part 176 will now include provisions for the transportation of military explosives by vessel. These

---

(Figure continues)

42   RULEMAKING

Figure 2-1   *(Continued)*

Federal Register / Vol. 55, No. 246 / Friday, December 21, 1990 / Rules and Regulations   52403

were previously contained in 46 CFR part 146, which is being revoked in a separate rulemaking.

Part 178, addressed primarily to container manufacturers, contains detailed construction specifications for a wide variety of packagings. The specification packagings found in part 178 range from paper bags to cargo tanks (tank trucks). The major portion of part 178 is devoted to non-bulk packagings (authorized capacities of 110 gallons or less) and includes approximately 100 specifications for carboys, drums, barrels, boxes, cases, trunks, tubes, bags and various sorts of inside containers or receptacles designed to be enclosed by larger containers. Not included in these 100 specifications are those covering cylinders for compressed gases and packagings designed solely for radioactive or explosive materials, none of which are addressed under this final rule.

Part 179 addresses specifications for tank cars. Part 180 contains requirements for the continuing qualification and maintenance of packagings.

Beginning with the creation of the Department of Transportation in 1967, the Department assumed responsibility for the HMR and embarked on a long-range effort to simplify and improve the regulations. In 1968, under Docket HM-7 [33 FR 11862; August 21, 1968], DOT stated its intent to revise the HMR to make them uniform for the various modes of transport and easy to understand and apply. DOT also stated it would improve hazard classification of materials to better describe their hazards and relate classification to appropriate handling and packaging designs, improve hazard communication through labeling, placarding and emergency response provisions, and prescribe packaging requirements in terms of performance standards rather than manufacturing specifications.

Major accomplishments of this effort to simplify and improve the HMR include adoption of labels and placards (1974) based on the United Nations Committee of Experts' Recommendations on the Transport of Dangerous Goods (U.N. Recommendations), development and widespread distribution of DOT's Emergency Response Guidebook, and adoption of identification numbers for hazardous materials (1980) based on the U.N. Recommendations. Numerous other rulemaking projects have addressed improvements to classification, hazard communication, and packaging. Docket HM-181 and related rulemaking projects represent the culmination of RSPA's

efforts since 1968 to improve the HMR and align them with an internationally-based performance standards system.

The importance of this rulemaking initiative has been recognized in the Department's National Transportation Policy which states that it is Federal transportation policy to:

• Adopt hazardous materials packaging standards that are based on performance criteria rather than detailed design specifications, to accommodate technical innovation, and

• Implement Federal hazardous materials standards for movements by the various modes that are, to the maximum extent consistent with safety, compatible with international standards, in order to facilitate foreign trade and maintain the competitiveness of U.S. goods.

II. Problems With the HMR

The development of the HMR has been an evolutionary process. Regulations originally were addressed only to the most acute transportation safety hazards such as the risks of explosives and flammable materials. As new materials presenting different risks entered the transportation system, new hazard classes were added. The HMR now address over 20 different classes of hazardous materials. Hazard communication and packaging requirements were added as the need arose, based on the occurrence of accidents or the development and adoption of industry standards. Packaging requirements were based on industry standards, with economic considerations sometimes taking precedence over safety considerations, rather than on a systematic assignment of packagings based on the hazards of the materials to be packaged and the suitability of the packaging. By the same token, hazard classifications were often made based on subjective criteria, with economic considerations occasionally taking precedence over safety considerations.

Because of the non-systematic and piecemeal fashion in which they were developed, the HMR tend to be unnecessarily complex and difficult to use. RSPA believes there is a need to amend the HMR to address deficiencies related to safety, complexity of regulations, inflexibility of packaging standards and incongruities between the HMR and international regulations for hazardous materials transport.

With regard to safety, correct classification of materials is essential for determining the hazards posed, appropriate hazard communication, and packaging. Classification procedures in the HMR were developed in a piecemeal

fashion over an eighty-year period and tend to be imprecise and subjective. The classification scheme proposed in Docket HM-181, based in large part on the U.N. Recommendations, is more precise than the existing system and would replace subjective hazard class definitions with objective criteria, particularly with regard to gases which are toxic by inhalation and flammable solids. Other safety initiatives embodied in Docket HM-181 involve enhancements to general packaging provisions for both bulk and non-bulk packagings, and improvements to the integrity of packagings for extremely hazardous materials such as those which are poisonous by inhalation.

The HMR have long been criticized as being too lengthy (1400 pages), complex, and difficult to use and enforce. It is impossible to eliminate complexity in regulations which, of necessity, must address the legal, technical and operational concerns for classification, hazard communication and packaging for thousands of hazardous chemicals. However, a new format and use of performance standards rather than detailed design specifications will make the HMR more "user friendly" and substantially reduce the number of HMR pages.

With regard to packaging flexibility, the detailed design specifications which are found in the HMR are generally based on industry standards, many of which were incorporated into the regulations in the 1920's and 1930's. They tend to be overly specific and are outdated in many respects, thereby stifling innovation and resulting in the need for numerous burdensome exemptions. Authorizations to use specific packagings for specific hazardous materials were often made based on economic considerations, operating convenience or historical precedence, rather than by assessing the risks posed by the hazardous material and selecting a packaging suitable for the material. Typical specifications found in part 178 include requirements for materials of construction, thickness, fastenings, capacity, coatings, openings, joints and carrying devices. Much of the information contained in a specification is given in great detail and is repetitious. For example, there are fourteen specifications for wooden boxes. Most wooden box specifications list each acceptable type of wood from which the box must be constructed. This list may be repeated in the next specification for a similar, but slightly different box. In addition to listing the acceptable types of wood, the regulations also specify the thickness and width of boards, kinds

Source: Federal Register, December 21, 1990, 52402-52403.

PROCESS AND SUBSTANCE

Given the vast scope of rules and that so much depends on their content, it should not be surprising that the process used to write them attracts a great deal of attention. During the past fifty years rulemaking has been the focus of considerable professional and political controversy. The way rules are written profoundly affects what they contain, and we have already established that the content of rules determines, to a very large extent, the quality of our lives.

The substance of rules and the process of rulemaking are linked in a number of important ways. The elements of the contemporary rulemaking process are reactions to great expansion in the substantive reach of rulemaking. We have seen that the New Deal and the decades of the 1970s and 1980s were periods of explosive growth in governmental programs that required massive rulemaking to meet ambitious objectives. These expansions of the subject matter of rulemaking stimulated intense interest in the manner in which rules were developed by the responsible agencies. In both periods there was concern about how agencies were making decisions about the contents of rules. What were agencies taking into account? To whom were they listening? To whom were they responsible? In both periods, these concerns led to many proposals, some successful, others not, to change the way rules were written.

Contemporary rulemaking is a highly developed process, generally subject to a complex web of legal requirements. Nevertheless, the subject matter of a particular rule can still exert a powerful effect on how the rule is developed. The types and amounts of information needed and the persons affected by a rule determine which of a large set of legal requirements will actually apply in a particular rulemaking. As important, the technical, administrative, and political dimensions of each rulemaking are determined almost entirely by the topic and scope of the rule to be written. A few simple examples highlight the differences.

A rule that deals with important aspects of the transport of hazardous materials necessarily involves a large number of issues, some of which require major research efforts to resolve. The rule will affect large and diverse segments of our population, each interested in it for different reasons. Those who ship goods, transport them, and consume them will all be concerned with the effect of the rule on them, as will environmental groups and organizations representing the workers who come in contact with the dangerous materials. Because the rule will have a large overall impact on the economy, certain legal requirements that would otherwise not apply must be met. Similarly, the rule's potential effect on the environment and small businesses triggers other specific legal requirements. Because the provisions of the rule mandate the keeping of records and periodic reporting to the government, a law that seeks to limit paperwork for regulated parties must also be considered. The number and diversity of interests affected by the rule alters rulemaking procedures in less formal ways also. The agency writing the rule must provide for participation by those affected, and this will be determined in part by what the law requires in this regard and in part by the agency's assessment of the political environment. Within and without the agency there are systems to review and approve rules before they take effect. Given the scope of the rule, the costs it will impose on regulated parties, and the inevitable controversy it will generate, it is certain that all in a position to affect its content will scrutinize it closely.

Contrast this with the making of a much less prominent and far more common rule. Virtually every week the Marketing Service of the Department of Agriculture issues rules that limit the amount of specified commodities that can be shipped to market during some predetermined period of time. The rule is developed by a standing committee of experts in the marketing of the commodity in question, and the decision is based on the clearly stated goal of supporting the price and quality of lemons, oranges, or the other half-dozen fruits and vegetables affected by this program. The interests most immediately and substantially affected are narrow and comparatively few in number, and the rule remains in effect for a very short period of time.[2] Its limited scope and impact allows the agency to avoid many of the legal requirements that apply in the case of the rule for transportation of hazardous materials. The routine and serial nature of this form of rulemaking generates less political and administrative scrutiny. Public controversies are rare and muted, if evident at all.

Substance and process are inextricably linked in rulemaking. The missions established for agencies in authorizing legislation determine what rulemaking must accomplish. These goals, in turn, determine the types and amount of information that must be collected. The legal requirements that apply to rulemaking do so on a contingent basis, triggered by the size and type of populations or activities affected by the rule being developed. For virtually every procedural requirement imposed on rulemaking, exceptions may be granted, an acknowledgment that few elements of process make political or economic sense in all rulemaking situations. Process is so modulated for reasons of politics and efficiency.

In the previous chapter we saw that a majority of actions classified as rules deal with narrowly defined subjects or affect only a small number of activities and people and are temporary in their effects. Their content may hinge entirely on technical considerations about which there is no debate. Such rules are not likely to stimulate affected parties to invest considerable time and effort to change the process by which they are written. Further, additional procedures will not improve or alter the decisions made during rulemaking sufficiently to justify the additional costs imposed on the agencies who write the rules. Variations in the substance of rules determine the extent and intensity of political attention that will focus on a given rulemaking, driving oversight by Congress, the White House, and the courts. All of these, in turn, influence the administrative and management systems that support and oversee rulemaking in the agencies. In rulemaking, when considering process we must always be aware of the leavening effects of a given rule's subject matter.

FROM THE FIRST CONGRESS TO THE ADMINISTRATIVE PROCEDURE ACT

Not much is known about how our early presidents actually wrote the rules they were authorized to issue under the laws enacted by the first congresses. Clearly, George Washington and many of his successors lacked the formidable executive office and massive bureaucracies that now support rulemaking. Even as the function of rulemaking migrated from the direct control of the president to cabinet secretaries, it was not until the latter part of the nineteenth century that sizable bureaucracies were available to put their collective expertise to the task of rulemaking. But presidents and cabinet secretaries did issue rules, sometimes numerous and complex, from the very start of the Republic. Take, for example, the extensive rules governing customs duties that the president was required to issue. Certainly, Washington was an accomplished man, but was he sufficiently expert to fix the level of duties on so large a number of goods?

Until the 1930s none of the main governmental institutions— Congress, the president, the courts—paid serious or sustained attention to rulemaking as a general public function. Still, it is also important to note that in particular instances Congress did provide guidance on how rulemaking in specific programs should work, and in some agencies it was remarkably well developed by the time of the New Deal. Consider the rulemaking techniques used by the Wage and Hour Division of the Department of Labor under the Fair Labor Standards Act. A study conducted in the late 1930s revealed a five-step process to establish rules governing wages. An "industry committee" consisting of representatives of labor and management was appointed. The committee then engaged in an investigation, after which it recommended a minimum wage rate for the industry in question. The recommendation would be the subject of a public hearing conducted by the administrator of the Wage and Hour Division, who, upon consideration of the recommendation and the results of the public hearing, would issue his or her final determination.[3] This whole procedure was something akin to what we would today call a permanent "regulatory negotiation" process.

Another example of 1930s rulemaking with a faintly contemporary ring involves rules written for fisheries by the Department of the Interior. The Attorney General's Committee on Administrative Procedure found in its research into the Interior Department that the fishing industry's dissatisfaction with the regulations had led to a crisis of enforcement. Widespread noncompliance and evasion of rules were reported. To deal with the dissatisfaction and revive these important regulations, the Department of the Interior held a series of public meetings around the country to collect information from affected persons about the deficiencies in the existing regulations and ideas for reform.[4] As we will see, forty years later the Carter administration relied heavily on such mechanisms for public outreach to reform what it considered an unresponsive rulemaking process.

THE POLITICS OF PROCESS

The process of rulemaking burst onto the political agenda during the early years of the New Deal. From its inception the New Deal was a lightning rod for critics. They decried the growth of the federal government and the intrusions into private affairs that the philosophy and individual programs of the New Deal represented. The criticism that a massive federal bureaucracy had become the "headless fourth branch of government" was certainly heard before the 1930s, but during the New Deal it became particularly focused and intense.

The most organized and persistent criticism of rulemaking came from the American Bar Association (ABA). The reasons that this was so may not be immediately apparent. After all, the ABA's members might commiserate with their clients about the influence on previously private affairs of a seemingly endless succession of agencies, but the effect of this growing body of regulation might also bring to attorneys an enormous increase in business. Still, however sincere their concern about the growth of government per se, the reasons for the organized bar's alarm about the way this rapidly growing bureaucratic state was making decisions are understandable.

Lawyers today are educated and trained to participate in government decision making in all its varied contexts, but the bar of the 1930s was very much identified with the judicial system. Based on the adversary model, which stressed formal rules of evidence and procedure, aggressive advocacy for both sides of a dispute, and a removed and objective tribunal with final authority to decide, the civil courts were a far cry from the bureaucratic institutions that were popping up like so many mushrooms. David Rosenbloom has observed that the rise of this "administrative state" represented far more than an irritating change in habits for the legal profession. It was, instead, "an especially severe challenge because it threatened the supremacy of the common law."[5] Through legislation, administrative agencies themselves possessed the power to "contravene" the common law. The strategies open to the lawyers faced with this apparent steamroller of expanding government were essentially two. They could stand in its path and hope that the collision would arrest its progress and then reverse its course. Or they could attempt to divert its progress to a different path, one more acceptable to the core values of the profession. Ultimately, they chose the second approach.

For a brief time in the mid-1930s it appeared as if the juggernaut of government would be derailed. A series of Supreme Court decisions suggested that the mechanism on which the administrative state depended for maintenance and growth and for delegation of authority would be severely curtailed. The cases involved challenges to the National Industrial Recovery Act, which, as noted in the previous chapter, granted sweeping regulatory powers to the president and a myriad of boards responsible for segments of the economy. Once under way, the actions of these boards and other institutions of the New Deal came under heavy attack by critics, who had found a largely sympathetic ear in the federal courts. Stephen Breyer and Richard Stewart report that in the early years of the New Deal federal judges were frequent allies of the critics, invalidating some statutes, curtailing the powers of agencies, and reversing individual decisions.[6]

The most dramatic confrontation between the new administrative state and the forces of the old order occurred in 1935 and 1936 in a series of three cases that appeared to knock out the underpinnings of the New Deal. In three cases—*Panama Refining Co. v. Ryan, Schechter Poultry Corporation v. United States,* and *Carter v. Carter Coal Co.*—it was found that authorities granted under the New Deal statutes amounted to unconstitutional delegations of legislative authority to the president, agencies, and other regulatory officials.[7] *Panama* involved powers granted the president in the NIRA to restrict the production of oil. *Schechter* contained a challenge to the "live poultry codes" authorized under the NIRA's "fair competition" provisions. In *Carter,* the Supreme Court was asked to rule on the legitimacy of a statute that empowered private groups consisting of coal producers and their employees to set binding conditions for this segment of the economy. In both *Panama* and *Schechter* the Court ruled that the sections of the NIRA on which the so-called "hot oil" and "sick chicken" authorities were based contained no discernible standards to guide and constrain the president and his administrative agents. Thus, they were invalidated. In *Carter* the Court found a different but no less fatal flaw in that the statute empowered private individuals to make binding public decisions. This too was ruled an unconstitutional delegation of authority by Congress. In these cases the Court questioned not only basic grants of authority but how they were exercised by the various instrumentalities that arose under the NIRA. Cited were instances of rules being written with little or no advance warning, of their being written with minimal consultation with affected parties, and even of their being unpublished or otherwise unavailable to the regulated parties.

The New Deal was shaken by this judicial assault, and the question of what constituted an acceptable delegation of legislative authority was opened.[8] Since much of the NIRA and other New Deal law was based on similarly broad grants of power, the prospects for a rapidly expanding government were very much in doubt. The implications for rulemaking, as a general governmental function, were particularly ominous. Each of the cases touched some aspect of rulemaking and left a clear message. In the future, rulemaking might be much more constricted, because Congress would be required to be more specific and restrictive in its grants of authority. Further, the rulemaking that remained to be done would be scrutinized closely on both substantive and procedural grounds.

As it happened, however, the threat was short-lived. The court's decisions triggered a firestorm of protest from the supporters of the New Deal, and Franklin Delano Roosevelt personally led the charge. Most students of American government are familiar with the constitutional crisis that ensued. Roosevelt, charging that an out-of-touch, overworked, and thoroughly unresponsive group of five of the nine Supreme Court justices was thwarting the will of the American people, launched an offensive to recoup what had been lost. His "court-packing plan" would add to the Court one justice for every sitting justice over seventy, giving him an immediate ten-to-five majority. Congress, however, outraged at the judicial decimation of their handiwork, was not willing to countenance this wholesale manipulation of another constitutional branch of government.[9] The court-packing plan failed, but Roosevelt still won the day. Shifts in voting by two members of the court changed a bare five-to-four majority against the New Deal into a vocal minority. Departures of sitting judges delivered FDR the opportunity he needed to remake the Court in his own image. He succeeded in the transformation; the New Deal and rulemaking were quickly restored to their previous states of health and influence.

The loss of their judicial ally hurt but by no means destroyed the critics of the new administrative state. On the contrary, the action shifted to the legislative arena, and the bar took the lead in attempting to recast the rulemaking process in a form more consistent with traditional lawyerly practices. In this political arena the tenor of the debate shifted from careful, scholarly arguments regarding the proper "channels" for legislative powers to less subtle and politically charged accusations that rulemaking and other administrative functions were manifestations of a creeping "socialism." The specter of unelected and essentially invisible bureaucrats writing, in near secrecy, laws that had the direct or indirect effects of curtailing freedom and confiscating property was a compelling, if somewhat melodramatic, argument for reforming the administrative process.

The ABA's original proposals for reform focused on the elimination of independent regulatory commissions and the transfer of all adjudicatory powers from the remaining agencies to the federal courts. Further, it argued that all administrative actions that stayed with agencies be subjected to judicial review in a special federal administrative court. Rulemaking would be transformed into a quasi-judicial activity, with each proposed rule subjected to a formal public hearing. The content of rules would be determined using standards of evidence like those used in civil trials. Many of these proposals were contained in the Walter-Logan Bill of 1940, which surprisingly passed both houses of Congress. According to Peter Woll, the bill "attempted to enforce common law due process, applicable only to adjudication, to the legislative process of administrative agencies." [10] Support for Walter-Logan in the wake of the New Deal was apparently not seen by members as contradictory, perhaps because they failed to see the link between the substance of programs and the processes by which they were administered. Clearly, however, the immobilization of the administrative state was again at hand. Intended or not, Walter-Logan would calcify the administrative process and render rulemaking on a large scale virtually impossible.

If Congress did not see the threat, Roosevelt most certainly did. He vetoed the bill, and the veto was not overridden by Congress. But the president knew he had a problem that would not go away. There was widespread belief, justified or not, that the administrative process needed attention. For example, it is certainly true that rulemaking procedures were well developed in a number of agencies, but it was not uniformly so. No generally applicable, procedural standards had been authoritatively established by legislation or any other means. What those standards should be was not immediately clear to FDR, but his recent experience with the Walter-Logan Bill probably convinced him that Congress should not be let loose on the task. So he did what all presidents have done when they faced difficult and politically dangerous decisions. He bought time, and prayed for answers, from an advisory commission.

The extraordinary work of the Attorney General's Committee on Administrative Procedure was discussed in the previous chapter. Their case studies of the practices in force in more than two dozen agencies in the late 1930s constitute an invaluable resource for scholars. More important, their findings laid the foundation for one of the landmark statutes of the twentieth century. The report of the Attorney General's Committee, *Administrative Procedures in Government Agencies*, was issued in 1941, and the recommendations developed in it became the springboard for what became the Administrative Procedure Act of 1946. Its passage was delayed by World War II, but enactment followed soon thereafter. Its enduring importance to contemporary rulemaking is debatable, but the act remains a historic statement of the principles of government for a bureaucratic age.

Martin Shapiro has characterized the APA as a "deal struck between opposing political forces" at a pivotal stage in the development of the national government.[11] On the one hand were the New Dealers, who were not quite yet the dominant force in American political life, and on the other were conservatives, who probably saw the handwriting on the wall but wanted to delay reading it for as long as possible. The New Dealers sought a large and active government capable of defining and refining policies quickly and able to implement them with dispatch. The conservative forces held on stubbornly to the notion that the common law and judicial processes were the best, if not the only, way to protect private property, individual rights, and capitalism itself from a rapacious public sector. The compromise ultimately struck was perfectly logical, but lopsided. In the APA the proponents of big and easy government won a great victory.[12] But they failed to rout the enemy thoroughly, and during the next several decades they would eventually lose the war.

Shapiro has observed that the APA divides all administrative procedure into three categories: rulemaking, which is when agencies act like legislatures; adjudication, which is when agencies act like courts; and everything else.[13] The final category is hardly trivial, since it contains the classic bureaucratic tasks of executing, administering, and otherwise delivering programs and policies to the public. In the simplest terms, the APA requires agencies to behave like a legislature when they write rules and like courts when they adjudicate disputes. Everything else is left essentially to the discretion of the agencies. Looked at from this perspective, the New Dealers succeeded in capturing much of the making and all of the implementation of policy and law for their political philosophy. America's historical penchant for an independent judiciary, with its distinctive and elaborate methods for making decisions, would, however, be preserved. Adjudication in agencies was to be conducted in the manner of a civil trial presided over by a judicial officer whose objectivity was to be guaranteed through his or her structural and functional separation from the other activities and personnel of the agency. The APA is vague on the matter of the situations in which adjudication was to be the required method for decision making, defining them only as "matters other than rulemaking . . . but including licensing." [14] For decades the struggle to define a clear and bright line between situations appropriate for rulemaking and those appropriate for adjudication has produced few hard and fast generalizations, leaving a substantial number of government actions in a procedural twilight zone. It is safe to say that adjudication is the preferred method in those situations when the rules or standards to guide decision making already exist. Hence, it is best used in situations when the status of an individual, as a petitioner, potential beneficiary, or regulated party, is in question and the application of known rules depends on facts about that individual or his or her activities that may be in dispute or in need of elaboration.

Adjudication works best with two-sided issues. Rulemaking, as a legislative process, is designed to sort through facts from multiple sources in order to select standards that will apply generally. That said, it does not take much imagination to think of situations in which "individual fact" might have a strong influence on the rule that an agency is considering. This is especially true when a regulated or beneficiary community is very small, or when the risk to the public posed by incorrect or incomplete facts is great. The APA takes these situations into account by leaving room for Congress to require formal adjudicatory procedure on certain classes of rulemaking when it authorizes agencies to carry out programs. In reality, Congress has used this option infrequently. The key rulemaking provisions of the APA, found in section 553, are very different:

> 553 Rulemaking
> (a) This section applies, according to the provisions thereof, except to the extent that there is involved—
> (1) a military or foreign affairs function of the United States; or
> (2) a matter relating to agency management or personnel or to public property, loans, grants, benefits, or contracts.
> (b) General notice of proposed rule making shall be published in the Federal Register, unless persons subject thereto are named and either personally served or otherwise have actual notice thereof in accordance with law. The notice shall include—
> (1) a statement of the time, place, and nature of public rule making proceedings;
> (2) reference to the legal authority under which the rule is proposed; and
> (3) either the terms or substance of the proposed rule or a description of the subjects and issues involved.
> Except when notice or hearing is required by statute, this subsection does not apply—
> (A) to interpretative rules, general statements of policy, or rules of agency organization, procedure, or practice; or
> (B) when the agency for good cause finds (and incorporates the finding and a brief statement of reasons therefor in the rules issued) that notice and public procedure thereon are impracticable, unnecessary, or contrary to the public interest.
> (c) After notice required by this section, the agency shall give interested persons an opportunity to participate in the rule making through submission of written data, views, or arguments with or without opportunity for oral presentation. After consideration of the relevant matter presented, the agency shall incorporate in the rules

adopted a concise general statement of their basis and purpose. When rules are required by statute to be made on the record after opportunity for an agency hearing, sections 556 and 557 of this title apply instead of this subsection.

(d) The required publication or service of a substantive rule shall be made not less than 30 days before its effective date, except—

(1) a substantive rule which grants or recognizes an exemption or relieves a restriction;

(2) interpretative rules and statements of policy; or

(3) as otherwise provided by the agency for good cause found and published with the rule.

(e) Each agency shall give an interested person the right to petition for the issuance, amendment, or repeal of a rule.

The procedures framed in section 553 have come to be known as "notice and comment" or "informal" rulemaking. They have been described by Kenneth Culp Davis, one of the most influential voices in the history of American administrative law, as one of the "greatest inventions of modern government." [15] What made administrative rulemaking so attractive to him was its speed, its economy, and that "it can be, when the agency so desires, a virtual duplicate of the legislative process." [16] In fact, as contemplated in the APA, administrative rulemaking was considerably less encumbered than the legislative process. Rulemaking authority, safely ensconced in the bowels of agencies, was attended to by specialized staffs with narrow ranges of responsibility and without the presence of constituencies holding the big stick of reelection in their hands. The most remarkable feature of rulemaking was the extraordinary freedom of action it appeared to grant the bureaucrat. History has shown it to be just that, an appearance. Freedom of action for bureaucrats is not rulemaking's most prominent characteristic. A grasp of the APA's original provisions is an important foundation for understanding current process, nonetheless.

THE CORE ELEMENTS OF RULEMAKING: INFORMATION, PARTICIPATION, ACCOUNTABILITY

The core elements of rulemaking as put forth in the APA can be expressed in three words: information, participation, and accountability. These are familiar principles, basic to our constitutional democracy. In the context of rulemaking, however, they assume forms and meanings different from those in other political and governmental settings.

INFORMATION

The most basic element of "information" in rulemaking is the notice provided to the public at large when a rule is being developed and when it becomes final and binding. Generally these notices appear in the *Federal Register*. Under the provisions of the APA the notice varied, depending on the stage of the rulemaking. For proposed rules, agencies needed only to tell the public, in general terms, what it was proposing to do and the authority under which it was taking action. The agencies had the option to serve the notice on persons individually and directly rather than using the *Federal Register*. For proposals, agencies could either provide the public a description of what it had in mind or the actual intended language of the rule. In the absence of other statutory mandates these decisions were left unequivocally to the discretion of the rule writers. The agency was also expected to provide information on the time and place of rulemaking, and for final rules a "concise, general statement of basis and purpose," and at least thirty days prior warning before its requirements took effect.

Another dimension of information is implied in the statement of basis and purpose. That is the information the agencies rely on to develop the rule. Beyond acknowledging its existence and the need to disclose it, the APA says little about what must be considered. More will be said, however, about this dimension of information later in the book.

An argument can be made that the information thus provided the public during rulemaking was at least the equal of what we have access to when Congress or a state legislature is considering a new law. What we learn of pending legislation comes from the selective and often superficial accounts in the media or from direct inquiries we make of our elected representatives, or from their increasingly frequent newsletters. There is no equivalent of a *Federal Register* notice for pending legislative votes. Still, agencies enjoyed considerable discretion when deciding how much information to disclose. All they needed to reveal was a general description of the rule they had in mind and, once it was complete, the statute that it was designed to implement and some discussion of the "basis" for the action they took. This left much discretion to the agencies when determining the quantity and quality of the information that the public would have to work with as it decided if and how it would participate in rulemaking.

PARTICIPATION

Agencies enjoyed considerable freedom when structuring public participation under the provisions of the APA. The agencies were obliged to allow written comments, but participation in any other form was not a matter of right. Surprisingly, the agencies were not instructed anywhere in the act to take heed of what they learned from the public in written comments, or whatever other form of participation they allowed. Clearly, participation was included in the APA for some purpose, but from the language of the act one cannot conclude that it was for any reason other than the education of the agency. No explicit linkage was drawn, for example, between the participation provisions of the act and the requirement that agencies briefly describe the "basis" for their decisions. In like fashion the APA allowed the public to petition agencies to write a rule but provided no additional mandates or guidance to agencies on how to handle or dispose of these petitions.

It is interesting that the framers of the APA chose to codify the least intrusive mechanisms for public participation that were already in use in rulemaking agencies. As noted above, by the time the act was passed in 1946 many agencies, clearly a majority of those writing a significant number of rules at the time, used a variety of procedures to interact with the public they were affecting. In some instances constant and intense interactions between the rulemakers and regulated parties were common. By establishing a floor, below which no agency could fall in its interactions with the public, the APA left it to existing or future legislation to add additional, general procedural requirements. Nothing in the act prevented the agencies themselves from innovating in their dealings with the public during the course of the development of regulation. On reflection, this approach is quite consistent with the views of some in the New Deal coalition that placed such great faith in the capacity of government. If agencies were up to the myriad of technical tasks required to produce a better society, they were certainly capable of fashioning the proper structures and procedures for public participation within the loose constraints of the APA. Those who fashioned the legislation were comfortable with entrusting the steward-ship of public participation to the agencies in which they had such faith.

ACCOUNTABILITY

The APA's substitute for the accountability fostered by the ballot box was the specter of judicial review. The act does not explicitly mention other, more powerful mechanisms for accountability. Congress and the president exert powerful influence over rulemaking in general and specific ways. But, these influences were not treated in the APA other than certain references to Congress to be discussed presently. The primary vehicle for accountability in the APA was judicial review. As outlined in section 706 of the act, judicial review is paradoxical. On the one hand, the act made the courts available to those who wished to challenge rules, repudiating earlier theories of judicial review that made the courthouse threshold difficult to cross. On the other hand, the standard against which agencies' rulemaking decisions would be judged was anything but strict. Rulemaking could be judged on both substantive and procedural dimensions, but in neither were agencies given difficult criteria to meet.

The substance of rules could not constitute an "arbitrary or capricious abuse of discretion." [17] According to definitions found in *Webster's New Collegiate Dictionary*, arbitrary behavior and capricious behavior should be very rare and difficult to establish when they did occur. *Arbitrary* means "at random," an "unreasonable act"; *capricious* means "impulsive," "unpredictable." Taken literally, few rules could be so devoid of "basis and purpose" that their contents would not pass so easy a test. The other avenue for challenging a rulemaking established in the APA was procedural. Given the rather minimal procedures outlined in the act, agencies should have had little difficulty meeting these standards as well. Of course, if Congress had increased procedural requirements for a particular program, or if the agency itself had adopted more elaborate procedures, these would have become the standards against which the rulemaking would have been judged. In this sense, the procedural basis for judicial review was potentially more formidable than the standards for review of the substantive content.

The New Dealers had reason to rejoice over their success in fashioning a rulemaking process that could serve as the vehicle for a rapidly expanding government. As noted above, however, the conservatives took firm control of agency adjudication. Based on long-standing principles of common law, and embodying the adversary model of decision making, adjudication in the provisions of the APA was structurally separated from other agency functions, including rulemaking. This was accomplished through the creation of an independent corps of hearing examiners, later to be called administrative law judges. Preserved was the principle that adjudication was special; when it was the appropriate form of governmental action, the full complement of administrative due process was essential to ensure the accuracy and fairness of the result.

While it is true that the basic rulemaking provisions of the APA have never been significantly amended in the forty-five years since passage, we should not conclude that the act thoroughly dominates the making of rules today. In fact, most important rulemaking is not conducted according to the minimalist model of the APA, if it ever was. Minor and routine rulemaking is also not carried out in tight accordance with the APA, but for different reasons. The fact that the relevant sections of the APA have never been extensively amended does not mean that Congress, the president, the courts, and the agencies themselves have not been busy altering rulemaking since soon after the act passed.

The political coalition that produced the rulemaking provisions of the APA has long since disappeared. The most enduring legacy of the act are the seeds of change its authors planted in the original legislation. The three fundamental elements of rulemaking procedure contained in the APA—information, participation, and accountability—have remained dominant themes throughout the past twenty-five years of virtually constant change. As mentioned briefly above, the APA allows for forms of rulemaking other than the notice and comment provisions of section 553. Specifically, if Congress indicated that rulemaking was to be conducted "on the record," the procedures that normally apply in adjudication would come into force.[18] In addition, when this type of rulemaking is invoked, the standard of review shifts from the permissive "arbitrary and capricious" standard to a considerably more demanding requirement that agencies demonstrate "substantial evidence" for the decisions embodied in the rule. Formal judicialization of rulemaking, which the ABA and its conservative allies fought so hard for in the late 1930s, was not strongly promoted by this provision in the APA, nor has this option been exercised frequently by Congress. The fact that it was retained as an option to exercise is significant nonetheless, perhaps betraying some nagging doubt about the adequacy of the procedures in section 553.

Whether or not the equivocation in the APA was due to discomfort over informal rulemaking is little more than an academic question at this point. For important rules, the events of the 1960s, 1970s, and 1980s have rendered pure notice and comment rulemaking a historical artifact. What happened to the rulemaking process during these years could be described as creeping judicialization. "Creeping" because many small, often uncoordinated alterations were enacted. "Judicialization" because their net effect has been to push rulemaking from a purely legislative mode of operation to one with more of the elements we have come to identify with decision making in courts. The forces pushing rulemaking in this direction are both external and internal to the agencies. Some were motivated by a profound mistrust of government regulation of private activity and the rulemaking that made it possible. Others were motivated by a concern for more rational and comprehensive decision making. Like the APA, all are united by their emphasis on information, participation, or accountability as preferred devices for changing rulemaking into a process more to the liking of the motley crew of reformers. Concentration on these three elements has been remarkably consistent over time.

In rulemaking, information and participation cannot be separated. Effective participation is simply impossible without accurate and complete information on what the agency intends to do, the reasons the agency has for doing it, and the likely effect a new rule will have.

As we have just seen, Congress, the president, and the courts have through time increased dramatically the information that may be generated and shared with the public during the course of rulemaking. They have taken a very similar approach to participation. In fact, these institutions have rarely expanded information requirements without simultaneously increasing the opportunities for the public to participate in the larger rulemaking process. Every increment of information on the need and justification for, and implications of, rules under development increases the ability of interested and affected parties to consider their position and present fully informed views to the agency. It should not be surprising, then, that the very vehicles that vastly expanded the information requirements in rulemaking also opened the process to additional involvement by the public.

INFORMATION: INCREASED LEGAL REQUIREMENTS

Information is a crucial element in any rulemaking. How it is handled by an agency will profoundly influence the content of the rule that is ultimately produced. Information in two general forms must be considered. The first is the information that any agency must collect, or develop, and then consider during the course of a rulemaking. The second is the information that the agency must provide to the public during and after the rulemaking. Both dimensions of rulemaking have changed dramatically since passage of the APA.

Up to 1946, authorizing statutes provided agencies the sum and substance of the direction regarding information they were expected to use when writing rules. Except for its single reference to the "basis" for a rule an agency is about to adopt, the APA provides no additional guidance to and imposes no new standards on the agency in relation to how it is to go about the assembly of the information on which a rule will be based. Authorizing statutes varied considerably in the direction they provided agencies, but as a general rule until the 1960s laws mandating or allowing rulemaking were vague as to the specific types of information to be used and the way it was to be collected.

INFORMATION THAT THE AGENCY MUST CONSIDER

AUTHORIZING STATUTES. Since the late 1960s, regulatory statutes have become increasingly concerned with the type of information an agency considers when deciding whether and how to write a rule. The pattern is most evident in the statutes that establish major programs of social regulation and, to a lesser extent, those dealing with economic institutions and transactions. The section of the Occupational Safety

and Health Act that grants the secretary of labor authority to promul-
gate rules to protect American workers is illustrative. After setting out
the goals that OSHA's rules are to promote, the statute turns to the
types of information that should be used during rulemaking.

> Development of standards . . . shall be based on research, demonstra-
> tions, experiments and such other information as may be appropriate.
> In addition to the attainment of the highest degree of health and
> safety protection for the employee other [information] considerations
> shall be the latest available scientific data in the field, the feasibility
> of the standards and the experience gained under this and other
> health and safety laws.[19]

In this way the APA establishes formidable information collection and
analysis responsibilities for OSHA when it writes rules. Not only is the
agency to rely on what is already known about health and safety
aspects of substances and activities, there is a clear mandate to create
and use new knowledge when what is available is insufficient. Further,
information that relates to health and safety must be supplemented by
information about "feasibility," which means, in this instance, what is
possible technologically, operationally, and financially.

Rulemaking to control the threat posed by toxic substances in the
environment is the responsibility of the Environmental Protection
Agency under the Toxic Substances Control Act (TSCA). A key element
in the TSCA scheme is the testing of substances that may pose a risk.
These tests are to be performed in accordance with regulations governing testing facilities promulgated by the EPA. The information that
Congress expects the agency to develop when writing test rules
includes "the relative costs of the various test protocols and methodologies which may be required under the rule and the reasonably
foreseeable availability of the facilities and personnel needed to
perform the testing required under the rule." [20] But the TSCA supplements these bits of practical information with an imposing list of
considerations related to the core purpose of the statute. When writing
test rules on substances, the EPA is required to consider a range of
health and environmental effects that are produced by various characteristics of the chemical under examination. These characteristics
include its "persistence, acute toxicity, subacute toxicity, chronic toxicity." In addition to information on these characteristics the TSCA also
expects the rulemakers in the EPA to consider a range of risks posed by
the chemicals that are tested. Risks that testing must be attentive to are
expressed in the form of effects such as "carcinogenesis, mutagenesis,
teratogenesis, behavioral disorders, cumulative or synergistic effects
and any other effect which may present an unreasonable risk to health
or the environment." [21]

The information provisions in the Occupational Safety and Health Act and the Toxic Substances Control Act that relate to the physical well-being of individuals are examples of a general approach to regulation known as "risk assessment." Many other statutes explicitly or implicitly require some form of risk assessment as a basis for rules.[22] Not all statutes treat the risk assessment issue identically. In fact, different statutes administered by the same agency often establish different criteria for risk assessment, which require different approaches to information collection. The best example of this inconsistency is provided by the programs administered by the EPA. Compare the standards for risk assessment found in three of the main statutes for which it writes rules: the Safe Drinking Water Act; the Federal Insecticide, Fungicide and Rodenticide Act (FIFRA); and the Toxic Substances Control Act. The Safe Drinking Water Act, under which the EPA writes rules governing the quality of potable water from public water supplies, requires establishment of "maximum contaminant levels . . . (at which) no known or anticipated adverse effects" could happen and which allow for an "adequate margin of safety." The law that authorizes the agency to write rules that control the dangers posed by pesticides—the FIFRA—requires the agency to develop the information needed to set standards that result in "no unreasonable adverse effect" but which take "into account the economic, social and environmental costs and benefits." The TSCA adopts an approach similar but not identical to that of the FIFRA by calling for the control of toxic substances to the extent that "unreasonable risk" is eliminated but using the "least burdensome requirements" to accomplish this goal.[23]

It is clear from these statutes that in authorizing agencies to protect the public from various types of risks present in the environment, the workplace, and consumer goods, Congress also insists on the development or collection and consideration of other types of information. Information requirements of the sort listed above reflect a strong congressional desire to please all affected constituencies. By mandating that rules be based on such information, Congress encourages, and sometimes requires, agencies to balance information on risks to health and safety with risks to economic well-being. This sets the stage for a rulemaking process characterized by the same types of trade-offs and compromises that dominate congressional lawmaking.

INFORMATION STATUTES. The information requirements established through individual authorizing statutes are significant because they give structure to the specific analytical tasks that rulemakers must perform. Rivaling this source of collection and analytical requirements, however, is what can be termed the *information statute*. This type of law does not apply to a single program or agency. Rather, these statutes apply generally to all agencies that write rules. The National Environmental Policy Act (NEPA), the Regulatory Flexibility Act (RFA) and the Paperwork Reduction Act (PRA) are good examples of congressional insistence that a particular type of issue be considered in all rulemakings undertaken by the federal government.[24] The vehicles to ensure adequate consideration of these issues are statutory provisions that mandate the collection or development, analysis, and use of information about the effects of a rule on particular interests or populations.

NEPA is a landmark statute in many ways. Passed in 1969 it is often viewed as the symbolic start of a period of environmental policy making that continues unabated to the present day. It has many notable provisions, but the ones most pertinent here are those that require agencies to consider the effect of rules on the environment. The law calls for what could be two stages of information collection and analysis on environmental issues that arise in the making of a single rule. First, there is a threshold assessment of whether the actions contemplated in the rulemaking, such as the setting aside of public lands for certain types of activities or the relaxation of emissions standards for nuclear power plants, constitute a potentially significant impact on the environment. If they do not, the agency issues a "finding of no significant impact." If the agency reaches the opposite conclusion, it must then prepare an environmental impact statement (EIS), which is a report on the likely effects of the rule and the steps the agency will take to eliminate or mitigate damage to the environment. The EIS is also prepared in two stages, draft and final, a system that is strikingly similar to that of proposed and final rules established in the Administrative Procedure Act.

The PRA and RFA are remnants of an ambitious but failed effort, primarily by the Senate of the United States, to overhaul the regulatory process with a single, massive statute.[25] The originally proposed legislation, which went through a number of iterations, ultimately failed to attract the support needed to make a new law. These two statutes emerged in 1980 as the progeny of those efforts. The PRA requires agencies to develop information on the extent of the paperwork burdens that will accompany new rules. The legislation was intended to reduce these burdens by forcing agencies not only to analyze the information collection and reporting costs they were imposing on the private sector but to use the studies to minimize the costs. Essentially the same approach was taken in the Regulatory Flexibility Act. Here the protected class was less global than that embraced by the Paperwork Reduction Act. The RFA sought to protect small businesses and organizations from the ravages of federal rulemaking by requiring agencies to develop and analyze information on the effect of rules on small entities. When the effects of a rule are likely to be substantial, the agency is expected to take steps that will reduce the burden. The agency can fashion devices that will scale back the actual requirements or somehow make it easier for the smaller entity to comply.

The similarities between the National Environmental Policy Act and the other two information statutes mentioned above that followed a decade later may not be immediately apparent. The Paperwork Reduction Act and the Regulatory Flexibility Act were both spawned during a period when Congress attempted, unsuccessfully, to enact comprehensive regulatory reform legislation.[26] The provisions of NEPA clearly call for government to adopt a more self-conscious, fiduciary stance toward the environment, a posture that would appear to require greater vigilance and regulatory intervention. The PRA and the RFA were born of different motives, ones driven by a desire for less intrusion and more freedom for the private sector. In actuality each of the three statutes represents an effort by Congress to minimize the negative effects of rulemaking and other governmental activities on resources, activities, and individuals deemed worthy of special protection by Congress. The basic designs of these three statutes are very much alike. Development and analysis of information is central to each. There is an unexpressed but obvious intent that the information will alone be a substantial force in altering the rulemaking behavior of agencies. We will see shortly, however, that Congress was not so naive as to think that information alone would be sufficient. In these and other statutes, Congress combined information with participation and accountability to ensure that the desired results were achieved.

INFORMATION REQUIREMENTS BY EXECUTIVE ORDER. Congress, although it has been the major source of expanding information requirements for rulemaking, has not acted alone. Presidents since Richard Nixon have imposed additional information requirements on rulemaking by agencies, and with time they have become broader and more rigorous. The major device for presidential intervention into the rulemaking process is the executive order, which enables the president to establish requirements for the agencies and departments under his direct authority and supervision. Nearly 13,000 executive orders have been issued by our presidents since the start of the Republic. Several of these have had important effects on rulemaking; one may be the most important reform of rulemaking since passage of the Administrative Procedure Act.

President Nixon started the process when he imposed a "quality of life" analysis on new rules, the meaning of which was never particularly clear. This gave way to his successor's inflation impact analysis requirement. The executive order of President Gerald R. Ford was followed by a more extensive set of reforms written into President Jimmy Carter's Executive Order 12044. Among the requirements in this executive order was a mandatory analysis of "regulatory alternatives" to force agencies to consider innovative and less restrictive and burdensome ways to achieve regulatory objectives. President Reagan followed the tradition with Executive Order 12291, arguably the most significant incursion by any president into the core processes of rulemaking. This order mandated a regulatory impact analysis for all rules whose estimated effect on the economy was $100 million or more. This amounts to full cost-benefit analysis with the additional feature that the proponents of any new rule were required to demonstrate a net gain to· society prior to its promulgation. Like Carter's 12044, Reagan's 12291 had a reformist dimension. It was accompanied by a set of regulatory principles that exhorted agencies to adopt nonregulatory options for accomplishing public policy objectives whenever possible and to use the least intrusive and burdensome regulatory devices when governmental intervention was the only realistic alternative. While other aspects of Executive Order 12291 have proved more important to the operation of rulemaking than the regulatory impact analysis requirement and the regulatory principles, they are nonetheless two more examples of using information requirements to influence the manner in which rules are written.

President Reagan did not stop with Executive Order 12291. During the course of his presidency he signed numerous other executive orders, which required the development of specific types of information during rulemaking. In 1983 the president signed Executive Order 12498, which required agencies semiannually to assemble and send to the White House agendas of the significant rulemaking that was under way or contemplated in the near future. Executive Order 12612 required agencies to conduct a "federalism assessment" of rules under development. The intention here was to ensure that federal rulemaking did not interfere with the "sovereignty" of the states. In effect, this executive order forced agencies to consider whether action by the states was a legal and feasible alternative to federal action and even when it was not, how the rule could be structured to minimize disruption to the authority and financial integrity of those governments.

The federalism initiative was followed by executive orders requiring consideration of the effects of rules on private property and on the family. These additional executive orders, like the more prominent and controversial Executive Order 12291, were manifestations of the mandate that President Reagan believed he had received from the American people in both 1980 and 1984. The types of information required to be collected and analyzed by these executive orders are predicated on a deep respect for the free market and private property, states rights and the family. Is there a better summary of the domestic policies of the Reagan presidency?

INFORMATION THAT AGENCIES MUST PROVIDE THE PUBLIC

There is, of course, another side to information. What the agency is required to produce to educate itself during the course of rulemaking is undoubtedly important, but what it is required to disclose and to whom establishes the crucial link between information and participation and accountability. We saw that the Administrative Procedure Act took care to provide for disclosure of information about rulemaking to the public through the vehicle of notice in the *Federal Register*. To this day the *Federal Register* remains the primary, but not the sole, official mechanism for communication with the public regarding rules under development. The content of notices of proposed rulemaking and notices of final rules is, however, vastly different today from what was contemplated by the drafters of the APA and by those who were initially involved in its interpretation and implementation. The APA appeared to allow agencies considerable flexibility in what went into a rulemaking notice. A manual prepared by the attorney general shortly after passage of the act went so far as to advise agencies against publication of the actual text of proposed rules. The attorney general instead recommended that agencies publish general descriptions of what the agency was intending to do, based on the dubious proposition that the actual text might simply confuse the public.[27]

The content of notices has developed in a very different manner and now routinely includes material that could not have been contemplated by the drafters or early interpreters and implementers of the APA. Notices of proposed rulemaking virtually always contain not only the full text of the rule that the agency has developed to that point but a preamble as well, which is frequently as informative as the rule itself. The publication of the full rule in the notice is a practice that is mandated by some statutes, such as the Federal Trade Commission Act, but is more often a matter of agency practice. Agency practice, in turn, is a result of intense pressure from the public, the White House, and the courts for rulemakers to be precise about what they are proposing to do. Preambles, in contrast, are mandated by the rules governing the *Federal Register*, which dictate a standardized format for all proposed and final rules. These rules, issued by the administrative committee of the *Federal Register*, call for a "preamble which will inform the reader who is not an expert in the subject area of the basis and purpose for the rule or proposal." [28]

Notices of proposed and final rules often contain a great deal of additional information arising from the statutes and executive orders discussed above. For example, agencies report in preambles the results of the reviews they are required to conduct under the Paperwork Reduction Act, the Regulatory Flexibility Act, and Executive Orders 12291 and 12612. Illustrations of this type of reporting can be found daily in the *Federal Register*. A recent final rule issued by the Internal Review Service, dealing with reporting on employee expense accounts, noted that the amount of time needed to fill out the required form is one-half hour. But it also noted that "individual record-keepers may require greater or less time, depending on particular circumstances." [29] It is very common for rules to report no impact on smaller entities. Often, when effects are found at all the agency determines they are positive. For example, in a rule that effectively deregulated the export of red cedar, the Department of Commerce reports that its new rule will save each small lumber company the funds associated with applying for an export license. [30]

Beyond the disclosure of information of this sort in proposed and final rules, agencies are required to summarize the "basis" for their decisions. This requires, in the preambles of rules, explanations of the information, data, and analyses the agency relied on when developing the regulation. As noted above, the information, data, and analyses that are given depend on what the authorizing statutes require and are either in the form of specified studies or the objectives they are expected to achieve. These sections can be quite extensive. Preambles are usually longer than the rules they precede, and those for major rules can be several hundred pages long.

Although the preambles of rules can be quite lengthy and detailed, they do not contain every bit of information that the agency reviewed and relied on during the course of its deliberations. For this purpose agencies maintain "dockets" or "records" into which all material pertinent to a rulemaking is placed. In some instances the docket or record is mandated by an agency's authorizing legislation. Such requirements can be found in legislation establishing environmental regulation, notably clean air and toxic substances, and consumer protection programs. Much of the widespread maintenance of records and dockets in other programs arises from the fear of litigation, during which agencies would be expected to document their actions. [31] As we will see subsequently, the rulemaking docket or record, like the information it contains, is a vital element in participation and accountability.

We know from the records of the period that those drafting the Administrative Procedure Act had consciously decided to leave to the discretion of agencies decisions about the type, quantity, and means of disclosure of information on which their rules were based. As Kenneth Culp Davis observed:

> In making rules of general applicability agencies were generally free, in the absence of a special statute, to develop factual materials or not to develop them as they saw fit.... Such freedom for the agencies was understood at the time of enactment in 1946. Nothing in the APA changed that presumption.[32]

What we have experienced since 1946 is a repudiation of this approach to information collection and use in rulemaking through the enactment of many special statutes, the imposition of numerous executive orders, and the adoption of a defensive posture by agencies because of the possibility of litigation. Now agencies engaged in significant rulemaking do not enjoy anything near the discretion Davis alludes to; a high threshold for information collection, use, and disclosure is now set for rulemakers by these actions of Congress, the president, and the courts. The agencies are free to exceed these requirements if they wish. Unless specifically exempted from their legal mandates, these laws, executive orders, and judicial decisions constitute a floor below which they cannot fall. As we will see, however, such exemptions are not rare.

PARTICIPATION: EXPANDED OPPORTUNITIES MANDATED BY LAW

The opportunity to participate in the development of rules lends the process an element of democracy not present in other forms of lawmaking. Participation is so important to rulemaking that an entire chapter is devoted to the topic later in this book. In that chapter we will examine actual patterns of participation in rulemakings, the perceptions of those involved as to the effectiveness of various forms of participation, and the relationships that exist between public participants and the agencies that write rules. There we will also take up the troublesome but crucial question of the efficacy of participation from the perspective of both the agencies and the external participants. In this chapter we deal with participation in rulemaking solely as a legal requirement. The objective here is to demonstrate how the opportunities for participation have grown and diversified since passage of the Administrative Procedure Act.

The story of participation in rulemaking begins long before the passage of the APA. The Attorney General's Committee that studied administrative practices in agencies in the late 1930s discovered that significant and apparently highly effective programs of public participation supported rulemaking in a number of agencies. One especially interesting form was used in the offices of the Department of Labor, which administered the wage and hour laws. A "conference" of affected parties, including representatives from both business and labor, met regularly with the agency to set and adjust rules governing wages and hours. This conference approach, both formal and informal, was not uncommon among the agencies that wrote rules.[33] These and many other early mechanisms for participation are discussed in a later chapter. But when the drafters of the APA decided on the form public participation would take, they opted instead for a much less direct and substantial approach. Except for those rare circumstances when formal, trial-type proceedings were mandated by authorizing statutes, agencies could limit, at their discretion, public participation to written comments in response to notices of proposed rulemaking. It is true that the legislative history of the APA reveals at least some concern for the adequacy of written comment as a means for the agency to educate itself and for the public to be able fully to articulate its concerns or opinions. The record shows that the framers of the APA expected agencies to reach out to the public in different ways when issues of great importance or difficulty were under consideration.[34] The point is, however, they did not define those circumstances in the act nor did they mandate the use of more elaborate forms of participation. They were satisfied to leave it to the informed discretion of agencies or to subsequent Congresses to add to the basic framework. Later Congresses, as well as presidents and courts, accepted the implicit invitation in the APA with considerable enthusiasm.

Contemporary authorizing statutes, particularly those creating or amending regulatory programs, are replete with examples of the conscious and aggressive expansion by Congress of opportunities for public participation to accompany new information requirements. The practice became so commonplace that by the 1970s academic and professional journals were acknowledging and generally endorsing the rise of a new, "hybrid" form of rulemaking.[35] The name derives from a notion that this new form displays a variety of options for public participation located somewhere between the minimal model of notice and comment rulemaking and the full-blown trial procedures of "formal" rulemaking. Indeed, diversity in modes of participation became the norm in laws establishing new programs. Some authorizing statutes built on the APA by specifying the amount of time that the public would have to comment on proposed rules. Invariably, the allowed time in these statutes was more generous than what had become the norm of thirty days among the agencies. The amount of time given the public to respond to a proposed rule can be crucial for several reasons. It takes time to assemble the essential information needed to evaluate and then respond to what can be highly technical and complex rules. As important in the contemporary political environment, time allows people to get organized, to build coalitions, and to orchestrate a response to the agency's proposals.

An interesting and highly significant question is what the agency does with the comments it receives from the public. On this the APA is essentially silent, except for the required statement of basis and purpose that must accompany the final rule. Obviously, Congress would not have required agencies to, at minimum, solicit written comments if they expected the rule writers to ignore what the public had to say. If public comments raise significant issues related to statutory objectives or requirements, the agency can ignore them only at its peril. Reviewing courts are responsive to arguments from the public that a matter of central importance to a rule was missed or mishandled by the responsible agency. In a subsequent chapter we will discuss this form of judicial review. It has become common practice for agencies to include a discussion of public comments in the preambles of rules. Not only are the nature and number of public comments reviewed and discussed, the actions the agency has taken, or chosen not to take, in response to them are detailed as well. The amount of attention paid to comments depends on the volume and seriousness of the comments received, but in many instances they dominate the preamble. There is little question that agencies take public comments seriously.

Other statutes sought to diversify participation by mandating that agencies provide the public different types of opportunities to express their views during rulemaking. Perhaps the most common of these means is the "legislative hearing," during which witnesses present testimony orally to those responsible for the rulemaking in much the same manner as congressional committees do their work. This allows for a give and take not possible through written comments. The legislative hearing was required in rulemakings authorized or mandated in statutes dealing with occupational safety and health, safe drinking water, toxic substances, clean air and water, endangered species, consumer products, energy conservation, and trade practices. Some statutes went even further, virtually to the edge of formal trial-type proceedings, by allowing for either rebuttal comments or actual cross-examination of agency personnel. The former is an option in rulemakings dealing with toxic substances and drinking water; the latter also occurs in rulemaking for toxic substances and in that for certain trade practices regulated by the FTC.

Many laws allow for or require a more institutionalized form of participation through the use of advisory committees. The role of advisory committees in rulemaking can vary considerably. In some instances the committee may be nothing more than a sounding board for agency ideas, in others it may help the agency set the rulemaking agenda, and in a few instances, such as the Safe Drinking Water Act, consultation with advisory groups is mandatory. Although the use of advisory committees is widespread and highly varied, several features of their operations are standard. The Federal Advisory Committee Act (FACA) established strict requirements that agencies must meet when using these types of groups during rulemaking. The provisions of FACA govern the composition of advisory committees by requiring that they be "chartered" in the *Federal Register* to inform the public of their functions and activities. Further, agencies must ensure that the committees are balanced in regard to the interests that will be affected by their rules, and the meetings of the committees must be open to the public.[36]

Some have commented that FACA has had a chilling effect on the use of advisory committees. But it is important to acknowledge that one of the primary intentions behind the statute was to ensure that principles of public participation were observed in the operation of these highly influential groups. The model established in FACA was essentially duplicated in the Negotiated Rulemaking Act of 1990, a statute that establishes the basic procedural requirements agencies must use when they develop rules using this innovative and highly promising technique. Negotiated rulemaking is an important development of the rulemaking process and will be discussed in the next chapter.

Other general statutes promote participation in rulemaking by expanding it in certain subject areas. The National Environmental Policy Act and the Paperwork Reduction Act are prominent examples of how this indirect approach to participatory rulemaking works. NEPA requires public input at two critical stages in the development of environmental impact statements. At the outset the agency preparing the EIS is required to conduct a "scoping session," at which plans for the study are discussed with the public. The public has the opportunity to help set the agenda for the research and analysis by identifying those environmental resources and values that might be significantly affected by the rule being written. The agency then prepares a draft EIS, which is made available for public comment. At this stage the public comments on the adequacy and accuracy of the agency's plans for avoiding or mitigating the potential environmental damage associated with the rule. The comments must be addressed in the final EIS that accompanies the final rule. In this sense, public comments on a draft EIS are treated in a manner quite similar to the public comments made on a draft rule.

Participation fostered by the PRA is different. In this case the public has no role in the preparation of the paperwork analysis or in the review conducted by the Office of Management and Budget. But where pertinent and required the agency's assessment of the paperwork burden is contained in the notice of proposed rulemaking, as is information on the availability of the analysis on which the estimates are based. The public is then free to review the agency's studies and conclusions, consider the estimated burdens, and comment on both along with the draft rule.

In general, the various executive orders promote participation as an important by-product of the information they require agencies to develop and disclose. The regulatory impact analysis required by Executive Order 12291 is available to the public. So too are the results of the OMB's review of the rule. These pieces of information can facilitate informed comment and other forms of participation by the public in a rulemaking that is under way. Similarly, if the agency prepares a federalism assessment or a family impact study, both covered by an executive order, those interested in these types of issues can use the information in their comments. Other executive orders provide different types of aids to participation or other forms altogether. Executive Order 12372 requires consultation with the states when agencies are undertaking actions that have an effect on the management of intergovernmental fiscal affairs. Executive Order 12498 requires agencies to develop and publish a planning document that outlines their regulatory programs. This assists participation by giving the public an advance look at what is in store for them and allowing them time to plan for effective participation in those rules that carry a high priority. All this presumes, of course, that critical information is accessible and used by those with an interest in participation. This topic will be discussed further in Chapter 5.

We will see, also in a subsequent chapter, that judicial review of rulemaking can promote participation as well. When an aggrieved party convinces a court that an agency has failed to take into account important information during the course of a rulemaking, there are several remedies that the judge(s) may order. One is to require the agency, in effect, to work with the successful plaintiff to correct the deficiencies in the rule. Simply by a court's finding that a rule is defective and its agreeing with the plaintiffs as to the reasons why, the agency, when it returns to the rulemaking to try again, will likely be quite attentive to the parties that brought the lawsuit. The patterns we observe in participation are essentially the same as those that emerge in the information dimension of rulemaking. The actions of Congress, the president, and the courts have increased and diversified the opportunities for participation. Information and participation are linked inextricably. One, information, has no practical significance unless it is used by those who wish to contribute to and influence the course of rulemaking, whether it is before the rule is issued or after, as in litigation and oversight. The other, participation, cannot be effective unless people have the information that is needed to determine if, how, and to what extent a rule under development will affect their lives.

So far we have concentrated on the formal requirements and avenues for information and participation, those mandated by law, executive order, and court decisions. These are significant to be sure. We will see in a later chapter, however, that there are other sources of information and paths of influence that are less formal and more numerous than those discussed above. Taken together, the formal and informal dimensions mean that the development of important roles is open, rich in information sources, and replete with opportunities to contribute to and influence the outcomes.

MECHANISMS OF ACCOUNTABILITY

A strong case can be made that the elements of information and participation outlined above would be of questionable significance if they stood alone with no mechanisms to hold agencies accountable for the rules they ultimately write. Like participation, these mechanisms of accountability are so crucial to contemporary rulemaking that an entire chapter of this book is devoted to them. At this point, however, it is important to establish the main forms of accountability. Like information and participation, they too have grown and diversified since passage of the Administrative Procedure Act.

Rulemakers are accountable to three external sources of authority. These are the primary institutions created in the Constitution. The actual mechanisms of accountability used by Congress, the president, and the courts take many forms. Some are direct and explicit; others are indirect and subtle. At times the line between participation and accountability blurs, as members of the institutions to whom rulemakers answer become active players in the development of rules. What is clear, however, is that the Congress, the president, and the courts review and routinely pass judgment on the products of the rulemaking processes. They are quite different from one another, however, in the criteria they employ, which creates a situation in which an agency in attempting to respond to the wishes of one may run afoul of another. In days of divided government the stresses placed on rulemakers attempting to respond to their squabbling sovereigns can be substantial.

Two crucial aspects of this accountability network deserve to be highlighted here. First, those who write rules are expected to be responsive to multiple superior authorities, each of which wields considerable but different power over the agency. Second, there are profound differences in the priorities and objectives of each of these authorities. Congress is driven by the interests of constituents and expects those who write rules to be responsive to them as well. The power exerted by Congress is fragmented and incoherent as many members of the House and Senate jockey for influence in the rulemaking process. House and Senate jurisdictions, drawn as they are, can result in agencies' reporting to multiple committees and subcommittees. The president is driven by what he perceives to be his mandate from the entire electorate or at least those segments who supported him. His priorities are more focused, as are the mechanisms he uses to ensure responsiveness. Judges have no constituents as such. Their purpose is to see that the law is observed and to resolve disputes accordingly. But in their behavior judges resemble Congress more than the president because of the varied backgrounds and judicial philosophies they bring to the bench. Although presidents like Reagan have put their clear stamp on the judiciary through the appointment process, there is never any guarantee of consistency or predictability in a federal court system as diverse as ours.[37] Each branch of government, and its practices, will be covered in much greater depth in Chapter 6.

HOW THE APA MODEL HAS CHANGED

It is evident from this review of contemporary developments in the process of rulemaking that the model established in the Administrative Procedure Act has been altered profoundly. The changes have been observed and documented even more fully by other scholars.[38] It is true that virtually all the requirements outlined above have exceptions, when the rulemaking agency is freer to act. Every case of rulemaking is different, and many instances are sufficiently minor and routine that the speed and flexibility contemplated by the APA actually characterize the process used by the agency. But there is no mistaking the general direction in procedural requirements for those rules that are not considered routine or minor, or for the comparatively rare instances of emergency action: Congress, the president, and the courts have come to prefer a more elaborate and procedurally encumbered model for rulemaking than that which was outlined in the APA.

It is striking how far we have moved from the model outlined in the APA, particularly in the category of information. One could argue that the net effect of the various legal developments related to information is the creation of a legislative equivalent of "open discovery"—when litigants can learn about the facts in each other's possession—and the deposition processes so familiar in civil litigation. As noted, numerous statutes and executive orders require the agency to produce information and documents on a range of standard questions, just as the attorney for the plaintiff might do during a deposition. This information, once developed, is placed with all the other information the agency considered during the course of a rulemaking into a formal record, or docket, which is then completely open for review by the public. The docket and the records it contains must, on examination, explain the decisions that led to the rule.[39] While critical features found in trial proceedings are missing, information requirements and the intensity provided by public participation, particularly when information in the record is challenged and agency witnesses are cross-examined, have gone so far as to transform some rulemakings into quasi-judicial proceedings.

We can see from these decades of legal developments that the coalition that embraced the simple and flexible requirements of section 553 of the APA soon lost its salience. The rulemaking process simply became too crucial, visible, and potentially dangerous. The political coalition that had advocated big government was, for a time, able to dominate both the substantive and the procedural dimensions of the debate. In order to extend the reach of government further, as occurred in the 1960s and 1970s, an implicit trade-off of substance for process was made. The advocates of more government got new laws and programs; those who opposed these initiatives or feared their negative consequences got new procedural requirements for rulemaking, which they could use to constrain, channel, and delay this crucial stage in the policy process.[40] As James O'Reilly notes, these "procedural victories took the sting out of substantive regulation."[41]

EXCEPTIONS, EXEMPTIONS, AND EVASIONS

At this stage the reader may feel as though he or she is sitting at a railroad crossing waiting for a freight train with no end in sight to pass. But before reaching what would be the eminently reasonable conclusion that contemporary rulemaking is hopelessly encumbered by massive and stultifying legal requirements, remember that like all things governmental there are no absolutes. Not all rulemakings entail every one of the legal requirements outlined above. In fact, only a minority do. The reasons why are many, and although the rulemaking process remains generally more complex than the minimum standards outlined in the APA, most rules can be developed without attention to all the analyses, reviews, and opportunities for public involvement outlined above.

There are three ways some or most of the legal requirements outlined can be suspended. First, some types of rules were exempted when some of these requirements were first enacted. Second, the subject matter of some rules makes certain legal requirements irrelevant. Third, if they are so inclined, agencies can evade certain requirements by engaging in *pro forma* compliance or by finding a way to characterize their actions so that the requirements do not apply.

Exemptions and exceptions have been written into many of the statutes that established the requirements now associated with rulemaking. The practice began with the Administrative Procedure Act itself. Provisions of the APA allow agencies to develop procedural and interpretive rules without prior public notice or participation. When, in the opinion of the agency, there is a compelling public interest, these same requirements, which are the core of the APA's rulemaking provisions, can be suspended for legislative rules as well.[42] The National Environmental Policy Act has been interpreted to allow for "programmatic exemptions" when a given type of frequent or routine agency action can be shown to carry no significant environmental effects.[43] Rulemaking apparently qualifies broadly for such exemptions, because one can read final rules published in the *Federal Register* for many days without once encountering a reference to NEPA. The Paperwork Reduction Act also allows exemptions for certain types of frequent, minor, and routine rulemakings.

Executive orders also exempt certain types of rules from their various analysis and review requirements. Executive Order 12291 specifically exempts regulations dealing with "emergency situation(s)" and when the involvement of the OMB would interfere with the ability of the agency to meet statutory or judicially imposed deadlines. Executive Order 12291 also allows for exemptions of entire classes of rules, a privilege that has since been extended to several programs administered by the Environmental Protection Agency, the Department of Agriculture, the Federal Aviation Administration, and others.[44]

As noted earlier, the subject matter of a rule can effectively eliminate many legal requirements. If a rule has no environmental effects, has no serious implications for smaller entities, has no impact on state and local government powers and prerogatives, or involves no new collections of information, then the procedural obligations that would otherwise apply have no bearing on the rulemaking process. Of course, each of these conditions involves some degree of interpretation. What constitutes a significant impact on state and local government or smaller entities is a matter of judgment. Agencies applying a liberal threshold for what constitutes "significance" will find themselves burdened with additional work; those with a more restrictive view will find the rulemaking task substantially eased.

We may be seeing the effects of evasion through interpretation in the case of the regulatory impact analysis requirements put forth in

Executive Order 12291. The order establishes that an analysis must be made only if the costs of complying with a rule equal or exceed $100 million or if compliance has "major" or "significant" effects on other levels of government or on various aspects of the economy. Regulatory impact analyses are, in fact, done infrequently by agencies that write rules. Ostensibly, this is so because agencies are estimating that the rules they write will not have effects of the magnitude set out in the provisions of the executive order. While there is no hard evidence to suggest that agencies are engaging in minimal or *pro forma* compliance, it is true that economic impact, federalism, and small entities are frequently dealt with in the preambles of rules with language that can only be described as boilerplate.

Another form of evasion is the avoidance of rulemaking altogether. Because of the difficulties agencies face in rulemaking, some have resorted to the use of "guidelines," "interpretations," and technical manuals and other vehicles to state or refine policy.[45] In the next chapter we will consider the controversy that has resulted from the use of these devices, which can be issued without benefit of any of the procedures outlined above, in lieu of rulemaking. Suffice it to say that the frequency of their use is testimony to the formidable task that rulemaking has become because of multiple procedural requirements.

The variable applicability of the procedural obligations that have accumulated since passage of the Administrative Procedure Act should underscore for us some important points about the state of contemporary rulemaking. First, rulemaking is an enormously diverse form of governmental action; no single set of procedures can be designed that is appropriate or even feasible in all circumstances. While we are correct to be concerned about the right to participate in a crucial legislative process, most of us also acknowledge that there are circumstances when even that cherished value must give way to the need for prompt action to preserve life or property. Second, we must acknowledge that bureaucratic routines and the sheer magnitude of the rulemaking process require attention to enforcement if procedural requirements are to be consistently observed. The pressures on rulemaking agencies are considerable, especially when powerful external or internal constituencies are clamoring for regulations. In a subsequent chapter we will explore how the review of rules and other forms of oversight by the White House, the courts, Congress, and even other agencies contribute to compliance with procedural requirements.

Even if most procedural requirements ultimately do not apply in a given instance, an agency must have the capacity to examine the rulemaking it is about to undertake to determine which of the obligations must be met and how to meet them. This requires that rulemaking agencies have systems not only to make these determinations but to ensure that, once established, these laws are observed to the letter. The best way to illustrate the number of decisions and steps that are commonly associated with rulemaking is to leave this discussion of formal legal requirements and take a more practical look at how a substantial rulemaking might proceed, from inception to conclusion.

THE STAGES OF RULEMAKING

Having established the legal dimension of the rulemaking process we can now take a more practical, operational look at how rules come into being. The rulemaking process is easier to understand by conceiving of it as a sequence of activities, each of which is affected by ones that precede it. Fortunately, James O'Reilly developed this way of examining the rulemaking process (Table 2-1).

STAGE 1: ORIGIN OF RULEMAKING ACTIVITY

Although not part of the actual rulemaking process, the writing of law by Congress is the true origin of rulemaking. No rule is valid unless it is authorized by law and is promoting a statutory purpose of some kind. Key features of such legislation are the substantive mission it establishes for rulemaking, the number and timing of rules the agency will be required to write, the degree of discretion the agency enjoys in determining the content of rules, and the procedural requirements imposed on the agency.

STAGE 2: ORIGIN OF INDIVIDUAL RULEMAKING

Although all rules can ultimately be traced to statutes, specific rules often have more proximate origins. Statutes vary considerably in the degree to which they mandate that particular rules be written. Laws may be very explicit and specific. They may also contain deadlines and provisions that will take effect if the agency fails to meet the schedule. These provisions are called *hammers* and will be discussed further in Chapter 6. When rules are not explicitly mandated, the potential sources of ideas for new rules are many. Some are internal to the agency, others are external. The political leadership of the agency may bring with it policy agendas that can be implemented only through rulemaking. Advisory committees attached to an agency can also be the source of ideas for rules, although their authority in this area varies markedly. Those closest to program operations in an agency are in the best position to spot the need for new or revised rules. Many agencies have well-developed systems for analyzing new legislation or amendments to existing statutory authorities in order to determine

TABLE 2-1   An Outline of Rulemaking Activity

Stage 1   Origin of Rulemaking Activity: Rules Mandated or Authorized by Law
                Degree of agency discretion
                Procedural requirements
                Volume and frequency of rules to be produced

Stage 2   Origin of Individual Rulemaking
                Content of legislation
                    Deadlines
                    "Hammer provisions"
                Internal sources
                    Political leadership
                    Senior career service
                    Advisory committees
                    Program office staff
                    Office of general counsel
                    Field staff
                    Enforcement officials
                    "Advance Notice of Proposed Rulemaking"
                External sources
                    White House
                    Congress (other than legislation)
                    Other agencies
                    Public action

Stage 3   Authorization to Proceed with Rulemaking
                Priority-setting system
                Agency approval process

Stage 4   Planning the Rulemaking
                Goals of the rule
                Legal requirements
                Information requirements--technical and political
                Participation plan
                    Internal agency constituencies
                    Affected groups, firms, and individuals
                Securing necessary resources
                Assigning staff

Stage 5   Developing the Draft Rule
                Collection of information
                Analysis of information
                Impact studies (paperwork, small business,
                    environmental, etc.)
                Internal consultations
                External consultations (informal)
                Draft language of preamble and rule
                Implementation plan

TABLE 2-1   *(Continued)*

Stage 6   Internal Review of the Draft Rule
             "Horizontal" review
                Other program offices
                General counsel
                Policy analysts
                Research and development
                Field and enforcement offices
                Advisory groups
             "Vertical" review
                Management "chairs"
                Political leadership

Stage 7   External Review of the Draft Rule
                Office of Management and Budget
                Congress
                Interest groups
                Other agencies

Stage 8   Revision and Publication of a Draft Rule
                Notice of Proposed Rulemaking transmitted to *Federal Register*

Stage 9   Public Participation
                Receipt of written comment
                Conduct of hearings
                Review and analysis of public input
                Draft responses to public input

Stage 10   Action on the Draft Rule
                Choice of alternatives
                (a) Prepare final rule with no change
                (b) Prepare final rule with minor change
                (c) Another round of public participation
                (d) Prepare final rule with major change
                (e) Abandon rulemaking and start over
                (f) Abandon rulemaking altogether
                If (f), prepare notice for *Federal Register*
                If (e), return to Stage 3
                If (d), return to Stage 5
                If (c), return to Stage 8
                If (b), draft revisions, repeat Stages 6 and 7; prepare Notice of
             Final Rulemaking for *Federal Register* and transmit
                If (a), repeat Stage 7, prepare and transmit Notice of Final
             Rulemaking for *Federal Register*
                (See a reproduction of an actual rule in Figure 2-1)

Stage 11   Post-Rulemaking Activities
                Staff interpretations
                Technical corrections
                Respond to petitions for reconsideration
                Prepare for litigation

Source: Adapted from James O'Reilly, *Administrative Rulemaking* (Colorado Springs, Colo.: Shepard's/McGraw-Hill, 1983), pp. 90, 131.

what rules will be required to carry out the new provisions. A good example of this is the work done by a task force within the Environmental Protection Agency in advance of passage of the Clean Air Act Amendments of 1990.[46] Months before the bill was actually signed by President George Bush, the EPA had in hand a detailed plan that contained information on the number, content, and scheduling of the rules by the new legislation. Efforts like these are usually led by a team consisting of agency lawyers and technical staff in the affected program areas. Finally, the agency officials in the field actually implement, administer, and enforce rules and come into direct and constant contact with regulated or benefiting communities and representatives from other agencies and levels of government. They are a likely source of ideas for new or revised rules to improve program operations.

There are many potentially important external sources for ideas for rules as well. The most visible is the White House. The Vice President's Task Force on Regulatory Relief, which functioned during the Reagan administration, was a frequent source of ideas for elimination of rules and alterations in others to make them less burdensome to the private sector. This body took a new form in 1991 and was called the Council on Competitiveness. It was abolished by President Bill Clinton early in 1993. Other agencies can be a source of ideas, and pressure, for new rules. For many years the Federal Energy Regulatory Commission (FERC) failed to develop regulations that established its approach to complying with the National Environmental Policy Act. In this it was virtually alone among the major agencies of the federal government whose work had environmental consequences. In time, pressure on FERC from a number of federal and state environmental and natural resource agencies mounted. FERC conceded and in 1988 issued its first comprehensive rule outlining how it intended to comply with the NEPA.[47]

External sources of ideas for rules need not be confined to the public sector. The Administrative Procedure Act allows anyone to petition an agency to make a rule. There is scant empirical evidence on the number of petitions received and how they are ultimately disposed of. It is safe to assume, however, they vary considerably in quality and seriousness. Agencies are required only to acknowledge the petition and consider the request. The attention these are given most certainly depends on the importance of the issue presented, the evidence provided with the request for a new rule, and the support for and source of the petition.

STAGE 3: AUTHORIZATION TO PROCEED WITH RULEMAKING

Given the multiplicity of sources and large number of potential rulemaking projects that most agencies could undertake, mechanisms may be in place to authorize the start of work on a new rule. Because the investment by an agency in the development of a rule can be substantial, senior management may want to be sure that available resources, which are always limited, are put to work on those projects of greatest importance. We will explore the priority-setting process for rulemaking in federal agencies at length in a subsequent chapter. For now it is enough to note that the mechanisms to authorize rulemaking vary dramatically. Some are highly structured and rigid, allowing only a fixed number of high-priority rules to be undertaken at any one time. Others are quite permissive, with authority delegated to relatively low levels of the agency. And there are many intermediate systems. Whatever the mechanism, this stage marks the transition in a rulemaking from ideas to action.

STAGE 4: PLANNING THE RULEMAKING

Some type of planning is needed for all rules, regardless of their scope or complexity. Whether it is done consciously or unconsciously, formally or informally, planning for rulemaking forces agencies to confront important questions. The first order of business is to determine who in the agency will be responsible for developing the rule. Assigning responsibility for a particular rulemaking is determined by a variety of methods in government agencies. As we will see in a subsequent chapter the responsibility is usually shared by several components of an agency. The importance of rules, the variety of issues that must be resolved during rulemaking, and the variety of perspectives within an agency affected by the results will determine whether the rule is written by a single individual or a small group from a single office or whether it will be a collective exercise involving many people from throughout the entire agency. Whatever the form, these staff members must be found and assigned to the task. The selection of individuals is obviously based on their expertise and areas of responsibility, but the availability of key people at any point in time may be an issue. Conflicting demands on available expertise is a chronic problem, so agencies must have some method for assigning people to rulemaking projects.

Once personnel are selected and assigned, the task itself becomes the focus of the planning effort. What is the objective of the rule being written? To answer this question the agency must review the statutory language and, perhaps, the legislative history to determine what Congress sought to accomplish with the legislation. Then the agency must determine which of the numerous potential procedural requirements apply to this particular rulemaking. By sorting out the objectives of the rule and the legal requirements that must be satisfied during its development the agency can begin to comprehend the information needed to complete the rulemaking. Knowing what information is required, the agency can then begin thinking about where and how to obtain it. This may well raise new resource issues. In addition to internal staff and information resources that are needed to complete the rule, this review may lead the agency to conclude that additional information must be collected. For this the agency may choose to use contractors. Sufficient monies must be available and the agency must set about to structure a separate process to meet the formidable legal requirements that apply when the government procures services from the private sector.

This stage is not too early to begin thinking about how the public will be involved. Each form of public participation requires different support. If the agency opts for written comments only, it must establish a system for docketing what it receives. If it intends to use an advisory group not already formed, the requirements of the FACA, discussed earlier, must be considered and arrangements made for the conduct of the group's meetings. Similarly, public hearings require considerable advance work. Sites and formats for the meeting must be determined, arrangements made to secure transcripts of the proceedings, and travel plans made.

At this stage of the rulemaking the responsible staff may also be getting another important bit of information. Guidance from senior officials and political leadership in the agency is most useful at this stage. While it may be confined to only the most important rules, policy guidance from the agency's leadership can establish both the substantive and procedural direction for the rulemaking. If it occurs early enough it can foreclose certain options and prevent investments of time and effort on alternative approaches to a rule that would be unacceptable to those in the agency with ultimate authority.

Clearly, this is an important stage in the rulemaking. Although the content of the rule may not be determined with any degree of specificity, the quality of work done at this point has an important influence on the ease and speed with which the rulemaking is conducted. Advance planning of this sort, especially in determining major policy issues, obtaining guidance from senior officials, and clarifying how essential information can be obtained can prevent delays later.

STAGE 5: DEVELOPING THE DRAFT RULE

The content of a rule is determined during this stage. So too is the agency's compliance with many of the various procedural requirements we have already discussed. There is a simple sequence that must be followed during this stage, since those working on the rule must determine to some extent what the rule will contain. Until some general idea of the content is formed, one cannot fully determine which of the myriad of potential legal requirements will apply. Will the rule have an effect on the physical environment? Will it have a disproportionate impact on small businesses and other entities? Does it curtail in any way the normal legal prerogatives of state and local governments? Will it necessitate the collection and reporting of additional information? The answers to these basic questions, and many others, determine whether particular types of analyses and external reviews will be needed. In any event, the work to determine the content of the rule and to meet the legal requirements that apply is actually done during this stage in the rulemaking.

Clearly this is a period of intense activity for those engaged in writing the rule. Extensive internal and external consultations are likely occurring for at least two important reasons. First, those responsible are combing known sources for the expertise and information needed to complete a draft of the rule. At the same time they are also attempting to keep key constituencies informed of the direction and progress of the rule. It is important to note that even though formal requirements for public participation usually do not take effect until a draft rule is completed, there is evidence of substantial contact between the agency and interested or affected parties well before this point in the process. Informal contacts of this sort will be explored at length in a subsequent chapter.

At the end of this stage the agency will have completed work on drafts of key elements of the rule. It will have a draft rule that contains the actual language it is proposing. It will also have completed the studies and reports needed to satisfy whatever other additional legal requirements apply. Finally, it will have a draft preamble to the draft rule that is a narrative explanation of the rule and its compliance with applicable procedural requirements. At this stage, although the rule may not be formalized, the agency has also considered how it will be implemented, administered, and enforced. In some cases the agency expends considerable effort attempting to assist those affected by the rules in their efforts to comply. A regular feature of the EPA's rulemaking process is the preparation of a draft "communications strategy" that outlines how the regulated community will be informed of its new responsibilities.[48] The Nuclear Regulatory Commission routinely prepares a technical assistance manual to help the operators of regulated facilities to comply with new regulations. These documents would be prepared in draft form during this stage, as well.

STAGE 6: INTERNAL REVIEW OF THE DRAFT RULE

The ease or difficulty of conducting internal reviews depends quite heavily on how stage 5 was conducted. Internal reviews of draft rules occur horizontally and vertically.[49] *Horizontal review* refers to that which takes place across the agency, allowing the various offices to determine if the rule has any effect on the areas under their jurisdiction and, if so, whether they agree with (or at least can accept) what is being proposed. The role of various offices in an agency during this internal review varies considerably, due in no small part to the relative power each enjoys in the bureaucratic pecking order. The office of general counsel, or its equivalent, usually plays a major role, since its lawyers are charged with ensuring that everything the agency does is legally permissible. What other offices will be involved depends entirely on the scope of the rule and the issues raised during its development.

Vertical review involves supervisors and senior officials. Since rules are usually developed at a relatively low level of the agency, this review is conducted to ensure that what is being proposed is consistent with overall program operations and general agency policy. We will see in a subsequent chapter that the number of levels of vertical review varies considerably across agencies. The number depends entirely on the location of responsibility in the agency for developing the rule and the way in which an agency is organized.

The use of a team approach in developing a rule can expedite both horizontal and vertical reviews. If all the offices affected by a proposed rule are involved in its development and if their representatives reflect the views of their superiors, then the review process should be *pro forma*. This is especially true if the rule represents the consensus of the team. The role of these agency rulemaking teams is important and will be explored at greater length later in the book.

STAGE 7: EXTERNAL REVIEW OF THE DRAFT RULE

A wide variety of agencies may be asked to review a draft rule, and those especially affected by its contents may have been consulted extensively during its development. In certain instances an agency may have a special role to play for a particular aspect of the rulemaking. This is the case for the reviews by the Council on Environmental Quality of environmental impact statements and the role of the Small Business Administration in the Regulatory Flexibility Act. It is widely agreed, however, that the most consistently important external review of draft rules is conducted by the Office of Management and Budget under the authorities granted it by the Paperwork Reduction Act and a variety of executive orders.

The powers of the OMB were discussed earlier, but it is important to note that this office does affect both the substance and process of rules. First, all the reviews take time, the amount varying according to the size of the rule and the policy issues it raises. The OMB has the authority to question the content of rules with the important proviso that it cannot prevent an agency from accomplishing an objective set in statute, either through alteration of its content or delaying its release for publication. The clout of the OMB is substantial. When it objects to something in a rule, agencies usually negotiate, as we will see later when the review of rules is focused on more closely. At this stage too, Congress and interest groups may be consulted again.

STAGE 8: REVISION AND PUBLICATION OF A DRAFT RULE

This may appear to be a routine matter but in fact the *Federal Register* is quite particular about the format and content of the proposed rules it publishes. Its guidelines are quite stringent, and agencies must frequently revise their original submissions to meet the *Register's* specifications.[50]

STAGE 9: PUBLIC PARTICIPATION

As mentioned earlier, the views of the public can be received in a variety of ways. The agency can call for written public comments or decide to conduct some form of public meeting or hearing or embrace some combination that involves all these options. Authorizing legislation may require a particular form of participation. When it does not, decisions with regard to the form and management of public participation depend heavily on the amount and intensity of interest the proposed rule is likely to generate. There is little reason to structure elaborate opportunities for public participation when a rule has little effect or is essentially noncontroversial. The choice between written comment and the conduct of public hearings often has more to do with politics and public relations than it does the quality of the input anticipated. In instances of complex or highly controversial rules, the public hearing may be selected because it allows agency personnel to go to the field and explain what they are doing to affected parties and make a case for it. At other times the opposition may be so intractable, and predictable, that public meetings would serve little purpose other than catharsis.

It is at this stage that the agency must actually manage the receipt of comments, ensuring that those that are submitted are retained and made available in a location accessible to the public. The content of public input must be reviewed and analyzed. Summaries are often prepared and responses to the comments, which will ultimately appear in the rule's preamble, are developed. The task is relatively simple when there is a limited number of comments and they call for clarification or further refinement of what is already in the rule. The task grows more complex and difficult when numerous substantive issues are raised by seriously involved commentators or when this type of input comes from particularly influential or important constituencies.

STAGE 10: ACTION ON THE DRAFT RULE

This is obviously a crucial stage. All essential information—technical and political—has been collected and all constituencies—internal and external—have been heard from. The still-unfinished rule has several alternative paths it might take:

(a) When no changes are needed, the agency has succeeded in producing a draft that can stand as is. All that remains is the preparation of the appropriate notice for the *Federal Register* (see Figure 2-1) and final clearance by the OMB.

(b) When only minor revisions are needed, those drafting the rule may circulate it for another round of internal and external reviews. If the revisions are truly minor they will be made as a matter of form. Review of the final rule by the OMB is required, however.

(c) Another round of participation is pursued only when comments by the public are unclear or raise issues that cannot be resolved internally. Normally, the notice that is issued will ask the public to respond to a specific set of questions.

(d) When major revisions are needed the agency will, in effect, reproduce the process starting with stage 5, because the changes constitute a new proposed rule.

(e) Abandoning the rulemaking and starting over is a more extreme version of option (d). Here the agency is convinced that all of its work was for naught and begins anew.

(f) A rulemaking is abandoned altogether if the agency is convinced that its decision to write a rule was wrong. It will notify the public that no rule will be issued through a notice in the *Federal Register*.

STAGE 11: POST-RULEMAKING ACTIVITIES

If rulemaking works perfectly, this stage is not necessary. If, on the other hand, it is flawed, once the rule is published in the *Federal Register* in final form the process of attempting to undo or revise it can take place almost immediately. The actions take a number of forms. The most dramatic is a lawsuit filed against the agency claiming that in issuing the rule it has somehow acted illegally. The potential grounds for such lawsuits are numerous, as we will see presently.

Many post-rulemaking revisions are less dramatic. Staff may be called on to interpret key provisions of the rule that are vague or unclear. Petitions for reconsideration may be filed by parties affected by a new rule who want some element of it changed or clarified. These are treated in a manner that most closely approximates petitions for rulemaking. Frequently, the agency itself will issue technical corrections or amendments to rules when it discovers shortcomings arising from omission or commission. Suffice it to say that it is unwise to consider the rulemaking as a process that has a definite start and finish. Elements of rules can be challenged and changed at any time.

VARIATIONS IN THE SEQUENCE OF ACTIVITIES

This portrayal of rulemaking as a sequence of stages must be qualified in a number of ways. The stages do not always occur in the sequence presented here. Some may be undertaken simultaneously, others reversed in order. The model captures the decisions and tasks that confront rulemakers; not all will apply in all cases. In fact, the majority of rules will be developed without one or more of the stages or subelements present. Very minor or routine rules will be exempt from many if not most of the requirements. The content of others will obviate the need for the steps related to planning, staffing, and public participation. Still, O'Reilly's basic design, as amended, provides an accurate and full description of a significant rulemaking. It is a complex, multidimensional activity that commands considerable resources and attention.

Rulemaking may be relatively simple or highly complex, depending on the nature of the issues involved and the parties affected. Rulemaking during the past twenty-five years has become increasingly encumbered with requirements arising from concerns of the three branches of government, which in turn reflect a more active and sophisticated citizenry. The analyses, reviews, and opportunities for public participation that now characterize the rulemaking process resulted from a growing recognition that what goes on during and emerges from rulemaking is at least equal in importance to any other element of our public policy process. Concerns expressed in the larger political system, be they about quality of our environment, the burden of government regulation, the vitality of state government, or the integrity of the family, find their way sooner or later to the rulemaking process.

What can be surmised about our larger political system from the current state of the rulemaking process? The lesson is as plain as it is perplexing. We, as a people, are apparently willing to accept the growing reach of government as expressed in the thousands of rules and regulations issued annually by agencies of government. But the process that manufactures these agents of governmental expansion— rulemaking—is designed to be difficult and slow, at least for the most important rules that agencies issue. However consistent this is with the plan for government established in the Constitution, our inconsistent approach to rules and rulemaking is bound to raise issues. It is to these issues and the contradictions that we now turn.

NOTES

1. Background on this rule can be found in "Performance Oriented Packaging Standards," *Federal Register*, December 21, 1990, pp. 52402-52465. Information on the process of writing this rule was gained through a personal interview with Department of Transportation staff.
2. James Anderson, "Agricultural Marketing Orders and the Process and Politics of Self-Regulation," *Policy Studies Review* 2 (August 1982): 97-111.
3. Attorney General's Committee on Administrative Procedure, *Administrative Procedure in Government Agencies*, S. Doc. 8, 77th Cong., 1st sess., 1941, part 1, p. 5 (hereafter cited as Attorney General's Committee).
4. Ibid., part 7, p. 67.
5. David Rosenbloom, "Public Law and Regulation," in *Handbook of Public Administration*, ed. Jack Rubin, W. Bartley Hildreth, and Gerald Miller (New York: Marcel Dekker, 1989), p. 532.
6. Stephen Breyer and Richard Stewart, *Administrative Law and Regulatory Policy* (Boston: Little, Brown, 1985), p. 31.
7. *Panama Refining Co. v. Ryan*, 293 U.S. 388 (1935); *Schechter Poultry Corporation v. United States*, 295 U.S. 495 (1935); *Carter v. Carter Coal Co.*, 298 U.S. 238 (1936).
8. Rosenbloom, "Public Law and Regulation," pp. 554-555.
9. Harold Spaeth, *Supreme Court Policy Making: Explanation and Prediction* (San Francisco: W. H. Freeman, 1979), p. 89.
10. Peter Woll, *Administrative Law* (Berkeley: University of California Press, 1963), p. 18.
11. Martin Shapiro, "APA: Past, Present and Future," *Virginia Law Review* 72 (1986): 452.
12. Ibid.
13. Ibid., pp. 453-454.
14. 5 U.S.C. 551 (6).
15. Kenneth Culp Davis, *Discretionary Justice: A Preliminary Inquiry* (Urbana: University of Illinois Press, 1976), p. 65.
16. Ibid.
17. 5 U.S.C. 706 2(a).
18. Phillip Cooper, *Public Law and Public Administration* (Palo Alto, Calif.:

Mayfield, 1983), pp. 185-186.
19. 29 U.S.C. 655(b)(5).
20. 15 U.S.C. 2603(b)(1).
21. 15 U.S.C. 2603(b)(2)(a).
22. Michael Kraft, "The Use of Risk Analysis in Federal Regulatory Agencies: An Exploration," *Policy Studies Review* 1 (May 1982): 666-675.
23. "Elements of Risk Assessment," in *Regulation Development in EPA* (Washington, D.C.: Environmental Protection Agency, 1988).
24. National Environmental Policy Act, 42 U.S.C. 4321-4347; Regulatory Flexibility Act, 5 U.S.C. 601-612; Paperwork Reduction Act, 44 U.S.C. 3501-3520.
25. James O'Reilly, *Administrative Rulemaking* (Colorado Springs, Colo.: Shepard's/McGraw-Hill, 1983), pp. 14-16.
26. Ibid.
27. Benjamin Mintz and Nancy Miller, *A Guide to Federal Agency Rulemaking* (Washington, D.C.: Administrative Conference of the United States, 1991), p. 173.
28. Ibid., p. 175.
29. "Employee Business Expenses—Reporting and Withholding Employee Business Expense Reimbursements and Allowances," *Federal Register*, December 17, 1990, p. 51684.
30. "Western Red Cedar," *Federal Register*, June 3, 1991, p. 25054.
31. William Pedersen, "Formal Records and Informal Rulemaking," *Yale Law Journal* 85 (1975): 66-70.
32. Mintz and Miller, *Guide to Federal Agency Rulemaking*, p. 204 at n. 1.
33. Attorney General's Committee, pp. 103-105.
34. Mintz and Miller, *Guide to Federal Agency Rulemaking*, p. 4.
35. Stephen Williams, "Hybrid Rulemaking under the Administrative Act: A Legal and Empirical Analysis," *University of Chicago Law Review* 42 (Spring 1975).
36. 5 U.S.C. app., 1-15.
37. Charles Johnson and Bradley Canon, *Judicial Policies: Implementation and Impact* (Washington, D.C.: CQ Press, 1984), chap. 2.
38. For example, see Thomas McGarrity, "Some Thoughts on De-Ossifying Rulemaking," *Duke Law Journal*, 41 (1992): 1385-1462.
39. Mintz and Miller, *Guide to Federal Agency Rulemaking*, chap. 5.
40. Matthew McCubbins, Roger Noll, and Barry Weingast, "Administrative Procedures as Instruments of Political Control" (Paper delivered to the Annual Meeting of the Midwest Political Science Association, Chicago, March 1987).
41. O'Reilly, *Administrative Rulemaking*, p. 335.
42. 5 U.S.C. 553(b)(1) B.
43. Richard Linoff, *A National Policy for the Environment: NEPA and Its Aftermath* (Bloomington: Indiana University Press, 1976), pp. 193-207.
44. Executive Office of the President, *Regulatory Program of the United States Government* (Washington, D.C., 1991), pp. 648-649.
45. Robert Anthony, "Interpretive Rules, Policy Statements, Guidances, Manuals and the Like: Should Agencies Use Them to Bind the Public?" *Duke Law Journal* 41 (1992): 1311-1384.
46. Environmental Protection Agency, *Implementation Strategy for the Clean Air Act Amendments of 1990* (Washington, D.C.: Office of Air and Radiation, Environmental Protection Agency, 1991).
47. *Federal Register*, December 17, 1987, p. 897.

48. Environmental Protection Agency, *Communication Strategy Document Development*, EPA Order 1510 (Washington, D.C.: Environmental Protection Agency).
49. Fred Emery, *Rulemaking as an Organizational Process* (Washington, D.C.: Administrative Conference of the United States, 1982).
50. Mintz and Miller, *Guide to Federal Agency Rulemaking*, pp. 273-278.

CHAPTER 3

Issues and Contradictions

Regarding government, we live in a time of paradox and contradiction. On the one hand, there is deep dissatisfaction with the performance of our public institutions. Their alleged failures are the stuff of headlines, documentaries, feature films, and doctoral seminars. The Three Mile Island accident, Superfund failures, the *Challenger* tragedy, the savings and loan fiasco, and the AIDS epidemic are prominent among the hundreds of disasters and disappointments laid at government's door. To its varied critics, government does too much or too little. Whatever government does is done badly. On the other hand, as our concerns grow, our disgust deepens, and our confidence erodes, we continue to turn with unabated insistence to the public sector to solve new and increasingly complex problems. The pall of disdain that surrounds our public institutions has obviously not discouraged us from seeking them out. Perhaps an apt analogy for our current national condition is the dependent person who despises the object of his or her addiction but cannot bear to give up the bottle, needle, or pipe.

The demand for governmental action was constant throughout the 1980s and early 1990s, as noted earlier. We may be losing faith in the ability of government to cure what ails the country, but we certainly have not fully embraced the only clear alternatives. We do not ignore problems, tough it out on our own, rely on the magic of the free market, or depend on the munificence of private individuals or institutions, even when these alternatives are championed by popular politicians.

And so it is with rulemaking. It should be no surprise that a process so vital to government would be among the most popular targets of the legions of dissatisfied. Indeed, considerable criticism has been heaped upon rulemaking and its results. In the last decade alone prominent scholars have used terms like *malaise, ossification,* and *atrophy* to describe the current state of rulemaking.[1] This will no doubt be curious to those who remember hearing throughout this same decade that the government was issuing far too many rules. A paradox is obvious. On one side, there are complaints that rulemaking has congealed into a state of disuse; on the other, there is concern that it is running amok.

The reader must remember while considering what follows that the demand for rules and the concomitant pressures on rulemaking have increased steadily during the past several decades. The level of discontent is indisputably high but certainly has not been sufficient for us to abandon rules as primary instruments of government. Nor have we even decided to depend less on rulemaking as the primary process for establishing our legal obligations and giving form and specific meaning to our public policy. We must evaluate what follows as critiques of an indispensable governmental process that persists despite its frailties and imperfections.

It is important to acknowledge that beyond the issues that are discussed in this chapter there are larger and more fundamental problems related directly to rules and rulemaking. Debates about the role of government in our lives and the way government should be conducted are as intense and important today as they were at the time of the founding of the country. These debates arise from contrasting visions of the purpose and proper scope of the public sector. They involve ideology, constitutional theory, and assessments of institutional capacity. As we focus on the more pragmatic and operational issues, we must keep the more fundamental ones in mind as well. Ultimately, they are more important.

Four general issues emerge from the various literatures devoted to rules and rulemaking. These issues are the volume of rulemaking, the quality of rules, the time it takes to write them, and the involvement of the American people in their development.

THE VOLUME OF RULEMAKING

THE STRAIN ON INSTITUTIONAL CAPACITY

The rules written each year number in the thousands. Their aggregate effect on the lives of Americans cannot be exaggerated; no instrument of government exerts such influence on the quality and conduct of our lives. Not surprising, then, that a common complaint is that there are simply too many rules. Those who believe there is too much government must focus on the volume of rulemaking to give their position substance. Beyond this general discontent lie potentially serious operational problems. When the amount of rulemaking undertaken by a single agency increases, questions of institutional capacity arise.[2] When the number of rules affecting a particular sector of the economy or society increases, similar questions about the ability and willingness of the private sector to comply loom large.[3]

Like so many important elements of rulemaking, the volume of rules written by a given agency is largely determined by the legislation it is administering. Some agencies exercise statutory authority that requires relatively few rules, whereas others must issue hundreds every year and maintain a sizable backlog of rules in various stages of development. In addition to the type of legislation, three additional sources of rulemaking have been identified. Each has been referred to earlier in the book. First, the agency itself can decide to undertake a program of rulemaking to address emerging issues or to renovate regulations that have become obsolete or ineffective. Second, the public may petition an agency to make a rule, and the agency may respond positively. Finally, new rules may be required when regulations are challenged successfully through litigation. These sources of rulemaking are indisputably important, but they usually add only marginally to the volume of rulemaking under way in an agency at any given time. Legislation, new or amended, is the major determinant of the size of an agency's rulemaking agenda.

It is meaningless to consider just the number of rules written without regard for their scope and complexity or for the resources available to the agency responsible for writing them. Whether the amount of rulemaking done becomes a problem for a given agency is determined entirely by situational factors such as the agency's resources, experience, expertise, and relations with external interests. Even a comparatively small number of rulemakings can put an agency with limited experience and resources under considerable stress. Conversely, agencies that issue hundreds of rules a year can manage with little difficulty, thanks to accumulated expertise, relatively smooth relations with affected parties, the development of effective and efficient bureaucratic routines, and the serial, if not routine, nature of the rules themselves. There is ample evidence that a mismatch between the volume of rulemaking and institutional capacity frequently becomes a real problem.

Programs of social regulation are especially susceptible to strains on institutional capacity, and the reasons are clear. Such programs are created to deal with problems that sometimes cut across the entire society and economy. They are often the first substantial undertaking for the national government in areas that have either been previously the preserve of state and localities or left entirely to private transactions or relationships. Usually enacted by Congress against a backdrop of widespread public approval and high expectations, these programs are depended on to accomplish in a short period of time what often prove to be monumental tasks.[4] The legislation that establishes the program is often long on lofty rhetoric and ambitious objectives but quite short on operational details and budgets.[5] And, as noted in Chapter 1, the agenda that such legislation sets for rulemaking is frequently daunting. The difficulties these factors can create for the agency responsible for rulemaking, and the difficulties the rulemaking agencies can create for themselves, are well illustrated by two land-marks in the history of social regulation—workplace safety and health and the management of hazardous waste.

When the Occupational Safety and Health Act became law in 1970 it included an unusual provision that allowed the responsible agency (OSHA) to adopt "consensus national standards" without using rulemaking procedures outlined in the APA.[6] The task set before OSHA by the original legislation was enormous. The demands for action from powerful and vocal constituencies that had lobbied effectively for its creation were unremitting. In an apparent effort to establish itself as an aggressive regulator, OSHA issued nearly 4,500 regulations in a period of five months.[7] Those remotely familiar with the normal pace of governmental decision making will agree that this level of productivity in rulemaking is absolutely breathtaking. Those who were the ultimate consumers of OSHA's regulations were also impressed. Unfortunately, the impression was anything but favorable. The rules were met with cascades of criticism, outrage, and worse, ridicule. More than one astute observer of the regulatory process has attributed much of OSHA's tortured history in rulemaking to this fateful approach that seemed to value volume and speed over profes-sionalism, relevance, and reason.[8]

In retrospect an unprecedented and since unmatched outpouring of rules was the result of a too fond embrace of Congress's tempting invitation to adopt consensus standards. Certainly this was the quickest way to drop a net of rules across its vast jurisdiction, but it was also one of the least effective. OSHA adopted as its rules thousands of standards set by professional organizations and trade associations. They had been developed through the decades in a process that muted potentially intense controversy by treating the resulting standards as nonbinding, advisory, and voluntary. In a rush to respond to a sweeping legislative mandate and a clamoring public, OSHA failed to study these standards carefully. Nor did it gauge the implications of transforming voluntary guidelines into government regulations that carried the threat of significant sanctions. Others have commented on the obsolescence, unnecessary complexity, and downright silliness that became part of our law because of the fateful decision to produce rules so carelessly.[9] OSHA had traded volume for quality. For the past twenty years the legacy of this massive blunder, certainly one of the greatest rulemaking fiascoes in American history, has haunted the agency in its pursuit of an unquestionably important mission.

The issue of hazardous waste management allows us to observe a related but different problem that can arise when agencies undertake a large number of rulemakings in a short period of time. The Resource Conservation and Recovery Act (RCRA) was passed by Congress in 1976 in an effort to regulate the generators, shippers, and ultimate disposers of waste materials, also known as garbage. For the rest of that decade and the first years of the next the Environmental Protection Agency's Office of Solid Waste and Emergency Response (OSWER) focused its attention on trash collection and disposal services provided by local governments, since these activities and facilities accounted for the greatest amount of trash. By the early 1980s, however, it was becoming increasingly clear to the agency and the interested public that a far greater threat to public health was posed by wastes that were toxic. These were introduced to the "waste stream" from a wide variety of sources, ranging from massive chemical plants to single households. The problems at Love Canal and the virulent pollution of ground water caused by leaching from similar hazardous waste disposal sites ultimately led Congress to attach major amendments to RCRA in 1980 and 1984. These were known as the Hazardous and Solid Waste Amendments (HSWAs), and they radically altered OSWER's mission and approach to rulemaking.

In a report titled *The Nation's Hazardous Waste Management Program at a Crossroads*, EPA personnel noted that the HSWAs "greatly expanded the magnitude of waste types and ... facilities requiring regulation ... approximately 81,000 waste management units ... [and] 211,000 facilities that generate hazardous waste."[10] In addition to a greatly expanded jurisdiction, OSWER was also put under tight deadlines for the production of the many regulations needed to implement the new statutory mandates. The result was that in the decade of the 1980s OSWER became the most efficient rulemaking "machine" in the EPA, producing regulations faster than any other program office in the agency. During the same period the volume of hazardous waste regulations increased by 150 percent. But in the course of responding to a clear and persistent congressional pressure, OSWER, by its own admission, paid a high price.

In the chapter of the report devoted to rulemaking, "The Regulations Machine: Too Many, Too Fast," the authors assess the consequences of OSWER's attempt to satisfy the external demands for rules. They state, "this success in developing regulations has been achieved at the expense of other important program objectives, and has resulted in high staff burnout and turnover in the RCRA program."[11] The "other objectives" that were sacrificed on the altar of high volume are absolutely central to the quality and credibility of any regulatory program. They include an ability to define an overall philosophy and direction for the hazardous waste program, control over the process of setting priorities for rulemaking, stable internal management of the rulemaking process, and an ability adequately to address issues related to compliance and enforcement in the rules that are produced.[12]

The portrait that emerges from this extraordinarily frank and thoughtful study is that of a regulatory program that came to define productivity as rules produced. The quality of the program the agency was creating suffered because of inattention. The preoccupation with production of rules prevented OSWER from appreciating that rules are worse than useless if they result in an inconsistent, incoherent regulatory program that cannot be understood by the regulated community or enforced by government agents in the field.

VOLUME AND IMPLEMENTATION

This final point is particularly important when discussing increases in rulemaking activity. Sudden increases in the volume of rules can have enormously disruptive effects on the ability of programs to implement and enforce regulatory standards or deliver government benefits and services. Government agencies are not monolithic, omniscient entities. In most agencies, the people engaged in the writing of rules are different from those who are charged with implementation and enforcement. Further, the rule writers are often separated both by physical distance and bureaucratic perspective on the nature of the agency's work from the implementers and enforcers. Those charged with producing regulations are rewarded for that activity, and they may not be particularly sensitive to the problems their work may create for other parts of the agency.

Rules that alter existing program requirements demand learning and adjustments on the part of personnel in the field. Their job is to ensure that a regulated community is doing what the law requires or that a group of beneficiaries, applicants for benefits, and those that deliver services are treated accurately and fairly under new standards. New rules that add to existing regulatory, eligibility, or service requirements imply the need for more resources in the field to ensure that the new obligations are met. Too often rule writers have no incentive to consider these resource issues, and they almost never have the authority to augment the staff and related budgets available to field offices. So the greater the volume of rulemaking, the greater the likelihood that the resultant rules are being passed on to implementation and enforcement staffs with inadequate training and resources. At times, agencies acknowledge they are overwhelmed. The Federal Communications Commission (FCC), for example, announced in June 1993 that the implementation of rules that could reduce the price of cable television would be delayed. The FCC chair stated bluntly that it was "too short staffed and too strapped for money to implement its new rules."[13] To the extent that implementation of new rules is delayed and such efforts require reallocation of existing resources that were devoted to enforcement of other rules, high-volume rulemaking could lead to the perverse situation in which the creation of more rules leads to less protection from whatever danger the overall regulatory or social welfare program was intended to reduce.[14] Overtaxing occurs in the private sector too when increases in rulemaking activity occur. Contemplate for a moment being on the receiving end of even a tiny fraction of thousands of regulations adopted in one grand, wrong-headed gesture by OSHA. The typical and now well-known problems of complying with government regulations are magnified and multiplied when volume increases suddenly. Research conducted in the early 1980s demonstrated that in normal times government regulation increases with the size of the company and that conflict between the public and private sector grows along with it. Smaller entities have complained that they are disproportionately affected by government requirements. A significant number have trouble learning what and how requirements apply to them. They must rely on accountants, lawyers, and other compliance professionals far more than they want or probably can afford to do. And some perceive their only choice as being either compliance with the law or keeping their business open.[15]

The Environmental Protection Agency personnel who wrote the report on hazardous waste regulation summarized the problems associated with increased rulemaking in the following way:

> The current hazardous waste system is plagued by a number of rules that are both difficult for industry to comply with and difficult for EPA and the states to implement—and the requirements continue to grow. In RCRA, *as in other programs*, a regulated hazardous waste handler *literally must do hundreds of things correctly to fully comply with the regulations, yet doing only one thing wrong makes the handler a violator.* (Emphasis added.)[16]

In this way the sheer volume of rules compounds what are clearly more fundamental problems with government regulation. Many of those who must comply with the rules feel insecure and exposed because of numerous complex requirements that are difficult to understand. They harbor a seething resentment as they watch their freedom of choice and autonomy continually eroded by government mandates. The impact of the sheer weight of regulation can be mitigated, however, by rules that are well-conceived and written. Heavy volume can be tolerated if rules accomplish objectives for which there is widespread public support. The quality of rules is therefore critical.

QUALITY IN RULEMAKING

Quality in rules, like so many other aspects of contemporary American government, is an elusive concept. The most exacting standard of quality in rulemaking is derived from the fundamental purpose of a rule. We should expect our rules to reflect perfectly the statutory purposes they are to implement and to promote these legislative objectives in the most effective and efficient manner possible. Here, *effective* would be defined as producing the program outputs, such as regulations and enforcement, that in turn produce the outcomes contemplated by the enactors of the statute being implemented.[17] High-quality rules would produce these intended effects in the proper amounts. *Efficiency* means that the rule calls for spending up to the point that the costs of implementation and compliance equal the benefits that society enjoys from the new conditions they create.[18] Since legislation often ignores or explicitly rejects this classical definition of efficiency, another, less rigorous approach can be employed. *Cost-effectiveness* is achieved when the results of the program, however defined, are produced at the least cost.[19]

The importance of these standards of quality in public policy is indisputable. Obviously, public policy is a failure if it does not accomplish the objectives established by Congress on behalf of the American people. Equally important, especially in a period of economic recession and tight public budgets, are standards that promote the best use of scarce resources. These visions of quality in rules and rulemaking can be articulated and their importance underscored, but an exploration of them here in a way that does them justice would require an analysis of factors and forces in public policy that far exceeds the scope of this book. First, there is the problem of matching rules to their legislative origins. The intent of Congress is not always clear in either the language of the statute or the legislative history on which it is based. The meaning of key statutory terms can be obscure, subject to alternative constructions, or seemingly contradictory.[20] Second, rulemaking must be evaluated in a manner consistent with its important but limited role in our overall system of government. We cannot, for example, credit or blame rulemaking for errors committed during the legislative process. If Congress writes law that is based on faulty premises or incorporates requirements that prevent rules from designing public programs that are effective or efficient, the fault cannot lie with rulemaking. Similarly, the work that follows rulemaking—implementation and enforcement—may undo good work embodied in rules. The converse is also true, of course. Legislation that is self-implementing reduces the significance of the rules that follow, since the rules do little other than mirror statutory terms. It is also possible for implementing and enforcing officials to correct, through interpretation and enlightened use of discretion, rules that would otherwise obstruct progress toward statutory purposes. Finally, there is the persistent problem of measuring the actual effects of public programs. Measuring the benefits and costs of entitlement or regulatory programs has proved difficult and controversial; our grasp of end results is tenuous at best.

This chapter focuses on more immediate and practical issues of quality. Rules from a wide variety of public programs have been severely criticized because they are unnecessarily difficult to implement, comply with, and enforce. No corner of the vast expanse of American rulemaking has escaped censure. Serious consequences can arise from rules that prove difficult or impossible to put in force because of deficiencies in the way they are written. It is often difficult enough for regulated parties or potential beneficiaries of public programs to meet their responsibilities when rules are unmistakably clear. When they are obscure or subject to multiple interpretations, the task can be overwhelming. Flaws that lead to problems in implementation, compliance, and enforcement come in a number of forms.

Colin Diver, now dean of the University of Pennsylvania Law School, argues that rules should have three qualities: transparency, congruency, and simplicity.[21] For a rule to be transparent it must mean the same thing to everyone who reads it. All should draw from it the same understanding of their legal obligations and what will happen to them if they fail to comply. The enemy of transparency is vagueness. It "leaves the reader to guess at the meaning of the rule and its application in a particular case." As a prominent example of vagueness, Diver points to the standards used by the Federal Communications Commission when considering whether to renew a broadcasting license or award it to a competitor. The standards place heavy reliance on whether the current holder can demonstrate a record of service that is "substantially attuned to meeting the needs of and interests of its area." Repeated efforts to clarify and specify the meaning of terms like *substantially, needs,* and *interests* failed and the rules remain, in Diver's terms, "a paragon of administrative opacity."[22]

Vagueness in rules can reduce important public programs to bickering between levels of the responsible agency and between the responsible agency and its clients or regulated parties. When the rule is unclear, implementing and enforcing officials must expend time and resources to develop an operational definition of key terms and concepts. This pursuit effectively transforms the implementer into a rulemaker. In complex public programs administered through a series of regional or field offices, such a situation raises the real possibility that a key term, poorly defined in a rule, will come to mean different things in different parts of the country, damaging consistency and perhaps raising questions about equal protection of the laws. Even if there is perfect consistency within the government in the way vague terms are being defined, it is highly unlikely that the same will hold with the external parties they serve or regulate. It is reasonable to assume that those in the private sector will adopt the interpretation of vague rules that best suits their interests. This difference in interpretation leads to inevitable conflicts with the agency and, in some instances, lawsuits challenging the agency's interpretations of its own rules. Such challenges, until they are resolved, cast doubt over the status of the program and, when successful, trigger a new round of rulemaking that is dominated by the views of the successful plaintiff or the judge in the case.

A rule is *congruent* when it states what the law it implements intended, nothing more, nothing less. To Diver, threats to congruence are "overinclusiveness" and "underinclusiveness." These conditions occur when the rule includes persons, things, or activities that should not be included or excludes those that should be included.[23] Perhaps the best example of both characteristics can be found in the thousands of standards issued by OSHA shortly after its creation in the early 1970s. These "overincluded" to such an extent that they held the agency up to ridicule for issuing standards that governed in excruciating detail the characteristics of safety devices and mandated, with no humor intended, portable toilets for cowboys. The underinclusion was probably more serious than the derision that greeted these types of standards. In its headlong rush to protect worker safety, the agency lost sight of the other dimension of its work. Among the thousands of standards issued, virtually all dealt with safety and hardly any with workers' health.

Overinclusive rules also have a corrosive effect on working relationships in the public sector and the posture of the private sector toward the program. Consider for a moment the inspectors responsible for enforcement of the blizzard of safety standards issued by OSHA in the early 1970s. If they were to take the regulations literally, they would be measuring the distance between the struts that attach hand railings to walls in every American workplace covered by the act. By pursuing these responsibilities aggressively, as research suggests they did, the OSHA inspectors were sure to encounter problems with the private sector.[24] Many in the private sector derided this approach to regulation and those who were attempting to force their compliance with it. The agency was soon dismissed as one far more concerned with bureaucratic standards of performance, such as the number of citations issued, than with the ultimate goal of protecting worker safety in the most effective and efficient manner. The damage done by this most dramatic example of overinclusiveness is evident to this very day. For nearly two decades the agency has attempted to eliminate or modify their irrelevant, obsolete, or excessively prescriptive rules. It has attempted to establish outreach programs to assist employers in developing compliance programs for the rules that remain. Still, the initial, overwhelmingly negative impression lingers.

It is important to note that a significant variant on overinclusiveness is what we might term *overspecificity*. It is evident that the OSHA rules treated the characteristics of common objects, such as railings, ladders, and protective clothing, as mysterious forms of new technology that required descriptions as impenetrable as the assembly instructions that accompany Swedish lawn furniture. OSHA's obsession with detail extended even to rules for their own employees. These rules contained excessively thorough instructions on how inspections were to be conducted, what would and would not be considered violations, and how citations were to be written when violations were observed. In its early years OSHA displayed what some would view as a deadly combination of failings: overinclusiveness and rigid enforcement.

Simplicity, to Diver, is achieved when there are few steps and relatively little information needed to determine the applicability of and establish compliance with a rule. Complexity is the threat to simplicity.[25] Complexity comes in many forms. It is manifested in contemporary rules that incorporate a myriad of qualifications, exceptions, exemptions, and considerations that complicate the processes of determining applicability and complying with its provisions. A previous example is illustrative: EPA's own report on hazardous waste regulations describes a situation in which a regulated entity is expected to do "hundreds of things to establish compliance." Perhaps even more complex are the rules issued by the Internal Revenue Service that implement the tax code. It is a standing joke that each attempt at "tax simplification" leads inevitably to the opposite.

Complexity produces many of the same general effects as vagueness and the lack of congruence. The damage occurs for different reasons, however. Complex rules present considerable difficulties for the private sector, especially smaller entities and private individuals. As they struggle to understand what is required of them to obtain benefit from a government program or to comply with a regulatory obligation, they find themselves increasingly dependent on others to tell them what must be done. An important study of the impact of government regulation on American business found that smaller firms relied heavily on attorneys, accountants, and other compliance professionals. One respondent in that survey remarked, "We formerly almost never consulted an attorney. Now it seems we have to get permission to go to lunch—to be sure we are not violating a new law." [26] This survey found complexity to be a significant problem that manifested itself in a number of ways. The comments of another respondent highlighted the issue of complexity in one agency's rules. "I can't believe they realize what a large negative effect they are having on those businesses [being] regulated. The Department of Labor is far-and-away the hardest to deal with. Not only are their regulations complex and vast but they often conflict with each other and serve no apparent purpose." [27]

In their examinations of the proposition that rules have a disproportionately large effect on very small businesses, studies have highlighted another, perhaps more serious, problem partially attributable to complexity. The same study cited above reported that government rules were written in such a way that larger firms were favored.[28] This suggests that complexity may be a tactic used by those with ulterior motives. For example, the rules governing eligibility for health care benefits under the federal Medicaid program are so complex that their effect, if not their intent, has been to frustrate applicants with so many qualifications that the government can always find some basis on which to deny benefits.[29] Entitlement programs like Medicaid are not the only programs that have been accused of issuing rules so complex that smaller and poorer entities are under a severe disadvantage. Licensing programs and other types of regulatory programs have been criticized in much the same way. For example, the rules governing the content of applications for hydroelectric power licenses have been cited as deterring all but the richest applicants because they contain requirements for many types of environmental, engineering, and economic studies and a multiplicity of bilateral consultations with other federal and state agencies.[30]

Complex rules hurt the government as well. It may be no easier for government officials charged with implementation and enforcement to understand a complex rule than it is for those in the private sector who are supposed to be complying with it. As mentioned earlier, contemporary rules usually contain preambles that are longer than the body of the rule itself. During the first six months of 1991, for example, preambles were, on average, two and a half times as long as the rules they prefaced.[31] As preambles and rules grow in length and complexity, the chances increase that a critical term or issue will be handled differently from one section to the next. When the complying community is left to decide which version is correct—the interpretation found in the preamble or the actual language found in the body of the rule—the credibility of the program is damaged and the potential for challenges to the rule's enforcement increases.

How common are these qualitative problems that frustrate implementation, compliance, and enforcement of the rules written by the federal government? When they occur, what are their root causes? Here we consider two factors that produce rules that are difficult to put into effect: poor information and ineffectual rule writers.

THE LIMITATIONS OF INFORMATION

Rulemaking is, in one sense, a process for changing information into law. Sometimes the information is obvious or easy to obtain; at other times the information is difficult to secure or simply nonexistent. When the Federal Aviation Administration prepares an airworthiness directive, it is usually based on information that has been provided through routine inspections of aircraft by its own personnel or those working in the regulated community. When a problem is discovered there are usually well-established ways to determine how to solve it and to explain to the regulated community what needs to be done. This is not to say that the system is infallible or without problems of clarity or specificity. In general, however, the FAA's rules are developed in what we might call an information-rich environment.

Some rules require no information other than what the agency issuing them wants to do. Agencies regularly use rulemaking to change their internal procedures for all types of programmatic activities. These rules are based simply on what the agency determines to be expeditious, convenient, or otherwise beneficial to the operation of their programs. This type of rulemaking can also be found in programs in which the agency traditionally enjoys considerable authority to protect health or safety. The frequent rules of the Coast Guard designed to maintain safe and efficient use of navigable waterways are examples of rules for which the only information really needed is the knowledge that a potential hazard or obstruction exists. Once identified the solution does not require much, if any, information collection, since the rule will be based on well-established policies and practices. The types of rules in which information is not much of an issue are usually quite easy to implement, although communicating the new obligation or restriction to the regulated community may be difficult. For example, the Coast Guard's rules may be quite clear, but because the boating community is so diverse the process of making it aware of the restrictions can be a problem.

Weaknesses in information can be a serious obstacle to writing high-quality rules. Certainly on occasion the responsible agency knows little about the nature of a problem, its causes, or the practices of the individuals, groups, or firms whose behavior or activities it must change to accomplish the goals of a statute. This was and is true of much social regulation.[32] The causes and consequences of threats to the environment and to human health and safety are extremely difficult to determine. Perhaps even more problematical is the sheer number of behaviors, activities, and practices that social regulation seeks to affect. When one combines the elusiveness of the problem with the indeterminacy of its cause and multiplies that by the number and diversity of the people whose lives the agency is attempting to change, the probability of error is very high indeed. The examples of agencies attempting, unsuccessfully, to write rules with less than complete or accurate information are numerous.[33]

Stephen Breyer, a noted scholar and prominent jurist, has identified four generic sources of information available to rulemakers. First, *industry*, broadly defined, is the most reliable source of information on its own processes, and products. Second, the agency has *in-house research offices*, but Breyer sees these staffs as limited in what they know or can learn in time to help on specific rules. Third, the agency has access to *outside experts*, but it may be difficult to find an expert on the right subject, and they can be expensive. Finally, there are *"public interest"* groups, but these often have less hard information than industry and carry with them a predictable point of view.[34] In general, Breyer sees information shortcomings as a "central and persistent problem" and concludes, "in technical areas the agency to some extent inevitably works in the dark." [35]

THE LIMITATIONS OF RULEMAKERS

As significant as limitations in information are the limitations of the people using it. As we will see presently, most agencies report that they assign the task of rulemaking to individuals with expertise in the subject matter in question. We would be surprised and alarmed to find that the contrary was true. Nevertheless, expertise on the subject matter in a given area of regulation does not necessarily mean that an individual also possesses a comparable level of practical experience and sensitivity to the nuances of regulatory language. The expert may know a given technology or industrial process, but can he or she write a rule that can be implemented with minimal effort, understood and managed by the affected parties, and enforced should it be violated? Some agencies have discovered that those writing regulations lack the essential perspectives and experience. The Environmental Protection Agency put it this way:

> Implementation and enforcement issues raised by regulations are not consistently identified or addressed as part of the rulemaking process.... Staff writing ... regulations are often not familiar enough with or do not have enough exposure to the types of facilities and industrial groups that they are trying to regulate.... Some staff members lack field experience and exposure to industry that limits their ability to design regulations that both are understandable and work in the field.... This is especially true, given the high turnover rates....[36]

There is no reason to believe that this problem is confined to a particular type of agency or governmental program, but large programs dealing with environmental, health, and safety issues are likely to be especially affected. Such programs are expected to produce large numbers of rules dealing with complex issues that involve vast expanses of the economy. The learning curve for those writing such regulations can be quite steep, since they must simultaneously understand the nature and consequences of the problem they are attempting to deal with and the operations of the particular industry that must be regulated. The problem of staff turnover is exacerbated by the increasing frequency of internally or externally imposed deadlines.

The regulations of most agencies are written at their headquarters, in Washington, D.C. There is usually no requirement that those writing the rules be experienced field personnel. Although these agencies have large field staffs, some of which have histories of long and intense interaction with the segment of the economy or society affected by a given rule, these staffs may not be consulted to the extent they should be in writing the rule. The reasons for this gulf between the Washington staffs who write the rules and the field staffs who must mold a program from them are numerous, and sometimes subtle.

At the most mundane level, some field staffs may simply be too busy with the task of implementing and enforcing an existing body of rules to worry about those that are under development. Since they will have to live with the problems created by unrealistic or poorly crafted rules, this attitude may seem quite shortsighted, but given the dynamics of program management it may be entirely rational. Field staffs are evaluated based on their performance in relation to existing rules. They are usually not rewarded for their efforts in making future rules better. Further, field staffs know intuitively that they ultimately control the process by which rules are actually put into effect. Many new rules require interpretation in the field, and through this process of fitting the language of the rule to the circumstances of the real world, implementation and enforcement staffs have substantial control on what the rule will actually mean. Consequently, field staffs must balance their expected yield from participation in the rulemaking with the probability that they will be able to fashion a rule they can live with through the discretion they enjoy in implementation and enforcement.

When enforcement staffs choose to become involved in rulemaking they can face two different types of obstacles. Resources may not be sufficient to allow for full participation in the rulemaking. Rules are often written by teams of agency personnel who interact on a regular basis, sometimes intensely.[37] The locus of this activity is almost always the agency headquarters. While there is technology that provides effective substitutes for the physical presence of participants, the logistical problems can be formidable. Communication and scheduling, which are difficult enough in a single location, become much more problematical when the input is coming from multiple remote sites.

When field personnel are willing to participate, the resources are available, and the logistics are manageable there may still be obstacles to incorporating the implementation and enforcement perspective into a given rule. Those responsible for writing the rule may not want suggestions or data from those in the field. Some argue that rule writers have a short- term perspective with little or no incentive to get it right.[38] The issues raised by those concerned with implementation and enforcement are often numerous and complex. The larger the number and the more difficult the issues presented during the development of a rule, the longer the process takes. More important is the fact that the resolution of the types of issues raised by field staff may require a level of specificity in the rule that would threaten the maintenance of consensus among the headquarters personnel involved. Elements of the legislative process in Congress are present in rulemaking. By avoiding certain issues or using vague language that is open to multiple interpretations, rulemakers may be able to satisfy various agency offices with different responsibilities, concerns, and perspectives whose opposition would otherwise block or delay issuance of the rule. It has also been suggested that rule writers could make a career of interpreting a rule they have written badly.[39]

For a variety of reasons, those in headquarters writing rules may mistrust the input from the field. They may view the positions of the field staff as either too friendly or too hostile to the segment of the private sector that will be affected by the rule. Headquarters personnel may respond to this type of criticism of the agency by writing rules that narrow the range of discretion, an approach that those in the field may find unrealistic or unworkable. Conversely, personnel in both regulatory and social welfare agencies have been accused of "going by the book" and rigidly applying the language of the rule with no effort to respond to unique or unanticipated situations.[40] In these instances, by writing general rules that must be molded to individual circumstances, headquarters personnel may force the field staff's exercise of discretion and at the same time give the regulated or benefiting community grounds to question the judgment of that field staff when adverse decisions are made. Clearly, this is not a situation that those in the field will always welcome, especially in programs where the number of parties to be dealt with is large and the diversity of their circumstances substantial.

It is important to note that the information needed to write rules that are attentive to the importance of compliance is not solely in the hands of the public sector. On the contrary, those who know the most about the area affected by the rule are those in the regulated or benefiting community. It is conceivable that rulemakers who ineffectively handle input from field personnel could still produce feasible and workable rules if they could gain the necessary insights from the private sector. The impediments to gaining these insights will be discussed presently.

TIMELINESS

After noting that many believe there are far too many rules, the reader may be wondering how it can be argued that the process by which they are written takes too long. But consider the following statement by Neil Eisner, the assistant general counsel for regulation and enforcement at the U.S. Department of Transportation:

> In recent years all three branches of government have been concerned with delay in the rulemaking process. Their efforts to eliminate or lessen it have been hampered because delay in decision-making is an age-old disease for which there is no cure; there is rarely agreement on whether the victim is ... ill.... Part of the difficulty in attempting to cure the problem of delay in the rulemaking process is its wide variety of causes.[41]

The general view that the pace of rulemaking is a problem is supported by several committees of the United States Congress, the Administrative Conference of the United States, the federal courts, and elements of the private sector. But before turning to the causes, we should first attempt to explain the apparent contradiction between the twin charges that there are too many rules and that their production is too slow. We should also review some of the evidence that, as Eisner put it, the "victim is ill."

Those who decry the time it takes to issue rules are likely to be the individuals, groups, or firms who view themselves as the beneficiaries of rules or in need of the guidance they provide. Certainly they are not the same people who complain about the volume of rules. For example, environmental groups of all sorts have turned to litigation against the

Environmental Protection Agency in an attempt to speed up the issuance of regulations favored by their members. If Congress has indeed identified a problem whose elimination would result in net gains to some members of our economic or social system, it stands to reason that delays in issuing the regulations that detail how the problems will be solved constitute a loss to those who would benefit. In other cases, businesses may suffer because of the uncertainty created when regulations affecting their operations are not completed in a timely fashion. Businesses are understandably reluctant to move into new areas or make changes in their operations and practices if a new regulation might make the activity unattractive. The government itself, and the taxpayers who finance its operations, can be big losers when essential regulations are delayed. A report by the General Accounting Office (GAO) issued in 1977 estimated that delays in issuance of regulations that established cost-sharing in the Medicaid program resulted in a loss of more than $81 million in just one fiscal year.[42]

On what basis is the claim made that rulemaking takes too long? The history of the rule attempting to deal with the problem of occupational exposure to the carcinogen benzene provides the type of case that tests the faith of the most optimistic supporters of government action. The efforts to write this regulation spanned the decades of the 1970s and 1980s and featured multiple studies, public petitions, emergency actions, failed negotiations, and seemingly inevitable lawsuits.

The story of the benzene rule is an admittedly extreme example of a common occurrence. The more than ten years it took the Department of Transportation to overhaul the rule dealing with the transport of hazardous materials is another. But there are hundreds of examples of rules that took extraordinarily long periods to complete or that were never finished at all. The authors of the General Accounting Office report that focused on Medicaid rules studied the rulemaking process of what was then called the Department of Health, Education and Welfare (HEW). It found that rulemaking in HEW routinely took much longer than both statutes and the department's own policies required. Of twelve regulations studied in the GAO report, one rule took twice as long as it was supposed to, five took between two and four times as long, three took between four and six times as long, and another three had still not been completed by the time the GAO's research was finished, so it could not measure how delayed these would ultimately be. More than a decade later the problem in the successor agency— Health and Human Services—apparently persists. The assistant secretary for the office that now administers Medicaid, the Health Care Financing Administration, was forced to design and implement yet another program to expedite the pace of rulemaking.

These examples demonstrate that the problem of delay spans the government. The Federal Energy Regulatory Commission's rule implementing the provisions of the National Environmental Policy Act in its hydroelectric power licensing program was nearly twenty years in the making. The inability of the Federal Aviation Administration to revise the rules that govern flight time for airline pilots and crews in a timely way forced the agency to issue thousands of individual "interpretations" that were needed so that the industry could function under regulations that were obsolete but still remained in force.[43] A recent study of rulemaking in the Environmental Protection Agency found that the average time that elapsed in rulemaking in the four major program areas—air, water, toxic substances, waste—ranged from slightly more than two years to just under five years.[44] Congress has grown so frustrated with the pace of rulemaking in the EPA that it imposed nearly one thousand statutory deadlines for the issuance of rules under a variety of statutes.[45] A very long list of individual examples could be developed, but it is actually quite difficult to determine the extent to which delay affects all rulemaking. Is it a widespread crisis or a localized irritant affecting relatively few rules? There are two factors that make it exceedingly difficult to assess the problem.

First, it is hard to measure the actual time elapsed in rulemakings. Second, we have no valid, objective standards to help us determine how long a rulemaking should take. There are few systems within the government that allow us to determine, without huge effort, when a rulemaking actually began. The first public notice of a proposed rule in the *Federal Register* might be preceded by weeks, months, or even years of work. Although many agencies have a process to authorize the start of a rulemaking, we cannot know how much time and effort has been expended on a given rule prior to these formal authorizations. In some cases we can obtain partial measures of elapsed time, such as the duration between the notice of proposed rulemaking and the publication of the final rule. But a review of the rules that emerged in the first six months of 1991 showed that a very large portion of final rules appear without benefit of a proposal, so in these many instances even a partial measure of elapsed time is not possible. The question of an objective standard against which the timeliness of rulemaking can be judged is even more difficult. The circumstances surrounding a rule determine the length of time it takes to develop it. And it is these circumstances that must be explored if we are to understand the sources of delay.

COMPLEXITY

Rules sometimes involve highly complex, difficult issues that simply take a long time to resolve. The benzene rulemaking involved a fundamental issue about which there was little unequivocally accepted scientific judgment. To write a good rule about benzene the Occupational Safety and Health Administration would have had to determine the level of benzene exposure that triggered the carcinogenic effects of the substance and then set a standard within the constraints of the statute and what was technologically achievable. The hazardous materials rule prepared by the Department of Transportation that was discussed earlier displays a different type of complexity. Here, rather than dealing with a couple of difficult scientific and technological questions, the agency was challenged to produce a single rule that dealt with hundreds of distinct but interrelated issues in a coherent and consistent manner. So any one issue might not have been particularly challenging, but the task of ensuring that taken together they formed a rule that was logical and understandable was daunting. Agencies of social regulation constantly deal with these types of complex tasks. This means that they are consciously or unconsciously balancing the quality of the rule they are writing with the timeliness of its issuance.

CONTROVERSY

Rulemaking agencies must accept and contend with controversy in the rules they write. The controversy can be internal to the agency, between external groups affected by the rule that the agency is writing, or between the agency and these external clients or constituents. Whatever the form, conflict holds the potential for extending the time it takes to issue rules. The political scientist William West has shown that the various offices in an agency involved in rulemaking are populated with individuals with distinctly different views on the technical and policy questions involved in rulemaking. A given rulemaking may involve technical specialists in the program area or areas covered by a rule, lawyers who are responsible for interpreting the authorizing statute, policy analysts charged with finding innovative or economically efficient ways to achieve statutory objectives, and personnel who specialize in implementation and enforcement of completed rules. Existing research demonstrates that these varied concerns and backgrounds translate into significantly different views about rulemaking and that these differences can lead to serious conflict.[46] The engineer's fondness for rules based on technology may run afoul of the preferences of the lawyers who worry about whether such an approach is permissible under a statute. An economist working in a policy analysis unit may favor clear statements of objectives in rules but great freedom for the regulated community in how they are achieved. Consequently, he or she will oppose specific and rigid technology-based standards.

We have already noted the differences in perspective between those writing rules and those who must see that they are put in force. Many agencies now administer multiple statutes, and occasionally a single rule can cut across two or more of them. The Environmental Protection Agency has long contended with the "multimedia" dilemma in which a possible solution to problems in air quality creates new problems for water quality or waste disposal. Each of these media is represented by different program offices in EPA, and each office deals with statutes that have significantly different standards that guide their rulemakings. The same situation holds in the departments like Interior, Agriculture, and Transportation, which house multiple and distinct yet interrelated programs.

The degree to which internal sources of conflict lead to delay depends to a great extent on the relative power of the various offices in a given agency and the organizational norms for rulemaking. If, for example, rulemaking authority is confined to the responsible program office and there is little or no opportunity for other offices to influence the process, then the effect of diversity of perspective on the pace of rulemaking will not be substantial. If the agency has a process that allows for broad internal participation by interested offices, however, then the effect on timeliness can be significant.[47] Time will be spent in managing the mechanisms of participation and in circulating and obtaining comments on drafts. If this norm of participation is combined with the expectation that the rule will represent the consensus of the agency, further delay is likely. Here time will be spent in each of the participating offices that must establish a position on the rule and in what may be extensive negotiations to iron out differences. When consensus is not achieved, the deadlock must be broken by senior agency officials, who may take time attempting to determine what should be done or who may force another round of lower-level negotiations.

We will see in a subsequent chapter that participation has become the prevalent standard across the government. The standard of consensus also exists, but not constantly. It is important to note that gaining consensus costs a great deal more than elapsed time. If the agency is committed to producing a rule with which everyone with a recognized interest can agree, the only way to break certain deadlocks is to produce a rule that ignores unresolved (or unresolvable) issues or deals with them through vague language whose meaning will be fought out during the implementation process. This is one potential cause of the qualitative problems that frustrate the enforcement of certain regulations.

There is another widely observed form of conflict within agencies that holds the potential for delaying the issuance of rules. The tension between career bureaucrats and the political appointees who lead the agencies is a persistent theme in the literature of public administration.

It manifests itself in rulemaking when the approach favored by the program office specialists runs afoul of the policy priorities of the political leadership. This type of problem has been evident for several decades, but it reached its peak during the Reagan years. Policy differences aside, this type of conflict is especially damaging to timeliness when it is not anticipated or dealt with until late in the rulemaking process. If the career staff develops a regulation without early input from senior agency officials, there is always the chance that it will produce a rule that is not acceptable. All or part of the time spent developing the proposal is wasted, and additional time will be spent reformulating the regulation, perhaps with a different cast of characters, or in what amounts to negotiation between the careerists and political appointees.

A special mention of an agency's relationships with its counterparts in the federal government and the states is in order. Comments referred to in the preambles of final rules confirm that agencies take a great interest in the rulemakings conducted by other agencies. The jurisdictions of our national bureaucracies overlap and collide. Rules issued by the Federal Energy Regulatory Commission regarding environmental protection at hydropower facilities have implications for resources under the care of fish and wildlife, public lands, and agricultural agencies. Similarly, EPA routinely issues rules that have enormous impact on other federal agencies, like the departments of Defense and Energy, as well as all local governments. Other elements of the public sector—notably Congress, the White House, and the courts—are key players in rulemaking; when they are unhappy they have means not always available to private organizations to exert influence. So it is reasonable to expect an agency engaged in rulemaking to attempt to accommodate its counterparts in the public sector. This takes time.

Richard Stewart of the Harvard Law School has written that the administrative process in governmental agencies is driven by the clash of external interests.[48] Those involved in decision making in a government agency, including decision making that is done during the course of rulemaking, strive for a result that can be embraced by the agency's external clients and constituents, whether they are beneficiaries or regulated entities. In order to satisfy external constituents the agency staff must take the time to learn their preferences. Once learned they must then be accommodated by the agency. When external parties are in conflict with one another the task becomes more difficult and time-consuming. The same holds true when the positions of the external parties are at odds with what appears to be permissible under the statute or in consideration of the preferences of powerful interests inside the agency. Participation is the means by which the agreement of external parties is secured. It will be covered extensively in subsequent chapters of this book.

PROCEDURAL REQUIREMENTS

The growth in procedural requirements, other than participation, is also responsible for delay in rulemaking. In the last chapter, I alluded to the mixed motives that likely lie behind these types of procedural reforms. Certainly, each can be justified by a noble purpose, be it better-informed rulemaking or empowerment of those who will be affected by its results or a greater degree of management control by the president over a sprawling bureaucratic state. These stated goals notwithstanding, delay can also be an unspoken objective. In the case of Congress this amounts to a seeming contradiction. Our legislators enact programs of regulation or social welfare but then encumber them with procedural requirements that will almost certainly stall their implementation. This simply confirms that political decision making is multidimensional. The combination of an aggressive and ambitious substantive mission combined with a cautious and painstaking process of implementation can satisfy different sets of constituents.

Some presidents who have made incursions into rulemaking have been quite explicit and direct about their intentions to delay the process. When he took office in January 1981 President Ronald Reagan ordered a moratorium on new rules until the provisions of his executive order mandating OMB review could become effective. Slowing the pace of rulemaking was a clear goal of his management program. President George Bush imposed a similar moratorium and then extended it during the waning days of his administration. But presidents, like Congress, engage in the politics of mixed messages when it comes to timeliness in rulemaking. President Bush was reported to have given some regulatory agencies, notably the EPA, more freedom of movement to issue rules than his predecessor had. Nevertheless, he also embraced the Council on Competitiveness and watched without intervention as it slowed the issuance of major rules from that agency and others. Research has demonstrated that in the context of administrative decision making generally, mandates from Congress, the president, courts, or officials of agencies about the rulemaking process are never neutral.[49] They elevate some interests or values over others. In the case of rulemaking, the value that is diminished by growth in procedure is timeliness.

SHORTAGES OF RESOURCES

Rulemaking requires resources, human and otherwise, and when they are in short supply delay is an inevitable result. There are basic structural issues that lead to a situation of insufficient resources. Massive deficits plague the federal government. Fundamental differences have divided Democratic Congresses and two Republican presidents about the proper role of government in American life. There is a lack of connection between the authorizing process that creates rulemaking responsibilities and the appropriations processes that provide the resources that agencies need to carry them out. The net effect of these and other factors is that rarely, if ever, are agencies with large agendas for rulemaking given the staff and access to the essential expertise that they think they need to get the work done. This is, of course, a common complaint and one that is exceptionally difficult to evaluate fairly. It is true, however, that at times Congress can take actions that are mystifying.

The Department of Transportation was the victim of a recent congressional decision that literally dictated that its rulemaking responsibilities would overwhelm available resources. Apparently shocked and appalled by a fatal subway accident in New York City allegedly caused by a drunken motorman, Congress, in an amendment to an appropriations bill, established mandatory alcohol testing for public transportation workers across the United States. It charged the Department of Transportation with responsibility for developing what will be a large body of complex rules to govern all aspects of the testing process and the procedures that would guide the new regulatory program. Equally shocked and appalled by the sorry state of the federal budget, the same appropriations committee refused to provide the department any additional funds or personnel for the rulemaking effort.

Still, our guardians of fiscal integrity did not stop there. When the overtaxed department sought and received help from another federal agency in the form of temporary assignment of staff with appropriate expertise, the appropriations committee intervened and pressured the agency willing to provide the help to rescind its offer. In a personal interview in 1992 with a staff member of the Interstate Commerce Commission, I was told that the reason for this otherwise inexplicable behavior was simply muscle-flexing by a Congress (or its staff) determined to show the agency that it meant business when it declared "no more money." It is not immediately clear how Congress planned to answer the millions of Americans who ride public transportation when they asked, "Where is the program you promised us?" We should not be surprised to hear phrases like "bureaucratic foot-dragging" echoing through those hallowed chambers, however.

MANAGEMENT OBSTACLES AND DEFICIENCIES

Another potential cause of delay is poor management of the rulemaking process by the agency. While this is probably more likely in agencies that have relatively few rules or high staff turnover, it can occur anywhere. Rulemaking can require the organization and direction of many different people and activities. Personnel from the different offices discussed above must be brought together, their work coordinated and supported by research, and their differences resolved. These things do not happen automatically or without substantial thought and effort. Breakdowns in communication, poor coordination of interrelated efforts, and inadequate supervision can lead to the types of misunderstandings and oversights that ultimately delay the issuance of a rule. Management of rulemaking is an important but largely unstudied governmental activity, so a subsequent chapter is devoted to how agencies of government are organized to manage rulemaking.

Short supplies of resources for rulemaking are likely to persist as long as there is deadlock over the budget deficit. Those resources that are available for rulemaking can be profoundly affected by changes in rulemaking priorities. A rule under development can be stalled or abandoned altogether when staff and money are reassigned to projects that are considered more important. Shifts in priorities occur for three reasons. First, Congress, through new legislation, amendments to existing statutes, and oversight activities, can cause the agency to undertake new initiatives. Given the proclivity of Congress to affix deadlines to these new rulemaking responsibilities, the shift of internal resources can be immediate. Second, court decisions can have a similar, if less dramatic, effect. Studies have documented the impact that judicial rulings have had on the priority-setting process for rulemaking agencies.[50] These decisions can cause the agency either to redo a rule that the court has found somehow in error or to undertake the development of a rule that the agency has not yet started, or even anticipated.[51] While Congress can be faulted for a lack of generosity when handing out new rulemaking responsibilities, new resources never accompany a judicial decision of this sort. Third, decisions by the agency itself may lead to a reordering of rulemaking projects. New political leadership with a different vision of what is important or staff work that uncovers serious problems or deficiencies that need attention can lead to work on new projects, leaving others on hold.

Inertia

Finally, delay can occur simply because the agency does not want to act. In many instances this type of delay is difficult to distinguish from that caused by conflict, be it internal or external. Realizing that any form of action will cause them untold grief, the responsible officials choose to wait, often using a study of some sort as a surrogate for action. The chronology of the benzene rule, for example, showed a five-year period consumed by risk analyses. Stalling tactics are attractive because in time a conflict may dissipate on its own, the contending parties may reach an agreement that the agency can then ratify, or the burden may pass to an unlucky successor.

It is evident that any or all of the many potential sources of delay could apply in a given case of rulemaking. Little systematic research has been undertaken that might establish which of these many potential causes are the most common or serious. The authors of the only known empirical study of the passage of time in multiple rulemakings examined nearly two hundred rules and developed measures for complexity, internal and external conflict, procedural requirements, and participation. It found that taken together these variables could account for as much as 60 percent of the variation in elapsed time in rulemaking. The ways these variables were measured, however, were far from ideal. For example, complexity was measured by the length of the rule, and the number of comments received from the public served as the surrogate for external conflict.[52] At this stage it is hard to know whether better results could be obtained with better measurement of these variables or if some unobserved variables are also contributing to delay. We do know, however, that the problem of delay is generally accepted as a major issue in rulemaking and that few simple solutions for it exist.

PARTICIPATION

Participation was discussed as a legal requirement in the preceding chapter. The actual development and current patterns of participation in rulemaking are the topics of Chapter 5. This considerable attention notwithstanding, participation is an important issue in rulemaking and here I will briefly outline the reasons.

Participation in rulemaking poses problems for both the public and the agency. The prerequisites that individuals, groups, and firms must possess in order to become involved in rulemaking in a way that holds some prospects for success include resources, organization, and sophistication. These prerequisites are not distributed evenly. Consequently, some fail to participate in rulemaking because they lack the ability or awareness. We will see presently that rulemaking demands a keen sense of timing and a grasp of the subtleties of bureaucratic decision making. These skills are not necessarily related to the size of an organization or company or the amount of money it has to spend on public affairs. Size and money help, to be sure, but an understanding of the process of rulemaking is more important.

Problems arise, however, even when participation is both extensive and balanced. Sometimes the quality of participation is poor. In other words, even though the agency solicits and receives the views of the public, the results do little or nothing to improve the rule. This occurs for several reasons. First, the information provided by the agency about the rule under development may be misleading or insufficient to allow interested parties to comment intelligently. As noted in earlier chapters, however, legal requirements and inbred agency caution make this a relatively minor problem. Second, given the fact that most rulemaking requires detailed and often technical knowledge, commenting parties may not possess the requisite expertise to be able to offer any additional information or constructive advice on rules. Finally, parties are often uninterested in improving a rule. They use the opportunity to participate to challenge the rule, per se, or to make their opposition a matter of public record that can be referred to in subsequent challenges to the rule.

The sheer volume of participation can be a significant problem for the agency developing the rule. A system for collecting the comments must be established, and the comments themselves must be read and analyzed. Then, the agency must have some mechanism to decide which of the comments have merit, which require changes in the rule, and what those changes will be. Finally, if the agency revises the proposed rule based on the comments it receives, it must prepare an analysis of the changes and why they were made. The magnitude of the task presented to the agency obviously depends on the number, length, and complexity of the comments.

There are near-legendary examples of rules proposed by federal agencies that generated massive outpourings of public comment. Several ill-fated efforts by the Department of Treasury's Bureau of Alcohol, Tobacco and Firearms to regulate handguns were greeted by tens of thousands of postcard responses, orchestrated by the National Rifle Association and related groups. The hazardous materials regulation generated more than 2,200 written comments, and many of these were extensive, containing multiple points and complex arguments. But lest it be thought that only politically charged issues, like gun control or rules affecting large swatches of the economy, generate this level of interest, consider the proposed rule of the Animal and Plant Health Inspection Service (APHIS) on the importation of ostriches. When it was published it stimulated more than 2,000 written comments, an extraordinary number when one considers that ostriches are not normally considered an issue with high political salience.[53] One can only guess at the response that APHIS will receive when it undertakes, as is planned, a more broadly based rule covering all "flightless birds." How long can it be before the distinctive sound of the mating call of emu interest groups is heard along the Potomac?

On a more serious note, participation in rulemaking displays the same proclivity for conflict and deadlock that characterizes other key elements of our public policy process. Phillip Harter, an important figure in the movement to reform the rulemaking process, has summarized the problems that can beset the development of major rules under the general title of "adversary process." He views rulemaking as too often characterized by the taking of extreme positions, both by the agency and by affected parties; waves of "defensive research"; and an inability or unwillingness of parties to the rulemaking to state and deal with "true concerns." Formal mechanisms for participation, such as written comment and public hearings, become stylized rituals from which neither side expects much more than an affirmation of what is already known. He notes that these forms are not conducive to the resolution of "polycentric" issues and they are not well suited to the type of give and take between parties that is so elemental to dispute resolution.[54] Accommodation of contending positions, if it occurs at all, happens behind the scenes in quiet negotiations. When conflict persists and is not resolved, rules are issued and the controversy spills into the federal courts, the halls of Congress, or the White House. Petitions for reconsideration are filed, and the initial rulemaking effort may be for nought.

Harter is careful to note that this description does not hold for all rulemaking. In fact, evidence will be presented in a subsequent chapter that disputes this general view of rulemaking. We will see that at least some of those who participate actively in the rulemaking process find it a valuable and fruitful activity and find the agencies they deal with responsive. Nevertheless, a great deal of evidence indicates that the dysfunctions in participation of the sort Harter identifies are clearly present in rulemaking. Although it may not be the best barometer of dissatisfaction with rulemaking, litigation challenging rules is certainly one indicator of the degree to which parties fail to get what they want from participation. The rates of litigation for some programs of rulemaking are extremely high. With one exception, every health standard issued by the Occupational Safety and Health Administration has been challenged in court, usually by both labor and management. The Environmental Protection Agency has estimated that some 80 percent of its rules stimulate lawsuits by dissatisfied parties.[55] Although there are no definitive corroborating figures, these and other agencies receive petitions for reconsideration in a high percentage of the rulemakings they complete.

Involvement of the public in rulemaking may be the most complex and important form of political action in the contemporary American political system. When it is blocked or otherwise does not occur, there are profound constitutional and practical implications. As we will detail in Chapter 5, because rulemaking is a form of lawmaking, participation by the public is important to the maintenance of democracy. Because rule writers are not omniscient, the information that the public possesses is badly needed.

BUREAUCRATIC DISCRETION

Like participation, the exercise of bureaucratic discretion is central to any consideration of rulemaking. Also like participation, bureaucratic discretion, more accurately its containment, is the topic of an entire chapter. Still, it is important to acknowledge here that it is a serious and persistent issue.[56] When a function as basic as the making of law and policy is conducted by persons with no direct electoral link to any constituency, conflict with fundamental constitutional principles results. Further, as we have seen in this chapter, the ability of a bureaucracy to perform well in the exercise of delegated authority through rulemaking has been questioned.

We have already established why bureaucracy is entrusted with rulemaking initially. In subsequent chapters we will examine how the constitutional branches attempt to retain control, ensure the faithfulness of bureaucrats, and influence the results of rulemaking. It will be evident that bureaucratic discretion as an abstract concept looms much larger than its actual occurrence in rulemaking. Far more important and interesting are the profound contradictions in our political system that express themselves so clearly in any serious consideration of rulemaking as a bureaucratic function. These contradictions deserve clarification.

INSEPARABLE ISSUES

The issues in rulemaking are serious, and their contradictions are perplexing. Presenting the issues as discrete problems is potentially misleading, because we must examine their interrelationships in order to expose their contradictions.

The most profound dilemma faced by those interested in rulemaking is how to address any one of these issues without further complicating another. If, for example, we seek to improve the quality of rules that are issued by ensuring they anticipate and fully resolve implementation, compliance, and enforcement issues, it is difficult to imagine that the rulemaking process will be faster or the resultant rule will be less complex. If, instead, we make a concerted effort to accelerate the pace of rulemaking, it is likely that time will be gained at the expense of internal and external participation or the reasoned deliberation that we believe to be essential to high-quality rules. Many other examples of contradictory expectations can be offered.

From the perspectives highlighted in this chapter we cannot escape the conclusion that in rulemaking we can observe the struggle between powerful and important values. The volume of rulemaking can be viewed as an agency's attempt to be responsive to legislative mandates. The quality of rules is linked to the faith, perhaps now lost, in the expertise and neutral competence of the bureaucracy. Concern for the speed of rulemaking is also linked to responsiveness, but in addition it is linked to values prevalent in the field of policy analysis that delay is waste, and waste in a time of scarcity is a tragedy. Each of these values has merit, but the foregoing survey of problems in rulemaking should remind us that outsized and clashing expectations put our basic institutions and decision-making processes under considerable stress. Rulemaking is a process that demands trade-offs; each of these important values is thus threatened by compromise.

NOTES

1. Phillip Harter, "Regulatory Negotiation: A Cure for the Malaise," *Georgetown Law Review* 71 (1982): 1; Thomas McGarrity, "Some Thoughts on Deossifying Rulemaking," *Duke Law Journal* 41 (1992): 1385-1462; Jerry Mashaw, "Improving the Environment of Agency Rulemaking" (Report to the Administrative Conference of the United States, August 1992).
2. Gary Bryner, *Bureaucratic Discretion: Law and Policy in Federal Regulatory Agencies* (New York: Pergamon, 1987).
3. Paul Sommers and Roland Cole, *Complying with Government Requirements: The Costs to Small and Larger Businesses* (Seattle: Battelle, 1981).
4. Bryner, *Bureaucratic Discretion*, chap. 9.
5. Ibid.
6. 219 U.S.C. 655(a).
7. Albert Nichols and Richard Zeckhauser, "OSHA After a Decade: A Time for Reason," in *Case Studies in Regulation: Revolution and Reform*, ed. Leonard Weiss and Michael Klass (Boston: Little, Brown, 1981), p. 214.
8. Ibid., p. 203.
9. W. Kip Viscusi, "Reforming OSHA Regulation of Workplace Risks," in *Regulatory Reform: What Actually Happened*, ed. Leonard Weiss and Michael Klass (Boston: Little, Brown, 1986), p. 248.
10. Office of Solid Waste and Emergency Response (hereafter, OSWER), *The Nation's Hazardous Waste Management Program at a Crossroads* (Washington, D.C.: Environmental Protection Agency, 1990), p. 7.
11. Ibid., p. 31.
12. Ibid.
13. Paul Farhi, "FCC Delays Reductions on Cable Television Rates," *Washington Post*, June 12, 1993, sec. D, p. 1.
14. OSWER, *Nation's Hazardous Waste Management Program*, p. 87; also see John Mendeloff, "Does Overregulation Cause Underregulation?" *Regulation*, September/October 1981, pp. 47-52.
15. Sommers and Cole, *Complying with Government Requirements*, p. 171.
16. OSWER, *Nation's Hazardous Waste Management Program*, p. 36.
17. Laura Langbein, *Discovering Whether Programs Work* (New York: Goodyear,

1980).
18. Edward Gramlich, *Benefit-Cost Analysis of Government Programs* (Englewood Cliffs, N.J.: Prentice Hall, 1981), chap. 2.
19. Ibid., p. 7.
20. David O'Brien, "The Multiple Sources of Statutory Ambiguity," in *Administrative Discretion and Public Policy Implementation*, ed. Douglas Shumavon and H. Kenneth Hibblen (New York: Praeger, 1986), p. 69.
21. Colin Diver, "Regulatory Precision," in *Making Regulatory Policy*, ed. Keith Hawkins and John Thomas (Pittsburgh: University of Pittsburgh Press, 1989), p. 200.
22. Ibid., p. 215.
23. Ibid., p. 200.
24. Peter Bardach and Robert Kagan, *Going by the Book* (Philadelphia: Temple University Press, 1982).
25. Diver, "Regulatory Precision," p. 200.
26. Sommers and Cole, *Complying with Government Requirements*, p. 123.
27. Ibid., p. 125.
28. Ibid., p. 123.
29. "Maze of Medicaid Rules Forcing Painful Choices," *Washington Post*, August 18, 1991, p. 1.
30. 16 U.S.C. 661.
31. It is interesting that case studies of single programs have also found overly long preambles to be a problem. See OSWER, *Nation's Hazardous Waste Program*, p. 37.
32. For example, see Mark Rothstein, "Substantive and Procedural Obstacles to OSHA Rulemaking: Reproductive Hazards as an Example," *Boston College Environmental Affairs Law Review* 12 (1985): 627.
33. Bryner, *Bureaucratic Discretion*.
34. Stephen Breyer, *Regulation and Its Reform* (Cambridge, Mass.: Harvard University Press, 1982), p. 109.
35. Ibid., p. 110. On this general point, also see Peter Manning, "The Limits of Knowledge," in *Making Regulatory Policy*, ed. Hawkins and Thomas.
36. OSWER, *Nation's Hazardous Waste Management Program*, p. 37.
37. Kerwin and Furlong, "Time and Rulemaking: An Empirical Test of Theory," *Journal of Public Administration Research and Theory* 2 (1992): 118.
38. Barry Boyer, "The Federal Trade Commission and Consumer Protection Policy: A Post-Mortem Examination," in *Making Regulatory Policy*, ed. Hawkins and Thomas, p. 113.
39. Ibid.
40. Bardach and Kagan, *Going by the Book*.
41. Neil Eisner, "Agency Delay in Rulemaking," *Administrative Law Journal* 3 (1989): 7.
42. *Fundamental Improvements Needed for Timely Promulgation of Health Program Regulations* (Washington, D.C.: U.S. General Accounting Office, 1977), p. i.
43. Neil Eisner, "Regulatory Negotiation: A Real World Experience," *Federal Bar News and Journal* 31, no. 9 (1984): 372.
44. Kerwin and Furlong, "Time and Rulemaking," p. 117.
45. Benjamin Mintz and Nancy Miller, *A Guide to Federal Agency Rulemaking* (Washington, D.C.: Administrative Conference of the United States, 1991), p. 15 (n. 54).
46. William West, "The Growth of Internal Conflict in Administrative Regulation," *Public Administration Review*, July/August 1988, pp. 773-782.

47. Kerwin and Furlong, "Time and Rulemaking," p. 118.
48. Richard Stewart, "The Reformation of American Administrative Law," *Harvard Law Review* 88 (1975): 1667-1711.
49. Matthew McCubbins, Roger Noll, and Barry Weingast, "Administrative Procedures as Instruments of Political Control" (Paper delivered to the Annual Meeting of the Midwest Political Science Association, Chicago, March 1987).
50. Rosemary O'Leary, *Environmental Change: Federal Courts and the EPA* (Philadelphia: Temple University Press, 1993), p. 168.
51. R. Shep Melnick, *Regulation and the Courts* (Washington, D.C.: Brookings Institution, 1983), chap. 4.
52. Kerwin and Furlong, "Time and Rulemaking."
53. Personal interview with staff of the Animal and Plant Health Inspection Service, January 18, 1993.
54. Harter, "Regulatory Negotiation," p. 450.
55. The origins of this statistic are obscure, but it has been quoted extensively in EPA training materials.
56. Theodore Lowi, "Two Roads to Serfdom: Liberalism, Conservatism and Administrative Power," *American University Law Review* 36 (1987).

CHAPTER 4

The Management of Rulemaking

The volume of rules and the diversity and complexity of the rulemaking processes pose serious management challenges for responsible officials. Rules are not equally important or equally advisable. Information for rulemaking is not always readily available, and it is never free. Personnel sufficiently expert and available to undertake a rulemaking do not appear magically. The multiple levels and types of review do not just happen. Each of these requires attention and direction. Without such attention and direction the problems and dilemmas outlined in the previous chapter are not likely to be resolved. In fact, rulemaking is actively and aggressively managed, another indication that it is a governmental function of central importance.

The management of rulemaking occurs at three distinct levels, and each will be examined in this chapter. The first level of management, and the one that has received the most public attention in recent years, consists of government-wide programs operated out of the White House to coordinate and control various aspects of all rulemaking. The second level of management is in the individual agencies. This level consists of structures and processes that have evolved in every agency, frequently through long periods of time, within the broader management frameworks established by recent presidents. Finally, management occurs at the level of the individual rule. Here, attention is focused on the techniques used to bring together the expertise and authorities needed to complete a particular rulemaking successfully. These efforts are strongly influenced by both presidential and agency management systems. Taken together these three levels of management exert a strong influence on the direction and content of a rulemaking.

PRESIDENTIAL MANAGEMENT

Henry Rosovsky, commenting on what it was like to serve as dean of the faculty at Harvard University, said it was similar to "herding frogs." On a much grander scale this is what a president confronts when he sets about to manage rulemaking across the government.[1] Even in earlier periods, when the volume of rulemaking was not what it has been in recent decades, a president seeking to control or merely influence the process of writing regulations faced considerable variety. Earlier we discussed the situation in rulemaking during the New Deal, when President Franklin Delano Roosevelt struggled with forces in Congress that appeared intent on transforming rulemaking into a pale version of judicial decision making. But beyond his successful efforts to resist extreme judicialization of the process, nothing FDR undertook during his terms could be properly called management of rulemaking. There is no evidence of any serious effort of this type in the years of Harry Truman, Dwight Eisenhower, John Kennedy, or Lyndon Johnson. During the presidencies of Richard Nixon and Gerald Ford, serious and sustained attention was given to the regulatory process, in general. Both administrations called on agencies writing rules to conduct studies to predict the effect of new regulations on various segments of the population or economy. Nixon established a "quality of life review" and Ford an "inflation impact statement." Neither administration went much beyond these analytical devices in an attempt to direct or coordinate rulemaking across the full range of programs administered by the federal government.

Serious and formal programs to manage rulemaking from the White House are, then, a relatively recent phenomenon. They coincide roughly with the rise of social regulation and the vast bodies of rules that came with that expansion of the federal government. Presidents came to realize that their grip on the course of domestic public policy hinged to a considerable extent on their ability to influence the course of the thousands of rules that put programs into action. It should not be surprising that it was Jimmy Carter who initiated what is arguably the most far-reaching and diversified program of rulemaking management undertaken by an American president. Throughout his political career he was known to be intensely interested in the management of government programs. In fact, he was frequently criticized for immersing himself too deeply in the specifics of policies and programs while losing sight of, and his grip on, the bigger picture. But Carter did focus on larger, more general issues. Like several of his predecessors and each of his successors, Carter was concerned with the role and effect of government regulation in American society. The program of management he devised had many elements, most of which survive, either intact or in modified form, to this day.

The Carter rulemaking management program was embodied in Executive Order 12044. The actions undertaken by Carter in this 1978 action were substantial indeed. The order created a "regulatory council," consisting of the heads of the agencies with the most substantial regulatory programs. The council was conceived of as a mechanism for the coordination of rulemaking activities across the entire government. It prepared a calendar of the most significant and important rules being developed in agencies and departments and attempted to identify areas of common interest or approach or potential overlap in these individual efforts. The council was also expected to conduct studies of the "cumulative effect of regulations on particularly vulnerable industries or sectors." [2]

Created along with the council was the Regulatory Analysis Review Group (RARG), headed by the Council of Economic Advisers and with representation from the same agencies that sat on the council. The mission of RARG was to "improve the quality of analysis supporting proposed regulations, identify and attempt to resolve common analytic problems among the agencies and assure adequate consideration of least costly alternatives." [3] The RARG was also used as a vehicle to allow all regulatory agencies to review and comment on the rules developed by a particular agency with the idea that this participation would increase available expertise and promote consistency in rulemaking.

The Carter executive order also created a role for the Office of Management and Budget. It was to review rules to ensure that agencies were faithfully adhering to the recently enacted Paperwork Reduction Act and that rules embodied the general principles outlined in the order. Although it had no power to change rules that it reviewed, OMB was to report to the president regularly on the performance of agencies in achieving the goals of the order.

The Carter approach to management of rulemaking was built on five principles: policy oversight of rulemaking by agency heads, increased participation by the public in the development of rules, regulatory analysis, "sunset review" to eliminate rules no longer needed and to update or revise those that had become obsolete or ineffectual, and the use of "plain English" in rules to make them more accessible to those who must comply with their provisions. [4] Each of these principles was developed in response to a common problem in rulemaking. The active involvement of agency leadership in the planning and development of rules was designed to counteract the nearly total lack of central direction to rulemaking in federal agencies that the Carter administration found when it took office. Central oversight of rules in agencies was called "the most important element of the Order and the key to the success of [Carter's] regulatory reform program." [5] Increased participation by the public was seen as a way to improve the image of rulemaking while simultaneously enriching the pool of information that agencies had to work with when developing rules. Regulatory analysis was developed as an effort to inject a degree of self-conscious rationality into the process of rule development. When done correctly and seriously, such analysis forced attention to alternative ways of accomplishing public policy objectives. "Sunset reviews" were a method of stimulating agencies to renovate bodies of regulations that had developed in piecemeal fashion, in some cases over many decades. Obsolescence was an inevitable by-product of this approach to developing rules. Anyone who has read the *Federal Register* or the *Code of Federal Regulations* will immediately understand what the "plain English" initiative was all about.

The Carter management program was in effect for fewer than three years. Despite its short life, it was able to stimulate change in each of the areas it targeted, and several of its basic principles and structures continue to influence rulemaking today. In a report on the implementation of the executive order in 1979 the Office of Management and Budget noted that overall progress was mixed, with some reforms showing well and others relatively poorly. In answer to the call for more systematic and aggressive oversight of rulemaking by agency leaders, several agencies established their own regulatory councils or steering committees. The composition and functions of the councils and committees varied, but there were examples of agency leaders playing an active role in both the initiation and final approval of rules. Considerable progress was reported in the area of public participation, a subject that is explored in the next chapter. There were truly dramatic results in the area of sunset review. Several agencies had undertaken reviews that led to major revisions of their body of regulations. The Occupational Safety and Health Administration, for example, reduced its fire safety standards from 400 pages to 30. The Department of Health, Education and Welfare reviewed more than 2,800 pages of rules. The result was that 719 pages were deleted outright and 500 pages were rewritten. Similar efforts were reported in the Department of Transportation. The campaign for plain English in most agencies focused on the use of preambles to rules, using them as what amounted to a layman's guide for translating the often inescapable technical and legal jargon found in actual regulations into words that nonspecialists could understand. Progress in the area of regulatory analysis was generally weak. The OMB report concluded that "some individual examples of good analyses are available, but no department can be commended for having a department-wide, continuously successful effort in place." [6]

Still, the performance of Carter's management program cannot be fully appreciated until we consider the enduring relevance and influence of many of its basic principles and structures. One could easily argue that many of the elements of his program were not original. The Regulatory Council, for example, was a more focused version of the old Council on Wage and Price Stability. Regulatory analyses can be viewed as the next logical step after the impact analyses of the Nixon and Ford administrations. Nevertheless, the breadth, coherence, and specific focus of Carter's program was distinctive and influential. When Ronald Reagan and George Bush fashioned their own regulatory reform efforts, they saw sufficient merit in Carter's programs to retain many of their basic elements while adding distinctive features of their own.

Reagan did not wait as long as his predecessor did to put his rulemaking management system in place. Shortly after taking office he issued Executive Order 12291, which instituted a sixty-day moratorium on new rules, a mandatory cost-benefit analysis for all major regulations, a requirement that all such regulations meet a "net benefit" criterion, and a review of all proposed and final rules by the Office of Management and Budget. The order was part of a general policy of the Reagan administration that sought to reduce the burden of regulation on the American economy by making it more difficult for agencies to issue regulations and to ensure that they could justify those that were written. The moratorium was an effort to prevent "midnight" rules from being issued by holdovers from the Carter administration who might possess a more expansive view of regulation than that of the Reagan team. The mandatory cost-benefit analysis and the "net benefit" rule codified more strictly the regulatory analysis program of Executive Order 12044. Mandatory review by the Office of Management and Budget as Reagan designed it carried with it the power to delay issuance of proposed or final rules that did not comport with the philosophy of the new administration. It too was an upgrading and strengthening of a review program that Carter had put in place. We will see in a subsequent chapter that this single act had a more profound effect on the rulemaking process than the entire Carter program. President Reagan also created the Vice President's Task Force on Regulatory Relief. In doing so he elevated a secondary function of Carter's Regulatory Council, consideration of the impact of regulations on particularly fragile sectors of the economy, to primary status. The Reagan administration also chose to continue the semiannual regulatory agenda and an annual version of the regulatory calendar containing summaries of the work of the OMB in review of agency rules.

When Bush became president he kept virtually all of Reagan's program intact, but significant changes occurred in the name and function of the Task Force on Regulatory Relief he had chaired as vice president. Renamed the Council on Competitiveness in 1991, it under-took the review of individual rules that were likely to have an especially significant impact on the economy generally or on particular sectors of the economy. President Bush continued one tradition by putting the council under the chairmanship of his vice president, James Danforth Quayle. It functioned like a super-OMB review by selecting rules with considerable potential impact or high visibility for special scrutiny. The council received staff assistance from the compo-nent of the OMB that normally conducted the analysis of regulations. The effects of and controversy surrounding the activities of the council will be covered in a subsequent chapter.

The major differences between the Carter program and those of his Republican successors are ones of emphasis and power. Carter was concerned with at least four major issues associated with rulemaking. First, he wanted rulemaking to be based on rigorous analysis of all reasonable alternatives for achieving public policy goals. Second, Carter sought consistency in the way rules addressed problems. Clearly, Carter was concerned that policies could be working at cross-purposes with, for example, regulatory decisions impeding broader economic initiatives. This is apparent in the stated functions of the Regulatory Council and the Regulatory Analysis Review Group, the functions established for OMB, and the heavy emphasis he placed on involvement of the most senior officials at the agency level. Third, he was concerned with the role of the public in two ways: he wanted every reasonable mechanism for public participation in the formula-tion of rules to be used fully and the results of rulemaking to be presented in language that the average American could understand. Finally, Carter wanted rulemaking to be managed proactively by the most senior officials in the various agencies.

The goals of Reagan's program were narrower. He was far less concerned with proactive management and broadly based public partici-pation. He was far more concerned with slowing the pace and volume of rulemaking as part of a conscious strategy to reduce the impact of regulation on the private sector. It would be unfair to argue that the imposition of regulatory analysis requirements and the "net benefit" rule did not reflect a sincere interest in the assessment of alternatives by the most rigorous means available. But it is fair to say that this was not as important to Reagan's program as it was to Carter's. The Bush program had few unique features and was characterized as half-hearted and fraught with mixed messages about the proper role of regulation in economic and social affairs.[7] The management program of William Clinton has focused on familiar issues and review mechanisms. As one would expect, the president has chosen to retain OMB review but open it to public scrutiny and limit it to "significant" rules. "Significant" is defined by economic impact, budget impact, inconsistency with other rules, or novel legal or policy issues. President Clinton has also vested Vice President Albert Gore with the authority to set the government-wide rulemaking agenda.[8] At this writing, the Clinton program has just been announced, so it is much too early to evaluate its implementation.

What is altogether clear is that presidential efforts to manage rulemaking as an identifiable government-wide activity have been sophisticated, substantial, and influential. To use a crude analogy, presidents have come to approach the management of rulemaking in a manner not unlike their efforts to manage an otherwise diffuse and fragmented national security apparatus. What is also clear is that the recent management systems operating out of the White House are very much the product of the synthesis of ideas, structures, and procedures that occurred during the Carter administration. But it was the Reagan administration that put real bite into presidential management of rulemaking. The dramatic advances it made, which will be documented in considerable detail in the chapter devoted to oversight, owe much to a foundation laid by a president from another party.

MANAGEMENT ON THE AGENCY LEVEL

Individual agencies have many good reasons to manage rulemaking. Most are quite independent of the interest a given president may take in one or another aspect of the process. As we have seen in previous chapters, rulemaking is the primary way agencies define the programs they implement and administer. They are under considerable pressure from sources other than the White House to produce rules. Congress, interest groups, other agencies, and their own staffs may be clamoring for new or revised regulations. The agency's ability to sort out these demands for rules and to be responsive depends to some extent on its management of the overall rulemaking process. There are other reasons for management. Political leadership of an agency will likely have a policy agenda. Whether it is the promotion of the president's larger program or a set of priorities that the secretary of a department or administrator of an agency brought with him or her, good management can supply the vigilance and discipline to ensure that rules issued are consistent with a given policy or approach. Finally, rulemaking uses resources. Some agencies devote significant shares of the budgets provided them by Congress to rulemaking. The Environmental Protection Agency estimates that roughly 40 percent of its multibillion dollar annual budget is spent on the development of rules.[9] In these days of massive deficits and budgetary stringency, careful management of a function that is so expensive is an obvious obligation to the public, which pays the bills.

THE ELEMENTS OF MANAGEMENT

Agency-level management of rulemaking goes well beyond the structures and procedures that have been included in various presidential programs. Whereas presidents have been concerned with broad issues and concerns, agency management programs encompass administrative activities as well as policy concerns. To examine the management of rulemaking at the agency level, one must first determine what the elements of such a system might look like. Drawing on available case studies of rulemaking and the general literature devoted to public administration, we are able to identify what the basic elements of a management system might include.

A word is in order here on how the information about rulemaking management practices in federal agencies was assembled for this chapter. Three sources were used. The first was guidance documents and internal reports on rulemaking prepared by agencies themselves (see Appendix B). To the extent that they were available, these internal studies and reports provided descriptions of some of the elements of rulemaking management in selected agencies. But these documents were not available or current in all cases, and where they did exist they frequently addressed only a portion of the activities and structures of the agency in question. To obtain a more complete picture of rulemaking management, I supplemented these sources with a survey of experts in thirty-five agencies of the federal government that have substantial rulemaking responsibilities, as measured by the volume of rulemaking reported in the 1990-1991 Regulatory Program of the president (Appendix C). The survey consisted of fourteen open-ended questions asked in telephone interviews (Appendix D). In certain instances research assistants conducted follow-up interviews to clarify points in the surveys. Note that in this section of the chapter, only quotations related to process or policy are footnoted. Other quoted terms were drawn from agency guidance documents or interviews. The sample of respondents and the nature of the questions asked require caution in making sweeping generalizations, but a clear picture of the major features of rulemaking management emerges from these various sources.

A PROCESS FOR SETTING PRIORITIES THROUGHOUT THE AGENCY.   By setting priorities throughout its domain, an agency can control the types and sequencing of rules that it produces. Priority setting enables the leadership of the agency to determine how it will respond to external demands for rules and how the agency's resources available for rulemaking will be spent. Agencies might vary considerably in their attention to setting priorities. At one extreme is a fully centralized system in which the priority order is set at the top of the agency; at the other is a fully decentralized system in which no overarching set of priorities is imposed on the various operating units of the agency. Between these extremes one might find a system in which agency leadership designates some number of rules as high-priority projects, leaving the operating units to determine the rest of the rulemaking agenda. Still another is an essentially decentralized approach that allows for intervention by agency leadership when an emergency, political or otherwise, arises.

Seventy-four percent of the agencies surveyed reported that they had systems to set the priority order for rulemaking. These systems vary considerably, however. Some do little more than what is required to assemble the semiannual regulatory agenda. Others are comprehensive and rigorous. At the Department of Housing and Urban Development (HUD), the Secretarial Oversight Group sets rulemaking priorities and reviews progress on existing projects each quarter. The most ambitious priority-setting system may be that in operation at the Federal Aviation Administration. At the FAA only fifty significant rulemaking projects are authorized to be in progress at any one time. As a rule is completed, the proposed rule project deemed to be the most important takes its place among the fifty. The priority setting is done by the Regulatory Review Board, which consists of the FAA's associate administrators and other senior officials. It operates under the direct auspices of the administrator as a forum for the discussion of major issues emerging in each office that will require rules. More important, it is a mechanism for developing consensus as to which of these needed rules are important enough to join the list of fifty.

In the Department of Education the priority setting is managed by the Division of Regulations Management (DORM) in the Office of the General Counsel. Each year the DORM meets with the program offices to determine which rules are needed during the next twelve months and the "relative priorities given to these regulations." The priority order is set, in part, according to the resources available in the department to write the regulation. It is interesting to note that program offices in the Department of Education are expected to anticipate the need for new regulations even before legislation is enacted. Department guidance requires program offices to conduct a "side by side" analysis when the two houses of Congress enact similar bills that may require new rules.[10] This type of study helps the department to determine if there are sufficient similarities to begin work developing regulations. Obviously, it also requires an assessment of the likelihood that a single bill will emerge and become law. Otherwise, the effort could easily be wasted.

There is, however, no evidence to suggest that these or other agencies use rigorous analysis to set the priority order of a given project. Most agencies reported that rules considered important to senior managers were given higher priority than others. The presence of political interest in the rule was the most frequently cited reason for a rule to be considered important. Agencies also reported that rules with mandatory deadlines, either congressional or judicial, were given priority over other projects. Of the agencies reporting no priority-setting system, one reported that the frequency and intensity of political pressure forced the agency to alter the priority order of rulemakings so often that the system once in place had become useless.

A PROCESS FOR INITIATING RULES.   We have seen that rules can be initiated in a variety of ways. Statutory mandates, judicial orders, petitions from the public, and agency determinations of need can all cause a rulemaking to begin. A requirement that those about to begin writing rules must secure permission to do so from senior agency officials, or simply must inform higher authorities that a rulemaking is being initiated, serves a number of purposes. Like a systematic mechanism for priority setting, control over the initiation of individual rulemakings can, in a negative sense, insert senior management into agenda setting and resource allocation. By denying authorization or delaying the start of a rulemaking, senior officials are affecting the priority of other projects and the resources available to complete them. Depending on the form it takes, it can also alert other offices in the agency that a rulemaking that affects or interests them is being undertaken.

A substantial majority of agencies (63 percent) reported that those wishing to initiate rulemaking must obtain prior authorization to do so from senior agency management. Virtually all of these require that the permission be requested in writing. Many require a memorandum, but some use a standardized form. The Environmental Protection Agency, for example, uses a standardized "start action request," which is forwarded to a "steering committee" of the agency. The EPA Steering Committee consists of representatives from all major program and nonprogram offices. It does not set priorities for rulemaking, but it does serve as a vehicle for authorizing the start of a rule and, more important, alerting the entire agency to an action that is being undertaken by a particular office.

In other agencies the start of rulemaking is regulated more aggressively and more centrally. The FAA's priority-setting system is designed in such a way that the initiation of work on new regulations is also controlled. At the Food Safety and Inspection Service (FSIS) the written approval of the administrator is needed to authorize the start of rulemaking. At the Nuclear Regulatory Commission it is the executive director that must give approval, and at the Bureau of Land Management it is a division of legislation and regulations management. Some agencies, such as the Social Security Administration, require authorization to start a rule only when the rule is discretionary and involves policy considerations.

EARLY INPUT BY SENIOR OFFICIALS. Since at least the Carter administration there has been concern that rulemaking lacks the benefit of a coherent, overall approach. To cope with this perceived shortcoming, a mechanism that allows senior officials to provide early technical or policy guidance can be quite significant. Assuming a degree of consistency in the senior leadership, this management device could ensure that all rules, or at least the most significant ones, reflect a common substantive or procedural philosophy. At a more practical level, it can also minimize the problems caused when a fully developed rule finally reaches senior officials for review and is found unacceptable by them. The costs of conflict, delay, and wasted resources that accompany these so-called "late hits" by senior managers can be substantial. Their insertion into the rulemaking process early enough for them to influence the direction of a rule can avoid these problems.

Agencies can be grouped in three categories: those that require guidance by senior officials for all rules, those that require guidance only on rules deemed important enough for senior management attention, and those that have no system of this sort. An overwhelming percentage of agencies—83 percent—reported systems that fall into the first two categories. The devices are as varied as those for priority setting. In some agencies, a senior official provides the direction, whereas in others, a committee or board with broad policy-making authority does so. The FSIS, for example, requires the completion of a "threshold analysis" that summarizes the salient features and issues associated with the rule that is to be developed. The analysis is reviewed by all senior officials, including the administrator, before the actual work on the rule begins. At the Department of Housing and Urban Development, a senior political appointee from each program office is designated the "policy contact person" for rulemakings. He or she receives and reviews "program office descriptions" of rules that are being considered for development and provides input at this very early stage. In those agencies in which guidance is provided only for a special few of the total rulemakings, it is not clear why or how the senior management or political leadership intervene. In at least one case the agency reported serious inconsistencies in the management of this guidance process. In this instance, there were complaints that although senior managers get involved at the beginning of rulemaking they rarely participate in or oversee the rulemaking consistently after the initial stages.

THE PREPARATION OF PLANNING DOCUMENTS.   The significance of planning documents may not be immediately apparent, but under certain circumstances they can be effective management tools. A detailed work plan forces those responsible for writing rules to make their intentions clear and known to all who read them. Combined with a system for approving the initiation of rules, a work plan can give senior management officials sufficient information to intervene at the early stages of a rulemaking if it appears that the rule writers are pursuing an unacceptable or nonfeasible course of action. Even when work plans do not serve as an instrument for oversight, they can still be useful. Depending on their content, they can force those writing the rule to consider the full range of policy, technical, operational, and resource issues that will arise and must be resolved during the rulemaking. Work plans are thus a mechanism for anticipating the types of problems for which rulemaking is often criticized.

The preponderant majority of agencies—66 percent—use some kind of planning documents to chart the course of all rulemakings, and a substantial portion of the rest use them selectively. In the latter category, agencies like the EPA and the Mine Safety and Health Administration have program offices that require planning documents for significant rules or those whose preparation is likely to be highly complex. The documents vary from agency to agency in both content and purpose but generally include background on the need for the rule, the type of information required to complete it, the availability and sources of information, the policy issues involved, public interest and involvement in the rule, and needed resources and schedules.

Many agencies require program offices to develop what amount to planning memoranda to accompany requests for permission to start rulemaking. These memoranda do not appear to be as extensive as the EPA planning document, but they contain sufficient detail about the purpose of, need for, and issues related to the rule to allow others in the agency to determine whether they wish to participate in some way in the rule's development. And there is evidence that these memoranda are taken seriously. The Department of Housing and Urban Development underscores the memorandum's importance by calling it "the foundation document of any new regulation. . . . it is the beginning of communication [on the rule]." [11] Such documents are also used to inform senior managers of some aspect of the rulemaking that is about to begin or already under way. In this sense they serve an oversight purpose. But the contents of some, such as those done by the EPA, suggest that they can also serve as a true planning tool. Among the topics addressed in these documents are the purpose of the rule being developed, the intent of the legislation that the rule will implement, the effects of existing rules on the one being developed (and vice versa), the information and resources needed to complete the rule, the impact of the rule on the affected population, deadlines that must be met, the forms of public participation appropriate for the rulemaking, and the likely points of controversy.

SCHEDULES. Experienced and thoughtful observers of the rule-making process contend that setting a firm schedule can reduce or eliminate delay.[12] A schedule provides a benchmark to measure the performance of those writing the rule, and if linked to a staff performance appraisal process, it can provide strong incentives to complete the rulemaking on time. When required to do so, and to be realistic, those setting a schedule cannot avoid dealing with and planning for the substantive and procedural issues whose resolution consumes the bulk of time in any rulemaking. Like a planning document, a schedule requires attention to key issues and how they might be resolved. For that reason one would expect to find schedules incorporated into planning documents.

With the exception of two, all agencies reported that they set schedules for all their rulemakings. An example of a schedule format used by the Federal Aviation Administration is shown in Figure 4-1. It identifies key milestones and the dates they were or are expected to be achieved. The FAA and many other agencies determine schedules on a rule-by-rule basis. The Nuclear Regulatory Commission (NRC) has set general policies for completing rules. The NRC expects all rules to be completed within two years of their formal initiation.

The frequency of scheduling reported by the agencies might be impressive, especially in light of the value some experts place on schedules as a way to combat delay, but it is important to note that a substantial number of agencies reported that schedules were routinely adjusted. In other words, in many agencies schedules slip. This is by no means an indictment of scheduling. The value of a schedule, as Neil Eisner has argued, does not lie primarily in whether it is adhered to religiously. On the contrary, a schedule is an objective. If it is not met, it requires another to be set and the assumptions that led to the first to be reexamined. That so many agencies set schedules and monitor progress in meeting self-imposed deadlines is significant for this reason alone.

BUDGETS. Writing rules costs money, and it can command a hefty share of the total budget of some agencies. It is not clear, however, how agencies allocate and manage the resources devoted to developing

Figure 4-1 Abbreviated Sample Schedule of the Rulemaking Process at the Federal Aviation Administration

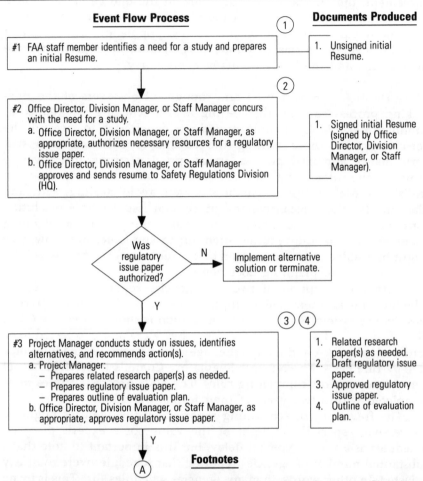

Event Flow Process

① **Documents Produced**

#1 FAA staff member identifies a need for a study and prepares an initial Resume.

1. Unsigned initial Resume.

②

#2 Office Director, Division Manager, or Staff Manager concurs with the need for a study.
a. Office Director, Division Manager, or Staff Manager, as appropriate, authorizes necessary resources for a regulatory issue paper.
b. Office Director, Division Manager, or Staff Manager approves and sends resume to Safety Regulations Division (HQ).

1. Signed initial Resume (signed by Office Director, Division Manager, or Staff Manager).

Was regulatory issue paper authorized? — N → Implement alternative solution or terminate.

Y

③ ④

#3 Project Manager conducts study on issues, identifies alternatives, and recommends action(s).
a. Project Manager:
– Prepares related research paper(s) as needed.
– Prepares regulatory issue paper.
– Prepares outline of evaluation plan.
b. Office Director, Division Manager, or Staff Manager, as appropriate, approves regulatory issue paper.

1. Related research paper(s) as needed.
2. Draft regulatory issue paper.
3. Approved regulatory issue paper.
4. Outline of evaluation plan.

Y

Ⓐ

Footnotes

① The resume and regulatory issue paper are developed simultaneously in some Directorates. (Directorates, in the FAA, include: ANE-100; ACE-100; ASW-100; ANM-100; and AWS-100.)

② In Headquarters (HQ), only the Office Director can approve the need for a study.

③ At this point the project team has not been formed. However, the individual that is assigned to prepare the initial resume is usually referred to as the Project Manager.

④ The need for an evaluation plan is based on a consensus of rulemaking theorists who believe that, in the future, evaluation plans will be required for new regulations. Currently, there is no standard format for an evaluation plan. There is, however, an intent to develop one.

-1-

Note: The document from which the figure is excerpted is nineteen pages long. For purposes of illustration, three of those pages—1, 7, and 19—are shown.   *(Figure continues)*

Figure 4-1   *(Continued)*

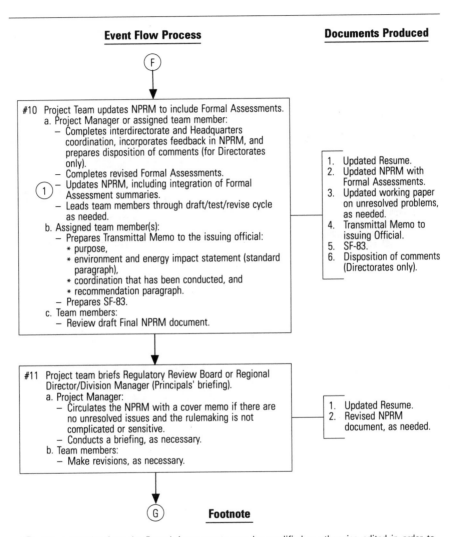

Event Flow Process   **Documents Produced**

(F)

#10 Project Team updates NPRM to include Formal Assessments.
    a. Project Manager or assigned team member:
        – Completes interdirectorate and Headquarters
          coordination, incorporates feedback in NPRM, and
          prepares disposition of comments (for Directorates
          only).
        – Completes revised Formal Assessments.
        – Updates NPRM, including integration of Formal
          Assessment summaries.
        – Leads team members through draft/test/revise cycle
          as needed.
    b. Assigned team member(s):
        – Prepares Transmittal Memo to the issuing official:
            * purpose,
            * environment and energy impact statement (standard
              paragraph),
            * coordination that has been conducted, and
            * recommendation paragraph.
        – Prepares SF-83.
    c. Team members:
        – Review draft Final NPRM document.

1. Updated Resume.
2. Updated NPRM with
   Formal Assessments.
3. Updated working paper
   on unresolved problems,
   as needed.
4. Transmittal Memo to
   issuing Official.
5. SF-83.
6. Disposition of comments
   (Directorates only).

#11 Project team briefs Regulatory Review Board or Regional
    Director/Division Manager (Principals' briefing).
    a. Project Manager:
        – Circulates the NPRM with a cover memo if there are
          no unresolved issues and the rulemaking is not
          complicated or sensitive.
        – Conducts a briefing, as necessary.
    b. Team members:
        – Make revisions, as necessary.

1. Updated Resume.
2. Revised NPRM
   document, as needed.

(G)   **Footnote**

(1) The summaries from the Formal Assessments may be amplified or otherwise edited in order to
    enhance the completeness of presentation of the findings.

-7-

Note: The document from which the figure is excerpted is nineteen pages long. For purposes of illustration,
three of those pages—1, 7, and 19—are shown.   *(Figure continues)*

Figure 4-1   *(Continued)*

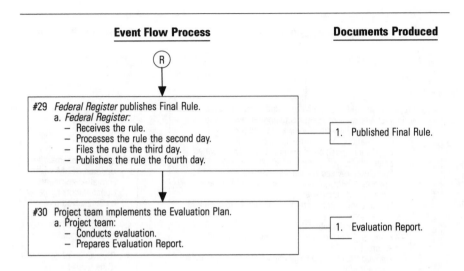

Event Flow Process	**Documents Produced**

R

#29 *Federal Register* publishes Final Rule.
    a. *Federal Register:*
        — Receives the rule.
        — Processes the rule the second day.
        — Files the rule the third day.
        — Publishes the rule the fourth day.

1. Published Final Rule.

#30 Project team implements the Evaluation Plan.
    a. Project team:
        — Conducts evaluation.
        — Prepares Evaluation Report.

1. Evaluation Report.

-19-

Note: The document from which the figure is excerpted is nineteen pages long. For purposes of illustration, three of those pages—1, 7, and 19—are shown.

Source: Federal Aviation Administration.

rules. They can budget for an entire rulemaking program or for specific rules. Budgeting, like scheduling, demands attention to the process and substance of writing rules; one cannot estimate the necessary resources if one does not understand the tasks that must be performed. So in addition to combating delay by ensuring that needed funds and personnel are available, budgeting could make a positive contribution to the quality of rules as well.

Only four of thirty-five agencies surveyed reported that they budget for rulemaking, and only one of these did so on an overall, programmatic basis. How the preponderant majority of agencies supply and account for the human and other resources needed to prepare rules remains something of a mystery.

For a variety of reasons budgeting for rulemaking at either the agency or individual rule level is fraught with uncertainties. At the agency level the total rulemaking workload can be quite unpredictable as new legislation, litigation, external demands, and new political leadership affect the volume and the relative priority placed on a given project. The priority order of rules is quite important, since every rule requires a different mix of personnel and resources to assemble the essential information. Nevertheless, resources for rulemaking are a visible concern in several agencies. For example, in the FAA system of setting priorities, the selection of rules for inclusion on its list of fifty constitutes an explicit commitment on the part of all the offices represented on the Regulatory Review Board to supply the personnel and related resources needed to complete the rulemaking on schedule. The FAA also reported a method of rulemaking management that applied resources to rulemaking projects based on the ability of the resources to help a given project meet a key milestone.

Although formal budgets may not be common, concern about the resources for new rulemakings may be dealt with through the systems used to initiate rulemaking. The FSIS requires that the start of rulemakings be authorized by the administrator in part because they require expenditure of resources. The same can be said of the National Highway Transportation Safety Board's procedures for initiating rules.

RESPONSIBILITY FOR WRITING RULES

As in all complex and important public functions, selecting the right people to accomplish the task is crucial to the eventual success of the enterprise. The complex nature of many rulemakings and the multiple interests, internal and external, drawn to them suggest that agencies must make choices about how to allocate responsibility for the development of rules. In those agencies in which rulemakings are less complex or which place a premium on speed and clear accountability, responsibility might be given to a single individual. Other agencies might choose to use a work group or task force when the rulemakings affect multiple interests and where consensus in decisions is important. Either of these general models of staffing for rulemaking, and each of the numerous variations on them, raises significant issues.

When single individuals write rules there is always the possibility that they lack a crucial element of expertise or skill. How they compensate for their shortcomings is not clear. In such a system, it is not immediately obvious how other offices that might have a legitimate and important interest in the rule get access to and responsiveness from the single rulemaker. Work groups or task forces, in contrast, can be used to assemble the needed expertise and to provide a forum for the airing of all significant points of view. But questions arise as to how members of work groups are chosen and how the work group itself is managed. Leadership and participation in work groups are key variables. Whether the work group functions as a mechanism for collective rulemaking with all members responsible for drafting sections of the rule or merely as an advise-and-consent body is also significant. We would expect these models to behave quite differently and bring about different results.

A majority of agencies (66 percent) reported that they use work groups or task forces to write all or some of their rules. Those that use work groups on a selective basis reserve them for major or especially complex rules. Agencies use a variety of devices to determine the composition of work groups. The process almost always starts with the program office responsible for the statute that the new or revised rule will implement. In most agencies the Office of the General Counsel is a regular participant in work groups because questions of legal sufficiency—both substantive and procedural—are the most common in rulemaking. Some agencies reported that the composition of their work groups generally did not vary. The Health Care Financing Administration, for example, uses a team that usually consists of program office personnel, members of the staff who are concerned with regulations, and a representative from the Office of the General Counsel. Agencies that include more variation in their work group membership select members in a many different ways. In some instances the program office essentially decides what other agency offices it wishes to invite to be part of the work group. Sometimes the program office and the Office of the General Counsel jointly determine who will be in the work group. This appears to be the practice in the Maritime Administration, the Health Resources and Services Administration, and the National Marine Fisheries Service. More often, a central office or permanent committee directs or coordinates the process of forming work groups.

The Regulations Division in the Department of Housing and Urban Development circulates descriptions of rulemakings about to be initiated to all offices "that may have an interest." The division then convenes a "predrafting meeting," the purposes of which are to allow an early identification of issues and to establish the formal membership of the rulemaking work group. In the Department of Education the assembly of the work group is the responsibility of the Division of Regulations Management. Here the process is more formal. The DORM notifies the various departmental offices of the rulemaking and asks whether each wishes to be a "reviewing office." The decision of each office is sent in writing to the DORM, whose staff maintains a record of these individual decisions.[13]

The Environmental Protection Agency's steering committee, which approves the start of rules, serves an even more significant function in the assembly of work groups. With representatives from all program and nonprogram offices, the steering committee decides which offices will be on each work group and names actual participants. Membership on EPA work groups is generally open to all offices in the agency that wish to join, although the system was altered recently for the rules being developed to implement the Clean Air Act. For this legislation the openness of participation in work groups will depend on how rules are initially classified, which in turn will depend on the extent to which they affect the interests of multiple offices. This decision was made to simplify and expedite what will be a large number of rulemakings, all operating under strict statutory deadlines.

Two agencies, the EPA and HUD, report the use of core work groups. These consist of a small number of people who have primary responsibility for developing the rules but who turn to members of a larger, secondary work group for discrete pieces of information and consultation. It is also interesting that several of the agencies that reported they did not use work groups also noted that the individuals assigned to complete the rule usually obtained assistance from others. The agencies reporting this type of arrangement during interviews were the Pension Welfare Benefits Administration, the Federal Highway Administration, and the Office of Surface Mining. These responses suggest that the percentage of agencies using some form of work group to write rules is quite high if informal mechanisms like these are included in the definition.

CONCURRENCE SYSTEMS

Securing the approvals of those with influence or authority is a potentially powerful aspect of rulemaking management. It means that all significant issues have been dealt with to the satisfaction of those in the agency who hold primary responsibility for each. It can be, however, a source of conflict and delay, especially if there are no mechanisms through which these actors can be informed and consulted while the rule is actually being drafted. Conflict at late stages in the rulemaking, the already noted "late hit," is a particularly devastating obstacle to timely and efficient rulemaking.

Two types of concurrence are identified in the literature devoted to rulemaking. Horizontal, or lateral, concurrence, involves offices other than the one with the primary interest in the rule being developed. Vertical concurrence involves senior managers and political appointees.[14] The overwhelming majority of agencies surveyed have systems to ensure that both types of concurrence happen. It is important to note that work groups are, among other things, mechanisms for horizontal concurrence. Theoretically, if the work group is properly constituted as regards the offices represented and performs effectively, additional horizontal concurrence will not be necessary. Theory notwithstanding, many of the agencies that use work groups to write rules have separate, and sometimes elaborate, mechanisms for horizontal concurrence.

At the EPA, for example, horizontal concurrence happens at a formal "work group closure" meeting that is chaired by a staff member from the Office of Standards and Regulations. At HUD, when a work group has completed the draft regulation, the Regulations Division takes control of the horizontal concurrence process. "Policy contact persons," those senior political appointees who provide early direction to a rulemaking, are also sent draft rules and supporting documents with deadlines for review, comment, and suggested revision. According to internal guidance documents at the FSIS, threshold analysis is sent to "all other deputy administrators and staff directors for simultaneous review and clearance." [15] With one notable exception, the system in the Department of Education is quite similar to that at HUD. There, in addition to a concurrence process that is coordinated by the Division of Regulations Management, a regulation quality officer reviews the draft to ensure that it is consistent with the department's *Regulation Quality Manual*. This document contains standards for both content and format.[16]

When conflict arises during the course of the deliberations of the work group, several agencies have procedures to resolve it before the draft rule moves to vertical concurrence. In the Department of Education, the Division of Regulations Management is expected to mediate the resolution of conflicts. A method used in several agencies combines negotiation and mediation with mechanisms to elevate the conflict to senior officials who have the authority to make decisions and resolve the dispute. At the FSIS, a directive states a clear expectation that conflict should first be negotiated at the work group level. But there is also a mechanism for prompt elevation of issues to the FSIS administrator, ostensibly to reduce delay caused by such conflict. At HUD, when issues arise during the drafting of a rule they are elevated immediately to a "Secretarial Review Group," consisting of the under secretary, three assistant secretaries, who have jurisdiction over policy and administrative matters, and the general counsel. This group recommends a resolution to the problem, but if it is not acceptable to the office involved it goes directly to the secretary for final decision.

All agencies reported the existence of formal vertical concurrence systems. An important issue in vertical concurrence is the number of levels at which a rule is reviewed. The number of steps in the vertical chain can vary considerably. In some agencies the review is not only by senior managers or political appointees but also by some form of policy board like the Secretarial Review Group that operates at HUD and the Regulatory Review Board at the FAA. The most common number of steps reported in the survey was three. In the case of the National Marine Fisheries Service, the agency conducts much of its rulemaking in the field and a requirement of headquarters approval multiplies the number of steps in the review chain. It is important to note that vertical concurrence frequently is not confined to a single management chain. When rules are written in work groups, a system of vertical concurrence in each participating office is common. Horizontal and vertical concurrence systems converge in agencies that write rules in this way.

PUBLIC PARTICIPATION

The management of public participation in rulemaking has two dimensions. Deciding on the mechanisms that will be used to solicit public participation and evaluating the comments and criticisms it generates are both important to rulemaking. Agencies generally enjoy more discretion on how they organize and manage their responses to public input than they do on the form that participation will take. Increasingly, statutes that mandate or authorize rulemaking contain provisions that require agencies to do more than give "notice and comment," as provided under the Administrative Procedure Act. Still, agencies are free to supplement what is legally required. Responsibility for dealing with public comment or testimony is significant, because the volume of such comment can be heavy and the agency has an affirmative obligation to take it into account when finalizing the rule. In short, it affects the substantive content of the rule and the response of the public to what is finally decided. So the mechanisms to ensure that the results of participation are incorporated or otherwise accounted for in the final rule are management devices worthy of attention.

Eighteen agencies (51 percent) reported that the program office developing the rule had authority to determine the form of public participation, although many of these reported that for this decision they either consult with or get the approval of other offices. The Office of the General Counsel is most frequently mentioned in this regard. In nine agencies (26 percent), offices other than the program office determine the form that public participation will take. These agencies give the authority to the Office of the General Counsel exclusively or in combination with various policy, information, and consumer offices. Two agencies, the Agricultural Stabilization and Conservation Service and the Federal Railroad Administration, reported that this decision is made at the highest levels of their agencies. A third category of agencies (23 percent) consists of those whose programs for public participation are determined by statute or long-standing agency policy. Eight agencies, including OSHA, the Mine Safety and Health Administration, HUD, the Bureau of Land Management, and the Department of Education, indicated that the form of public participation is predetermined in this manner.

Evaluation of the results of public participation, whether in the form of written comments or transcripts from informal or formal hearings can also be grouped into three categories. In fourteen agencies (40 percent), the staff that develops the rule has primary responsibility for evaluating the results of public participation and incorporating them into the regulation. Nineteen agencies (54 percent) split this responsibility between the staff and some other office. Once again, the Office of the General Counsel plays an important role in this regard. Offices with general policy responsibilities are involved as well in some agencies. Some agencies have systems to ensure that the results of public participation are reviewed broadly. At HUD, the Regulations Division collects public comments, summarizes the significant ones, and circulates them to all interested offices. This group also circulates the responses made to public comments by those developing the rule. Two agencies, the Bureau of Land Management and the Federal Railroad Administration, remove responsibility for evaluation and incorporation of public comments entirely from the staff developing the rule.

THE USE OF CONTRACTORS

The scope and complexity of rulemaking responsibilities may exceed the resident expertise and staff resources of agencies. Both can be supplemented, however, by the use of contractors. The presence of contractors in the rulemaking process raises many interesting issues. How well contractors perform tasks related to rulemaking and the types of tasks they are asked to perform are two such issues. The first relates to the quality and timeliness of rules produced. The second relates to ongoing concerns that basic governmental functions are being inappropriately delegated to private parties. It is, therefore, important to learn how extensively agencies use contractors during rulemaking.

Although more than 70 percent of the agencies surveyed reported that they used contractors in rulemaking, many of them noted that they did not do so on a regular basis. Two agencies, the Coast Guard and the Office of Surface Mining, had used contractors but abandoned the practice altogether because of poor quality work and problems in managing the procurement process. When contractors are used, it is almost always to supplement existing staff resources or to provide otherwise unavailable technical expertise. In only one instance did an agency's response suggest that contractors were used actually to develop the content of regulations. To the extent they are used, contractors appear to be largely confined to support functions. This is not to say that their role is not occasionally substantial. A recent report by the General Accounting Office found that between fiscal years 1986 and 1988 the Occupational Safety and Health Administration spent more than $11 million on contractors to support their rulemaking effort. Nearly 90 percent of these funds were spent on mandatory "regulatory analysis." [17]

THE CONDUCT OF REQUIRED ANALYSES

A given rulemaking may require several separate analyses in addition to the collection of information for the content of the rule itself. Paperwork, regulatory flexibility, and regulatory impact analyses are all common. How the agency is organized to conduct these studies is potentially significant. There are essentially two options. The responsibility can be given to the individual or group writing the rule, or specialized units can be formed to conduct the analyses for all rulemakings. Management issues associated with each of these are not difficult to identify. In the first case, the individual or group writing the rule must become familiar with the legal requirements and gain access to the information needed to do the study. This process can take time and divert the individual or group from the central task. It can also result in poor quality reviews. In the second case, the workload of a specialized unit and the costs associated with its maintaining the essential communication with the rulemakers may be important management issues. One would expect, however, that such a unit's experience and familiarity with available information would lead to comparatively faster and better studies.

Rulemaking requires frequent and extensive contacts with the OMB, which was granted multiple authorities in the Paperwork Reduction Act and various executive orders. Agencies and the OMB come in contact with one another in the latter's overall review of proposed and final rules, regulatory impact analyses, and requests to collect information. These contacts, which can influence the review process, may be managed by those responsible for writing the rule or by a central office in the agency. Similarly, Congress may take an interest in a rule under development, creating, at minimum, a liaison function and, at maximum, a political dimension that could influence profoundly the content of the rule. The extent of congressional contacts and the ways these are managed are at least as important as how the relations with OMB are carried out.

More than 60 percent of the agencies expect the staff that develops the rules to conduct paperwork and regulatory impact analyses. Several of these agencies reported that the staff gets assistance from other offices on an as needed basis. The remaining agencies place the responsibility for conducting these studies in specialized offices.

In contrast to these patterns, only two agencies, the Food and Nutrition Service and the General Services Administration, allow the staff developing the rule to maintain liaison with the OMB on matters pertaining to these required analyses or other aspects of the rulemaking. In the other thirty-three agencies this function is performed by a variety of offices, including the general counsel, the budget office, policy and planning staff, and the staff of the senior manager or political appointee.

The agencies were evenly divided between those that reported contact with Congress during rulemaking and those that reported such contacts were either nonexistent or exceedingly rare. Only one agency, the National Highway Transportation Safety Administration, attempts to keep interested members of Congress appraised of the progress being made on rules. Some reported they confine such contacts to cases in which a specific request is received. There is little evidence from the survey that Congress is heavily or even consistently involved in rulemaking. Other evidence, however, contradicts these findings, and it is discussed in a subsequent chapter.

DRAFTING THE RULE

Responsibility for drafting the actual language of the rule cannot be taken for granted. In the preceding chapter it was noted that poorly crafted rules can lead to problems. Some of these problems relate to sloppy drafting or the inability to capture in words exactly what the rule seeks to accomplish. The choice of drafter is important.

Virtually no agency relies exclusively on technical staff to develop the content of rules to put them in the format and language that will ultimately appear in the *Federal Register*. In seventeen agencies (49 percent) the language and format of proposed and final rules are developed jointly by the staff and some other office, usually the Office of the General Counsel. Other agencies (52 percent) have established offices with specialists in regulation drafting. The FAA, for example, employs a corps of "writer-editors." A writer-editor is deployed to each rulemaking. More than mere writers of drafts, the FAA writer-editors also serve as "assistant managers" of the rulemaking. They get involved in all phases of the rulemaking, including preparing summaries of public comments and responses to them. They are senior civil servants with training in group facilitation and team building. The Social Security Administration and the Health Care Financing Administration appear to use similar arrangements.

SUMMARY

It is evident from the survey of agencies and from available documents that rulemaking management systems are well developed in many federal agencies. Included in such systems is the capacity to set priorities, to control the initiation of new rules, to provide early guidance on important policy matters to the rule writers, to ensure horizontal and vertical concurrence, and to maintain a degree of discipline in the rulemakers' dealings with the OMB on proposed and final rules. It is significant, and somewhat reassuring, that rulemaking appears to be given a level of management attention comparable to other major bureaucratic functions, such as budgeting, finance, procurement, and personnel. Not all the literature relevant to rulemaking management has been covered here. For example, work has been done on the overall approach that certain agencies take with regard to rulemaking. The most interesting deals with differing organizational cultures and the effects they have on the structure and process of rulemaking.[18] This literature is considered carefully in the final chapter.

What is not so clear is how well these agency management systems actually work, or even the criteria we should use to judge their performance. In a previous chapter the general criticisms of rulemaking were discussed, and it is clear that agency-level management systems could be both sources of and solutions to certain problems. If procedures for setting priorities and initiating rules work well, they should reduce the number of unnecessary rules. Mechanisms for obtaining early policy guidance, work groups, and concurrence systems and effective liaison with the OMB can increase the quality of the content of rules and decrease the conflict in rulemaking processes.

Scheduling and monitoring can expedite the rulemaking process, thus reducing delay in the issuance of important rules.

Still, several elements of management systems at the agency level can contribute to delay in rules if they work poorly. Volatility in priorities must be avoided in systems designed to set priorities. Frequent changes in the priority order of rules leads to erratic application of resources to individual projects, delaying those that are suddenly downgraded. Similarly, initiation procedures and concurrence systems can lead to long delays. Some studies point to excessively layered concurrence systems as factors contributing significantly to delay in issuing rules. The author of one of these studies, devoted to rulemaking in the EPA under the provisions of the Clean Air Act, counted more than fifty "sign-off" points in the development of a single regulation.[19] Although there may be good reason for each and every one of these reviews and approvals, the effect on timeliness in the rulemaking is obvious, especially when one considers that many rules would undoubtedly be going through such a gauntlet at any one time.

MANAGING INDIVIDUAL RULES

Work groups and concurrence systems were created to ensure that all vital information, perspectives, and interests associated with a particular rule could be captured and represented during the course of its development. The other side of this important function is conflict. Available research suggests that when the net is cast broadly across an agency during rulemaking the likelihood of conflict increases. The issue is not the occurrence of conflict. The agencies that write rules house multiple interests and perspectives that are bound to clash when something as important as rulemaking is undertaken. The real issue is how well this conflict is managed and resolved during the development of individual rules.

The management of individual rules occurs within the constraints imposed by the systems that operate out of the White House and at the various agencies. Unlike those systems that rely on established structures and general procedures, the management of individual rules is heavily affected by the idiosyncrasies of the particular rule being developed. For a given rule, the two key variables affecting management of the process are information and people.

TYPES OF ESSENTIAL INFORMATION

Managing the information dimension of rulemaking involves three general tasks. The first is determining what information is required to complete the rule. The second is obtaining the needed information. The third is incorporating that information into the final rule that is published by the agency.

A rulemaking may involve as many as five types of information. The first is legal information. Those writing the rule must understand the provisions of the statute that the new rule will implement. These establish, in effect, the objectives of the rule. In addition, the rule-makers must understand the procedural requirements that apply in their particular case. As noted previously, these procedural requirements are established by general statutes, specific authorizing statutes, judicial orders, executive orders, and the agency's own procedural regulations.

A second type of information is policy. Presidents can establish general policy guidelines for rulemaking. For example, President Reagan's policies required that rules be written so that they would impose as little burden as possible on affected sectors of the economy and that they use marketlike mechanisms whenever possible. The leadership of individual agencies may have their own policy initiatives and directions that they wish to see reflected in rules. When William Reilly became administrator of the Environmental Protection Agency he announced his strong support for "waste minimization" as a strategy for reducing pollution of all forms. He ordered that the agency consider this approach when writing rules.

The third type of information is what can be called technical. That is the information that will form the substance and content of the rule. This type of information will also provide the basis for the various impact analyses that may be required. Technical information is determined entirely by the objectives of the rule, which in turn are determined by the substantive provisions of the statute that the rule will implement. And these will determine the types of analyses—small business, paperwork, cost-benefit, federalism, and the like—that the agency will have to conduct as an adjunct to rulemaking. Technical information is tied inextricably to the substantive legal information mentioned above. The technical content of the rule commonly includes information on various alternatives that can be considered and the impacts of each. When the best alternative is selected, the focus then shifts to what is allowed or required, who is affected and who must comply, the means by which the provisions will be implemented and enforced, and the consequences of failing to comply.

The fourth type of information is political, consisting of the views and positions of the internal and external interests affected by the rule under development. In many instances this type of information may not be easily distinguishable from policy or technical information. Since it is provided by other parts of the agency or external groups and institutions during the course of rulemaking, it is frequently presented as critiques of a particular approach or of certain supporting data, or in regard to the negative effect the rule would have on existing programs or conditions. Consequently, what is essentially a political reaction to a proposed rule is couched in policy or technical terms.

Finally, there is managerial information. The rulemakers must have a knowledge of the agency's internal management system and the requirements it imposes on their particular rulemaking.

In the last chapter it was noted that other scholars have viewed information as an ever-present issue in rulemaking. It was also noted that Stephen Breyer, and others, have identified the various internal and external sources of information.[20] Here these five types of information are discussed in more detail.

Legal information pertaining to the substance of the rule is obtained directly from the statute and the interpretations of the agency's general counsel. Information about procedural requirements based in law is also obtained from the general counsel, and it is quite common for agencies to develop guidance documents on common obligations—for example, those associated with the various executive orders and general legislation, such as the Paperwork Reduction Act. Rulemakers use these sources to determine which of many possible requirements apply and how to comply with them. When an agency program involves the writing of multiple versions of the same general rule, substantive and procedural legal requirements are widely understood. Rules such as the FAA's airworthiness directives, the Department of Agriculture's marketing orders, and even the EPA's new source performance standards for air and water pollution require relatively little original legal information. When an agency undertakes to write rules for a new statute or amendment to an existing law, or when it moves into a new area covered by established legislation, the amount of legal information it requires will increase. With the increase the influence of agency attorneys in the rulemaking will grow, at least in the early stages.

Policy information is obtained through the management systems outlined above. White House guidelines are published and distributed broadly across all agencies. These primary documents are usually accompanied by agency supplements that provide further explanation of the requirements and how they apply in rulemaking. Agencies have similar documents covering their own policy priorities and initiatives. In addition, many agencies appear to have procedures that require or allow senior officials to review rulemaking projects at some stage in their development. It is during this review that the policy priorities of both the White House and the particular agency are reinforced.

Officials of the Federal Trade Commission, when asked about where they obtain the information needed for the content of the rules they had written, responded simply, "wherever we can get it." [21] Although this answer may seem facetious, it is not. Since the nature and amount of information needed during the course of a rulemaking can vary so much, the sources must be assembled on essentially an ad hoc basis in many cases. There are, however, certain generic sources of information that agencies draw upon that will play a greater or lesser role, depending on the particular needs of a given rulemaking. Agencies may have their own databases and archives from which to draw information. When these are insufficient they always have the option to create new information, either through the work of their in-house research and development organizations or contractors. Another important internal source of information is the agency's own staff, each of whom brings education, experience, and external contacts that may contribute to a particular rulemaking effort. This expertise is tapped by using work groups to develop rules. Finally, information can be drawn from outside the agency as well. One source, already discussed, is the advisory committee. Another source, and far more influential for the great majority of individual rules, is the segment of the public affected by or interested in the rulemaking. Agencies rely heavily on external groups for information. This information is obtained through written comments on proposed rules, hearings of various sorts, and a great deal of informal, bilateral contact between agency personnel and those representing affected interests.

The sources of political information are many of the same ones that supply technical information. The political positions of those inside the agency are made known through concurrence systems and work group participants. The political positions of external parties are made known through public comments, during public hearings, and through the numerous informal contacts that occur between represen-tatives of external interests and agency personnel.

Finally, rulemakers can obtain information about the agency's management system in two ways. Internal guidance documents and procedural regulations outline the management system for rules. Many agencies, particularly those in which rulemaking is identified as a major function, have training programs for staff. For example, both the Environmental Protection Agency and the Federal Aviation Adminis-tration have instituted large-scale training programs for those involved in rulemaking. The EPA program focuses heavily on the elements of its internal management system. The program was started in 1988, and by the end of 1991 more than 1,200 staff members had been through the program. Other agencies have different methods of training their personnel. In the Department of Education, for example, the Division of Regulation Management, in cooperation with the departmental regulations quality officer, provides training in rulemaking on an as-needed basis to those writing rules. This training includes information on the department's rather elaborate system for managing the process of developing regulations.

The information required for the development of a rule can be extensive and varied. Of the types listed above, that which is most consistently troublesome for most agencies is technical information. The nature and amount needed can be highly variable, and sometimes it may simply not be available from any existing source. The lack of information brings with it the need to create it and the likelihood that when it is developed it will not be complete and will be open to challenge. In this situation the importance of policy and political information tends to increase, since these considerations enter any vacuum created by technical or scientific uncertainty. But no type of information is unimportant. Insufficient understanding of any dimension of information mentioned above can damage, delay, and, in some instances, destroy a rulemaking. It is therefore important that those writing rules understand these information needs and meet them.

THE ROLE OF WORK GROUPS

Information demands converge on and must be managed by the people involved in writing the rule. Available evidence suggests that increasingly these people develop rules collectively through work groups and task forces. These temporary collections of agency personnel are influential in the development of rules in many agencies. Consequently, their management is important, and often crucial, to the overall management of rulemaking. The work group approach has been in use in the Environmental Protection Agency since its early years, and recently conducted research sheds considerable light on the strengths and weaknesses of the approach in that agency.[22] Generalizations must be undertaken with caution, but this research does provide insights of unquestionable relevance to other agencies that use this type of mechanism for writing rules.

Work groups are likely to be found in all agencies that have significant rulemaking responsibilities. Their composition and size, however, are functions of the programs the agency administers and its internal organizational culture.[23] In agencies that have limited statutory responsibilities, a work group might consist of a representative from the program office, an attorney from the Office of the General Counsel, and, perhaps, an economist or other type of policy analyst. The work group will be small; management of the work group will not likely be a very serious problem.

In larger, more complex agencies administering multiple, overlapping statutes, work groups are likely to be larger and have a more diverse membership.[24] In these cases many program offices may be represented. In addition to attorneys from the Office of the General Counsel, lawyers concerned with the enforcement dimension of the rule may also participate. Attorneys from the Office of the General Counsel will be concerned with the congruence between the rule and what the statute it will implement requires or allows. Attorneys from the offices concerned with enforcement will want to ensure that the rule avoids some of the common problems that promote noncompliance or make enforcement actions difficult to defend in court when they are challenged.

Representatives from offices concerned with research and policy analysis are likely to be members of the work group. The research office will be concerned that information they have developed and maintained is used in the development of the rule. The policy analysts will push for full consideration of all reasonable alternatives and for a complete assessment of their economic effects.[25] The field personnel that are responsible for implementing the rule once it is complete may wish to be involved to ensure that what is written is feasible and easy to administer. They too will be concerned with enforceability and with the effects that the new rule will have on others they implement and their resources.

Work groups of this latter sort can present formidable management problems. The experience of the Environmental Protection Agency during the past two decades indicates that the management of work groups hinges on three key variables: leadership, membership, and integration with senior management of the agency.[26]

LEADERSHIP. The leaders of work groups are usually selected because of their expertise in the subject matter of the new rule. But technical expertise is only a part of the job. These individuals must perform many important and sometimes difficult functions. Further, these functions are often performed in the face of strong and conflicting pressures exerted by others in and out of the agency. In addition to possessing technical expertise, the work group leader must be a careful planner, a skillful manager of resources and group processes, a shrewd politician, a diplomat, and, at times, a scavenger. He or she must locate, bring together, and accommodate the information and views that will define the content of the rule and ultimately determine the success of the rulemaking.

Once selected, the work group leader must determine the goals of the rule, the substantive and procedural legal provisions that apply, and what information is needed to achieve these goals. Senior officials must be consulted on policy matters and agency attorneys on the legal issues. The leader is then in a position to assemble or influence the membership of the work group. As we saw in the previous section, agencies vary in their procedures for assembling work groups. In some agencies, like the EPA, the work group leader suggests those offices and individuals whose participation is needed. In other agencies a central office takes complete responsibility for assembling the work group through a canvassing of the various offices. In either system the work group leader can influence the composition of the work group to some extent either by requesting help directly or by encouraging others to answer the call for participants that comes from a central office.

It is in the work group leader's best interests to ensure that membership is determined carefully. Leaving an important office off the work group can deprive the rulemaking of valuable information and insights. It can also lead to serious problems later in the process, when the group attempts to obtain concurrence from an office that has a real interest in the rule but was not at the table during its development. Although membership should be open to those with a significant interest in the rule, gratuitous participation is to be avoided. Large work groups are more difficult to manage than smaller ones. Communication, the logistics and conduct of meetings, development of consensus, and the concurrence process grow more complicated with each new office that joins the group. So the leader has an interest in ensuring that the work group includes everyone with a legitimate concern but excludes the merely curious. This said, it is difficult to exclude those who make a claim that their program or responsibility is affected unless senior officials enforce a degree of discipline.

Once the work group is constituted, the leader must brief it on the purpose of the rule, its legal dimensions, any decisions that have already been made regarding policy or actual content, and the schedule for its completion. Then the leader should discuss with the members how the work group will function and what each individual will be asked to produce. Work groups may meet frequently or infrequently, depending on what is needed from the members and the nature of the issues that arise. Frequent meetings may be needed when there are multiple issues on which consensus must be reached and when the members are expected to make substantive contributions to the content of the rule. Infrequent meetings may be more appropriate when there are few issues and the membership is expected to serve only as a means of securing the approval of the offices they represent for draft materials that the work group leader develops. Whatever the style of the group and the role of the members, they should be made clear at the outset so that there is agreement on how the group will function and the members can plan accordingly. If there is disagreement on either of these elements, the leader must act promptly to resolve it.

After the rulemaking has begun, the leader must maintain full communication with the work group in accordance with the operating principles established at the beginning. In addition to scheduling meetings and circulating drafts of the rule, the leader must set agendas, conduct the meetings effectively, and ensure that drafts are accurate and complete. During the process of rule development the leader should monitor the work group closely and be aware of members who are not performing as expected or who show signs of disagreement and conflict. When members are not responding promptly or substantively to drafts, or when they are missing meetings or presenting personal views rather than the position of their office, the work group leader must intervene. Poor performance may be a sign of inexperience or overextension. Whatever the cause, it means the member is not delivering what is needed.

The member who pursues an agenda not authorized by his or her office is a matter of particular concern. The work group leader needs to know how much authority a given member enjoys and the extent of the member's bargaining power for his or her own office in negotiations over the rule. If members do not faithfully represent the management of their offices, there is a risk that a draft rule, when it is finally reviewed at these higher levels, will not be acceptable. This is the "late hit." In extreme cases it may necessitate a complete reworking of the rule, with all the wasted resources and toll on internal working relationships that such a circumstance generates. At the very least it leads to delay. It is, of course, the responsibility of each member to represent his or her office, but it is in the best interest of the work group leader to confirm that the member actually does so. Such confirmation may require a direct confrontation with the member in question or a discreet inquiry through the respective management chains, but whatever the form it is usually worth the temporary discomfort it might cause.

While the rule is being developed the work group leader must assemble the information needed to complete it and any required analysis. Whatever information is not coming in directly from the work group membership has to be obtained from other sources. The leader's responsibility with regard to ancillary analyses, such as paperwork, regulatory impact, and regulatory flexibility, will be determined by the system followed in the agency. In some agencies the work group leader must do some or all of these analyses; in others they are conducted by one or more central offices. We can find this same variation in the management of internal concurrence, public participation, and the relationship with the OMB for the mandatory reviews of proposed and final rules. The work group leader must also draft the rule in language and format acceptable to the *Federal Register* or work closely with those who perform this function.

As the work group leader performs these many and varied functions he or she must contend with the strong pressures mentioned earlier. The nature and strength of these pressures are determined by the controversy that attends a given rule and the manner in which the work group leader is evaluated. If he or she is thought to be successful if the rule is completed on schedule and within budget, any controversy that may occur, especially within the agency, will threaten the leader's ability to perform to expectations. Similarly, if the criterion for success is qualitative, such as the production of a rule that represents internal consensus, proves to be easy to implement and enforce, or survives court challenge, controversy may be a sign that one or more of these objectives is in danger.

According to anecdotal evidence from a substantial number of those involved as work group leaders in the EPA and other agencies, meeting a preordained deadline is a more common criterion for success than any of these qualitative standards. This makes intuitive sense if we consider the nature of rulemaking and bureaucracies in general. Performance in relation to a schedule can be measured easily. Producing a consensus may or may not be valued by the leadership of a given office. Its importance may be heavily determined by preferences of the most senior political officials of the overall agency or department. If they want rules that reflect a consensus, then the proclivities of a given office may not matter. But if individual offices are given more discretion as to how they will proceed, some may see other organizations within the same agencies as rivals, adversaries, or both. They may be indifferent to consensus or directly opposed to it. Measures of implementability and enforceability may be elusive. Complaints about these dimensions of a given rule can sometimes be dismissed as efforts by field staff to avoid work and responsibility or as the whines of chronically cautious or dissatisfied lawyers. In some agencies these dimensions may be seen as concerns separate and distinct from rulemaking—in short, someone else's problem. The ability to survive litigation may be even more remote to the rulemaker. It happens after the rule is published, and the case may not be resolved for a very long time, usually well after the rulemaker expects to have left his or her current position.

Time pressure increases the difficulties leaders confront in attempting to meet any other standard that might be used to measure performance. It limits efforts to collect the best possible information, to involve work group members fully, to stimulate serious discussion of alternatives, to expose potential flaws in the rule as it is developing, and to resolve conflicts to everyone's satisfaction. Of course, not all rulemaking is done under time pressures of this sort.

MEMBERSHIP.   Work group members too have many functions that they must perform if this collective type of rulemaking is to be successful. Most of these are suggested by the foregoing discussion of the role of the work group leader. Ideally we might expect that the work group members would function as true intermediaries between their offices and the work group leader, balancing their interests with the goals of the rule. This is not a reasonable expectation. Members are there to represent an office and its particular concerns. This means they must be fully conversant with the goals of the rule and the statutory provisions it will implement. They need not concern themselves with procedural requirements, whether they are imposed by law or by the agency's internal management system, unless these somehow bear on the interests of their office. Members must understand the policies of their own office and what their superiors wish to accomplish in the rulemaking. To that end they must also be clear about the limits of their own authority and the room they have to negotiate on substantive issues in the name of their office. When there is doubt on such matters they must undertake to resolve it promptly.

Beyond this, members must also be alert to developments in the rulemaking that threaten the interests they are there to protect. This means faithful and attentive participation in work group meetings and careful reading of draft materials. They must be able and willing to seek advice and counsel from others in the office when they are unclear about the implications of a particular approach or wording and when office policy on a given matter is not apparent. They must make every effort to recognize potential or real problems as early as possible and move immediately to get them acknowledged and resolved. In this they must be willing and able to negotiate, drafting alternative language when they object to that proposed by the work group leader or another member. Whenever possible that alternative language should strive to accomplish the objective embodied in the original language while ameliorating that which offends the member's office. While maintaining a flexible and cooperative stance the member must also recognize intractable conflict or a situation in which the concerns of his or her office concerns are not being dealt with. Then the only answer is to elevate the issue to superiors, who will deal with their counterparts in the other office or offices involved.

In performing these functions members, like the work group leader, are likely to face certain pressures. In this case, however, the pressures are most likely to be related to their own workloads. Membership in work groups is often an "add-on" responsibility. Frequently, members are not rewarded or punished for their participation. So when other responsibilities compete for their time, their professionalism may be the only incentive to read draft materials promptly, to attend and participate actively in work group meetings, to be sensitive to potential problems, and to seek out the type of help they might require.

Workload pressure and the lack of potential sanction for poor performance, however, are not the only obstacles to effective participation. Those selected as members of work groups, especially in agencies that produce a large volume of rules, may lack the experience and expertise to represent their offices adequately. Unable to spare more senior staff, the offices may be forced to place newer employees in work groups, particularly in those groups whose rules do not enjoy high priority. Further, a member may not have access to the additional resources or expertise that he or she needs to participate effectively. Sometimes a member is taken off a work group for assignment to a rule with a higher priority or to a completely different set of responsibilities, and a new member must act as substitute. This type of turnover, especially at the middle and late stages in a rule, can be particularly problematical, because the new member must struggle with a steep learning curve in a compressed period of time. Finally, a member may not be given clear authority to represent the office. This is a tolerable situation if the member is astute enough to recognize a serious issue when he or she sees one and has ready access to those in the office who do have the authority to make decisions.

THE ROLE OF SENIOR MANAGEMENT.   The last major element in the management of work groups is their integration with senior management across the agency. It should be readily apparent from the discussion of work group leaders and members why this is so crucial to the rulemaking process. Senior managers and political leadership must be involved at the inception of work group operations, throughout the rule development process, and at the point of completion. At the outset they must set the overall direction of the rule whenever it is in doubt, making office or agency policy clear as regards the rulemaking in question. This means that they must be certain of the appropriate policy and the objectives they wish to achieve in the rulemaking. Once this is done they are able to set the limits of discretion that their representatives in the work group can exercise. As the rulemaking progresses they must be available to provide guidance to work group leaders or members on issues that were not anticipated at the beginning. To ensure expeditious rulemaking they must be able to respond promptly to such requests for guidance and to those situations in which an issue is elevated to their level because the work group has reached an impasse. In the latter instances they must have open lines of communication to their counterparts in other offices so that the conflict can be discussed and resolved and the rulemaking can move forward.

Finally, when the rule has been written the senior officials must complete the concurrence process promptly and in a manner consistent with the positions they have taken at earlier stages in the development of the rule.

Like leaders and members of work groups, these officials in the management chain are working under pressure, the sources of which, at this level, are time and politics. These officials may be tracking many rules, and rulemaking is far from their sole concern. They are working at the levels of an office or agency where external political pressure is expressed most directly and intensely. This political pressure can cause their priorities in rulemaking to shift and their positions on individual rules to be altered. These factors may make it difficult for some work group leaders or members to get the attention of these officials. Or they may cause resources to be taken away from one rulemaking project and allocated to another. Inaccessibility, delay in responding to requests for guidance, assistance in resolving disputes or final approval, and shifting priorities and policy positions create problems for work groups and for rulemaking generally.

The management of individual rules involves a set of functions performed by work group leaders, members, and senior officials. The roles of each, and the importance of the work group as a device, will vary with the subject matter of rule, the complexity of the rulemaking, and the amount of interest both generate. But it is highly likely that the most important rules written in federal agencies will be developed in work groups, because they are often substantively and procedurally complex and attract a considerable amount of interest. For this reason alone, the three major elements of work groups are important to the management of rulemaking.

Rulemaking is intensively managed at all three of the levels examined in this chapter. While there is considerable overlap, each level of management focuses on distinctive concerns and objectives. Presidential management seeks to ensure that the substantive policies and political agenda of the administration are reflected in the rules issued by federal agencies. Agency-level management is concerned with the president's program but may also reflect distinctive policies and procedures and seek coherence, consistency, timeliness, and a disciplined use of the resources available for rulemaking. At the individual level these general concerns are also present, but a stronger focus is likely to be placed on completing required tasks, managing bureaucratic relationships, meeting deadlines, and advancing or protecting one's career.

Although we have evidence of an enormous amount of management activity, we have little evidence of its effects on the rules that are finally issued. Does management make a difference? Do different management systems yield systematically different results? Currently, answers to these key questions are woefully incomplete. The problems start at the most fundamental level of analysis. We simply lack most of the basic information needed to evaluate various levels and systems of managing rules. We can measure how long it takes to complete a rule, but we rarely ask, in a disciplined manner, how well it works. To understand fully the quality of rules, we must ultimately link their content to the performance of the public program that they define. Only then can we begin to determine whether the manner in which rulemaking is managed has any effect on the quality of rules.

NOTES

1. The history of presidential management of rulemaking presented in this chapter is necessarily brief and draws on a number of extensive studies. See Howard Ball, *Controlling Regulatory Sprawl: Presidential Strategies from Nixon to Reagan* (Westport, Conn.: Greenwood Press, 1984), and National Academy of Public Administration, *Presidential Management of Rulemaking in Regulatory Agencies* (Washington, D.C.: National Academy of Public Administration, 1987).
2. Office of Management and Budget, *Improving Government Regulations: A Progress Report* (Washington, D.C.: Executive Office of the President, 1979), p. 6.
3. Ibid., p. 7.
4. Ibid., pp. 8-27.
5. Ibid., p. 9.
6. Ibid., p. 19.
7. Cornelius M. Kerwin, "Introduction," in *Federal Regulatory Directory*, 6th ed. (Washington, D.C.: CQ Press, 1990), pp. 42-43.
8. "White House Shifts Role in Rulemaking Process," *Washington Post*, October 1, 1993, p. 1.
9. This figure is quoted in the training course devoted to rulemaking attended by EPA employees. Also see *Regulation Development in EPA* (Washington, D.C.: Environmental Protection Agency, 1988), sec. 1.
10. Department of Education, "Administrative Communications System," Departmental Directive OGC: 1-100 (Washington, D.C., March 3, 1988), p. 12.
11. Department of Housing and Urban Development, "Operating Plan for Development of HUD Regulations" (Washington, D.C., n.d.), p. 2.
12. Neil Eisner, "Agency Delay in Informal Rulemaking," *Administrative Law Journal* 3 (1989): 7-52.
13. Department of Housing and Urban Development, "Operating Plan," pp. 3-7.
14. Fred Emery, *Rulemaking as an Organizational Process* (Washington, D.C.: Administrative Conference of the United States, 1982).
15. Department of Agriculture, Food Safety and Inspection Service, "FSIS Directive 1232.1" (Washington, D.C., 1985), p. 7.

16. Department of Education, "Administrative Communications System," p. 10.
17. General Accounting Office, *Use of Contractors in OSHA Rulemaking* (Washington, D.C.: General Accounting Office, 1989).
18. Thomas McGarrity, "The Internal Structure of EPA Rulemaking," *Law and Contemporary Problems* 54 (1991): 57.
19. Michael Berry, *A Method for Examining Policy Implementation: A Study of Decisionmaking for the National Ambient Air Quality Standards, 1964-1984* (Ph.D. diss., University of North Carolina, Chapel Hill, 1984).
20. Stephen Breyer, *Regulation and Its Reform* (Cambridge, Mass.: Harvard University Press, 1982), pp. 109-110.
21. Personal interview with professional staff member, Federal Trade Commission, February 1991.
22. Wesley Magat, Alan Krupnick, and Winston Harrington, *Rules in the Making* (Washington, D.C.: Resources for the Future, 1986), p. 24.
23. McGarrity, "Internal Structure of EPA Rulemaking," and William West, "The Growth of Internal Conflict in Administrative Rulemaking," *Public Administration Review*, July/August 1988, pp. 773-782.
24. McGarrity, "Internal Structure of EPA Rulemaking."
25. West, "Growth of Internal Conflict."
26. Information on the various elements of work groups comes from a variety of sources. See Magat, Krupnick, and Harrington, *Rules in the Making*; McGarrity, "Internal Structure of EPA Rulemaking"; West, "Growth of Internal Conflict"; Emery, *Rulemaking as an Organizational Process*. Also see "Workgroup Operations" in *Regulation Development in EPA*. The agency also conducted several surveys of work group leaders and members, the results of which were made available to me.

CHAPTER 5

Participation in Rulemaking

Because we are a representative democracy, and because lawmaking is the ultimate power granted our government under the Constitution, rulemaking presents us with a profound dilemma. On the one hand, we have established that in order for government to be truly responsive to the incessant demands of the American people for public programs to solve private problems, rulemaking is essential. It frees Congress to attend to many more problems than it would otherwise have time to deal with. It relieves Congress of the burden of maintaining and managing enormous staffs who possess the expertise essential to refining the operating standards and procedures for a myriad of programs. Finally, it is the best means yet found to break legislative deadlocks and to avoid difficult political decisions. On the other hand, as an indispensable surrogate to the legislative process, rulemaking has a fundamental flaw that violates basic democratic principles. Those who write the law embodied in rules are not elected; they are accountable to the American people only through indirect and less-than-foolproof means. Our elected representatives have confronted this dilemma on numerous occasions and decided that one answer is direct participation by the public in rulemaking.

The legitimacy of the rulemaking process is clearly linked to public participation. Phillip Harter, a prominent observer of rulemaking, noted, "To the extent that rulemaking has political legitimacy, it derives from the right of affected interests to present facts and arguments to an agency under procedures designed to ensure the rationality of the agency's decision." Harter is also a staunch advocate for using more consensual techniques for developing rules, arguing that their most important benefit is enhancement of public participation and "the added legitimacy a rule would acquire if all parties viewed [it] as reasonable and endorsed it without a fight." [1]

THE PURPOSES OF PARTICIPATION

Harter's remarks infer, correctly, that participation contributes more than legitimacy to the rulemaking process. By referring to "rationality" he is suggesting that participation can also enhance the authority of the rule. The credibility and standing a rule enjoys with those who will be regulated by it or enjoy the benefits it bestows depends heavily on the accuracy and completeness of the information on which it is based.[2] Agencies rely on the public for much of the information they need to formulate rules. Therefore, if participation is hampered by hostility, intransigence, secrecy, or incompetence on the part of the agency, the rule will be deprived of information that is crucial in establishing its authority with the affected community. Put another way, stupid rules do not beget respect.

Another reason for participation is less frequently cited but potentially important, nonetheless. The content and tone of expressions from the public can help rulemaking agencies plan for the circumstances they will confront when the rule is written and the next phase, implementation, begins. If one remembers that rulemaking is not an end in itself but the critical bridge between the aspirations articulated in law and the reality expressed in program operations, one can comprehend the special significance of participation.

The contribution of public participation to the content of a rule is easy enough to understand. Agencies are not omniscient, and they are not sufficiently endowed to conduct the research needed for all the rules they are expected to write. Comments from the public also alert agencies to gaps in their knowledge and provide them with an understanding of the conditions in the private sector they are attempting to ameliorate or regulate. Such comments are especially useful if the agency is dealing with a sector of the population it has not dealt with in the past or with an otherwise unfamiliar activity. Agencies can also begin to understand how much learning will be required of regulated and benefiting parties and how much and what form of teaching will be required of implementing officials.

Public comments also help agencies determine the degrees of acceptance and resistance in the affected communities to the rule under development. This information can be crucial in many ways. In regulatory programs the results of public participation help agencies design monitoring and enforcement systems. If the affected parties appear from comments to be generally accepting of the new rules and compliance appears to be relatively easy to achieve, the enforcement program might rely on self-reporting or some other nonintrusive, low-key means of guaranteeing compliance. If, however, the response of the affected public suggests significant opposition to the rule, hostility, and evidence that compliance will be difficult, a more aggressive and expensive enforcement program may be unavoidable. Comments from the public also help the agency gauge the likelihood of a lawsuit challenging the rule prior to its implementation. Litigation of this sort has a profound effect on the rulemaking programs of many agencies. Because of public participation, a lawsuit need not come as a surprise.

Various aspects of public participation were considered in earlier chapters. It has been noted that participation is one of the three fundamental elements in the law of procedure. In the discussion of the management of regulation, attention was given to the systems in agencies to solicit and evaluate the results of public participation. In this chapter a different view of the subject is taken. First, we will examine in a more focused manner the efforts undertaken by government agencies and officials during the past sixty years to broaden and diversify the mechanisms for public participation in rulemaking. Then we will turn to the actual patterns of public participation that occur in rulemaking to determine how those interested in rules under development take advantage of the opportunities to contribute afforded by the agencies.

Although public participation can contribute much to the quality, acceptability, and ultimate success of the rule, it can also complicate rulemaking and place the agency squarely between powerful, contending forces. It is therefore important to get some historical perspective on how the current mechanisms and practices of public participation in rulemaking came into being.

THE ORIGINS AND HISTORY OF PARTICIPATION

It stands to reason that there was some kind of participation by persons outside of agencies from the very start of rulemaking. The number of areas in which rulemaking occurred was initially quite small, but those who wrote rules were no more omniscient than they are now. Often, as now, those who knew the most about the subject of the rulemaking were those it would affect. It is likely that the public did participate in these early years, but we have no record that they did so. With the coming of the twentieth century, scholars started to focus on rulemaking more systematically. The record of participation by the public in the development of rules then began to change.

EARLY INATTENTION

The Attorney General's Committee noted that for at least half the history of rulemaking Congress paid virtually no attention to how it was being conducted by officials of the executive branch. Participation by the public in the act of creating law was effectively ignored. When the change came it was likely due more to the growing prominence and power of groups and associations representing business and professional interests than to any sense of concern for the constitutional ramifications of lawmaking by unelected surrogates in administrative agencies. The origins of these groups is a fascinating political history, worthy of a great deal more attention than we can give them here. The interest group phenomenon dominates the politics of the last quarter of this century and it has certainly left its deep imprint on rulemaking. Interest groups are deeply and aggressively involved in the development of rules, and their impact is great. But success begins with opportunity, and it is the opportunities for participation in rulemaking and the ways they developed over time that must first be considered.

PARTICIPATION AT THE TURN OF THE CENTURY

The earliest systematic research into the process of rulemaking was concerned in part with what, if any, legal status the Congress conferred on those affected by the rules agencies wrote. Thanks again to the work of the Attorney General's Committee we know of statutes at the turn of this century that encouraged or required officials of the executive branch to consult with various groups before issuing rules. These laws are quite important because they begin to form the basis for patterns of public participation that persist to this very day. For example, the committee discovered an appropriation statute enacted in 1902 that provided funds "to enable the Secretary of Agriculture, in collaboration with the Association of Official Agricultural Chemists, and such other experts as he may deem necessary, to establish standards of purity for food products." [3] Although often not required by law, the committee found this type of interaction between rulemakers and interested groups at a variety of agencies, including the Federal Reserve Board (now called the Federal Reserve System), the Federal Communications Commission, the Maritime Commission, and the Children's Bureau. From these informal communications between agencies and their clienteles participation grew and diversified. By the time the committee conducted its research in the latter half of the 1930s, a rich variety of formal and informal means of participation was in place.

THE SITUATION AT THE END OF THE NEW DEAL

The committee concluded after its survey of agency practices that five basic forms of participation were in wide use by the close of the 1930s. They were oral or written communication and consultation;

investigations; specially summoned conferences; advisory committees; and hearings, of which there were two general types.

In its meaning of the term, an investigation was any systematic collection of information to determine whether a rulemaking was necessary and the general content that such a rule might contain. Although investigations were often considered as activities that were internal to the agency and not particularly conducive to public participation, the committee found quite the opposite to be true. Many agencies worked closely with groups and individuals outside the agency at this crucial early stage in rulemaking. The committee noted, for example, that the Bureau of Biological Survey in the Department of Interior "has always been in close touch with state officials, conservationists and sportsmen." [4] This precursor to the Fish and Wildlife Agency used these contacts as the basis for all its rulemaking. This interaction was formalized to some extent when the bureau moved to submit its findings and conclusions relevant to the new rules to the International Association of State Game, Fish and Conservation Commissioners. A similar approach was used by the Food and Drug Administration. According to the Attorney General's Committee, it "employs a Food Standards Committee which collects information on products for which standards are to be proposed." [5] The Food Standards Committee consisted of members from industry. A similar arrangement was in place at the Interstate Commerce Commission for certain rules governing dangerous cargo, but the ICC took the approach one step further by delegating this exploratory work entirely to the Bureau of Explosives of the American Railway Association.[6] We see that at these earliest stages of rulemaking, the decision to act and the initial consideration of options, the public was actively involved. It is interesting to note that this early involvement of the public is one of the principles that make up the foundation of a rulemaking reform that enjoyed considerable attention some forty years later, during the administration of Jimmy Carter.

Oral and written communications and consultations need little further elaboration. They were the oldest and perhaps most common form of participation at the time the committee conducted its research and in all likelihood they remain so today. Even when statutes, then and now, require other forms of participation, informal contacts of this type will occur. They may be the most preferred and effective mode of participation for both the public and private sectors. Examples of this type of consultation were numerous by the late 1930s. The Attorney General's Committee noted, for example, that the "Securities and Exchange Commission ... has rarely failed to submit its proposals to those regulated before promulgating rules." Similarly, "The Federal Communications Commission ... has found it possible to dispose of a large portion of its rulemaking problems by consultation with the industry it regulates." [7]

Conferences were a more structured and focused form of participation and, in the opinion of the Attorney General's Committee, "[introduce] an element of give and take on the part of those present." [8] This type of interaction is not possible when consultation is essentially a set of bilateral contacts between an agency and an interested or affected party. The key to this form of participation was the ability to locate the interested or expert parties and to keep the number of participants manageable. Once again, several agencies were using conferences on a regular basis. The committee found the Federal Reserve Board's practices "particularly noteworthy because of the Board's virtually complete reliance on conferences . . . as a means of enabling affected parties to participate in the rulemaking process." The Federal Reserve Board conducted conferences "with the public directly and through the American Banker's Association." [9]

Advisory committees were as common as conferences and proved to be a more resilient and popular mode of participation. The Attorney General's Committee found advisory committees at work in a wide variety of agencies, and in some instances these bodies were far more than a resource from which the agency could draw information, expertise, and opinion based on experience. Several examples demonstrate the degree of influence that the committee found was exerted by advisory committees during the course of rulemaking. The Bureau of Marine Inspection and Navigation used an advisory committee comprised of "consultants drawn from the industries affected who met continuously with the Bureau's officers and participated in the drafting of particular sets of regulations governing the construction of vessels." [10] Statutes relating to taxation and game in what was then the territory of Alaska established similar groups with direct and active participation in rulemaking.[11] But, the most extraordinary influence of any of the advisory committee arrangements the committee studied was that exerted under the mandates of the Fair Labor Standards Act. It required that "wage orders of the Administrator varying the statutory minimum wage rates in particular industries shall originate with committees of the employers, employee and public representatives." [12] This is remarkable in a number of ways. The law effectively transforms the agency into a ratifier of decisions made by a group of external parties. It also includes a "public" member, a feature notably absent in other advisory committee schemes of the time.[13] And, most interesting, it establishes a structure for rules to be developed through negotiation by parties with contending interests. This form of participation called for in the Fair Labor Standards Act was a precursor of regulatory negotiation, the important reform of rulemaking that did not emerge until some forty years later.

Hearings, as a form of participation, come in two types. Informal hearings are patterned after the familiar legislative sessions. Witnesses are summoned to appear, are sworn, present testimony, and are questioned by the representatives of the agencies who are presiding. Informal hearings are decidedly one-sided. Their clear purpose is the collection of information that the agency will use in developing the rule. It is not to answer questions or challenges from those who are testifying. In this sense, informal hearings would appear to offer little substantive or procedural advantage to potential participants over the even less formal conferences mentioned above. In fact, it is easy to see how the limited formalities of legislative hearings might significantly reduce the "give and take" that is so important if public participation is to provide all it can to rulemakers. Nevertheless, these types of hearings were popular when the committee conducted its study and remain so today.

Legislative hearings were both mandated by statute and undertaken voluntarily by agencies. In the former instance, provisions in various statutes that called on the Interstate Commerce Commission to write rules included the conduct of hearings as a condition of the authority. These hearing requirements can be found in statutes written as early as 1903. The Attorney General's Committee found mandatory hearings common in transportation statutes, generally, and in agencies dealing with certain types of wages, trade and tariffs, prices, and marketing. Voluntary use of hearings was adopted by many business-related regulatory agencies, including the Federal Power Commission, the Federal Communications Commission, and the Department of Agriculture.[14]

Formal hearings are adversary proceedings based on the model of a civil trial conducted in a court of law. The procedural accoutrements of the adversary hearing are formidable and well-known: formal notice, compulsory process to obtain information and testimony, strict rules of evidence, direct and cross examination, a verbatim transcript of the proceedings, and a neutral third party making the decision strictly on the basis of the record developed in the proceeding. At the time the Attorney General's Committee conducted its research, this type of hearing was required for certain rules or rulemaking situations, such as when there were disputes over matters of material fact. The Fair Labor Standards Act, the Bituminous Coal Act, and the Food, Drug and Cosmetic Act all carried provisions for what has come to be called formal rulemaking. Many other agencies voluntarily used this type of proceeding for individual rules.[15]

Then, as now, formal rulemaking was a cumbersome, difficult, time-consuming, and expensive process. The Attorney General's Committee presented evidence on the use of adversary hearings for rulemaking under three of the statutes mentioned above. A coal price order by the Bituminous Coal Board was issued only after generating "a record and exhibits ... total[ing] over 50,000 pages; the trial examiner's report of approximately 2,800 pages in addition to exhibits and a Director's report of 545 single-spaced legal sized pages." Under those provisions requiring a formal hearing in the Fair Labor Standards Act, the agency produced rules based on records that ranged from 600 to 10,000 pages. Hearings under the Food, Drug and Cosmetic Act took from five to eleven months to complete and only after they were done could a rule be issued.[16] Although formal rulemaking was more common in the 1930s than now, when formal procedures are undertaken in contemporary rulemaking the supporting paper and elapsed time dwarf that of the former years.

It should be evident from the foregoing that at the start of the Second World War public participation in rulemaking was a well-developed activity. But if we adopt the currently prevailing ethic of public participation, the situation could cause concern, if not alarm. Today we live with a persistent concern that agencies will be captured by those they regulate or who serve as beneficiaries. The apparent coziness between rulemaking agencies and the industries or groups they regulated that emerges from the work of the Attorney General's Committee is striking. Contacts between public officials and representatives or consultants from industry were the norm. In several instances, the influence of the latter over the decisions of the former was substantial. Involvement of members of the general public, if it was occurring at all, was certainly not prominent in the report of the committee. In no small part the system of participation, so skewed in favor of regulated or benefiting interests, was due to the nature of the programs being managed by federal agencies at that time and the fact that professional and industrial interests were comparatively well organized. Their counterparts, representing broader social interests, were not. The reason notwithstanding, read in a contemporary context, public participation in the 1930s had all the earmarks of capture by powerful private interests, which became a common criticism of government programs in later years.

Aside from the imbalance in the population of participants, what may be most striking about the findings of the Attorney General's Committee is the rich diversity of participatory forms and practices in place more than fifty years ago. One would be hard pressed to find a mechanism of participation in rulemaking currently in force that cannot be traced back to this period. This is notable because, as we will see, it is a later era that is credited with a great expansion of public participation in government decision making, generally. Although rulemaking was certainly affected by the movement, the basic modes of participation were not profoundly altered.

The Attorney General's Committee was conducting its work at a time when rulemaking and the behavior of administrative entities were also receiving considerable attention from Congress, the courts, and the White House. The Walter-Logan Bill, vetoed by President Roosevelt, would have pushed much of the administrative process to the adversary model mentioned above.[17] And New Deal programs and activities, including rulemaking, were experiencing difficulties in the courts. Shortly after the completion of the committee's work the nation was thrust into a war effort that put consideration of administrative reform on hold. But shortly after the Second World War, Congress returned to the subject and enacted a landmark statute.

THE ADMINISTRATIVE PROCEDURE ACT

The rulemaking provisions of the Administrative Procedure Act, reviewed in a previous chapter, may seem curious in light of the information about participation that was available to Congress. The Attorney General's Committee found many different forms and models of participation in its study of agency procedures, but Congress chose to adopt a minimalist approach to public involvement embodied in section 553 of the act. These "notice and comment" provisions codify a limited form of what the committee termed *consultation* as the basic mode of participation the public could expect from rulemaking agencies. Congress also provided for formal rulemaking but restricted it to those situations in which an individual statute mandated its use. At the same time, the act ignored the other forms of participation uncovered by the committee. Further, it allowed agencies to write rules without benefit of any participation in emergency situations or when it was deemed, by the agency, to be in the public interest.

It would be wrong, however, to view the Administrative Procedure Act, its specific provisions notwithstanding, as a repudiation of the diverse forms of public participation already operating in most agencies. The act is a general framework, bounded by notice and comment provisions at one end and trial-type procedures at the other. Within those boundaries, existing statutes, future legislation, and the exercise of agency discretion define administrative procedures more specifically, allowing systems of participation to develop that make the most sense for particular programs. By establishing notice and written comment as the minimums, Congress provided the regularization of rulemaking procedure that critics had found so badly lacking during the New Deal era. In one sense, this action appears in retrospect to be of greater symbolic than instrumental importance. Unless the Attorney

General's Committee conducted woefully inadequate research, by the late 1930s most agencies with any appreciable program of rulemaking were reaching out and interacting with the public, albeit the well-organized public. The real significance of the Administrative Procedure Act was its statement that participation in rulemaking would henceforth be open to anyone who wished to become involved. It provided those interested the minimum information and access needed to get involved.[18] Organization, resources, and political sophistication would still, however, be prerequisites to effective participation, and it would take the larger political movements and actions of government of the 1960s and 1970s to bring a greater number and more diverse voices to rulemaking.

CONVERGING FORCES: THE "PARTICIPATION REVOLUTION" AND THE RISE OF SOCIAL REGULATION

Their origins are difficult to date with precision, but there is no question that during the 1960s and 1970s the nation was host to two major developments that would alter the status and process of rulemaking. The first was a movement to involve citizens in governmental decision making in ways that were more direct and intended to be more effective than the ballot. The second, discussed in detail in Chapter 1, was the vast expansion of social regulation that extended the reach of government in such a way that previously unorganized interests now had more than ample incentive to come together for collective action. Once in motion, the convergence of these two forces on the rulemaking process was both inevitable and important.

The revolution in participation was not a single, coherent movement. It drew support from people with different motives, consisted of many disparate initiatives, and had highly variable effects from program to program. At its base, however, was a lack of faith in the ability of established governmental officials, institutions, and procedures to understand properly or to respond seriously to the popular will. In retrospect, this posture is not difficult to comprehend. The 1960s and 1970s saw a seemingly interminable and frequently violent struggle for civil rights, unsatisfactorily explained assassinations of revered public figures, an unpopular war, shocking political scandals, and a growing opinion that government was unable to accomplish ambitious social objectives. The motives of those seeking to expand public participation ranged from a near-paranoid mistrust of government's own motives to a simple belief that direct citizen input would improve the quality of official decisions. Also prominent was a faith in participation as a means of empowering and involving the disenfranchised and unrepresented among the population. Depending on their underlying motives, members of the public emphasized and targeted for action different aspects of government decision making.

CONGRESSIONAL ACTION TO PROMOTE PARTICIPATION

A variety of legislative efforts were undertaken to open government decision making to public scrutiny. The Freedom of Information Act allowed private citizens to review the way agency officials made their decisions. The Privacy Act allowed individuals to gain access to the information the government might have about them, to learn the uses to which the information was being put, and to correct errors in those records while requiring the responsible agency to take steps to prevent unauthorized disclosures. The Government in the Sunshine Act opened many agency meetings and deliberations to the public. The Federal Advisory Committee Act required that membership on those potentially powerful groups be balanced in regard to affected interests and opened their deliberations to public scrutiny as well.

Other efforts sought to provide for more direct participation of the public in government decision making. The Great Society programs of Lyndon Johnson adopted this approach, and the movement for direct citizen action continued through the 1970s. By one estimate, hundreds of programs required "some form of citizen participation" by the end of that decade.[19] In some instances the displacement of existing governmental institutions and processes was nearly complete. The Model Cities Program, a crown jewel of the Great Society, mandated a governance structure consisting of separately elected citizen boards that completely bypassed local executive and legislative officials. Alternative governments, often competing with establishment officials for power and influence, were rapidly becoming the order of the day.

EXPANSION OF SCOPE, DIVERSIFICATION OF FORMS

The citizen participation movement was in full flower when the era of social regulation dawned in the late 1960s. The National Environmental Policy Act, which many see as the symbolic start of that era, embraced fully the participation ethic of the time. Both elements of the movement, full disclosure of the information on which government bases its decisions and direct public involvement, provide the cornerstones of NEPA. Government agencies were required to develop detailed impact statements of all the effects their contemplated actions would have on the environment. The statements were to be prepared only after a public "scoping session" at which citizens could voice their concerns and opinions about likely effects. Then, once completed, the statement was subjected to another round of public participation before it could be declared final. While the assessments of the effects of the NEPA provisions have varied considerably, there is evidence that the act contributed to significant changes in many federal agencies.[20]

The hundreds of statutes establishing and amending programs of social regulation embraced the concept of expanded public participation as well. But in each instance Congress tailored participation provisions to the program in question. Some statutes expanded on the basic provisions of the Administrative Procedure Act, effectively giving the public more of the same types of opportunities the APA had already established. For example, laws establishing programs of social regulation called for extended periods of public comment, replacing the norm of thirty days that had evolved since passage of the act. The 1977 amendments to the Clean Water Act, for example, allowed for sixty days for public comment on efficient guidelines for toxic water pollutants.[21] One motive for this type of provision was to give organizations, groups, and individuals new to the rulemaking process additional time to analyze and respond to the frequently complex proposed regulations needed to implement programs of social regulation. But other motives may have been at work too. The extended periods delay the issuance of rules and give opponents more time to alert and activate congressional, administration, and private sector allies who might help in blocking or altering the new rules.

Other statutes expanded the APA's notice requirements by calling on agencies to release to the public analyses on which they were relying for the content of their proposed rules. These disclosure requirements can be found in the Federal Trade Commission Improvements Act of 1980 and the Consumer Product Safety Act Amendments of 1981.[22] Again, the motives behind these provisions were mixed. Certainly, additional information can assist the public in determining whether to participate and in focusing their comments or stated opinions. Still, it can also delay the issuance of the proposal. More important, it exposes the agency to challenge. The studies and reports disclosed in this manner may be criticized from many different perspectives, and if their reliability or validity is called into question, the entire rule may be in jeopardy. Perceived weaknesses in supporting documentation may be used by opponents as a means of activating allies in Congress, the White House, and the private sector. The studies, and the agency's response to criticisms of them, may form the basis for a subsequent lawsuit.

Several of the general models of participation that were observed by the Attorney General's Committee in the 1930s reappeared in statutes of social regulation in the 1970s. Especially popular were provisions requiring agencies to go beyond the written comments called for in the APA and to allow interested parties to present information and views orally. These legislative-type hearings were included in the Occupational Safety and Health Act, the Consumer Product Safety Act, the Safe Drinking Water Act, the 1977 amendments to the Clean Water Act, and the 1978 revisions of the Endangered Species Act.[23] The provisions varied with regard to the triggering mechanism. In some, the hearings were required whenever the agency wrote a rule under the authority of the statute. In others, hearings were conducted only if a request was received from an interested party. A few statutes, notably the Magnuson-Moss Warranty—Federal Trade Commission Improvement Act and the Toxic Substances Control Act, went well beyond the legislative model by allowing for cross-examination of witnesses by participating interests.[24] Like other mechanisms to expand participation, hearings can serve the purposes of those with several different motives. It is thought that hearings provide a direct and compelling form of participation because they put agency personnel into direct and sometimes intense contact with those members of the public who will be affected by their rules. But hearings are also time-consuming and expensive to manage. Although they can generate a wealth of information and views, this is not an unequivocal benefit to those writing the rules. The agency must subsequently take this information into consideration when finalizing the rule. In addition, because the transcripts of hearings become part of this material "record" of the rulemaking, they can be used to mobilize political support or opposition and thus may figure prominently in subsequent litigation attacking the rule.

Innovations in participation were not confined to the latter stages of the rulemaking process. Some legislation, like the Federal Trade Commission Improvements Act and the Energy Policy and Conservation Act, required advance notices of proposed rulemaking.[25] This is a mechanism for early input by the public that will be discussed at greater length a bit later. At least two statutes—the Consumer Product Safety Act and the Medical Device Amendments to the Food, Drug and Cosmetic Act—contained "offerer provisions." [26] These provisions authorized nongovernmental groups and organizations to develop and propose rules to agencies, which would then decide whether to issue the rule in the form proposed.

Overall, Congress was a major force in promoting greater participation in rulemaking proceedings. Legislation was an important element in both the "participation revolution" that swept government in general, and the larger "procedural revolution" that altered rulemaking in recent decades. But other institutions were also heavily involved in the process of opening rulemaking to direct influence by the public.

PRESIDENTS AND PARTICIPATION

THE CARTER REFORMS.   Congress was not the sole agent of increased public participation. Jimmy Carter assumed the presidency determined to improve the operation of regulatory programs. He put considerable faith in the ability of enhanced public involvement to produce the desired change. His regulatory reform program consisted of numerous elements, most of which were contained in his Executive Order 12044, issued in 1978. As discussed in an earlier chapter, in addition to calling on agencies to find ways to get the public more involved in the development of rules, the order called for more oversight and coordination of rulemaking by senior agency officials, better regulatory analyses of rules under development, use of "plain English" in rules to make them more accessible, and programs to review existing regulations to determine whether they might be abandoned or improved. To these elements of the Carter program was added the Regulatory Analysis Review Group.

The means of increasing public participation could take many forms. One simple means was to increase the period for public comment on proposed rules from the usual thirty days to sixty days or longer. Better and earlier information on agencies' plans for rulemaking was to be supplied through the publication of regulatory agenda and calendars. These would provide early warning to the public of rulemaking projects in early stages of development or being contemplated. A more ambitious approach to achieving the same objectives is the *advance notice of proposed rulemaking*. This is a device that involves the public in the development of individual rules at a very early stage. The advance notice announces either the agency's intent to write a regulation or its concern that an issue or problem may require a rule. The agency solicits the views of the public on the need for the regulation or its ideas on how the issue or problem that will be addressed in the rule might be resolved. In effect, it is an invitation to join the agency at the very beginning of the rulemaking process.

The Office of Management and Budget was charged by the president with evaluating the progress that agencies were making in implementing the provisions of the executive order. In this task the OMB relied on the agencies' own reports, its independent inquiries, and responses from a survey of interest groups who were asked to comment on the performance of the agencies they dealt with in the area of participation. The summary assessment, done roughly one year after the executive order was promulgated, was "mixed" in most areas.[27]

Semiannual agendas were being produced by most agencies and were generally viewed as a positive development by the external groups that were surveyed. While they provided useful information that did help groups plan the agendas of individual agencies, they varied considerably in their quality and accuracy. In some instances the agendas were produced on something less than a semiannual schedule. In others the descriptions of problems or circumstances and the rules that were being developed to deal with them were skimpy or vague. Poor explanations and descriptions made it difficult to discern what the agency was actually considering and why the action was being contemplated. Another problem, one discussed at length earlier in the book, was the anticipated schedule for development of the rule. Groups complained that the schedules announced in the agendas were frequently inaccurate, tending to be overly optimistic about how quickly the work would be completed.[28]

Since its inception during the Carter administration the regulatory agenda program has continued to develop, and the quality of agency submissions is more uniform. The descriptions are now quite clear and sufficiently informative that external parties can easily understand why an action is being undertaken and how the agency is thinking about the problem. The program has been retained by the presidents who followed Carter, but its primary focus has shifted from a device for participation to one of accountability to the White House. Nevertheless, agendas still aid those who participate.

The OMB evaluators found that several agencies that had not used advance notices of proposed rulemaking in the past were experimenting with them. The response from the public to the use of these devices for early participation was generally positive but not unanimous. In a somewhat surprising turn, some groups appeared to resent the fact that agencies were using advance notices to the extent they were, viewing it as "a 'cop-out' to have the public do the [agencies'] work for them." [29] No more explanation of this position was provided, but it can be interpreted in at least two ways. One is that the groups expressing this opinion simply disliked the additional burden on their resources that early involvement in rulemaking entails. Another is that these groups saw the advance notice as a form of political cowardice on the part of agencies unwilling to take a position on a difficult issue, preferring to adopt whatever consensus emerged from the responses to the advance notice.

The sixty-day period for comments was found to be generally observed by agencies, but the effect on the public was marginal. The extension was an improvement over the thirty-day practice, which in the case of lengthy or highly technical proposed rules was clearly inadequate, but the sixty-day period afforded only a modest amount of additional time. In those instances in which the OMB found more extensive periods of public comment to be particularly useful, the agencies involved were far more generous, allowing, in some cases, as much as half a year or longer for responses.[30]

The OMB study did report on many innovative approaches to outreach during rulemaking that had been developed by agencies. These initiatives fall into a couple of general categories. The first consists of efforts to diversify the ways agencies communicate with the public on actions they are planning to take. However improved, notices that appear only in the *Federal Register* or in a semiannual agenda will have limited circulation. And, in contemporary parlance, they are anything but user-friendly. Agencies experimented with a variety of techniques and media more familiar, accessible, and understandable to the general public. Among these were notices in newspapers or television and radio and mass mailings. Another general thrust consisted of efforts to bring the rulemaking process to the people in ways less antiseptic and remote than the simple reception of public comments. Efforts sought to give the public a sense that the agency cared about their views. These were various forms of public hearing around the country.[31]

The overall performance of government under the Carter reforms may not be as instructive as the experiences of individual agencies. A series of case studies done in conjunction with the OMB evaluation provides important insights into the status of public participation in individual departments and agencies in the late 1970s. These studies review the situation in five departments—Agriculture; Health, Education and Welfare; Labor; Interior; and the EPA. They cover a wide variety of subject matter, and their missions touch virtually every person in America. Hence, the individual experiences discussed in each one help us understand the dynamics of public participation from the agency's perspective.

The Department of Agriculture has more than twenty major operating units, most of which issue regulations, some in large numbers. There was probably as much variation within the department in the late 1970s with regard to public participation as there is across the entire government. The experience of one of its rulemaking programs, the one that established agricultural marketing orders for various types of commodities, provides an interesting case study of how public participation evolves with time. The program came into being as part of the New Deal. It sought to stabilize the markets for agricultural products through many different means, the primary remaining device being rules that establish quality standards and limit the amounts of various commodities that can be shipped to market. For most of its history it was a classic example of a "captured" regulatory program. Rules regulating the amounts of a given crop, oranges for example, were initiated at the request of producers. Although the marketing orders were formally issued, after a hearing, by the Agricultural Marketing Service, they did not take effect until they passed a "producer referendum" by a two-thirds or three-fourths vote, depending on the commodity in question. From available reports it appears that the hearings associated with the marketing order rulemakings were rarely attended by consumer interests, nor did those interests actively oppose the program, which, it would appear, was stacked against them.[32] The inactivity of consumers is explained by conventional theories of regulation, notably those of the economist Mancur Olson and the political scientist James Q. Wilson, that underscore the advantage that a highly specialized and small group, producers in this case, enjoys over a group that is large, diverse, and difficult to organize, such as consumers.[33]

The participation revolution caught up with the agricultural marketing order program in the midst of the Carter rulemaking initiatives. Either at the initiative of the program or as the result of prodding from the outside, the Department of Agriculture "discovered a significant amount of outside interest in the marketing order programs that was not being accommodated through the formal hearing process."[34] Whether this was a sudden and unprecedented surge in interest from previously unconcerned groups or whether it simply took the program more than forty years to "discover" them was not discussed in the OMB evaluation. The response of the department was significant in that it established a "prenotice public participation requirement." In effect, this was a preliminary investigation of public attitudes and views on a planned marketing order through a solicitation of comments mailed directly to interested groups. The Agricultural Marketing Service would annually update the mailing list. Responses to the prenotice would "frame the issues to be covered" in the marketing order rulemaking.[35] This reform of a long-established and largely closed rulemaking process resembles to a remarkable extent the "scoping" requirements in the National Environmental Policy Act. In NEPA, this early involvement established the scope of the environmental studies to be done; in the Agricultural Marketing Service rulemaking, the prenotices determined the issues that the marketing order rule would address and resolve. It represented a major effort to open a captured program to nonproducer interests.

Participation in rulemaking was an area of major change for the Department of Health, Education and Welfare (HEW), now the Department of Health and Human Services. It too housed many programs, which, as in the previous case, touched the lives of every American. In programs like those of the Food and Drug Administration, Medicare, Medicaid, and Aid to Families with Dependent Children, the impact is profound. The issues facing the department involved reaching and listening to enormous numbers of potential participants. The initiative undertaken in response to the Carter program suggests the magnitude of the task. In an effort to bring the rulemaking process to the people, HEW conducted a series of public meetings outside of Washington and sent out special mailings about rules that were under way. In 1978 alone the department reported that more than 3,100 persons attended the public meetings and that it had sent more than 110,000 individual letters. In an effort to get the public to participate in the development of rules concerning food labels, the Food and Drug Administration sent out more than "40,000 letters," distributed "500,000 pieces of literature," and did an "experimental television survey" in Columbus, Ohio. The efforts were both successful and sobering. The good news was that the FDA initiatives generated more than 10,000 public comments on the labeling regulations.[36] The sobering fact was that each of these had to be read and decisions had to made about how to respond, if at all, to each of them in the final regulations. The experience of the FDA and HEW reminds us that the price one pays for participation in regard to staff time, delay, and opportunity costs can be dear.

The efforts of the Department of the Interior to implement the Carter executive order demonstrate some of the benefits and costs of the early participation of the public in rulemaking. The department reported several instances in which advance notices of proposed rulemaking were used and had a demonstrable effect on the regulation under consideration. It provided examples of rules whose scope of coverage expanded as a result of the early public input and many instances in which the number of affected parties or activities was reduced. Among other things, early involvement of the public appeared to be particularly useful in weeding out unnecessary provisions in regulations. In one case the number of eligibility criteria for a grant program was reduced from 100 to just 6, and the number of items included in an application for right of way on public lands went from 20 to 5.[37] It is not clear why this impressive reduction in apparently useless requirements was attributed to early involvement, but it demonstrates the potential power of participation, nonetheless.

As was noted above, strategies to involve the public early are not without their critics. In the case of the Department of the Interior, the unhappiness centered on advance notices of "technical or complex" rules. The OMB evaluation concluded that these did not result in "substantive, useful comments." According to one industry interest group it was because, "Notices of intent give a phony appearance of public participation—technical rules need specifics. If they don't . . . you can't comment." [38] Here it is apparent that either the public receiving these early invitations to participate misunderstands the request or that advance notices are simply infeasible for certain types of rules. The comment suggests that the people in this group may not have realized that they were being asked to help design a rule from the ground up. Alternatively, they did understand the request but were loath to invest substantial resources in an effort that might provide them no benefits whatsoever.

The Department of Labor's most important and controversial rulemaking organization is the Occupational Safety and Health Administration. The firestorm of controversy it generated when it issued thousands of workplace safety regulations that were based on consensus standards developed by professional organizations was discussed in an earlier chapter. The public input to that process was virtually nonexistent, and OSHA suffered as a result of the obsolete and often silly rules that were allowed to become law. We will see in a subsequent chapter that its health rules, which are far fewer in number, are no less controversial. In this environment one would predict that new opportunities for participation would be enthusiastically received, but in fact OSHA had an experience similar to that of the Department of the Interior when it attempted to introduce early public input into its rulemaking process.

The OMB evaluators found that the various agencies in the Department of Labor tailored their methods of outreach to the public to fit their particular constituencies. OSHA officials concluded that their "constituent groups apparently believe they can have the most impact by addressing issues raised in a specific proposal." The OMB review team concluded that OSHA found its "constituent groups reluctant to use their limited resources on relatively undeveloped concepts identified early in the process." [39]

The Environmental Protection Agency presents contrasting tendencies in its record on public participation in rulemaking. In some areas its efforts were unmatched anywhere else in the government. Yet it also behaved in a manner that appeared to be insensitive to the need for public involvement. According to the OMB report, the EPA "had a tradition of effective public participation." [40] For years the agency had been using advance notices and distributing supplemental information to the public on rules under development. But these notices and supplements were frequently not as informative as they might have been. The executive order pushed the EPA to improve its performance in this regard. The agency also developed a set of regulations that bound it to use various forms of public participation when developing rules for its solid and hazardous waste, drinking water, and clean water programs. It received more than five hundred comments on these procedural regulations, a significant percentage of which were received over a special toll-free long-distance telephone system. The new regulations established public meetings, hearings, and advisory groups as the three major means for obtaining the input of the public in these three important regulatory programs.[41]

Still, some groups accused the EPA of circumventing requirements for public participation by using devices other than rules and regulations for setting regulatory policy. The devices took a number of forms, including "policy circulars," "guidelines," "technical corrections," and the like. These were issued by the agency without any of the procedural steps normally associated with rulemaking. The public was both confused and irritated by these official but somewhat obscure pronouncements from the EPA. Confusion arose as to their status. Were they equal in legal terms to an actual rule or regulation? If so, should not normal rulemaking procedures, including public participation, apply to their development? One who criticized their use reflected a widely held view: "Where these . . . have major effects the public should have an opportunity for comment."[42] As it happens, the EPA was not the only department that may have been avoiding public participation requirements.

Time has only increased the use of, and the controversy associated with, these instruments of public policy as alternatives to rules. The courts have insisted that when agencies take actions that create or alter obligations borne by the public they must use appropriate procedures. Yet, nearly fifteen years after the OMB study, a study supported by the Administrative Conference of the United States found the use of guidelines, advisories, and the like still very popular among a large number of rulemaking agencies. The analysis, like prevailing judicial policy, calls on agencies to engage in rulemaking whenever there is a question about the action it is taking. Nevertheless, the study also concludes it is likely that agencies will continue to engage in the use of these devices in marginal cases.[43] First, there are always going to be instances when agencies do not perceive the action they are taking as any more than a clarification of existing rules or policy. Of course, any clarification will have the effect of transforming a gray area into one that is black and white, and this change alone may be enough to trigger a protest. Second, as noted in a previous chapter, what McGarrity calls the "ossification" of rulemaking under the weight of multiple, complex procedures creates incentives for agencies to find quicker, easier ways to manage their programs.

The last years of the Carter administration represent the high-water mark for participation in rulemaking as a public policy concern. Much can be learned from the initiatives undertaken during this time. It is apparent that even a short-lived program out of the White House can produce dramatic results. In point of fact, there was not enough time during the Carter administration for the program ever to be fully implemented. Nevertheless, the OMB study demonstrates that with the force of the presidency behind it an effort like the public participation initiative will be taken seriously by agencies and produce results. As we will see, efforts by President Carter's successors, while substantially different in form and thrust, also had substantial payoffs.

The Carter program underscores some fundamental principles of public participation in rulemaking. Above all others it reminds us that the goal of public involvement in the development of rules is costly, and the expenses take many forms. Public funds are expended on the design and maintenance of mechanisms to solicit public input and to incorporate it into rules when it occurs. Participation takes time, and delays in the issuance of regulations postpone the flow of benefits expected from the programs affected. The costs of delay may be partially or fully offset by better-quality regulation, of course. Participation requires resources for those who wish to become involved. They must expend effort to learn about the rule under development, to determine its likely effect on their interests, to assemble support for their position, and to communicate their views in an effective manner to the rulemakers.

The relation between information and resources for those participating in the development of a rule appears to be particularly important. The reluctance to become involved in the early stages of rulemaking that the OMB study found among some respondents demonstrates how groups and organizations use information to ration their rulemaking assets. Although some of the skepticism about advance notices and similar devices was based on the view that agencies were attempting to offload difficult or politically dangerous work, other responses suggested that such involvement was thought to be riskier than participation based on a firm, specific proposal developed by an agency. No group or business has unlimited funds and staff to expend in rulemaking; priorities must be set. Participation in the earliest stages of rule development carries the possibility that a group's investment will be for naught if the agency chooses a different approach from the one the group advocated or drops the matter altogether.

By the end of the Carter administration most of the major avenues for public involvement in rulemaking had been explored. The strengths and weaknesses of each were well understood, and it was apparent to any serious observer that further efforts could do little more than articulate and support the most general principles. Ultimately, programs of public participation in rulemaking have to be tailored to the subject matter and constituencies of the programs for which the rules are being written. This type of tailoring was highly developed in most agencies, but it is important to note that in many of the departments and agencies such a tailoring process had been in use for more than fifty years.

THE REAGAN CHANGES: PARTICIPATION OF A DIFFERENT SORT.   The transition from Carter to Reagan brought dramatic change. The new administration took a very different view of public participation. Jeffrey Berry, Kent Portney, and Ken Thomson, experts in the field of citizen participation in government, summarize President Reagan's position in the following way:

> In rather sweeping fashion, the Reagan administration pursued its policies under the belief that federally mandated citizen participation caused the bureaucracy to become unresponsive to officials elected by the people and that citizen participation therefore actually became antidemocratic. In a call for the return to the orthodox view of administrative responsiveness, the Reagan administration suggested that agencies had become responsive to clients and special interests in a way that was inconsistent with what the general citizenry wanted. In contrast, advocates of citizen participation argued that there is nothing antidemocratic about citizens working with agencies to fulfill the spirit and intent of the programs enacted by Congress. The debate continues today.[44]

Nevertheless, the 1980s saw two major developments, both of which had the potential to change how the public influences the rulemaking process.

The Reagan administration did not disdain all participation, only the type that sought expansion of certain government benefits and most regulations. The Reaganites viewed most of the initiatives of the 1960s and 1970s as empowering those very organizations and groups that had a strong vested interest in big government. They were correct. Reagan succeeded in rolling back a few of the mechanisms for public participation in rulemaking, notably public funding. But his major accomplishments were halting further expansion of participation opportunities and installing counterweights to the influence exerted by advocates of big government.

The main offsetting mechanism was review of all proposed and final rules by the Office of Management and Budget. The developments leading up to the Reagan program, and the Reagan program itself, were discussed in a previous chapter. What is significant here is the new form of participation that the OMB review program stimulated. The OMB staff members who reviewed proposed regulations became another point of decision making for organizations and groups to influence. Again, if it is true, as Theodore Lowi has stated, that politics flows to the point of discretion, the Reagan program created just such a point.[45] Certainly, the various review programs instituted by previous presidents created similar opportunities, but none was so sweeping as the charge given the OMB under Executive Order 12291. The authority of OMB officials was not confined to particular types of rules, or rules with particular types of potential effects, or rules already on the books. Here, for the first time, was a comprehensive program to review all rules with the implicit charge to alter those whose content contradicted, or failed to promote, the policy goals that President Reagan took as his mandate. In short, the president known as a skeptic of public participation had created one of the most inviting opportunities for involvement in rulemaking in American history. But in the opinion of many the invitation was extended only to a privileged few.

The logic of focusing one's available resources on these high-level bodies is both compelling and obvious. Theoretically, at least, important changes in a rule, valuable delay, and even complete defeat of a proposed regulation could be achieved through effective lobbying of the right officials in OMB. If a given interest group was confident about securing a sympathetic ear, it could pursue a strategy of nominal involvement during the agency phase of rulemaking while putting heavy pressure on the OMB staff and officials responsible for the review of the rule. In this way the interest group could attain its goal at a comparatively low cost.

Given the general policies of the Reagan administration, the willingness of the OMB staff to listen to those with concerns about proposed and final regulations depended very heavily on who was speaking. Critics of the OMB program accused the Reagan administration of creating a backdoor through which influence peddlers representing big business and antiregulation forces could slip and change or block outright those rules they failed to influence satisfactorily by dealing directly with the responsible agencies. They charged further that contacts between lobbyists and OMB staff members constituted an illegal violation of the long-standing principle that all information used to determine the content of a rule be known and subject to review by the courts and the public in general.

The charges were vehemently denied by those in the administration, but their protestations were not sufficient to silence the critics. Several years after the OMB program was instituted, the head of the Office of Information and Regulatory Affairs, the office that conducted the reviews, issued a set of binding guidelines that established standards for contact with the public and for recording the results of meetings or other forms of communication. Restrictions were placed on the communication between the staff and external interests, and that which occurred was to be consistent with the principle of a rulemaking record; that is, it had to be open to public review and, during litigation, to judicial scrutiny.[46]

President George Bush, having headed the Task Force on Regulatory Relief in the Reagan administration, sought to revive this mechanism that served as a forum for those critical of proposed and existing rules. His solution was to continue a more rarefied version of the review process that had been installed by his predecessor in the form of the Council on Competitiveness. It was given authority to review any rule it deemed sufficiently important to the operation of the American economy. The criteria it would apply about what to review were vague, and the council operated without benefit of the procedural restrictions that were imposed on the OMB. Provided with ample staff support from the same unit in the OMB that conducted reviews of rules, the council set about aggressively to alter regulations it thought to be unnecessarily burdensome on the economy. The same, albeit more intense, criticism was leveled at the council as that which had greeted the OMB review a decade earlier. Now, however, there were direct claims that preferential treatment was being given to those who supported the president's 1988 campaign and to those whose support the administration coveted for 1992. It became common to refer to the operation of the council as a form of regulatory pork barrel politics in which the White House doled out economic benefits in the form of reduced compliance costs. Nonetheless, the council won major battles with those agencies who persisted in their views. The effect of the council on important rules was sometimes quite dramatic. In a highly publicized struggle with the leadership of the Environmental Protection Agency, the council succeeded in rolling back proposed notification requirements in rules developed under the 1990 Clean Air Act. The action meant that polluting firms would not have to notify the public when incidents of excess emissions occurred, and thus it relieved affected businesses from potentially high costs and public scrutiny.

Critics issued withering assessments of the council's practices in this regard and the secrecy with which it conducted its business. In a joint report on the council, two organizations frequently critical of the approach of both Reagan and Bush to regulation stated:

> By directly meddling in ongoing regulatory actions, the Quayle Council undermines the entire system of federal regulation. Over the years, Congress has charged expert agencies such as the Environmental Protection Agency (EPA), the Food and Drug Administration (FDA), and the Occupational Safety and Health Administration (OSHA) with the task of safeguarding the public's health and safety. These agencies, in turn, are governed by an elaborate legal structure designed to ensure that they are open to the public, that they hear from all sides, and that they base their decisions on complex scientific or technical matters only on substantive merits. (These rules are embodied, primarily, in the Administrative Procedure Act

and the Freedom of Information Act.) By contrast, the Quayle Council invites regulated corporations unhappy about the results of regulation to quietly turn to the White House for relief. In the two years since the Council has been in place, it has already intruded in such detailed matters as the establishment of quality control standards for pap smears to determining just how much toxic formaldehyde workers can be exposed to safely. Because it acts in utter secrecy, the Quayle Council has set itself up as a channel for improper industry influence in regulatory decision-making. If it continues to expand its operations, the nation's health and safety standards will be in tatters.[47]

REGULATORY NEGOTIATION: PARTICIPATION AT ITS MOST INTENSE

Another form of participation in rulemaking, one that stands in stark contrast to the Reagan initiatives, was developing during the 1980s. Regulatory negotiation, or *reg neg*, as it has come to be called, offers the public the most direct and substantial role in rulemaking of any reform of the process ever devised. Its origins can be traced back nearly sixty years to the Fair Labor Standards Act, which established committees consisting of management, labor, and other interested parties who would, in effect, work cooperatively to make rules that affected wages and other important conditions of work in a variety of sectors and industries. As it happened, the more contemporary manifestation of the basic idea that regulations could be developed through negotiations also occurred in a department of the federal government responsible for various aspects of employment policy. John Dunlop, a Harvard professor of economics and then secretary of labor, proposed in 1975 that rules and regulations that established various standards for conditions in the workplace be determined by some form of consensual process that involved in a direct and substantial way those interests with a stake in their content. Dunlop, long a prominent theoretician and practitioner of mediation, believed that the same general principles that guided collective bargaining for wages and other conditions of employment could be profitably applied to the process of rulemaking.

This fundamental idea began to take more specific shape in the early 1980s as a substantial body of scholarly and professional literature devoted to the topic emerged. In these writings academics and practitioners set out the basic rationale for regulatory negotiation, its likely benefits, the conditions for it to be successful, and the obstacles to its implementation. The most influential of these was Phillip Harter, whose article "Negotiating Regulations," which appeared in the *Georgetown Law Journal* in 1982, is perhaps the most frequently cited and influential exposition of the case for regulatory negotiation.

Harter's argument proceeds from a withering critique of the methods of rulemaking that it would supplant. His survey of the state of contemporary rulemaking found it a fundamentally adversarial process in which affected parties jockeyed with each other and the agency for influence and advantage. The process of developing the information that would provide the content of the rule had become a ritual dance in which the various participants would stake out extreme positions and offer what they knew selectively to bolster their particular position or cause. The distortion of information and the tendency for participants to use the comment process simply as a means of establishing a basis in the rulemaking record for a subsequent lawsuit were, to Harter, an indication that a profound "malaise" had settled over this most crucial instrument of government. Much of the blame, he believed, could be attributed to a design that separated the interested parties in a rulemaking from each other and the agency through an antiseptic process of written comment or the limited exchanges of a legislative-type hearing or the stylized adversariness of formal rulemaking. The results of these modes of rulemaking were, to Harter, predictably depressing. Issuance of rules was frequently delayed, their quality was often flawed, they enjoyed little support from key constituencies, implementation was difficult, and compliance was anything but automatic. Believing they had only the most remote involvement in their development, affected parties and interest groups had no stake in their success. Put simply, the legitimacy and authority of rules were questionable because the process used to develop them was flawed.

The general accuracy of the Harter critique is a matter for debate, but there is little doubt that he captured the situation for a substantial portion of our most significant rules. He offered an alternative process, one in which conflict was acknowledged but resolved through face-to-face negotiations. As he put it "the parties participate directly and immediately in the decision. They share in its development and concur with it rather than 'participate' by submitting information." [48] What was being proposed was a fundamentally different model of rulemaking. It explicitly altered the role of agency officials by reducing them to the status of participants in the group that would negotiate the content of the regulation. Further, negotiated rulemaking would be applied to a much broader range of programs and issues than had been contemplated in the past. It should not be surprising that the early examples of regulatory negotiation were concentrated in programs dealing with labor relations. The tradition of collective bargaining involving labor and management was well established by the time Secretary Dunlop proposed a modified version of it for rulemaking. But the Harter proposal was not confined to a particular set of policy areas. Hence, it sought to bring together interest groups that might not have anything but the most episodic relationships with one another. The idea, if not revolutionary, did represent a dramatic departure from previous reforms.

Harter and other advocates of regulatory negotiation were quick to point out that it was neither feasible nor necessary for certain types of rules. It is unnecessary when there is little controversy associated with the development of a rule. When the course of action is clear and undisputed, or when there is little interest in the result, investment in regulatory negotiation would be frivolous. But even when the rule and the conflict surrounding it are substantial, there are criteria by which to determine whether regulatory negotiation has a reasonable chance to succeed.

Perhaps the most basic criterion for selecting candidates for regulatory negotiation is to choose those rules that do not entail conflict over fundamental, deeply held values. Where the basic dis-agreement is not about how much or little to regulate, or about the means to achieve a particular objective, but rather about the morality of government intervention, per se, the prospects for regulatory negotiation diminish substantially. As Harter notes, "In the regulatory context, the more the parties agree on fundamental principles that shape the decision, the more likely it is that negotiations will be successful. If the fundamental issues cannot be resolved because the regulatory statute is vague, the situation may closely resemble a debate over the superiority of various religions." [49] When the inevitable result of a rulemaking is litigation over the constitutionality or simple legality of government involvement in a particular area, the undertaking of a regulatory negotiation is simply a waste of time and resources.

Other important criteria deserve a quick review.[50] First, issues for regulatory negotiation must be what Harter terms "mature" or ready for resolution. The issue may not be ready for many reasons, including insufficient information about the issue, an inability to identify inter-ested parties, or a lack of agreement within individual organizations about the position they might take on the issue. Second, and perhaps self-evident, the parties to the rulemaking must perceive the possibility of gain from the negotiations. If there is little to win or no chance of even partial victory, the rational individual will pass on participation. Finally, the potential parties to the negotiation must believe that if they do not participate in the negotiation a decision will be made regardless, one in which their prospects for influence will be signifi-cantly reduced. In effect, this is the same type of incentive structure that leads prosecutors and defense attorneys to plea-bargain and litigants in civil cases to accept settlements.

The success of a regulatory negotiation hinges on the composition of the group that will work together to develop the rule. Forming such a group entails identifying interested and informed parties and persuading them to participate in the negotiation. In most instances the parties with interests at stake and information to provide in a rulemaking are well known to agency personnel. But the composition of the groups is so crucial to the success of a negotiation that agencies are well advised to use formal outreach, through the *Federal Register* and other media, to inform members of the public about the proposed negotiation and invite them to request the opportunity to participate. Willingness to participate alone is not sufficient. Groups and organizations must have sufficient resources to invest in the negotiation process, and, on occasion, the agency might face the delicate task of denying membership to an organization or individual whose involvement is unnecessary or inappropriate. Once the groups that will be parties to the negotiation are selected, the individual organizations must choose the individuals who will represent them. This, too, is a crucial decision. Not only must the individuals selected be knowledgeable in the area of public policy affected by the rule, they must also have the authority to speak for the group they represent and to negotiate on its behalf. Without this authority, the negotiations will bog down in endless cycles of consultations and approvals or will fail when an apparent agreement is vetoed by the real powers in a particular group.

Although every effort must be made to identify interested parties, the search may prove too successful. Harter has noted that there is a limit to the number of discrete interests that can be accommodated in a regulatory negotiation session. The number is by no means firm, but Harter sets as a general guideline fifteen participants at most. As he notes, "Negotiations will clearly not work among an auditorium full of people. The give and take of issues and positions can only occur with a limited number of participants." [51]

Another key criterion is the willingness of the responsible agency to accept the role of participant in the regulatory negotiation. This represents a profound alteration of an agency's usual role in the rulemaking process. Traditionally, other interest groups strive to influence the agency whose officials have the authority and power to determine the ultimate content of the rule. In regulatory negotiation the agency's role is reduced to that of one party attempting to influence the consensus that emerges from the negotiation sessions. Here the balance the agency must maintain is delicate. On the one hand, the agency cannot be party to an agreement that it determines to be illegal or bad public policy or simply infeasible. On the other, the agency cannot be in the position of reserving the right to reject the consensus after it has been reached simply because it is not all the agency wished to accomplish. If the agency should adopt this latter stance the process could not be termed a negotiation and, in fact, is not substantially different from a modified public hearing that is commonly used in informal rulemaking.[52]

Once the basic criteria are satisfied and a regulatory negotiation is undertaken, operating principles become important. Most who have written on the topic agree that a regulatory negotiation requires the presence of a skilled *convenor*, who facilitates group meetings and moves the group to consensus.[53] The most important qualifications that the individual convenor must possess is objectivity, both real and perceived. However effective an individual's facilitation skills might be, they will be of little consequence if he or she is perceived to be favoring one or more interests. The convenor may adopt an aggressive style, but his or her role must be confined to identifying areas of real or potential agreement and moving discussions along. The convenor is also needed to maintain the operating protocols for the negotiation. Each such group must, at the outset of the deliberations, establish a set of guidelines for the conduct of meetings and a decision rule as to what will constitute a consensus for the group. This is obviously crucial. A supposed benefit of regulatory negotiation is that its results—the rule—is developed and accepted by the group. This is supposed to promote better information about the rule and ultimately higher rates of voluntary compliance. This goal will be difficult to achieve if those involved in the negotiations do not make an initial commitment to accept the consensus of the group, however it is defined.

The values and ideas that underlie the concept of regulatory negotiation have much to commend them. They represent a significant departure from the way rules are usually written. But it took time for regulatory negotiation to be accepted by those involved in rulemaking. As noted earlier, the roots of regulatory negotiation can actually be traced to the early years of this century when, under the authority of the Fair Labor Standards Act, representatives of labor and management routinely met with agency officials to set rules on workplace matters. The idea gained momentum in the 1980s, spurred by a formal endorsement of regulatory negotiation by the Administrative Conference of the United States and consideration by Congress of a bill that would provide general authority for its use in rulemaking. The Negotiated Rulemaking Act ultimately became law in 1990.[54] It did not mandate regulatory negotiation, but it did encourage its use and, more important, it established a set of principles and operating guidelines for agencies to follow when they chose to use the technique.

Several authorizing statutes now mandate the use of regulatory negotiation for rulemaking affecting certain programs. Among these are several programs in the Department of Education and rules dealing with the use of radioactive isotopes in health care issued by the

Nuclear Regulatory Commission.[55] An interesting and potentially significant variation on the technique was recently enacted in authorizing legislation for the Federal Aviation Administration. In that bill the Aviation Rulemaking Advisory Committee (ARAC) was established. As designed, it would be an advisory committee, composed and convened in the traditional way, that would have responsibility for actually developing FAA regulations in many different areas using the same principles of consensual decision making that form the basis for regulatory negotiation. As of mid-1992 the advisory committee was considering thirty-one areas in which rules were being contemplated, and, as an official document states, the plan is that "ARAC ultimately will be the primary source of the FAA's rulemaking program." [56]

At this writing most major departments and agencies of the federal government have at least experimented with regulatory negotiation, and some, such as the Environmental Protection Agency, have made a major commitment to its use. The subject matter of rules for which negotiated rulemaking has been attempted varies widely, from the EPA's limitations on emissions from woodstoves to limitations on the flight time of crews on commercial airliners. There have been many successes and notable failures. Two highly publicized instances of the latter were rules dealing with the protection of farm workers from pesticides and the occupational exposure to benzene. In the case of the farm workers, the groups that joined the negotiation were deeply divided on fundamental values; in the latter, complex and difficult technical and scientific issues could not be fully resolved. But even in these instances, both the participants and the agencies that were affected acknowledged that the information and insights gained during the bargaining sessions were very helpful and contributed to better proposals when they were finally issued by the agency.[57]

Negotiated rulemaking is now a mature concept with a considerable, and largely positive, track record in the development of rules. Still, even though the process may save money and time in the long run, participants, who generally report positively about their experience with the technique, do have some common and persistent complaints. By far the most significant is the extraordinary commitment of time that a participant in a regulatory negotiation must make. Preparation for negotiation sessions, which includes consultation within one's own organization regarding positions and bargaining strategies, and the regulatory negotiation sessions themselves are demanding activities that can wreak havoc with normal work responsibilities and travel budgets.[58] Thus, when deciding whether to become involved, participants must weigh the benefits and costs against what they might gain from a more conventional rulemaking.

These issues and obstacles notwithstanding, it is apparent that regulatory negotiation will continue to provide special opportunities for widespread and substantial participation for the foreseeable future. The technique is grounded in principles that are unassailable. When the process works well all current indications are that litigation rates are quite low. No systematic evidence is available about ease of implementation and compliance, but the twin strengths of voluntary concurrence with the rule and full information about its content and intent certainly promote the flow of these intended benefits. Whether used on a case-by-case basis or institutionalized in a manner similar to the FAA model, participation in the form of regulatory negotiation is a permanent part of contemporary rulemaking.

ACTUAL PATTERNS OF PARTICIPATION

Let us now shift our focus to the participants themselves. The opportunities notwithstanding, participation in rulemaking still requires a great deal from those who would seek to influence its results. Opportunities to participate do not ensure that participation will actually occur, and the act of participation does not guarantee the participant success. So it is important to determine who participates in rulemaking, why they do it, the devices they employ, and the successes they achieve.

There are prerequisites to participation in rulemaking: an awareness that a rule is being developed, an understanding of how the rule will affect one's interests, a familiarity with the opportunities available for participation, the resources and technical expertise needed to respond, and, when necessary, the ability to mobilize others to join in the effort to influence the agency decision makers. These requirements mean that in most instances the most frequent participants in rulemaking will not be single individuals but, rather, groups, organizations, and firms. These collectivities are more likely to be aware of the importance of rules, possess detailed knowledge of how rules under development will affect their interests, be familiar with the means for influencing agency decisions, and have the resources needed to participate effectively. For this reason I will focus on interest groups, broadly defined, in this examination of the participants in rulemaking. For our purposes, interest groups will be defined as any organization that attempts to influence public policy. This includes companies, business and trade associations, unions, other levels of government, and the so-called public interest groups.

Most of what is known about participation in rulemaking comes from three sources: case studies of individual rulemakings and rulemaking programs, analyses of official records of government agencies, and surveys of interest groups. There are now a substantial number of case studies of rulemaking. Analyses of official rulemaking records and surveys of interest groups pertaining specifically to their involvement in the development of rules are as rare as hens' teeth. Therefore, for this book I undertook two such studies, and the results are reported in the paragraphs that follow. The first is an analysis of all rules published in the *Federal Register* from the beginning of December 1990 through June 1991. The preambles of published rules contain information on the public's response to the notice of proposed rulemaking and on the changes made in the original proposal as a result of this participation. The selection of the time period was arbitrary, but it was long enough to draw a reasonable sample of rules written by the federal government. I examined patterns in the solicitation and receipt of public comments and the manner in which agencies responded to the comments that were received. To supplement the material in the *Federal Register*, I conducted a survey of Washington-based interest groups in order to get a more complete picture of interest group participation in the rulemaking process. Approximately 180 groups and organizations responded, representing all sectors of the interest group community and paralleling closely the composition of groups in earlier surveys that have examined the involvement of interest groups in various types of political action. As important, the groups that responded to the survey interact with virtually every significant rulemaking agency of the federal government, ensuring representativeness on this important dimension as well. Consequently, the results of the survey should fairly represent the general situation regarding interest group participation in rulemaking.[59]

DOES PARTICIPATION ACTUALLY HAPPEN?

Simply because a large number of opportunities exist for a group to get involved in rulemaking does not mean that it actually does so. Groups may lack the concern and capabilities listed above, there may be fewer opportunities than there appear to be, or the agencies may take actions to avoid or otherwise frustrate participation. Evidence of avoidance of rulemaking in favor of other policy-making devices was noted earlier, as was the infrequency with which certain procedures are actually used. And, in fact, the available evidence we can examine to determine whether participation actually occurs is somewhat mixed.

If we were to rely solely on case studies, we would immediately conclude that participation by interest groups is a prominent part of all rulemaking. In his classic study of the rule that mandated warning labels on cigarette packages, *Smoking and Politics*, A. Lee Fritschler recounts the efforts of the tobacco industry, the advertising industry,

TABLE 5-1   Number of Rules, Rules with Notices, and Rules with
Comments, January-June 1991

	Rules	Rules with notices of proposed rulemaking	Rules with prior notice that generated public comment
January	338	162 (48%)	91 (56%)
February	227	106 (46%)	62 (58%)
March	367	175 (48%)	101 (58%)
April	409	141 (34%)	93 (66%)
May	343	138 (40%)	89 (64%)
June	301	127 (42%)	74 (58%)
Total	1,985	849 (43%)	510 (60%)

health groups, and consumer groups to influence the Federal Trade
Commission. A major study of the effluent guideline program, which
produces rules limiting water pollution, found constant involvement
by interest groups attempting to adjust the level of regulation. Ross
Cheit's case studies of four separate rulemakings that established safety
standards found participation to be common, as has research into the
development of agricultural marketing orders and the setting of
health-related workplace rules. William West analyzed rulemaking at
the Federal Trade Commission and also found participation by groups,
albeit those who were well-organized and with ample resources.[60]
Conversely, if one were to rely solely on the information found in the
preambles of final rules published in the Federal Register, one might
reach a very different conclusion (Table 5-1).

The infrequency of notices of proposed rulemaking as shown in
the table is disturbing. Concerns have been raised in other studies that
agencies failed with some regularity to comply with the APA's notice
requirements.[61] An alternative explanation is that many rules are
exempted from prior notice requirements under one of the APA
provisions mentioned in Chapter 2. Another is that the agencies simply
neglected to mention the prior notice in the final rule. There is, at
present, insufficient information to determine whether these figures
are the result of evasion, legitimate exemptions, or a simple failure to
mention the notice in the final rule.

Even when notices are issued it does not appear that participation
is as frequent as the available case studies would lead us to believe. A
couple of factors should be considered, however, before we reach any
conclusions on this point. One likely reason for this discrepancy is the
type of rules and rulemaking programs that attracts the attention of

TABLE 5-2   Comparative Importance to Interest Groups of Involvement
in Rulemaking (percent)

Degree of importance	Lobbying Congress	Grassroots work	Political contributions	Litigation
Far less	9.8	12.2	16.3	13.5
Somewhat less	23.3	20.6	13.8	7.9
About the same	34.6	20.6	6.5	17.5
Somewhat more	17.3	29.0	18.7	16.7
Far more	15.0	17.6	44.7	44.4
As important or more important	66.9	67.2	69.9	78.6

scholars. In all the case studies cited above, the rule or rulemaking
programs being examined are prominent, with large potential effects
and frequently controversial issues. For these reasons they were highly
likely to attract serious attention from interest groups. The *Federal
Register* sample contains all rules, and we have seen that many rules are
quite minor, routine, and noncontroversial. These are not likely to
attract serious attention from interest groups because their individual
effects are small. For rules that are issued routinely or in serial fashion,
groups focus on influencing the general standards and procedures that
structure the entire program rather than trying to influence each
individual rule. Another possible explanation for these data that
indicate low participation rates is that other means by which groups
can affect rules do not appear in the preambles of rules. The information presented below demonstrates that responses to formal notices of
proposed rulemaking likely provide a very incomplete picture of the
forms and frequency of interest group participation.

Evidence from the survey of interest groups sheds more light on
the question of participation. Of the nearly 180 groups that responded,
approximately 80 percent reported that they participate in rulemaking.
Further, when asked what priority they placed on rulemaking, they
rated it as shown in Table 5-2. These results are significant for several
reasons. First, other studies of interest groups have demonstrated that
such groups take the work of administrative agencies seriously. But
they consistently rank work with agencies second to influencing
Congress or even lower in priority. The data in the table indicate that a
large majority of the groups in the survey rate work on rulemaking on
a par with or of greater importance than lobbying Congress, and it
clearly exceeds other forms of political action. Lowi has coined the
term *corridoring* to describe groups' efforts to persuade agencies to do

their bidding.[62] When stalking the corridors these groups are clearly in search of rules.

It is also interesting to note that it is common for these groups to take an interest in rules written by many different agencies. The respondents reported a range of one to ninety-nine, with a median figure of five.

Overall, evidence from case studies, the *Federal Register,* and the survey provide support for the notion that public participation in rulemaking is more than an ideal. Although it is not universal and its occurrence depends on the characteristics of the rule being developed, all the sources indicate that it is common and taken seriously by the interest group community. Opportunities to participate that have been developing for nearly one hundred years are being exploited, but by whom?

WHO PARTICIPATES?

The conventional wisdom and some scholarship would lead one to hypothesize that groups representing business interests participate in rulemaking more often than other types of groups. There are at least two reasons why this imbalance in participation is a reasonable expectation. First, business organizations have long been thought to have superior political resources and skills and are thus better positioned to influence a process that requires sophistication and staying power. Second, in an era of big government, the business community has more to lose than other groups—the poor, the elderly, environmentalists, consumers—who are often perceived to be the primary clients of the agencies writing rules. As James Q. Wilson has noted, people are more likely to get involved in politics and governmental decision making to save something that is threatened than to gain something new.[63] Rules and regulations often restrict the discretion businesses enjoy and impose costs for compliance. Business often has something real at stake when rulemaking is undertaken.

There are, however, reasons to doubt both of these propositions and to take an alternative view. As outlined above, many steps were taken in the 1960s and 1970s to facilitate participation by groups that might otherwise lack the capacity to get involved. In this way, Congress, the White House, and the courts moved to offset the traditional advantages enjoyed by business in the rulemaking process. Further, the Reagan-Bush years brought policies hostile to the traditional clients of many rulemaking agencies, giving nonbusiness groups plenty of good, defensive reasons to participate in rulemaking. Suddenly, they too had a lot at stake. The available evidence, once again, presents a mixed view on who participates.

TABLE 5-3   Interest Groups Reporting Participation in
Rulemaking Activities, by Type of
Organization (percent)

Type of organization	Rate of participation
Trade association	90
Business	88
Labor union	80
Citizens' group	59
Government	100
Other	55

As noted above, Fritschler found evidence of involvement by many types of groups. Business was certainly present but so too were health and consumer interests. Still, the study of effluent guidelines written by the EPA found participation by regulated industries far more common than participation by environmental groups. The authors of the study argue that the reason for this apparent imbalance may be a combination of ingrained bias and tactics. They note that environmental groups perceived the rulemakers in the EPA as kindred spirits who could be trusted to protect their interests. In effect, a different form of "capture" occurred that ensured environmental groups the results they wanted without the burdens of direct participation. A slightly different conjecture was that these groups concluded that their lack of comment and involvement would expedite the rulemaking process and ultimately lead to more and quicker pollution control than if the EPA was bogged down by having to respond to both industry and environmentalists.[64] Cheit, in his study of safety standards, also finds more frequent and more intense involvement by the regulated industries than by workers and consumers. But he too cautions against drawing conclusions from his observations. In several instances consumers were represented in rulemaking proceedings by those acting effectively as surrogates, such as the National Academy of Sciences. Cheit's work also makes it plain that business interests were not monolithic and were sometimes divided among themselves.[65] Substantial participation by both producers and handlers of the affected commodities, described by an analyst as "self-regulation," was found even in the agricultural marketing order program. These groups do not always see eye to eye. It does appear from this particular study, however, that the involvement of the ultimate consumers of the products regulated by the programs was nominal, at best. It calls into

TABLE 5-4   Budget and Staff Time Dedicated to Rulemaking, by Type of Organization (percent)

Type of organization	Average budget	Average staff
Trade association	15.5	20.2
Business	17.3	19.1
Labor union	2.8	10.6
Citizens' group	9.4	14.3
Government	41.7	42.7

question the effectiveness of the Carter administration program in opening these rulemakings to influence by the general public.[66]

The *Federal Register* reports on participation in such a way that patterns in participation by certain groups are difficult to discern. Frequently, the agencies publishing the final rules focus on the substance of comments received rather than the type of group from which they came. When groups are identified it is often a single, generic reference. There is, however, ample evidence of participation by groups other than business interests in the form of comments on proposed rules.

My survey of interest groups also provides evidence that participation in rulemaking is not the sole province of business interests. Table 5-3 lists the percentage of respondents in various group categories that reported being regularly involved in rulemaking, and Table 5-4 shows the percentages of budgets and staff time they dedicated to this activity.

These data indicate clearly that businesses and the trade associations that represent businesses are more often involved in rulemaking than are other groups and devote greater slices of their probably larger budgets and staffs to rulemaking. Is this evidence of clear dominance or possible disadvantage? A plausible, albeit speculative, case can be made for each. Like other surveys, this one revealed that businesses and trade associations outnumbered other types of groups. They reported larger budgets and staffs and had been in existence longer than other groups. With virtually all such business and trade association groups reporting involvement in rulemaking, a strong case can be made that their superior financial and human resources and experience leads to a degree of influence in rulemaking that others cannot match. But these data are not sufficient to establish such a case. The reason that fewer citizen organizations, a category that includes environmental and consumer groups, are involved in rulemaking could be because

TABLE 5-5 Concerns of Interest Groups When Participating in a Rulemaking, by Frequency Reported (percent)

Frequency	Quality of information supporting the rule	Clarity of the rule	Options for compliance	Time for compliance	Cost of compliance	Agency authority to issue the rule
Never	0.0	0.0	1.0	3.1	4.5	18.3
Occasionally	16.5	24.6	13.6	24.4	18.2	54.2
Almost always	83.4	75.4	85.6	72.5	77.2	27.5

these types of groups specialize more than business groups. Perhaps business and trade associations are so frequently threatened by rulemaking that comparatively fewer can afford to devote their attention elsewhere. Other data from the survey do indicate that businesses and trade associations are more likely than are citizens' groups to rank rulemaking ahead of other forms of political action. Still, is this evidence of their "defensive" posture or simply greater sophistication? Unfortunately, we just do not know.

So it appears that participation in rulemaking is a priority for many different types of groups. Both business and nonbusiness organizations have found substantial enough reasons to invest their time and energy in rulemaking. But what are the general issues that bring interest groups to rulemaking? To learn more about the concerns of groups, one of the survey questions asked the respondents to estimate how often they were concerned about a particular type of issue when they chose to get involved in rulemaking. What the respondents reported is shown in Table 5-5.

It is apparent from this table that rulemaking regularly presents interest groups with multiple issues that concern them. The frequency of concern about compliance issues provides another bit of evidence that may help to explain the higher rates of participation observed earlier by trade associations, businesses, and other levels of government. These are the most frequent targets of regulations that raise compliance issues and threaten to impose compliance costs.

MONITORING RULEMAKING, INFLUENCING RULES

It was noted earlier that for groups to be successful in the rulemaking process they must know what the agency is preparing to do and must use the mechanisms at their disposal to influence it. Neither the case study literature nor material found in the *Federal Register* is particularly instructive on the question of how interest groups monitor rulemaking agencies. In the case study literature, authors are generally concerned with the substance of the rulemaking in question rather than the details of how interest groups go about their work. And one would not expect to read about the monitoring behavior of interest groups in the preambles of final rules published in the *Federal Register*.

With regard to the use of available mechanisms to influence the course of rulemaking, the case study literature indicates substantial interaction during the course of a rulemaking, usually in the form of written comments, public hearings, and other, unspecified, forms of communication. The *Federal Register* usually refers to comments received. Since neither case studies nor the *Register* provides insights into the frequency with which various monitoring and influence mechanisms are used, or whether groups consider them effective, other sources must be explored.

The interest group survey included questions about monitoring and efforts to influence. First, respondents were asked the frequency with which they used various devices for monitoring rulemaking (Table 5-6). It is evident that groups use a host of different devices to monitor rulemaking, but some are used more often than others. The survey indicates that the *Federal Register*, professional newsletters, and networks of colleagues are used very often. Consultants are relied on infrequently. As we will see, the colleague networks are also prominent in efforts to influence rulemaking (Table 5-7).

The results shown in Tables 5-6 and 5-7 are quite interesting for a number of reasons. From Table 5-6 it is evident that interest groups do not rely on a single tactic; they employ several devices on a regular basis. Again, some tactics are preferred over others. The *Federal Register*, coalition formation, and contact with the agency both before and after the notice of proposed rulemaking appear to be used most often. More interesting, and potentially significant, are the interest groups' ratings of the effectiveness of the various tactics (Table 5-8). Here the results are somewhat different from the results on the techniques the groups actually use.

Coalition formation and informal contacts before the notice of proposed rulemaking is issued are perceived to be the most effective. On reflection, these results should not be surprising. Contact with an agency before it has committed itself to a particular proposal allows the interest group to influence the earliest thinking about the content of the rule.[67] Coalition formation increases the number of groups that will communicate a consistent message to an agency. Comments in the *Federal Register* and grass-roots mobilization are also viewed as effective. However effective informal contacts may be, groups can ill-afford to fail to put their views on the public record by providing written comments. Filing petitions, advisory committees, and participation in public hearings are not included in this table but emerged in the survey as the least effective, although not entirely useless. It is notable that nearly half of the respondents rate informal contacts after the notice of proposed rulemaking as highly effective. This may point to situations in which agencies are surprised by the results of public comment and work informally with interest groups to fix the proposed rule.

Informal communication between the interest group and the agency need not flow solely in one direction. Consequently, the respondents were asked how often, if ever, agencies contacted them during the course of rulemaking and the reasons for the contact (Tables

TABLE 5-6 Devices Employed by Interest Groups to Monitor Rulemaking, by Frequency of Use (percent)

Frequency	Federal Register	Agency digests	Consultants	Professional newsletters	Informal contacts with agency	Colleagues in other groups
Once a year or less	4.4	7.6	43.8	4.5	0.8	0.0
Couple of times a year	7.4	12.9	23.4	4.5	12.0	6.8
Once a month	11.1	26.5	14.1	18.0	31.6	22.7
Once a week	16.3	25.8	10.9	27.8	33.8	28.8
More than once a week	60.7	27.3	7.8	45.1	21.8	41.7

TABLE 5-7 Devices Employed by Interest Groups to Influence Rules, by Frequency of Use (percent)

Frequency	Written comments	Attendance at hearings	Formation of coalitions	Mobilization of grassroots support	Informal contact with agency before notice	Informal contact with agency after notice
Never	1.5	7.0	3.1	11.5	8.4	4.6
Occasionally	11.5	34.1	9.9	17.6	18.3	18.5
Regularly	9.9	20.2	26.0	25.2	22.1	21.5
Very frequently	23.7	23.3	40.5	25.2	21.4	26.2
Always	53.4	15.5	20.6	20.6	29.8	29.2

TABLE 5-8 Ratings by Interest Groups of the Effectiveness of Techniques (percent)

Effectiveness	Written comments	Attendance at hearings	Formation of coalitions	Mobilization of grassroots support	Informal contact with agency before notice	Informal contact with agency after notice
Least effective	4.6	12.5	0.8	7.8	6.8	10.9
Somewhat effective	11.5	24.2	8.5	17.8	8.3	21.1
Effective	29.8	30.5	21.5	24.8	13.6	18.8
Very effective	38.2	21.1	38.5	34.1	37.9	32.8
Most effective	16.0	11.7	30.8	15.5	33.3	16.4

TABLE 5-9   Agency-Initiated Contacts Reported
by Interest Groups, by Frequency
(percent)

Frequency	Interest groups reporting
Never	6.1
Infrequently	40.9
Regularly	33.3
Frequently	16.7
Always	3.0

5-9 and 5-10). These results suggest that public participation occurs on a regular basis in rulemaking even when interest groups do not initiate the involvement. Agencies are proactive at least regularly 50 percent of the time. It is not surprising that the most common reason for these contacts is to get information for the rule under development. Agencies need this kind of help, especially when dealing, as they often do, with production processes and technology or business practices. Some legislation contains specific provisions empowering agencies to collect this type of information. But these data suggest that agencies are attentive to politics, possible legal challenges, and the conditions they are likely to confront when they attempt to implement and enforce the rule under development. These are the major reasons why an agency would be concerned with a group's reactions to a proposed rule. Getting a group's reaction is not an uncommon reason for initiating contact. It enables an agency to predict the degree of difficulty it will confront if it chooses to move forward with its proposals. Interest groups are not shy about telling agencies when they are unhappy nor are they loath to threaten political and legal action should the agency proceed on an unacceptable course.

What is striking about these elements of the survey is the multidimensional nature of both monitoring and influencing behaviors among interest groups. Although the frequency of use and perceived effectiveness varies widely, no source of information or technique of influence has been abandoned entirely by the interest group community. The overall approach appears to be both sophisticated and substantial. The data on the relative effectiveness of influence mechanisms are especially compelling. They show that informal mechanisms and difficult-to-observe mechanisms for communicating views to agencies are used a great deal and are thought to be as or more effective than the traditional means—such as written comment—that figure so prominently in the procedural law and academic literature that per-

TABLE 5-10 Reasons Given by Interest Groups for Contact by Agency, by Frequency of Reason (percent)

Frequency of reason	Information for rule	Guidance content	Group's reaction	Group's support of rule
Never	5.6	15.2	10.5	42.3
Infrequently	30.2	37.6	29.8	28.5
Regularly	26.2	31.2	30.6	15.4
Frequently	23.8	10.4	23.4	9.8
Always	14.3	5.6	5.6	4.1

tains to rulemaking. But a final issue remains. Does all this effort devoted to participation in rulemaking yield any results?

DOES PARTICIPATION MATTER?

In his influential article that appeared in the *Harvard Law Review*, titled "The Reformation of American Administrative Law," Richard Stewart argued that "interest representation" was the primary function of our contemporary bureaucracy and the administrative procedures it uses to make decisions.[68] If his analysis is correct, we would expect participation to be the single most important element in rulemaking, for it is through this device that bureaucrats learn what these varied interests want. It is important, then, to learn how agencies act when the preferences of interest groups are revealed. It is difficult when interests are at odds, because some must win and some must lose.

Determining whether interest groups that participate get what they want is an analytical task as difficult as it is important. Much must be known about the law that established the boundaries of the rulemaking, the true preferences of the groups affected, the accuracy of the communication of those preferences to the decision makers in the agency, and the benefits the rule bestows and the costs it imposes. For each of these dimensions, questions arise. How does the authorizing statute increase or limit the prospects for those who would participate in the rulemaking? In addition to the obvious procedural provisions that establish opportunities for comment and hearing of various sorts, other parts of a statute can be important. If, for example, the law requires agencies to base their rules on rigorous assessments of risk to human health and safety, the fact that some of the information needed to conduct such studies is in the possession of the regulated community may increase their ability to participate. As Harter has argued, the current rulemaking process often leads interests to distort their true positions for strategic purposes.[69] Finally, only the most rigorous form of program evaluation can establish the real benefits and costs that emerge from a rulemaking. For these and other reasons, linking participation to outcomes for selected interests is a most formidable undertaking. A definitive statement on the issue is well beyond the scope of this book. Still, the *Federal Register*, the case studies, and survey results provide some insights into the effectiveness of participation in rulemaking.

At the most basic level it is important to learn whether agencies take public participation as seriously as interest groups do. Evidence from all sources indicates clearly that agencies take public comments very seriously indeed. As noted above, interest groups believe that their comments, whether in writing or delivered less formally, are effective and that agencies frequently seek out their views. An examination of the *Federal Register* confirms that comments are carefully recorded and agencies respond to their contents in the preambles of final rules. This is not to say that agencies agree with all or even the bulk of the comments that are submitted. For the first half of 1991 an analysis of agencies' responses in the preambles of individual rules found that they disagreed with comments nearly twice as often as they agreed with them. Taken alone, however, these statistics are not very useful. There was no way of categorizing accurately the source of many comments, nor was there any way of knowing how important a given issue was to the group making the comment. So a review of the *Federal Register* will not answer these types of important questions. It does, however, resolve the question of whether agencies take comments from the public seriously.

Case studies provide yet another view on the matter. Most case studies deal with rules that have substantial consequences for businesses of one kind or another. Thus, the question they are most likely to address is whether business interests dominate or succeed disproportionately in their efforts to influence rulemaking. The case study literature is instructive, not because it yields an unequivocal answer to this important question but because it demonstrates the complexity of the issue. There are examples of programs that are seemingly dominated by what we would call business interests. One example is the agricultural marketing order program. The analysis of that rulemaking program made it quite clear that the producers and handlers of the regulated agricultural commodities dominated the committees from which the rules originated. But, at the same time, there was a degree of conflict between these different business interests that effectively prevented either of them from dominating the process. And, although representatives of consumers were rather few and far between, the study concluded that the Department of Agriculture, which holds the ultimate authority for issuing the marketing orders, served, at least on occasion, as an effective check on those business interests. The dominance of decision-making processes and rulemaking outcomes by business is not apparent in other studies, however. The cigarette labeling case is a prominent example of strong opposition by a powerful industry that was ultimately unsuccessful. Cheit's case studies provide additional examples of business interests faring poorly at the hands of rulemakers. Safety standards set for grain elevators by the Occupational Safety and Health Administration that he examined were opposed by operators "with vigor." [70] Three different trade associations became involved with the Consumer Product Safety Commission's rule relating to woodstoves, but Cheit found that collectively "they were barely more effective than no association at all." [71] When that same commission issued a rule related to ventilation for gas-fired space heaters, the Gas Appliance Manufacturers Association immediately petitioned to have it revoked.[72] When the Federal Aviation Administration, reacting to a recent disaster in which fire killed passengers on an Air Canada flight, issued regulations governing fire extinguishers, congressional pressure for action completely eclipsed any influence of the industry.[73] In their study of water pollution rules written by the Environmental Protection Agency, Wesley Magat and his colleagues at Resources for the Future found that affected industries commented on the standards far more often than environmental and other nonbusiness groups. Their comments were usually critical of the rules, but Magat and his colleagues found they had, at best, limited success in obtaining the changes they desired.[74]

Should we conclude from these cases that business lacks influence in the rulemaking process? Certainly not. These are but a handful of studies from which no generalizations about the overall influence of business interests can be drawn. Case studies, as noted earlier, are often done on rules selected because of their prominence and the controversy that attended their development. Business interests may be powerful, but they are not politically omnipotent. More important, the case studies demonstrate that business interests do gain important concessions in rulemaking even when they are not able to achieve all they wanted. The cigarette labeling rule did not, at least when it was first issued, make the warning to consumers as strong as it might have been. The grain elevator rule contained a standard which, although opposed by industry, was eight times less stringent than the most demanding alternative that OSHA had considered. In the matters of the unvented gas space heaters, the trade association representing the manufacturers was ultimately successful in getting the commission's rule revoked, but the manufacturers then faced the uncertainty of state and local level regulation. The gas space heater rule is also interesting because industry itself was split on it. While the trade association clearly opposed it, Cheit notes that "some major retailers saw a clear advantage in federal regulation." [75] What prompted this unexpected support was the fear of what might happen if state or local governments began acting on the issue. Finally, in the case of water quality regulations, the analysts found evidence of success for a portion of the companies studied. It appears from their data that companies represented by large trade associations with plentiful resources obtain somewhat less stringent standards than other types of firms. [76]

One of the most important things the case studies demonstrate is that the relationship between rulemaking agencies and business groups varies from program to program and probably from rule to rule. Conditions can be remarkably different. The amount of discretion the statute being implemented allows; the amount of pressure on the agency from Congress, the White House, and the courts; the quality of information at the agency's disposal and who controls it; the degree to which business perceives benefits or costs; the ability of the business community to organize a response to the agency's initiative; and the degree of opposition to the business position from other organized interests are some of the factors that vary from rule to rule.

Before leaving the matter of influence through participation, we should review survey data. Groups who participate in rulemaking do so to get what they want. Success, or the lack of it, will certainly affect future participation. Accordingly, it should be interesting to determine what groups think about their ability to influence the content of rules when they get involved in rulemaking. Respondents were asked how often they achieved what they had set out to achieve. The results are summarized in Table 5-11. Virtually no group characterized itself as completely successful or unsuccessful. More than 80 percent consider themselves able to influence the particular agency 50 to 75 percent of the times they get involved in rulemaking. This is a very optimistic assessment, and there are several reasons to question these self-evaluations that point to high levels of success. Organizations in the business of representing the interests of their members before the government have clear incentives to present themselves as successful in their efforts. If an organization reported that it lost consistently, the members might wonder about the shrewdness and influence of the Washington representative. At the same time, if it were to present itself as the winner in all cases, the members might begin to question the difficulty of the task they were paying to support. So another perspective of effectiveness of interest groups is needed. Research done recently by Scott Furlong as a doctoral student at The American University provides an alternative set of views on the effectiveness of

TABLE 5-11   Success in Influencing Rulemaking
Reported by Interest Groups
(percent)

Frequency of success	Interest groups reporting
Never	0.0
One-quarter of the time	15.9
Half of the time	40.9
Three-quarters of the time	42.4
Always	0.8

interest group participation in rulemaking. Instead of asking the groups, he directed the question to the rulemaking agencies. He asked agency respondents to estimate on a scale of 0 (never) to 10 (always) the frequency with which they made changes in rules under development as a result of comments from various types of groups. The results were averaged for each type of organization. Table 5-12 contains a summary of the results.[77]

The rulemakers are somewhat less sanguine about the ability of interest groups to influence their decisions than are the groups themselves. It is interesting to note how little difference there is between the various types of groups (with the exception of labor unions) with regard to the influence they believe they carry with the rulemakers themselves. Of course, these numbers must be considered in light of another kind of potential bias. Agency rulemakers are by now quite sensitive to charges of "unresponsiveness" and "capture" by special interests. Very low or very high scores on this question could be interpreted as an unwillingness to listen to the public or, alternatively, a willingness to serve as a doormat. The responses group curiously around the mid-point between agencies' turning a deaf ear to clienteles or regulated entities and doing whatever it is they are told. But it should be noted that the type of even-handedness suggested in the survey has been observed in other studies of regulatory decision making as well.[78]

The diverse, but still far from complete, body of evidence on participation in rulemaking lends support to Stewart's concept of "interest representation." It is clear that the opportunities to partici-pate, which have grown and diversified during the past several decades, have created a rulemaking process in which interest groups are major forces. The case studies, information from the *Federal Register*,

TABLE 5-12 Frequency of Changes by Agencies to
Rulemakings Based on Participation by
Interest Groups, by Type of
Organization

Type of organization	Average number of changes
Trade association	4.6
Business	4.0
Labor union	2.1
Citizens' group	4.1
Other government agencies	4.7

Source: Scott Furlong, *Interest Group Influence on Regulatory Policy*
(Ph.D. dissertation, School of Public Affairs, The American University,
1992).

and results of surveys confirm that the vast majority of interest groups
are aware of the importance of rulemaking. They devote resources to it
and use a variety of devices to monitor what rulemakers are doing.
Groups employ numerous tactics to influence the course and outcomes
of rulemaking. They consider themselves quite successful in achieving
their objectives. The rulemakers acknowledge their presence, listen
attentively to what they have to say, and are convinced by their
arguments with some degree of regularity. The outcome of each
rulemaking is influenced by many variables. Participation by the
public is clearly one of the most important of these.

There are other influences that have not yet been discussed at
great length, however. Each of the major branches of government—
Congress, the president, and the judiciary—have compelling reasons to
take an interest in the development of rules. Their review of rules
during and after their development by agencies constitutes another
major influence on the rulemaking process. It is to the review of these
three branches that we now turn.

NOTES

1. Phillip Harter, "Negotiating Regulations: A Cure for the Malaise," *Georgetown Law Journal* 71 (1982): 17, 31.
2. Ibid., p. 14. See also Glen O. Robinson, *American Bureaucracy* (Ann Arbor:
University of Michigan Press, 1991), pp. 128-129.
3. Attorney General's Committee on Administrative Procedure, *Administrative
Procedure in Government Agencies*, S. Doc. 8, 77th Cong., 1st sess., 1941, p. 103
(hereafter cited as Attorney General's Committee).
4. Ibid., part 7, Department of the Interior, p. 66.

5. Ibid., p. 114.
6. Ibid.
7. Ibid., p. 104.
8. Ibid.
9. Ibid.
10. Ibid., p. 105.
11. Ibid., pp. 103-104.
12. Ibid., p. 104.
13. Ibid.
14. Ibid., pp. 105-108.
15. Ibid., pp. 108-111.
16. Ibid., p. 110.
17. David Rosenbloom, "Public Law and Regulation," in *Handbook of Public Administration*, ed. Jack Rubin, Bartley Hildreth, and Gerald Miller (New York: Marcel Dekker, 1989), p. 556.
18. For interesting perspectives on the significance of notice and comment provisions of the Administrative Procedure Act by two men who were deeply involved in the Attorney General's Committee, see Kenneth Culp Davis and Walter Gelhorn, "Present at the Creation: Regulatory Reform before 1946," *Administrative Law Review* 38 (1986): 511-533.
19. Jeffrey Berry, Kent Portney, and Ken Thomson, "Empowering and Involving Citizens," in *Handbook of Public Administration*, ed. James Perry (San Francisco: Jossey-Bass, 1989), p. 209.
20. See, for example, David Mazmanian and Jeanne Neubauer, *Can Organizations Change? Environmental Protection, Citizen Participation and the Corps of Engineers* (Washington, D.C.: Brookings Institution, 1979).
21. Office of the Chairman, *A Guide to Federal Agency Rulemaking* (Washington, D.C.: Administrative Conference of the United States, 1983), p. 70.
22. Ibid., pp. 67, 68.
23. Ibid., pp. 67-70.
24. Ibid., pp. 67-68, 69.
25. Ibid., p. 68.
26. Ibid., pp. 67, 68-69.
27. Office of Management and Budget, *Improving Government Regulations: A Progress Report* (Washington, D.C.: Executive Office of the President, 1979), p. 9.
28. Ibid., pp. 13-15.
29. Ibid., p. 15.
30. Ibid., pp. 15-16.
31. Ibid., p. 16.
32. James Anderson, "Agricultural Marketing Orders and the Process and Politics of Self-Regulation," *Policy Studies Review* 2 (1982): 97-111.
33. Mancur Olson, *The Logic of Collective Action* (New York: Schocken Books, 1965); James Q. Wilson, "The Politics of Regulation," in *The Political Economy*, ed. Thomas Ferguson and Joel Rogers (New York: Sharpe, 1987), pp. 84-88.
34. Office of Management and Budget, *Improving Government Regulations*, p. A6.
35. Ibid.
36. Ibid., pp. A29-A30.
37. Ibid., p. A45.
38. Ibid.
39. Ibid., p. A55.

40. Ibid., p. A78.
41. Ibid., pp. A78-A79.
42. Ibid., p. A79.
43. Robert Anthony, "Interpretive Rules, Policy Statements, Guidelines, Manuals and the Like—Should Agencies Use Them to Bind the Public?" *Duke Law Journal* 41 (1992): 1131-1384.
44. Berry, Portney, and Thomson, "Empowering and Involving Citizens," pp. 209-210.
45. Theodore Lowi, "Two Roads to Serfdom: Liberalism, Conservatism and Administrative Power," *American University Law Review* 36 (1987): 295-322.
46. Executive Office of the President, *Regulatory Program of the United States Government* (Washington, D.C.: 1991), app. 3.
47. Christine Triano and Nancy Watzman, *All the Vice President's Men: How the Quayle Council on Competitiveness Secretly Undermines Health, Safety and Environmental Programs* (Washington, D.C.: OMB Watch/Public Citizen, 1991), p. i.
48. Harter, "Negotiating Regulations," p. 28.
49. Ibid., p. 49.
50. Ibid., pp. 45-67.
51. Ibid., p. 46.
52. Ibid., pp. 57-67.
53. Ibid., pp. 70-71.
54. 5 U.S.C., 581-590.
55. David Pritzker and Deborah Dalton, eds., *Negotiated Rulemaking Sourcebook* (Washington, D.C.: Administrative Conference of the United States, 1990), p. 346.
56. Federal Aviation Administration, *Regulatory Course: ARM Presentation* (San Antonio, Texas, 1992), p. 21.
57. Pritzker and Dalton, *Negotiated Rulemaking Sourcebook*, pp. 331, 336.
58. Ibid., p. 859.
59. The composition of the respondent pool for this survey is similar to that found in Kay Scholzman and John Tierney, *Organized Interests and American Democracy* (New York: Harper and Row, 1986). They compare as follows:

Organization type	Kerwin study (%)	Scholzman and Tierney study (%)
Trade association	54	45
Business	11	21
Labor union	3	3
Citizens' group	13	14
Government	2	3
Research, think tank	3	NA
Religious	1	NA
Other	13	13

Note: Three respondents did not identify themselves in the Kerwin study; $N = 178$ (Kerwin study); NA = not applicable.

60. A. Lee Fritschler, *Smoking and Politics*, 4th ed. (Englewood Cliffs, N.J.: Prentice Hall, 1989); Wesley Magat, Alan Krupnick, and Winston Harrington, *Rules in the Making* (Washington, D.C.: Resources for the Future, 1986); Ross Cheit, *Setting Safety Standards: Regulation in the Private and Public Sectors* (Berkeley: University of California Press, 1990); Anderson, "Agricultural Marketing Orders"; Mark Rothstein, "Substantive and Procedural Obstacles to OSHA Rulemaking: Reproductive Hazards as an Example," *Boston College Environmental Affairs Law Review* 12 (1985): 627; William West, *Administrative Rulemaking: Politics and Processes* (New York: Greenwood Press, 1985).

61. West, *Administrative Rulemaking*, pp. 84-85.

62. Lowi, "Two Roads to Serfdom," p. 307.

63. Wilson, "Politics of Regulation," p. 85.

64. Magat, Krupnick, and Harrington, *Rules in the Making*, p. 40.

65. Cheit, *Setting Safety Standards*, p. 141.

66. Anderson, "Agricultural Marketing Orders."

67. Stephen Breyer, *Regulation and Its Reform* (Cambridge, Mass.: Harvard University Press, 1982), p. 107.

68. Richard Stewart, "The Reformation of American Administrative Law," *Harvard Law Review* 88 (1975): 1667-1711.

69. Harter, "Negotiating Regulations," pp. 449-450.

70. Cheit, *Setting Safety Standards*, p. 58.

71. Ibid., p. 110.

72. Ibid., p. 141.

73. Ibid., pp. 71-72.

74. Magat, Krupnick, and Harrington, *Rules in the Making*, pp. 39, 147-148, 157.

75. Cheit, *Setting Safety Standards*, p. 141.

76. Magat, Krupnick, and Harrington, *Rules in the Making*, p. 157.

77. Scott Furlong, *Interest Group Influence on Regulatory Policy* (Ph.D. diss., School of Public Affairs, The American University, 1992).

78. Terry Moe, "Control and Feedback in Economic Regulation: The Case of the NLRB," *American Political Science Review* 79 (1986).

CHAPTER 6

Oversight of Rulemaking

Holding those who write rules accountable for the decisions they make and the manner in which they make them is critical to the maintenance of our democracy. Earlier we discussed the shaky constitutional status of a governmental process in which bureaucrats, for whom no one votes, formulate law. But the legitimacy of rulemaking is bolstered considerably when the people are secure in the knowledge that rulemaking is being conducted under the close scrutiny of elected officials and judges sworn to uphold the Constitution and laws of the nation. Mechanisms of accountability can ensure that the original intent of congressional statutes is truly reflected in implementing regulations. The will of national majorities, expressed every four years in presidential elections, can be translated into rules if presidents can find means to hold the rulemakers accountable. The judiciary, with whom we entrust the structure and operation of a constitutional democracy, can preserve basic legal principles if given the opportunity to examine the content of rules and the processes by which they are formulated.

In this chapter, I will describe the mechanisms of accountability that the constitutionally established branches of government—Congress, the president, and the judiciary—have developed and use to keep rulemaking in check. Some of these are quite direct and are obvious and familiar even to casual students of government. Others, as recent studies have argued, are more subtle, implicit, and maybe more effective. A more difficult question, which will be explored but not fully answered, is how well these various mechanisms actually function in directing the work of rulemakers. A full consideration of accountability must go beyond simple descriptions of devices at the disposal of the three branches of government and general assessments of how well they work. In this chapter the objectives of each of the branches as they attempt to influence the course of rulemaking will also be explored, and we will find that each branch seeks to accomplish different objectives when it oversees rulemaking. These differences in perspective and priorities lead to a struggle for control of the entire rulemaking process. This contest for supremacy in rulemaking has occasionally erupted in confrontation and conflict between the branches, most often between the president and Congress. But the courts have joined the fray as well, sending messages to rulemakers that at times make it difficult for them to act as the obedient agents of their legislative and executive superiors.

There is more to learn in this interbranch struggle for the hearts and minds of rulemakers than another lesson in petty politics or institutional hubris. This competition has had a profound effect on the rulemaking process and the contents of the rules it produces. More significant, perhaps, is what these frequent and increasingly visible fights tell us about the status of rulemaking and its importance to the branches of government that the Founding Fathers established to control the course and content of public policy. The amount of attention devoted to holding rulemakers accountable and the effort each branch has invested to gain supremacy together stand as profound testimony to the degree to which rulemaking has come to occupy the center of our public policy process. In its behavior, each branch has acknowledged during the past several decades that their symbiotic relationship with the rulemaking process can easily slip into one of dominance and dependence. In a very real sense these institutions are struggling to prevent the servant from becoming the master; to prevent what is supposed to be a secondary function from becoming one that overwhelms their constitutionally established powers and authority. Each branch's activities will be considered separately, and a brief section at the end will highlight the rivalries, and occasional cooperation, that characterize efforts to hold rulemaking accountable. We begin with the institution in which all rulemaking originates: Congress.

ACCOUNTABILITY AND THE CONGRESS

Congress has many devices at its disposal to hold those who write rules accountable. At the most fundamental level it can render the issue of accountability moot by the care it takes in drafting statutes. Congress is able to write laws so precisely and completely that no rules are needed to achieve the purpose of the statute. Alternatively, Congress can establish clear expectations regarding the types of rules agencies write, the content of those rules, the methods by which they are developed, and the time taken to complete the rulemaking task.

Once the delegation of authority to write rules has been crafted, Congress has at its disposal numerous oversight techniques. Some of these are direct; others are indirect and subtle. In the latter instance the effectiveness of indirect means of control has only recently been explored seriously in the literature. Whatever the approach, experience demonstrates that each of the oversight devices is potentially effective.

LIMITING DISCRETION THROUGH PROSPECTIVE STATUTORY CONTROLS

The best way for Congress to ensure the accountability of those who write rules is to eliminate or severely constrict the range of discretion they enjoy. As we have seen in earlier chapters, Congress has in fact clearly moved in this direction in one of the two critical dimensions of rulemaking. Chapter 2 documented the ever-increasing strictures that Congress has placed on the process of rulemaking. These obligations to employ certain procedures for public participation, particular types of analyses as bases for decisions, and specific criteria for establishing standards have grown remarkably during the last several decades.

THE IMPORTANCE OF PROCEDURE.   There is no question that each additional procedure a rulemaking agency is required to use restricts its freedom of action and causes it to produce information that it must then take into account in formulating the substance of the rule. Social scientists have argued persuasively that these additional procedures are anything but neutral. They assert that in imposing them on rulemakers Congress is not simply seeking some scientifically objective means for establishing a regulation or providing freer access to rulemakers by the general public. On the contrary, the procedural tinkerers in Congress are seeking to use process to achieve a substantive political result they are unable or unwilling to secure in the clear language of the statute. As the team of Matthew McCubbins, Roger Noll, and Barry Weingast put it in 1987: "Together, the legal constraints imposed by procedures and the incentives created by threat of sanction establish a decision-making environment that stacks the deck in agency policy in favor of constituencies important to political overseers."[1]

Still, we must acknowledge that precious little empirical evidence exists to indicate whether these additional procedures truly restrict rulemaking agencies on a regular basis. Evidence presented in Chapters 3 and 5 calls into question whether these additional procedural requirements, and even the minimal provisions of the Administrative Procedure Act, are actually observed by agencies in most rulemakings. Further, it is an exceedingly difficult task to determine whether procedures intended to rig rules to favor certain interests accomplish their intended purposes even when they are used. Given the fact that Congress often hides its intentions behind the twin veils of vagueness and procedural complexity, it may be very hard to determine just exactly which interests it was seeking to benefit in the first place. And if and when this detective job is accomplished, the analyst then faces the daunting task of determining which interest(s) won or lost, and to what extent.

Critics of Congress assail it for not being more specific in the substance of its delegations of authority to implementing departments and agencies. It could, according to these critics, avoid the disingenuousness of complex procedure and exorcise the demons of bureaucratic discretion by simply writing the laws so specifically that no important decisions are left in the hands of rulemakers. Theodore Lowi, a political scientist and long-standing skeptic of administrative discretion, prefers a system in which legislation evolves from the general to the increasingly specific.[2] This is, to a large extent, what has happened in many statutes that undergird contemporary social regulation. Many environmental programs, first enacted in the early 1970s, have by now been reauthorized and amended on several different occasions. Appropriations bills often provide additional substantive direction as well. The statutory bases for clean air and water programs are considerably more detailed today than they were two decades ago, because Congress has specified more fully the substances to be regulated and the techniques by which pollution control is to be achieved.

Despite this constant legislative activity the volume and importance of rulemaking has not abated. Congress has not achieved the type of prospective control over the content of rules that critics like Lowi would clearly prefer. The reasons for rulemaking that were outlined in the first chapter remain important. The demands from the public for action on an ever-increasing list of problems, technical and scientific complexity and uncertainty, conflict over goals, and political timidity combine to ensure that if Congress is to hold rulemakers in the bureaucracy accountable it will have to find ways other than the literal law to accomplish this objective.

DEADLINES AND HAMMERS.   Another prospective device to limit the discretion of those writing rules is the use of *deadlines* and *hammers.* The term *deadlines* is self-explanatory; hammers are provisions in statutes that will take effect on a certain date should the agency fail to issue an alternative regulation. Hammer provisions usually embody regulatory requirements that no one, including Congress, truly prefers. They are used to put pressure on agencies to expedite the rulemaking process. The Resource Conservation and Recovery Act, for example, called for a total ban on land disposal of wastes if the EPA did not produce alternative policies in the form of rules.[3] One can see why the various players involved—the agency, the affected parties, and Congress—might endeavor to make the completion of rules with hammer provisions a high priority.

Threat or not, and with or without accompanying hammer provisions, deadlines have become an increasingly popular accountability tool of Congress. A study cited by Benjamin Mintz and Nancy Miller estimated that as of 1987 Congress had enacted hundreds of statutory deadlines for the EPA alone.[4] The intent and effectiveness of such deadlines has been a matter of considerable discussion. In one very important sense a deadline may be the classic example of Congress's using an indirect method to achieve a substantive result. Many have noted that congressional deadlines are often hopelessly unrealistic. In addition to the normal inertia that attends any function that must be carried out in a large bureaucracy, rulemaking is an activity that Congress rarely funds at levels commensurate with the magnitude and complexity of the tasks involved. Congress imposes deadlines fully cognizant of the fact that agencies will be unable to meet them or in so doing will almost certainly produce an incomplete or flawed product. If Congress is seeking tactical advantage for a particular set of interests, a missed deadline or a bad rule is a fine outcome indeed. Why? Because these failures of the rulemaking process are subject to nearly immediate, and as we will see, searching, judicial review. The current dynamics of such review can lead to situations in which the litigating party, presumably a representative of the group that Congress seeks to benefit, may achieve a highly favorable judicial ruling. Recent research indicates that such decisions may effectively position the party bringing the lawsuit to exert a dominating influence over the content of the rule at issue.[5] The looming presence of the judiciary, combined with the unmistakable legislative intent of a fixed deadline, make this device the most powerful, and arguably the most predictable, indirect mechanism of accountability at the disposal of Congress.

MONEY.   We would be remiss if we were to overlook the power of the purse in our consideration of prospective mechanisms of accountability available to Congress. In the business of rulemaking the influence of budgeting has been passively negative. Theoretically, at least, budgets can be used to endow more generously those rulemaking projects that members of Congress want completed and to penalize those agencies who have failed to provide them the types of rules they prefer. When it comes to rulemaking, the budget is a very blunt instrument. There is no evidence, however, that Congress systematically funds particular rulemaking projects, or for that matter programs, in a way to suggest favoritism. It appears that all rulemaking projects are treated with equal amounts of neglect. Whatever additional funds agencies need to meet new rulemaking obligations in authorizing statutes must be drawn from regular appropriations for program operations. In recent years there has been what amounts to an inverse relationship between the rulemaking responsibilities established in authorizing legislation and the funding provided in appropriations. Although there is little evidence that Congress uses the budget process in a systematic way to punish agencies that produce rules not to the liking of their legislative masters, Congress does use appropriations bills to send substantive and procedural messages to agencies.[6] As we will see presently, our elected representatives use other means to register their displeasure with agency rulemakers. Hence, although it is a potential source of prospective control, the budget process does not appear to be a major mechanism of accountability.

PRINCIPALS, AGENTS, AND THE SUBTLETY OF PROSPECTIVE CONTROL

Political scientists who are concerned more generally about the relationship between Congress and the bureaucracy have debated about which party in that crucial relationship really exercises control. On one side are scholars like Lowi and William Niskanen, who view the bureaucracy as dominant, partially because of the degree of authority it has been delegated and partially because bureaucrats are thought to have certain strategic advantages in the relationship. Among the most important of these advantages was thought to be the possession of information about what public programs cost and how they actually work.[7] It has been a common assertion that oversight of the bureaucracy by Congress is flimsy, nonsystematic, and easily frustrated by canny bureaucrats.

More recently a different perspective has emerged in what has come to be called the principal-agent theory of legislative-bureaucratic relations.[8] In this model the principals are the elected officials in Congress and the White House; their agents are the bureaucrats, who are supposed to be carrying out their wishes and, ostensibly, the will of the people. Principal-agent theory acknowledges that each side of the relationship has distinctive goals and objectives, responds to different incentives, and has different tools at its disposal. Elected representatives seek to stay in office by providing for their constituents or avoiding blame when they fail to do so. Bureaucrats may be operating from a more complex set of objectives, ranging from the avoidance of work to the pursuit of their own personal policy agendas. The fundamental issue in principal-agent theory is if and how the former can effectively control the latter.

Scholars have argued that carefully structured administrative procedures, discussed above and in Chapter 2, and informal oversight, discussed below, are important and influential and that they are frequently ignored or denigrated by commentators who have simply not looked into the matter closely enough.[9] Some would argue that there are subtle forces at work in the relationship between Congress and the agencies when the latter performs its most important functions, including rulemaking.[10] These studies admonish scholars to avoid the error that occurs when they assume that, because bureaucrats are observed making decisions without any direct input by Congress, they are exercising meaningful discretion.[11] On the contrary, these scholars see an extensive network of subtle but powerful influences emanating from Congress that effectively curtails the exercise of bureaucratic discretion. As Randall Calvert, Matthew McCubbins, and Barry Weingast concluded in a frequently cited article:

> The analyst of agency policymaking must ask why the agency has the particular structure, procedures, jurisdiction, and personnel that it does; why particular leaders are in office at any given time; and what unspoken expectations agency personnel have about the conditions under which their elected overseers might invoke sanctions.[12]

This line of thinking strongly suggests that we cannot blithely dismiss prospective controls on rulemakers. On the contrary, those who write rules may, in many instances, be the faithful agents of legislators, neither exercising a great deal of choice nor desiring to do so.

OVERSEEING RULEMAKING PERFORMANCE

The intriguing and extremely important debate about the extent to which bureaucratic discretion in critical functions like rulemaking is truncated by prospective legislative controls does not foreclose a serious consideration of efforts by Congress to oversee agency performance. However effective, prospective controls are not likely to be foolproof, so "keeping a watchful eye," as one author puts it, is something Congress cannot avoid.[13] For some time it was fashionable to dismiss congressional oversight of administrative agencies as erratic, superficial, politically motivated, and largely ineffective. Now a new and quite different view is emerging. Advanced theoretical work, case studies, and more rigorous empirical efforts to study oversight argue that it is a formidable tool in the hands of Congress.

The major theoretical development in recent years that has promoted a different view of oversight is a challenge to the implicit assumption in earlier work that the function must be comprehensive and systematic in order to be meaningful. If we think about it for a moment, comprehensiveness in oversight is a mind-boggling prospect. Congress could do nothing else and still not cover the vast federal establishment in depth and on a regular basis. Expecting a truly systematic approach, however, is not unreasonable, and there is now reason to believe that there is in fact a method to what may appear unsystematic, if not random. Matthew McCubbins and Thomas Schwartz distinguish between two types of oversight—*police patrol* and the *fire alarm* variety.[14] *Police patrol* oversight is proactive, with Congress setting its own agenda for programs to review. As such, it would consist of the characteristics that the earlier critics found so lacking in oversight. *Fire alarm* oversight is a congressional response to a complaint filed by a constituent or other politically significant actor. When the alarm is sounded, Congress responds with one of many possible actions, ranging from a simple inquiry about the issue to a full-blown investigation, replete with hearings preceded by reports by the General Accounting Office. The authors argue that the fire alarm form of oversight is highly likely to be the most prevalent because it is the most efficient and effective for individual members of Congress. First, the mere fact of a complaint provides reason for inquiry, whereas a general police patrol may turn up nothing of concern. Further, the fire alarm type is really a hybrid of oversight and constituency service, an activity of compelling and enduring attractiveness to elected representatives. Finally, fire alarms can accumulate and provide Congress with good reasons to initiate oversight that more closely resembles the police patrol model in which whole programs of rulemaking, rather than a single rule, is the focus of the inquiry.

Case studies and more general assessments of oversight confirm that both the fire alarm and police patrol models of oversight are at work with regard to rulemaking. In his book *Signals from the Hill,* an award-winning analysis of congressional oversight of regulatory programs, Christopher Foreman provides the following list of activities that committees overseeing the Food and Drug Administration had engaged in:

- examine and pursue an "orphan-drug" program;
- take more effective action against pesticide residues on imported foods;
- delay action to ban the sugar substitute saccharin, "notwithstanding any other provision of law";
- study ways to expedite the approval of veterinary drugs for use in minor species;
- exercise caution in changing food labeling regulations;
- require the baby food industry "to monitor and report heavy

TABLE 6-1   Frequency of Use of Oversight Techniques, Ninety-fifth Congress

Technique	Mean	Number of cases	Rank
Staff communication with agency personnel	1.274	91	1
Member communication with agency personnel	2.802	86	9
Oversight hearings	2.561	89	3
Program reauthorization hearings	2.685	73	5
Hearings on bills to amend ongoing programs	2.756	70	7
Review of casework	3.551	87	13
Staff investigations and field studies (other than for preparation of hearings)	2.644	90	4
Analysis of proposed agency rules and regulations	2.800	90	8
Agency reports required by Congress	2.813	91	10
Program evaluations done by congressional support agencies	2.382	89	2
Program evaluations done by the agencies	2.954	87	11
Program evaluations done by "outsiders" (nongovernmental personnel)	3.227	88	12
Program evaluations done by committee staff personnel	2.696	89	6
Legislative veto	4.304	82	14

Source: Joel Aberbach, *Keeping a Watchful Eye* (Washington, D.C.: Brookings Institution, 1990), p. 132.

metal content—with particular emphasis on lead—of the food as it is received and after it is packaged." [15]

It is also revealing to examine the inventory of reports provided to Congress by the General Accounting Office. The GAO has occasionally supported congressional oversight investigations of whole rulemaking programs. Popular among the concerns of Congress when taking on programmatic issues are delay in the issuance of rules and the competence of a given agency with regard to its rulemaking responsibilities.[16]

TABLE 6-2   Effectiveness of Oversight Techniques, Ninety-fifth
Congress

Technique	Mean	Number of cases	Rank
Staff communication	1.430	86	1
Member communication	1.626	83	2
Oversight hearings	1.714	84	4
Program reauthorization hearings	1.688	61	3
Amendment hearings	1.750	60	5
Review of casework	2.694	72	14
Staff investigations and field studies	1.780	82	6
Analysis of proposed regulations	2.279	86	10
Agency reports	2.534	86	12
Congressional support agency program evaluations	2.000	88	8
Agency program evaluations	2.541	85	13
"Outsiders" program evaluations	2.523	84	11
Committee staff program evaluations	1.891	83	7
Legislative veto	2.085	35	9

Source: Joel Aberbach, *Keeping a Watchful Eye* (Washington, D.C.: Brookings Institution, 1990), p. 135.

There is also evidence of great variation in the devices that Congress uses to keep in touch with agencies that write regulations. In his book *Keeping a Watchful Eye,* Joel Aberbach surveyed congressional staff and, among other things, asked them to identify and rank in order of frequency and effectiveness various oversight mechanisms. Tables 6-1 and 6-2 summarize his results.

What is striking in these data, which refer to oversight as a general activity, is where the review of regulations ranks as regards both frequency and effectiveness. It is also quite possible, if not probable, that the issue that triggers many of the other forms of oversight is a rule or a rulemaking. No systematic analysis of these potential interactions are available, however.

Aberbach also provides his readers with information on the overall growth in oversight activity by Congress. Figure 6-1 charts increases in oversight days and compares them with the number of pages in the *Federal Register.* Aberbach cautions against any conclusions from this obvious correlation, but it is evident that a

Figure 6-1   Oversight Days and Pages in the *Federal Register,* 1961-1983

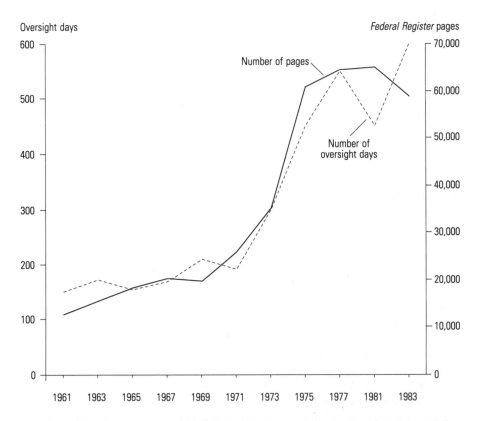

Oversight days   *Federal Register* pages

Number of pages

Number of
oversight days

1961   1963   1965   1967   1969   1971   1973   1975   1977   1981   1983

Source: Joel Aberbach, *Keeping a Watchful Eye* (Washington, D.C.: Brookings Institution, 1990), 45.

dramatic increase in the rate of oversight was coincident with the period associated with the explosion of social regulation in the 1970s.

The review of individual regulations cited in Aberbach's survey brings to mind an oversight mechanism that combines elements of the police patrol and fire alarm models and was the most powerful mechanism of accountability yet devised. The legislative veto was the most aggressive, intrusive, and potentially effective means of holding rulemakers accountable. Appearing first in this country in the 1930s, statutory provisions began to require government agencies to submit proposed rules to Congress for review and approval. At the peak of its use there were some 350 separate statutory provisions that allowed for the legislative veto.[17] Like the overall incidence of oversight, the greatest increase in the use of legislative veto provisions occurred during the period in which we experienced major increases in rule-making: the New Deal and the explosion of social regulation, as Table

TABLE 6-3   Legislative Vetoes Passed by Congress, by Decade

Decade	Number of acts	Number of provisions	Percentage increase in provisions over preceding decade
1932-1939	5	6	—
1940-1949	19	20	230
1950-1959	34	36	80
1960-1969	49	70	94
1970-1980	248	423	507

Source: Barbara Craig, *The Legislative Veto: Congressional Control of Regulation* (Boulder, Colo.: Westview Press, 1983), p. 27.

6-3 demonstrates.

The legislative veto combined elements of the police patrol and fire alarm models of oversight. Because they were directed at whole programs of rulemaking and were generally comprehensive in their scope, the police patrol model applied. But the mere existence of legislative veto provisions does not mean they were used. A fire alarm pulled by an interest group or a constituent could focus the power of the veto on a single rulemaking and stimulate members of Congress to invoke its authority.

Legislative veto provisions were richly varied in their form. Some called for congressional approval, others disapproval. Some vested power for action with both houses of Congress, others in just one, and still others granted authority to committees. Table 6-4 summarizes the various forms and the frequency of their use in statutory provisions.

Christopher Foreman provides insights into the dynamics of the legislative veto through several case studies. He examined two separate rules issued by the National Highway Transportation Safety Agency dealing with automobile passenger safety, two considered by the Federal Trade Commission covering used cars and the funeral industry, and the so-called saccharin ban considered by the Food and Drug Administration. Each case involved a distinctive form of the veto and ended differently. The NHTSA's interlocking-seatbelt rule was killed through a provision in the agency's 1974 reauthorization bill, but its subsequent rule requiring air bags survived an effort to invoke a two-house veto provision. The FTC's used-car rule was eliminated by a two-house veto in 1982, but its rule on funeral homes survived a persistent challenge in the House of Representatives. Intense opposition to the ban on saccharin forced the FDA to modify its approach, replacing a prohibition with a warning label. Foreman concludes that the political salience of the issue and the relative power of affected interests had

TABLE 6-4   Extent of the Legislative Veto, 1983

Types of legislative vetoes	Laws	Percentages	Provisions	Percentages
Congressional disapproval procedures, by rank				
1 Disapproval by either house passing a single resolution	60	47.6	103	53.1
2 Disapproval by both houses passing a concurrent resolution	45	35.7	64	33.0
3 Disapproval by both houses or alternatively by one house if such action is not disapproved by the other house	2	1.6	4	2.0
4 Disapproval by both houses passing and the president approving a joint resolution	6	4.8	9	4.6
5 Disapproval by committee (or committees) of either house	11	8.7	12	6.2
6 Disapproval by committees in both houses	2	1.6	2	1.0
7 Disapproval by both houses passing a concurrent resolution for certain regulations and by passing a joint resolution for other resolutions	0	0.0	0	0.0
8 Disapproval by two-thirds of both houses of Congress	0	0.0	0	0.0
Total	126	100.0	194	99.9[a]

(Table continues)

TABLE 6-4   *(Continued)*

Types of legislative vetoes	Laws	Percentages	Provisions	Percentages
Congressional approval procedures, by rank				
1 Approval by both houses passing a concurrent or simple resolution	19	17.9	36	21.8
2 Approval by the Senate or both houses	0	0.0	0	0.0
3 Approval by both houses passing and the president approving a joint resolution	10	9.4	14	8.5
4 Approval by both houses passing and the president approving a bill	4	3.8	5	3.0
5 Approval by committee in either house	2	1.9	2	1.2
6 Approval by committees in both houses	61	57.5	98	59.4
7 Approval by "come into agreement" by committees in both houses	5	4.7	5	3.0
8 Approval by a joint committee of both houses	1	0.9	1	0.6
9 Approval by a sub-committee in both houses	2	1.9	2	1.2
10 Approval by a committee chair of one house	1	0.9	1	0.6
11 Approval by a congressional agency—e.g., Office of Technology Assessment	1	0.9	1	0.6
12 Approval by two-thirds of both houses of Congress	0	0.0	0	0.0
Total	106	99.9 [a]	165	99.9 [a]
Total	232		359	

Source: Adapted from Jaime Gazell and Darrell Pugh, "Voiding the Legislative Veto," *Glendale Law Review* 7 (1985): 6-8.

[a] Less than 100 percent due to rounding.

much more to do with producing these outcomes than any general element in the relationship between rulemaking agencies and Congress.[18] Foreman also observes: "A fundamental point to remember in all the legislative veto cases considered is that such cases are rare." [19] We might be distressed by such a finding, but we should not be surprised. It is curious that a mechanism so popular with Congress in the abstract would be practiced so infrequently. But the simple fact is that it was rather ungainly. More important, according to Foreman, the effort required to invoke the veto, even vetoes vested in committees, is usually unnecessary.[20] Table 6-1, taken from the Aberbach study, confirms that its use was relatively infrequent and that its effectiveness as an oversight device was rated quite low.

The legislative veto was invalidated by the Supreme Court in 1983 in the case *Immigration and Naturalization Service v. Chadha*.[21] The demise of the veto should not be viewed as a major blow to congressional oversight of rulemaking. While it was a particularly dramatic and conclusive form of congressional intervention, in many of its various forms that are listed above it was quite difficult to invoke. As Foreman notes, its use, in relation to the outpouring of new rules from agencies each year, was exceedingly rare. Provisions that require one or both houses of Congress to act to roll back an offending rule do appear to be throwing megatonnage at a mouse. The existence of the veto is more significant than its use. It signals a degree of congressional concern with rulemaking that contradicts notions that our elected representatives routinely eschew detail. The veto was a formal way for Congress to keep its options open and to keep the attention of rulemakers focused on the preferences of the Hill. Like many other forms of oversight, the threat of sanction is more efficient and likely as effective as the sanction itself.

It is evident that Congress is deeply involved in a variety of activities to hold those who write rules accountable. By such endeavors the members are attempting to ensure that their "agents" in the bureaucracy are toeing their line. But all this effort does not guarantee success. The scope of the oversight task is vast, and Congress has serious competitors for the attention of the rulemakers. It is to one of these, the president, we now turn.

ACCOUNTABILITY TO THE PRESIDENT

In Chapter 4, devoted to the management of rulemaking, the mechanics of presidential-level review of proposed and final rules was discussed. In this section attention is focused on the subtleties of the relationship that has developed between the White House and the rulemaking agencies. We will also explore in a bit more detail the conflict this interaction has triggered between the presidency and the Congress.

OBJECTIVES

The rationale for establishing a system of accountability to the president may not be as obvious as that to Congress. If Congress is taking proper care to see to it that its statutes are being implemented by agency rulemakers, what role is there for the president? There is more than ample justification for the president to be involved in overseeing those who write rules. Presidents are elected by all the people and can boast a mandate different from that of members of Congress and a perspective that is broader than the subcommittees and committees where legislation originates and develops. If what has been termed *macromanagement* of public policy is to be undertaken to any extent, the president is the most likely candidate to undertake such an effort. But, this "coordination ... on a grand scale" is severely limited by the paucity and poor quality of information about the effects of policy on society as a whole.[22] What can and now does occur is a much less ambitious but still important form of oversight based on clearly articulated principles and fixed procedures.

Earlier it was noted that presidents since Nixon have become increasingly concerned and involved with the regulatory process. Gradually, through a series of evolutionary steps, presidents have come to focus their attention primarily on rulemaking as the most promising target for their efforts to channel or curtail regulation. Since the Carter administration, each president has articulated a set of principles, often in the form of an executive order, that would become the basis for review of individual rules by White House staff. Two general purposes have been articulated for the review of individual rules. The first is to link individual acts of rulemaking to the broader mandate a given president perceives for himself. This is evident in the executive orders affecting rulemaking issued by both Carter and Reagan. Another general purpose for White House review of regulations is to resolve conflicts and inconsistencies in rules written by different agencies. There are many examples of such conflict.

A now classic example of conflict between the rules issued by the Occupational Safety and Health Administration and the Department of Agriculture dealt with the condition of floors in meat-packing houses. The former called for floors to be dry at all times to protect the safety of workers; the latter called for floors to be hosed regularly to protect the purity of the meat. More recently, the Department of Agriculture and the Federal Trade Commission were locked in a protracted dispute over the contents of labels on foods. And, there is the already-noted problem of varying the levels of acceptable risk that are allowed under different environmental, health, and safety laws. Some agencies fix the acceptable level at one additional death per hundred thousand people, whereas others fix it at one additional death per million. Clearly, there is a role for the president in the resolution of such conflicts, but close examination frequently reveals that the origins of the conflict can be traced to statutes that provide inconsistent guidance on the same general topic to different agencies. The president can force resolution of such situations when agencies have the discretion to interpret the statutory provisions that are causing the conflict. But when the statutes are explicit or appear strongly to support different interpretations, the president's prerogatives will either be more limited or more controversial.

THE OMB's RECORD OF REVIEW

The review of rules issued by agencies based on principles or criteria outlined in executive orders has proven considerably more controversial than presidential involvement to eliminate conflict and inconsistency. It has also proven far more common. As we saw, Carter's principles emphasized rational decision making, sound management practices, and involvement of the public during the course of rulemaking. Reagan's principles also stressed rational decision making but in the form of cost-benefit analysis. Reagan's program also emphasized reducing the burden of regulation on business. This latter criterion was viewed by critics as simply an attempt to reward an important constituency and led to charges that the review of individual rules was being carried out solely to cut back programs of social regulation. The debate about the Republican president's program continues on several levels, so it is useful to review its actual results.

Tables 6-5 through 6-8 summarize the nature of the actions taken by the president's agent—the Office of Management and Budget—when it reviews rules and the experience of different agencies of government in the process for 1988 and 1989. Table 6-9 is a summary for the government as a whole from 1981 through 1989.[23] These tables provide important insights into the working of the presidential oversight process, yet they also raise intriguing questions. It is apparent that the OMB has become increasingly critical of the performance of rulemaking during the period studied. We see, for example, that the number of rules that were considered acceptable to the OMB on first review declined during the decade of the 1980s (Table 6-9). With this information in hand, we should not find it surprising that the frequency of changes in rules as a result of OMB review increased by approximately the same amount. We can also see that the numbers

TABLE 6-5 Types of Actions Taken by the OMB on Agency Rules during 1988

Agency	Total reviews	Consistent without change	Consistent with change	Withdrawn by agency	Returned for reconsideration	Returned, sent improperly	Emergency	Statutory or judicial deadline
Dept. of Agriculture	441	364	56	5	10	0	5	1
Dept. of Health & Human Svcs	320	209	101	5	3	1	0	1
Dept. of Transportation	257	169	79	3	2	0	1	3
Environmental Protection Agcy	210	107	58	6	7	0	1	31
Dept. of the Interior	152	132	14	5	1	0	0	0
Dept. of Commerce	145	96	19	2	1	0	4	23
Dept. of Education	123	82	39	2	0	0	0	0
Dept. of Hous. & Urban Devel.	105	57	31	11	0	0	0	6
Veterans Administration	82	68	12	1	1	0	0	0
Dept. of Labor	77	37	36	2	1	0	0	1
Off. of Personnel Management	74	62	11	0	0	1	0	0
Gen. Services Administration	57	42	12	1	1	0	0	1
Dept. of Justice	52	44	8	0	0	0	0	0
Small Business Administration	37	20	12	2	1	1	0	1
Dept. of the Treasury	37	32	5	0	0	0	0	0
Fed. Emergency Management Agcy	30	18	7	5	0	0	0	0
Dept. of the Environment	20	14	4	0	1	0	0	1
Nat'l Archives & Records Admin.	17	13	0	4	0	0	0	0
Nat'l Aeronautics & Space Admin.	17	16	1	0	0	0	0	0
Dept. of State	17	14	2	0	0	0	0	1
Railroad Retirement Board	14	14	0	0	0	0	0	0
Dept. of Defense	12	10	2	0	0	0	0	0
U.S. Internat'l Devel. Corp. Agcy	9	8	1	0	0	0	0	0

Nat'l Science Foundation	8	7	1	0	0	0	0	0
Other temporary commissions	7	6	1	0	0	0	0	0
U.S. Information Agcy	7	6	0	1	0	0	0	0
Immigration & Naturalization Svc.	6	5	0	1	0	0	0	0
Arch. & Trans. Barriers Compliance Bd	4	4	1	0	0	0	0	0
Fed. Mediation & Conciliation Svc.	4	3	1	1	0	0	0	0
Nat'l Endowment for the Arts	4	2	1	1	0	0	0	0
ACTION	3	3	0	0	0	0	0	0
Nat'l Endowment for the Humanities	3	1	2	0	0	0	0	0
Pension Benefits Guarantee Corp.	3	3	0	0	0	0	0	0
African Development Foundation	1	0	1	0	0	0	0	0
Commission on Civil Rights	1	1	0	0	0	0	0	0
Equal Employ. Oppor. Commission	1	1	0	0	0	0	0	0
Office of Management and Budget	1	0	1	0	0	0	0	0
Penn. Ave. Development Corp.	1	1	0	0	0	0	0	0
Peace Corps	1	1	0	0	0	0	0	0
Selective Service System	1	1	0	0	0	0	0	0
Tennessee Valley Authority	1	1	0	0	0	0	0	0
Total	2,362	1,674	518	57	29	3	11	70
Percentage of total	100.0	70.9	21.9	2.4	1.2	0.1	0.5	3.0

Source: Executive Office of the President, *Regulatory Program of the United States Government* (Washington, D.C., 1991), p. 637.

TABLE 6-6 Types of Actions Taken by the OMB on Agency Rules during 1988, by Percentage

Agency	Total reviews	Consistent without change	Consistent with change	Withdrawn by agency	Returned for recon- sideration	Returned, sent improperly	Emergency	Statutory or judicial deadline
Dept. of Agriculture	441	82.5	12.7	1.1	2.3	0.0	1.1	0.2
Dept. of Health & Human Svcs	320	65.3	31.6	1.6	0.9	0.3	0.0	0.3
Dept. of Transportation	257	65.8	30.7	1.2	0.8	0.0	0.4	1.2
Environmental Protection Agcy	210	51.0	27.6	2.9	3.3	0.0	0.5	14.8
Dept. of the Interior	152	86.8	9.2	3.3	0.7	0.0	0.0	0.0
Dept. of Commerce	145	66.2	13.1	1.4	0.7	0.0	2.8	15.9
Dept. of Education	123	66.7	31.7	1.6	0.0	0.0	0.0	0.0
Dept. of Hous. & Urban Devel.	105	54.3	29.5	10.5	0.0	0.0	0.0	5.7
Veterans Administration	82	82.9	14.6	1.2	1.2	0.0	0.0	0.0
Dept. of Labor	77	48.1	46.8	2.6	1.3	0.0	0.0	1.3
Off. of Personnel Management	74	83.8	14.9	0.0	0.0	1.4	0.0	0.0
Gen. Services Administration	57	73.7	21.1	1.8	1.8	0.0	0.0	1.8
Dept. of Justice	52	84.6	15.4	0.0	0.0	0.0	0.0	0.0
Small Business Administration	37	54.1	32.4	5.4	2.7	2.7	0.0	2.7
Dept. of the Treasury	37	86.5	13.5	0.0	0.0	0.0	0.0	0.0
Fed. Emergency Management Agcy	30	60.0	23.3	16.7	0.0	0.0	0.0	0.0
Dept. of the Environment	20	70.0	20.0	0.0	5.0	0.0	0.0	5.0
Nat'l Archives & Records Admin.	17	76.5	0.0	23.5	0.0	0.0	0.0	0.0
Nat'l Aeronautics & Space Admin.	17	94.1	5.9	0.0	0.0	0.0	0.0	0.0
Dept. of State	17	82.4	11.8	0.0	0.0	0.0	0.0	5.9
Railroad Retirement Board	14	100.0	0.0	0.0	0.0	0.0	0.0	0.0
All other	78	82.1	14.1	3.8	0.0	0.0	0.0	0.0
Total	2,362	70.9	21.9	2.4	1.2	0.1	0.5	3.0

Source: Executive Office of the President, *Regulatory Program of the United States Government* (Washington, D.C., 1991), p. 638.

TABLE 6-7 Types of Actions Taken by the OMB on Agency Rules during 1989

Agency	Total reviews	Consistent without change	Consistent with change	Withdrawn by agency	Returned for reconsideration	Returned, sent improperly	Suspended	Emergency	Statutory or judicial deadline
Dept. of Agriculture	405	339	58	4	1	0	1	2	0
Dept. of Health & Human Svcs	283	187	82	7	5	0	2	0	0
Dept. of Transportation	250	195	48	3	1	0	0	1	2
Environmental Protection Agcy	201	97	59	5	11	0	4	1	24
Dept. of Commerce	195	177	12	5	0	0	0	1	0
Dept. of Justice	100	87	6	2	0	1	0	2	2
Dept. of the Interior	97	82	11	2	2	0	0	0	0
Veterans Administration	95	85	8	2	2	0	0	0	0
Dept. of Education	82	51	26	4	0	0	1	0	0
Dept. of Hous. & Urban Devel.	78	27	30	14	3	0	3	0	1
Gen. Services Administration	61	46	10	3	2	0	0	0	1
Dept. of Labor	60	22	33	0	2	0	2	0	1
Off. of Personnel Management	53	43	5	2	2	0	0	0	1
Dept. of the Treasury	47	37	9	1	0	0	0	0	0
Small Business Administration	39	30	8	0	0	0	0	0	1
Fed. Emergency Management Agcy	29	16	10	3	0	0	0	0	0
Railroad Retirement Board	21	19	2	0	0	0	0	1	2
Dept. of the Environment	19	12	2	2	0	0	0	0	1
Nat'l Aeronautics & Space Admin.	16	11	3	0	0	0	1	0	0
Dept. of State	15	14	1	0	0	0	0	0	0
Nat'l Archives & Records Admin.	8	7	1	0	0	0	0	0	0
U.S. Information Agcy	7	6	0	1	0	0	1	0	0
Dept. of Defense	6	3	1	1	0	0	0	0	0
Equal Employ. Oppor. Commission	5	4	1	0	0	0	0	0	0
Nat'l Science Foundation	5	5	0	0	0	0	0	0	0
U.S. Internat'l Devel. Corp. Agcy	4	3	1	0	0	0	0	0	0

(Table continues)

TABLE 6-7 (Continued)

Agency	Total reviews	Consistent without change	Consistent with change	Withdrawn by agency	Returned for reconsideration	Returned, sent improperly	Suspended	Emergency	Statutory or judicial deadline
Fed. Mediation & Conciliation Svc.	3	2	1	0	0	0	0	0	0
Other temporary commissions	3	3	0	0	0	0	0	0	0
ACTION	2	2	0	0	0	0	0	0	0
African Development Foundation	2	2	0	0	0	0	0	0	0
Immigration & Naturalization Svc.	2	2	0	0	0	0	0	0	0
Peace Corps	2	2	0	0	0	0	0	0	0
Selective Service System	2	2	0	0	0	0	0	0	0
Arch. & Trans. Barriers Compliance Bd	1	0	1	0	0	0	0	0	0
Commission on Civil Rights	1	0	1	0	0	0	0	0	0
Nat'l Endowment for the Arts	1	1	0	0	0	0	0	0	0
Nat'l Endowment for the Humanities	1	1	0	0	0	0	0	0	0
Office of Management and Budget	1	1	0	0	0	0	0	0	0
Pension Benefits Guarantee Corp.	1	1	0	0	0	0	0	0	0
Fed. Acquisition Regulations	1	1	0	0	0	0	0	0	0
Fed. Credit System Assistance Bd	1	1	0	0	0	0	0	0	0
Federal Home Loan Bank Board	2	0	0	0	0	0	0	1	1
Inter-American Foundation	2	2	0	0	0	0	0	0	0
Office of Government Ethics	1	1	0	0	0	0	0	0	0
Panama Canal Commission	7	7	0	0	0	0	0	0	0
Resolution Trust Corp.	1	1	0	0	0	0	0	0	0
U.S. Trade Representative	1	1	0	0	0	0	0	0	0
U.S. Office of Special Counsel	1	0	1	0	0	0	0	0	0
Total	2,220	1,638	431	61	29	1	15	9	36
Percentage of total	100.0	73.8	19.4	2.7	1.3	0.1	0.7	0.4	1.6

Source: Executive Office of the President, Regulatory Program of the United States Government (Washington, D.C., 1991), p. 636.

TABLE 6-8 Types of Actions Taken by the OMB on Agency Rules during 1989, by Percentage

Agency	Total reviews	Consistent without change	Consistent with change	Withdrawn by agency	Returned for reconsideration	Suspended	Emergency	Statutory or judicial deadline
Dept. of Agriculture	405	83.7	14.3	1.0	0.2	0.0	0.5	0.2
Dept. of Health & Human Svcs	283	66.1	29.0	2.5	1.8	0.7	0.0	0.0
Dept. of Transportation	250	78.0	19.2	1.2	0.4	0.0	0.4	0.8
Environmental Protection Agcy	201	48.3	29.4	2.5	5.5	2.0	0.5	11.9
Dept. of Commerce	195	90.8	6.2	2.6	0.0	0.0	0.5	0.0
Dept. of Justice [a]	100	87.0	6.0	2.0	0.0	0.0	2.0	2.0
Dept. of the Interior	97	84.5	11.3	2.1	2.1	0.0	0.0	0.0
Veterans Administration	95	89.5	8.4	2.1	0.0	0.0	0.0	0.0
Dept. of Education	82	62.2	31.7	4.9	0.0	1.2	0.0	0.0
Dept. of Hous. & Urban Devel.	78	34.6	38.5	17.9	3.8	2.8	0.0	1.3
Gen. Services Administration	61	75.4	16.4	4.9	3.3	0.0	0.0	0.0
Dept. of Labor [b]	60	32.3	55.9	1.7	1.7	0.0	0.0	1.7
Off. of Personnel Management	53	81.1	9.4	3.8	3.8	0.0	0.0	1.9
Dept. of the Treasury	47	78.7	19.1	2.1	0.0	0.0	0.0	0.0
Small Business Administration	39	76.9	20.5	0.0	0.0	0.0	0.0	2.6
Fed. Emergency Management Agcy	29	55.2	34.5	10.3	0.0	0.0	0.0	0.0
Railroad Retirement Board	21	90.5	9.5	0.0	0.0	0.0	0.0	0.0
Dept. of the Environment	19	63.2	10.5	10.5	0.0	0.0	5.3	10.5
Nat'l Aeronautics & Space Admin.	16	68.8	18.8	0.0	0.0	6.3	0.0	6.3
Dept. of State	15	93.3	6.7	0.0	0.0	0.0	0.0	0.0
Nat'l Archives & Records Admin.	8	87.5	12.5	0.0	0.0	0.0	0.0	0.0
All other	67	80.6	10.4	1.5	0.0	6.0	1.5	0.0
Total	2,221	73.8	19.4	2.7	1.3	0.7	0.4	1.6

Source: Executive Office of the President, *Regulatory Program of the United States Government* (Washington, D.C., 1991), p. 638.

[a] Includes one returned exempt.

[b] Includes one returned sent improperly.

TABLE 6-9 Types of Actions Taken by the OMB on Agency Rules, 1981-1989

	Percentage in year								
Action taken	1981	1982	1983	1984	1985	1986	1987	1988	1989
Consistent without change	87.3	84.1	82.3	78.0	70.7	68.3	70.5	70.9	73.8
Consistent with change	4.9	10.3	12.7	15.1	23.1	22.9	23.7	21.9	19.4
Withdrawn by agency	1.8	1.2	1.6	2.4	3.1	2.8	2.5	2.4	2.7
Returned for reconsideration	1.6	2.1	1.3	2.7	1.5	1.4	0.4	1.2	1.3
Suspended	NA	NA	NA	NA	NA	NA	NA	NA	0.7
Sent improperly or exempt	3.1	0.9	0.0	0.0	0.3	0.2	0.2	0.1	0.4
Emergency, statutory, or judicial deadline	1.4	1.4	2.0	1.7	1.2	4.3	2.5	3.5	1.6
Total[a]	100.1	100.0	99.9	99.9	99.9	99.9	99.8	100.0	99.9

	Percentage change								
	1981-1982	1982-1983	1983-1984	1984-1985	1985-1986	1986-1987	1987-1988	1988-1989	1981-1989
Consistent without change	-3.2	-1.8	-4.3	-7.3	-2.4	2.2	0.4	2.9	-13.5
Consistent with change	5.4	2.4	2.4	8.0	-0.2	0.8	-1.8	-2.5	14.5
Withdrawn by agency	-0.6	0.4	0.8	0.7	-0.3	-0.3	-0.1	0.4	1.0
Returned for reconsideration	0.5	-0.8	1.4	-1.2	-0.1	-1.0	0.8	0.1	-0.3
Suspended	NA	NA	NA	NA	NA	NA	NA	NA	NA
Sent improperly or exempt	-2.2	-0.9	0.0	0.3	-0.1	0.0	-0.1	-0.3	-2.7
Emergency, statutory, or judicial deadline	0.0	0.6	-0.3	-0.5	3.1	-1.8	1.0	-1.9	0.2

Source: Executive Office of the President, Regulatory Program of the United States Government (Washington, D.C., 1991), p. 639.

Note: NA = Not applicable.

[a] Percentages may not add to 100.0 percent due to rounding.

returned for reconsideration or withdrawn by the agency, which are the most extreme results of presidential review, are stable throughout the period and quite small. These data can be interpreted in several ways. By and large, the White House agrees with the results of agencies' rulemaking efforts. At their least successful, agencies were still obtaining approval of rules without change in over 70 percent of the cases. But this also means that in the best years, during the early 1980s, when the White House review program was still relatively new, several hundred rules submitted to the OMB required change. It is also interesting to note the steady decline in the performance of agencies in relation to OMB standards during the first six years of the program and its stabilization at about 70 percent. There is reason to expect the trend to be in the direction of greater levels of agreement between the agencies and their overseers in the OMB.

Examining the tables, we find that there is considerable variation in the results of White House review for individual rulemaking agencies. Care must be taken in drawing inferences from these data. The rules that were changed by the agencies in question or that were subject to more serious actions by the OMB cover an enormous range of subject matter. For example, Table 6-10 is a list of rules that the OMB returned to the agencies for reconsideration during 1989. There is no easily discernible pattern in this list; a diverse group of agencies was affected and the subject matter covers a great deal more than the types of regulation that were targeted by the Reagan administration. Still, there is some circumstantial evidence that the White House review program focused more heavily on agencies with programs that the Republicans viewed with considerable suspicion.

In 1988 and 1989 the Environmental Protection Agency and the departments of Housing and Urban Development, Education, Labor, and Health and Human Services all experienced comparatively high rates of changes in the rules submitted for OMB review. Each of these departments houses programs that the Reagan administration criticized and, in one instance (a program in the Department of Education), vowed to abolish. And there are several now notorious cases of reviews in which critics charge that the OMB review singled out important forms of social regulation for especially harsh treatment. Harold Bruff, professor of law at the University of Texas, analyzed two such cases in detail.[24]

In one case, the Environmental Protection Agency withdrew two proposed regulations in the mid-1980s that would have imposed stringent controls on the production and use of asbestos. Subsequently it became clear that the withdrawal was prompted by heavy pressure from the OMB, whose officials took the position that the EPA should defer to other agencies for the regulation of asbestos. Ironically, when

TABLE 6-10   Regulations Returned to Agencies by the OMB for
Reconsideration during 1989

Agency	Regulation	Stage of rule-making at return
Dept. of Agriculture	Loans, Purchases, and Other Operations	Final
Dept. of Health & Human Services	Mental Disorders in Children	NPRM
	Income Parent to Child Deeming	NPRM
	End-Stage Renal Disease Program: Revised Composite Rates	Final
	Reciprocal Offset	NPRM
	Hospice/Case Management, Medicaid & Medicare	NPRM
Dept. of Housing & Urban Development	HUD Procedures for Implementing Executive Orders 11988 & 11990	NPRM
	Prepayment of a HUD-Insured Mortgage by an Owner of Low-Income Housing	Final
	Deregulation of Mortgagor Income Requirements	Final
Dept. of the Interior	Valuation Benchmarks in Gas Regulations	NPRM
Dept. of the Interior	Dual Accounting Requirement in Gas Valuation Regulations	NPRM
Dept. of Labor	Ionizing Radiation Standards for Underground Metal and Nonmetal Mines	Final
	Respiratory Protection	NPRM
Dept. of Transportation	Civil Supersonic Aircraft Noise Type Certification Standards	NPRM
Environmental Protection Agency	CERCLA Manual on Compliance with Other Laws	NPRM
	Surface Impoundment Clean Closure Guidance	NPRM

TABLE 6-10   *(Continued)*

Agency	Regulation	Stage of rule-making at return
	Carbon Monoxide Controls for Hazardous Waste Incinerators	NPRM
	Hazardous Waste Incinerator Standards	NPRM
	Metals and Hydrogen Chloride Controls for Hazardous Waste Incinerators	NPRM
	Liner/Leak Detection Rule	NPRM
	Open Burning Permits for Holston Army Ammunition Plant	NPRM
	Refueling and Evaporative Emissions for Gasoline and Methanol-Fueled Vehicles, Light-Duty Trucks, and Heavy-Duty Vehicles	NPRM
	NSPS for SOCMI Reactor Processes	Final
	NSPS for SOCMI Distillation Unit Operations	Final
	NSPS for SOCMI Air Oxidation Unit Processes	Final
General Services Administration	Governmentwide Real Property Asset Management	NPRM
	Assignment and Utilization of Space Amendment D	NPRM
Office of Personnel Management	Disability Retirement	NPRM
	Excepted Service—Schedule A Authority for Employment of Summer Aides	NPRM

Source: Executive Office of the President, *Regulatory Program of the United States Government* (Washington, D.C., 1991), p. 639.

Note: NPRM = Notice of proposed rulemaking.

another agency did undertake to regulate asbestos the resultant rule was stricter than the EPA proposal, but at that point the controversy surrounding the OMB's involvement prevented it from intervening effectively.

In another case, efforts by the Occupational Safety and Health Administration to regulate worker's exposure to ethylene oxide, a chemical used to sterilize hospital equipment, was thwarted by the OMB. In this case, a proposed rule that fixed short-term exposure limits was forwarded to the OMB for review. The office responded the next day with a detailed analysis of the regulation, stating that in its current form it did not meet the cost-effectiveness criteria established by President Reagan. One day after receiving the OMB response, OSHA forwarded an amended rule to the *Federal Register* simply deleting the sections related to short-term exposure limits. OSHA admitted in a subsequent lawsuit that it had made the changes in the rule primarily because of the OMB's response to the draft. Others who have commented on the case point out that the speed and detail in the OMB critique to the short-term exposure limits make it plain that the office had been in contact with the agency well in advance of the date that the proposed rule was forwarded for White House review.

Another, highly visible instance of White House intervention involved the Council on Competitiveness, chaired by Vice President Dan Quayle. In this instance the council effectively vetoed an EPA regulation that would require polluting firms to inform the public whenever their discharges exceeded the limits established in clean air regulations. Unlike the previous examples of White House intervention, this was not a case in which the agency's leadership openly cooperated with the White House or tacitly accepted its position. The EPA leadership fought and lost.[25]

THE OMB AND DELAY IN RULEMAKING

Another dimension of the White House review function is the time it takes and the effects of delay. As noted in an earlier section, the courts have insisted that White House review be conducted so that deadlines for issuing rules that are established in statutes or judicial decisions are met. Beyond this, the executive order establishing OMB review set time periods for review of proposed and final rules at sixty and thirty days, respectively. Table 6-11 summarizes the performance of the OMB in meeting these targets for review time. While there are some notable exceptions, the OMB has, on average, complied with the review time provisions of the executive order. Nevertheless, these average figures obscure a large number of cases in which the OMB held proposed or final rules for long periods of time. It is interesting to

TABLE 6-11 Average Review Time by the OMB of Rules under Executive Order No. 12291

Agency	1981-1989			1989			1988			1987			1986		
	M	N	A	M	N	A	M	N	A	M	N	A	M	N	A
Dept. of Agriculture	19	15	15	31	18	19	13	19	19	19	19	19	13	18	18
Dept. of Commerce	46	15	16	6	15	15	144	35	36	NA	19	19	127	15	15
Dept. of Defense	11	24	23	NA	92	92	NA	22	22	4	12	11	30	28	28
Dept. of Education	42	18	19	NA	33	33	NA	32	32	NA	15	15	14	13	13
Dept. of the Environment	41	18	19	52	98	92	125	42	47	NA	24	24	34	15	17
Dept. of Health & Human Svcs	44	30	30	46	36	36	48	32	33	162	36	37	19	37	36
Dept. of Hous. & Urban Devel.	30	21	22	83	29	31	21	31	31	35	21	22	44	32	33
Dept. of the Interior	10	16	16	3	30	29	32	22	23	4	20	19	7	11	11
Dept. of Justice	2	10	10	1	12	12	NA	17	17	2	6	6	NA	8	8
Dept. of Labor	114	43	50	179	71	86	133	84	87	132	46	54	76	47	49
Dept. of State	28	13	13	NA	11	11	NA	20	20	NA	12	12	NA	5	5
Dept. of Transportation	41	23	23	71	23	24	58	41	41	21	32	31	32	19	19
Dept. of the Treasury	24	16	16	NA	28	28	NA	17	17	NA	16	16	NA	7	7
Veterans Administration	NA	22	22	NA	17	17	NA	30	30	NA	38	38	NA	44	44
Environmental Protection Agcy	64	26	28	104	49	52	51	48	49	49	35	37	41	41	41
Other agencies	47	20	20	28	25	25	66	28	28	42	26	26	74	24	25
All government	40	21	21	59	28	29	44	32	32	29	24	24	29	24	24

(Table continues)

TABLE 6-11 (Continued)

Agency	1985 M	1985 N	1985 A	1984 M	1984 N	1984 A	1983 M	1983 N	1983 A	1982 M	1982 N	1982 A	1981 M	1981 N	1981 A
Dept. of Agriculture	15	19	19	11	19	19	15	13	13	17	10	10	22	8	8
Dept. of Commerce	NA	12	12	316	14	17	5	11	11	22	9	10	8	8	8
Dept. of Defense	NA	30	30	NA	30	30	NA	16	16	NA	6	6	NA	9	9
Dept. of Education	NA	16	16	39	18	19	NA	11	11	32	12	13	NA	8	8
Dept. of the Environment	30	7	8	77	9	12	45	7	9	26	6	7	7	7	7
Dept. of Health & Human Svcs	74	46	47	3	33	33	35	18	19	21	10	11	8	7	7
Dept. of Hous. & Urban Devel.	NA	27	27	10	18	17	12	15	15	NA	11	11	NA	14	14
Dept. of the Interior	5	19	19	7	17	17	12	17	17	13	10	10	6	8	8
Dept. of Justice	NA	9	9	NA	10	10	NA	14	14	NA	7	7	NA	6	6
Dept. of Labor	173	55	61	NA	43	43	121	18	29	37	10	12	26	6	9
Dept. of State	NA	16	16	NA	5	5	28	10	16	NA	7	7	NA	9	9
Dept. of Transportation	80	34	36	42	20	21	24	15	15	37	12	12	8	8	8
Dept. of the Treasury	16	13	13	17	18	18	NA	12	12	60	13	14	1	8	8
Veterans Administration	NA	23	23	NA	15	15	NA	15	15	NA	11	11	NA	10	10
Environmental Protection Agcy	78	33	35	58	30	31	14	22	22	88	17	19	12	9	9
Other agencies	105	23	25	26	20	20	35	14	14	40	13	14	5	10	10
All government	64	26	27	31	22	22	28	15	16	28	11	12	13	9	9

Source: Executive Office of the President, Regulatory Program of the United States Government (Washington, D.C., 1991), p. 647.
Note: M = Major; N = Nonmajor; A = All; NA = Not applicable.

note in the table that the average review time for Department of Labor rules is nearly twice that called for in the executive order. And there have been persistent complaints that rules of other agencies of social regulation, notably the EPA, have been stalled at OMB.[26]

The rules that experience significant delays are generally important rules in the sense that they impose substantial compliance costs on the private sector. Such delays are significant for a number of reasons. Obviously, the longer the delay in the issuance of the rule, the longer the period of relief from compliance costs for the affected sector or industry. Also, the passage of time may see a change in agency priorities or in external pressure for the issuance of the regulation, leading to abandonment or formal postponement of the rulemaking. Hence, review time is an apparently passive but actually potent dimension in the White House review program.

THE OMB AND THE AGENCIES

The relationship between the White House and rulemaking agencies is complex and variable. Harold Bruff has also explored the subtleties of these relationships in depth. Even more than is the case with Congress, the agencies possess what on the surface appear to be significant advantages in their relationship with White House overseers. The agencies have greater expertise and vastly superior numbers of staff when compared with the Office of Information and Regulatory Affairs (OIRA), the arm of the OMB that conducts rulemaking reviews. The OIRA staff members who are actively engaged in the review process are generally young, number no more than a few dozen, and have educational backgrounds in general policy analysis rather than the scientific and technical subjects that lie at the base of so much contemporary rulemaking.[27] The large number of rules each is expected to review requires them to be selective in their allocation of time. Hence, they pick those rules they deem to be the most important, devote the lion's share of their efforts to these, and conduct cursory and quick reviews on the rest. But as a counterweight to this mismatch of resources and expertise, the OMB possesses many advantages, some of which depend on the relationships between career staff and political appointees in the agencies that write rules, and others of which relate to the position and powers of the OMB.

Bruff notes four advantages that the OMB enjoys in the review process. First, "the power of persuasion 'depends on' the cogency of its positions and the power of those asserting them." Second, he notes the power created by the threat of delay, which he deems considerable. Third, the OMB can summon allegiance to the administration on the part of senior political appointees in agencies in which proposals developed by career staff conflict with White House policy. Finally, by linking its recommendations on agencies' budgets to the degree to which agencies produce rules that comply with the executive order, the OMB can increase its leverage over rule writers.[28]

What emerges from studies of OMB review is a relationship that operates at two levels. The staff-to-staff working relationships are likely to vary a lot. It is extremely difficult for OMB desk officers to develop close working relationships with all agency rulemakers because of their sheer numbers. Consequently, the degree of conflict between an agency and the OMB at this level is a function of the general attitudes about OMB review, the working style and negotiation skills of the two parties, and the bureaucratic incentives facing the rulemaker and the OMB analyst. Some agencies have developed a culture of hostility to OMB review, whereas others have accepted it as a legitimate and even valuable function. Some agencies dismiss OMB analysts as politically motivated dilettantes; others accept their role as generalists with concern for administration policy. Bureaucrats who place a high premium on autonomy and the technical content of rules may bristle at what they see as interference that is irrelevant or worse. Others, more concerned with bringing the rule to a successful conclusion, may compromise their professional values in order to expedite the review process. Of course, the analysts at the OMB have professional values and different incentives as well. By and large, however, the sheer volume of rules and numbers of rulemakers and the differences in the perspectives of the two sides leads to frequent disagreements that require some form of resolution.

When agency staff and OMB analysts reach an impasse, the issues are elevated to superiors in both organizations. Here, because the numbers are smaller and the organizations are bound by an apparent commitment to the same administration, a proclivity to negotiated agreements is more likely to be the norm. As Bruff puts it, "Because agency heads and OMB officials deal with each other on a multitude of issues, each has a strong incentive to reach compromise on controverted issues . . . rather than spending limited institutional capital . . . over a particular regulation." [29] In general, then, we can anticipate a White House review process with numerous incidences of conflict at the staff level that are ameliorated as issues move up the two organizations for resolution. But we should also anticipate periods of adjustment, especially when presidential administrations change and along with them the political leadership of both the agencies and the OMB.

The relationship between the White House and rulemaking agencies has become institutionalized, but the conflict over presidential oversight has not subsided. Few aspects of rulemaking have received more attention from students of public administration and policy than

OMB review. Scholars have debated the constitutionality of the process. They have examined the motives of those conducting reviews, the effectiveness of the various elements of the process, and the implications it has for the relationship between the White House and Congress. Courts have ruled that presidential management of rulemaking is constitutional as long as it does not interfere with explicit congressional or judicial mandates.[30] The motivations that drive White House review are, like any significant governmental function, complex and varied. Goals ranging from the perfection of the rulemaking process to the securing of short-term political or economic advantage have been articulated and pursued.[31] Scholars have offered a variety of constitutional theories to rationalize the respective roles of Congress and the president in rulemaking and its oversight.[32]

Throughout the 1980s and early 1990s clashes between the White House and Congress were frequent and occasionally intense. Cases like the asbestos, ethylene chloride, and public notice rules convinced many in Congress that OMB review and the Council on Competitiveness were little more than backdoors for politically powerful interests intent on frustrating normal and statutorily authorized regulatory processes. Congress retaliated with hearings, investigations, cutoffs of funding for OIRA review functions, and refusals to confirm nominees to head that office. A temporary truce in the interbranch war was achieved in 1986 when OIRA leadership issued a set of guidelines governing staff communications with external parties and disclosure of such communication. A detailed version of an "administrative agreement" between Congress and the OMB on regulatory review procedures and information disclosure was entered into the *Congressional Record* in November 1989. In turn, Congress reauthorized the Paperwork Reduction Act, which provided the OIRA with the power to review and approve collections of information attendant to new rules, and refrained from writing legislation that would drastically limit the ability of the OMB to review rules. Congress did not, however, authorize funding specifically for regulatory review and continued to consider proposals to exempt particular types of rules from the OMB process.

Presidential oversight of rulemaking review has received at least the qualified support of many influential organizations and numerous scholars who have considered the issue. The National Academy of Public Administration, the American Bar Association, and the Administrative Conference of the United States have each acknowledged the legitimacy and potential value of presidential oversight. Each, however, has suggested reforms of the process that would lead to better working relationships and results. The recommendations include full public disclosure of OMB communications and actions, increased numbers and training for OMB review staff, enhanced communication and coordination between the OMB and rulemaking agencies, and a statute that specifically authorizes and sets the parameters of presidential review. Although we can expect further refinements of the process and inevitable disagreements about the substance, at this writing OMB review of proposed and final rules is an accepted and, as we will see, effective method of presidential oversight.

The same cannot be said, however, about mechanisms like the Council on Competitiveness. The general consensus of those who studied the council was that its failure to disclose the basis for its selection of rules for review or its communications with those outside government during the course of review threatened its legitimacy. President Clinton rendered the issue moot when he abolished the council soon after he was inaugurated.

The effectiveness of presidential oversight of rulemaking is a matter of some dispute. Some have concluded from case studies that the actual influence OMB and related reviews provide the president is limited and that agencies have at their disposal means to resist that which they consider unwise or untoward.[33] Most of those who examine White House review programs and the reaction to them in many quarters suggest that presidential oversight of rulemaking is effective. Existing research and the behavior of key institutions and organizations tend to support this conclusion.

Although there is no definitive empirical study of the rules that are affected, the process housed in the OMB results in changes, reconsiderations, or withdrawals of several hundred proposals from agencies per year. These numbers do not include the number of rules that were changed prior to submission because of informal communications with OMB staff. Even more difficult to discern is the change in the rulemaking agencies that has occurred as a result of more than a decade of presidential oversight. The threat of presidential oversight, like the legislative veto, may be sufficient in some instances to alter the course and content of rules. We also have the implicit acknowledgment of the potential power of presidential oversight in the actions of Congress, the National Academy of Public Administration, the Administrative Conference of the United States, and a host of interest groups. Congress has engaged in an ongoing struggle with the White House for control of rulemaking agencies virtually since the inception of OMB review and related oversight devices. The National Academy undertook a major study of the issue, and the Administrative Conference has promulgated recommendations on its conduct. The American Bar Association has done the same. Organizations like OMB Watch and Public Citizen have issued reports replete with dire warnings about the threat that regulatory review in general and the Council on Competitiveness in particular pose to the integrity of the regulatory process. Other interest groups have challenged individual actions resulting from presidential oversight in court.

The overall conclusion one is compelled to reach is that the president is every bit as active a player in the rulemaking process as the Congress. Harold Bruff notes that this view is shared by the primary beneficiary of the process when he writes, "From the point of view of the administration . . . the program enjoyed unprecedented success in imprinting regulation with the President's own principles." [34]

President Clinton apparently agrees. Early in his presidency his senior staff affirmed the new administration's commitment to the principle of presidential management of rulemaking. Review of rules by the OMB would be retained but would be conducted on a more selective basis, focusing on the most important rules. Clinton's staff also announced that it would take steps to open the process of OMB review to full public scrutiny and to promote even greater levels of public participation.

A note about the continued use of cost-benefit analysis is appropriate here. Promoted in the policies and executive orders of numerous presidents, it has been a fixture in rulemaking for nearly two decades. Its most ardent supporters would have it dominate the rulemaking process by using economic analysis to point decision makers to the most rational content for rules. A substantial literature exists on cost-benefit analysis in general and its application to rulemaking.[35] Three themes in this literature are important. The first is that the information needed to do comprehensive cost-benefit studies is often as hard to obtain as the scientific and technical data on which many rules are based. Second, profound skepticism greets the use of cost-benefit analysis by those who view it as a device to prevent, delay, or reduce any form of government intervention. Third, the criteria for its use have allowed agencies to avoid conducting such studies in most cases.

As a reform, cost-benefit analysis has contributed to better rules in many cases. It has not, however, dominated the process or rendered other dimensions unimportant. Still, at this writing President Clinton has voiced qualified support for its continued "enlightened" use as a component in the rulemaking process.

Whatever their principles, future residents of 1600 Pennsylvania Avenue will seek to do the same. Presidential oversight is a permanent fixture in the rulemaking process. Whatever form it takes, it gives presidents their best hope for a broad and deep impact on public policy.

ACCOUNTABILITY TO THE COURTS

No institution of government has been as persistent in its over-sight of rulemaking for a longer period of time than the federal judiciary. Before Congress concerned itself in any meaningful, systematic way with the rulemaking process it set in motion, the courts were reviewing its results and determining whether they were lawful instruments of governmental authority. Decades before any president sought to oversee the rulemaking that occurred in departments and agencies, judges were remaking the process of rulemaking and reformulating the substance of rules through decisions in individual cases. The courts remain extremely important overseers of rulemaking.

OBJECTIVES

The objectives of the president and Congress when conducting oversight are political and, occasionally, institutional. Both the president and Congress attempt to make rulemaking produce results that promote their respective policy preferences and, when controlled by different political parties or philosophies, these branches vie for control over the rulemakers. The primary concerns of the judiciary are more complex. At the very least, their role in relation to rulemaking is to ensure that as the function is performed it is done in accordance with basic constitutional principles and that the law, both substantive and procedural, is observed. Judges are not without legal and political philosophies, however, and when they review the handiwork of rulemakers, they do so through the prism of these beliefs. Although not linked to a constituency that votes them in or out of office, judges are creatures of the political system. This must be taken into account, along with a number of other characteristics of the judicial system, if the role of judges as overseers of the rulemaking process is to be properly understood. In America we have few options when seeking an institution to protect the integrity of our constitutional system. Because the executive and legislative branches of government are inherently political, they have each demonstrated a frightening capacity to subjugate constitutional protections to the transient whims of a vocal electorate. We have, for better or worse, deposited the Constitution with the federal judiciary and attempted to remove those who occupy the bench from the temporary and partisan motives that too often drive the other branches.

A few important facts about the people who occupy the federal bench, the structure of the court system, and the remarkable powers that can be exercised by our judges are worth reviewing. Federal judges hold lifetime appointments after they are nominated by the president and confirmed by the Senate. Politics plays an important role in the screening of candidates for the bench, but once they are confirmed judges become the least constrained of our public officials. Because we vest in them the power to declare the acts of the other branches, including the making of law, null and void, it is vital that they be removed from the political arena. Lifetime tenure, protection from reduction of their salaries, and removal from office only through an elaborate impeachment process insulate federal judges from the pressures that might be exerted by Congress, the president, and interest groups. The courts are certainly not immune to criticism or attacks from external sources, but of all the branches they are the best equipped to withstand such attacks.

The political profile of the federal bench in the early 1990s is distinctive. At this writing nearly two-thirds of the sitting federal judges were named by Presidents Reagan and Bush. Still, President-elect Bill Clinton had more than one hundred vacancies on the federal bench awaiting his action when he took office. This demonstrates a remarkable but little analyzed aspect of our political system. In many ways, the most enduring legacy a president can leave is the federal judges he appoints during his term. Even the most dramatic and far-reaching programs of social or regulatory policy are altered almost from the moment they are enacted. Soon they barely resemble what was initially created. Appointments to the federal bench endure, however, changed only by the intellectual development of the individuals holding these lifetime jobs. This creates in our system an inherent tension. Even when the White House and Congress are controlled by the same party and are working in concert, there is no guarantee that coherent policy will be the ultimate result. Litigation, being so common, ensures that the policy initiatives of a given administration or Congress will be subjected to the scrutiny of a federal judge, or federal judges, who were likely appointed by a previous president and confirmed by a previous Congress, sometimes with quite different ideas about what is legally permissible and constitutionally sound.[36] So if previous presidents screened their candidates for the bench carefully, with an eye to putting a distinctive philosophical stamp on the judicial branch, conflict is bound to be the result. The diversity of views held by the more than one thousand federal judges, sitting in hundreds of courts geographically dispersed, militates against consistency and coherence in the outcomes of litigation. Since litigation over rulemaking is not uncommon, we can expect these judicial characteristics to influence the ultimate content of rules.

The power of the judiciary is expressed in a multitude of ways, some so subtle that they are very difficult to observe. Like Congress and the White House, the mere existence of the judiciary and the threat of litigation exerts a powerful deterrent effect on the behavior of rulemaking bureaucracies. Those writing rules have learned that when their work affects persons and groups with sufficient sophistication and resources to sue, litigation is a distinct possibility. They also know that judges are not reluctant to obliterate years of work if the court is convinced that the law has been violated in some way.[37] In the chapter devoted to the management of rulemaking it was noted that a representative of the Office of General Counsel is always included in agency work groups assigned the task of writing regulations. One reason for this inclusion, often the most important, is to advise those developing the content of the rule how to avoid litigation or how to survive it should it occur. The presence of courts not only fosters a healthy respect for the myriad of legal principles and issues that attach to rulemaking but may also be a powerful force pushing agencies to consider more seriously the views of those who might challenge the rule in court.

When litigation does occur, judges are frequently not the ultimate decision makers. Those familiar with the operation of courts are aware that settlements are a common means of ending a lawsuit. There is no empirical evidence that suggests that litigation involving rules is more or less likely to end in settlement than are other types of disputes. Rather, the point here is that with regard to rulemaking, the power of the court may be in its role as a context for the resolution of a dispute between an agency and a private party and as a ratifier of the agreement the litigants have reached. When a lawsuit is not settled and it falls to the judge to make the decision, the power of the judiciary is most in evidence. A rule may be fully vindicated, partially invalidated, or totally rejected by a reviewing court.

The federal court system includes three levels: district courts, courts of appeals, and the Supreme Court of the United States.[38] The courts at each of these levels perform a distinctive role in the judicial system. District courts are trial courts; their primary mission is the resolution of the disputes that created the cases in the first place. Trials in district courts are presided over by a single judge, whose primary task is to move the cases from an active to terminated status. Courts of appeals, as their title suggests, usually review cases that have already been decided in another court. Their function is to review previous decisions when one of the parties believes that the result was incorrect. For some types of cases, including most of those involving rulemaking, the courts of appeals function essentially as trial courts, being the first tribunal of the federal judicial system to hear the case. Cases in the courts of appeals are heard by groups of judges called panels. Most often three judges hear cases, but on some occasions it can be all the judges assigned to the court. Finally there is the Supreme Court of the

United States, consisting of nine members. Much of its caseload is discretionary, and it grants full hearing to only a few hundred cases each year. Challenges to rules are not often heard by the Supreme Court.

Decision making in courts of appeals is collective. Variations in legal philosophy and political predilection are likely to be more pronounced at the trial court level, since judges there need not accommodate their views to others in order to reach a resolution of the dispute. At the appellate level judges do not hear witnesses directly; they work from the transcript of trials, written briefs, and oral arguments from attorneys. Their task is to ensure the correctness and quality of decisions reached in trial courts or administrative tribunals. They often return cases to trial courts for further litigation or reconsideration and express their decisions in written opinions that are frequently quite lengthy.

The effect of judicial oversight on rulemaking can vary quite dramatically, depending on the level of court that has issued the ruling. Decisions by trial courts apply to the individual cases in which they were rendered. If the decisions are used as precedent for future decisions, their effect is often confined to the federal judicial district in which the court operates. Some districts encompass entire states, but many cover only a portion of a state. Since individual decisions of trial courts are not always accompanied by lengthy judicial opinions from which judges in future cases can take guidance, the effects of a trial court decision may be limited to the parties involved and the thinking of the judge who rendered the decision.

Decisions by appellate courts are quite different in their effect. Like district courts, courts of appeals and the Supreme Court pass judgment in cases that may raise issues about rulemaking in general or a statute that affects a broad spectrum of rules. The difference is that decisions by these higher courts apply to a much larger geographic area. The decisions of appellate courts become precedent for multistate regions, known as circuits, and the decisions of the Supreme Court apply to the nation as a whole. Some courts of appeals hear more rulemaking cases than others simply by virtue of their location. For example, the Court of Appeals for the District of Columbia Circuit has become a major force in the law of rulemaking, since its location in Washington makes it the court of choice for a large portion of the litigation challenging rules.[39] The decisions of courts of appeals and the Supreme Court are written and can be referred to by other courts and agencies. To the extent courts in future cases take guidance from these decisions and to the extent agencies pattern their behavior according to the principles outlined in written opinions, a single decision by one of these courts can be a powerful form of oversight of rulemaking.

We must now consider the major issues associated with judicial oversight of rulemaking. There are four large categories of issues.[40] First, we must establish who has the right to challenge a rule in court. Second, once the qualifications of those who can litigate are understood, we must consider the types of complaints that they may bring to the court. Third, the standards that the courts apply when they consider challenges to agency rulemaking are crucially important. Last, we must summarize the actual effects of judicial oversight on the conduct of rulemaking and its substantive results. We begin with the question of who may sue.

The qualifications a person, group, or organization must possess in order to bring a lawsuit in federal court are covered by the principle of *standing*. Until the 1940s it was exceedingly difficult for those unhappy with an action taken by a government agency to obtain a hearing in federal court. The judiciary had embraced a test for standing that came to be known as legal interests.[41] Under this test a party was required to show that harm would result from the action the government had taken or was contemplating and that the damage would be done to an interest that had explicit legal protection in statute or the common law. Generally, the latter was confined to a rather narrow concept of real private property. Challenges to rulemaking occurred, as we noted in the famous cases that invalidated large portions of the New Deal. But the interests affected in these instances fell under the narrow version of real private property.

The ability of litigation to stand as a check against the abuses of unrestrained executive or bureaucratic power persuaded Congress to encourage the courts to adopt a more liberal test for the law of standing. The judiciary opened its doors a bit more in the 1930s and 1940s, when it noted that in certain instances individuals who might otherwise not qualify for standing would qualify if they were acting as "private attorneys general." [42] The notion here is that an individual might be able to bring to the courts a dispute with an agency that allowed the judges to consider the broader question of whether the government was carrying out its functions in a legally permissible, constitutional manner. Of course, this principle left it entirely to the judges to determine which circumstances would qualify an individual to serve as a private attorney general.

The most prominent example of congressional encouragement of a more liberal doctrine of standing came in the Administrative Procedure Act of 1946. In it Congress extended judicial review to "persons aggrieved" by a given agency decision.[43] It provided no further definition of the term, nor examples of what types of interests other than real private property might be included under it. In time, however, the courts moved in the direction of what Congress sought.

In fact, some might argue that they went well beyond its goal. Along with the rise of interest groups and the explosion of social regulation, the decades of the 1960s and 1970s saw the eventual opening of the judicial system to virtually any person or organization who could articulate a complaint with an action taken by government. Congress was an active party to this movement and included "citizen lawsuit" provisions in many statutes that created programs of social regulation.[44]

The high-water mark in the liberalization of the law of standing can be observed in a case involving a rate decision issued by the Interstate Commerce Commission. A group of Georgetown Law School students, organized temporarily as something called "Students Challenging Regulatory Agency Procedures," otherwise known as SCRAP, took issue with the rate because it would, in their considered judgment, hamper the transport of recyclable materials. This, they argued, would damage their members in direct and indirect ways, including the effect on their recreational activities and their aesthetic enjoyment of the landscape. The Supreme Court agreed that the members of SCRAP were in fact aggrieved and stated that individuals and groups could expect to be granted standing when the Court accepted what it called the "attenuated line of causation" between the ICC's action and the harm the group allegedly would incur. The Court granted standing and allowed the group to try to convince a trial court that harm would in fact occur and that the commission was acting illegally when inflicting it on them.[45]

Courts appeared to back off from this extremely permissive view of standing in other cases. In one, a rule issued by the Internal Revenue Service (IRS) reduced the amount of free services a hospital had to extend to poor persons in order to qualify for tax-exempt status. A welfare rights organization challenged the rule, arguing that it would have the effect of reducing available health care for its members. The Supreme Court denied standing and stated that the group's issue was with hospitals and not with the IRS.[46] This decision raised fundamental questions of whether indirect effects of the sort that were considered relevant in SCRAP could any longer be considered as a basis for granting standing. The Court shortly answered that question in the affirmative when it allowed an environmental group to challenge a law that limited the liability the operators of nuclear power plants could suffer as a result of an accident. The group claimed that this limit to liability was in fact a form of subsidy without which nuclear plants would not be built. The Court agreed and granted standing. The difference between this and the earlier case involving indirect effects is that the Court was convinced that the action being challenged—the building of a nuclear plant—was causally linked to the limitation on liability.[47] It was not convinced that hospitals would deny care to the poor simply because of the IRS ruling. The Court has also made it clear that groups alleging harm must establish it clearly and relate it to the challenged government action.

The law of standing has many complexities and subtleties. For the ability to challenge rules, however, it is safe to say that if a group, person, or organization can demonstrate actual or potential harm that is attributable to decisions made during the course of rulemaking, that person, group, or organization will be granted the right to sue. The principle of standing is crucial to the conduct of judicial oversight of rulemaking because courts lack the authority to initiate cases by themselves. Unlike the oversight conducted by the other branches, the exercise by judges of any supervisory powers over rulemakers must await the arrival of a lawsuit. While standing tells us little about what a court will decide when reviewing the content of a rule or the process by which it was determined, it does establish how judicial oversight of rulemaking may begin.

Establishing the standing to sue an agency that has issued a rule does not, in itself, establish the timing of the lawsuit. Although an individual or organization may bring an issue to a court that qualifies the court to challenge a rule, it is not permitted to do so at any stage in the rulemaking process. On the contrary, courts are careful not to be drawn into disputes between agencies and affected parties until the rulemaking process has run its course. The principles at work here are "finality" and "ripeness for review." Together they forestall judicial review until the agency has completed its work and the rule is published in its final form in the *Federal Register* or, when available, petitions for reconsideration are exhausted. The logic of these rules is straightforward and compelling. The courts should not intervene in a basic function of another branch of government until it has completed its work. As long as the rule remains a proposal or under development there is a chance that the issues of concern will be resolved. The principle of withholding judicial oversight until the agency is done prevents the usurpation of agency authority and allows the courts to devote their scarce resources to controversies for which no alternative means of resolution are available.[48]

The second large category of issues is comprised of those related to what is known in administrative law as the scope of review, and an early authoritative statement on it is found in the Administrative Procedure Act. Section 706 of the act states:

> To the extent necessary to decision and when presented, the reviewing court shall decide all relevant questions of law, interpret constitutional and statutory provisions, and determine the meaning or applicability of the terms of an agency action. The reviewing court shall—

(1) compel agency action unlawfully withheld or unreasonably delayed; and
(2) hold unlawful and set aside agency action, findings, and conclusions found to be—
(a) arbitrary, capricious, an abuse of discretion, or otherwise not in accordance with law;
(b) contrary to constitutional right, power, privilege, or immunity;
(c) in excess of statutory jurisdiction, authority, or limitations, or short of statutory right;
(d) without observance of procedure required by law;
(e) unsupported by substantial evidence in a case subject to sections 556 and 557 of this title or otherwise reviewed on the record of an agency hearing provided by statute; or
(f) unwarranted by the facts to the extent that the facts are subject to trial de novo by the reviewing court.
In making the foregoing determinations, the court shall review the whole record of those parts of it cited by a party, and due account shall be taken of the rule of prejudicial error.[49]

Of these provisions most have continuing significance for contemporary rulemaking.

The first provision relates to actions that are unreasonably delayed. It was noted in a previous chapter that the amount of time it takes agencies to issue rules is a persistent problem. Of course, what constitutes a delay that is "unreasonable" is a matter of judgment unless clear standards are set. With the increased use of deadlines in authorizing statutes that specify quite clearly when Congress expects particular rules to be issued, the question of reasonableness is rendered effectively moot. If Congress imposes a deadline and the rulemaking agency misses it, there is no doubt that the courts will entertain a lawsuit, and it is highly likely that those attempting to force the agency's hand will prevail. When no deadlines exist but legislation establishes a clear expectation that an agency will produce a rule in a given area, it will be at the discretion of the judge whether to hear the case and to determine if the rule in question has been unduly delayed.[50]

That a rule that allegedly violates the Constitution is a proper matter for judicial review needs little elaboration. No act of government that violates the tenets of that document can stand. Because the ultimate responsibility for protection of the Constitution resides with the judiciary, there is little question that it should extend to rules and how they are written. Issues of constitutionality are not common in challenges to rulemaking, but they do occur, as in cases noted above involving the legislative veto and OMB review of rules.

In section 706(2)(c) of the APA, Congress takes care to establish in the court system both a check against a runaway bureaucracy and a safeguard for its lack of precision. It is elemental that agencies cannot write law unless authorized to do so by the legislature. When the authority of an agency to write a rule is challenged, the courts must look to the legislation that delegated responsibility for the program in question. On occasion, but relatively rarely, agencies knowingly step beyond the bounds of the authority they have been granted. More common are situations in which the authority to write a given rule is unclear but the agency, sometimes under pressure from external interests or the political leadership of the agency, writes it, nevertheless. This provision of the act requires the courts to be the arbiter of congressional intent when rules are challenged on the grounds that their development is an illegitimate exercise of bureaucratic power.

Section 706(2)(d) of the act requires courts to consider the process by which a rule is developed. We have seen in this and previous chapters that Congress has added much procedural complexity to the original design for rulemaking established in the Administrative Procedure Act. By adding new requirements to consider general issues, such as the environment, paperwork, and small businesses; by increasing the types of studies and analyses on which rules are based; and by affording greater opportunities for public participation, Congress has invited lawsuits under this provision of the APA. When such issues are raised in a lawsuit, the courts must consider them.

The avoidance of rulemaking in favor of other procedures is also an issue that might arise under this provision. For example, scholars have observed a tendency in governmental agencies to use many different devices, such as guidelines, technical manuals, and policy statements—to establish new standards and expectations. Sometimes the motivation is to avoid the procedural rigor, participation, and openness in decision making that characterize rulemaking by using mechanisms that can be developed internally. Courts review such documents when litigants agree that they are, in effect, rules. If convinced, courts force agencies to conduct some form of rulemaking to replace the rejected document.

Finally we come to section 706(2)(a), which grants our federal courts the right to question the judgments of our rulemakers. The language of this provision does not appear to establish a particularly rigorous standard for those who write rules. The dictionary meanings of *arbitrary* and *capricious* would appear to give rulemakers considerable freedom to fashion rules without the fear of being repudiated by a judge.[51] The term *abuse of discretion* lacks any inherent meaning and is entirely dependent on the context provided by the statute that authorizes rulemaking in the first place. But, as we will see in a moment, these words and phrases have been given meanings by the courts, which create a set of criteria for rulemaking agencies to meet that are more exacting than their literal meanings might suggest.

The scope of judicial oversight is broad. It encompasses every significant aspect of rulemaking. Courts are free to determine whether an agency has the authority to write a rule in the first place, whether it has acted quickly enough with the authority it has, whether it has observed proper procedure when doing so, and if the result is sound law and public policy. This final element of the courts' oversight power is far and away the most potent and controversial. When courts make decisions about the content of rules, they are inevitably substituting their judgment for those of administrative officials whom Congress charged with the development of rules. Such actions, when taken by unelected officials with lifetime appointments, cannot be taken lightly in a democracy. Hence, the standards that the courts employ when reviewing a challenge to agency rulemaking is crucially important.

The criteria that courts use to determine whether an agency has performed its rulemaking task in a legally permissible manner vary with the issues in dispute. All require judgments by reviewing judges. If the issue is the constitutionality of a given rule, the judges first have to be convinced that a constitutionally protected right or principle is at issue. If they decide that it is, they must then exercise judgment as to whether it has been violated. Constitutional issues do arise in rulemaking, and when they do the courts usually balance the interests of the government against those of private parties. On occasion the courts are asked to resolve a constitutional issue that involves the balance of power between the branches of government. This occurred in the successful challenge to the legislative veto and the largely unsuccessful challenges to presidential review of rules. The dispositions of these types of cases hinge on the judges' conception of the principle of the separation of powers. These types of cases are sufficiently uncommon and the circumstances are sufficiently diverse that outcomes are determined by the unique blend of facts and judicial philosophy that is present in each instance.

When litigation over rulemaking involves questions about the authority of an agency to write a rule, the court must go to the statute and, if it is unclear, to its legislative history to determine the intent of Congress. If the issue is the adequacy of the procedures used to develop a rule, the court must once again return to statutes, but in this case more than the authorizing law may be involved. At minimum the court refers to the Administrative Procedure Act, the authorizing statute the rule seeks to implement, and any general statute that might be relevant given the subject matter of the rule. Some of the more prominent of these—the National Environmental Policy Act, the Paperwork Reduction Act, the Regulatory Flexibility Act—were discussed in earlier chapters. If the issue is whether the substance of the rule is consistent with the statutory provisions it seeks to implement, the court must take cognizance of all the issues raised above, since all of these bear on the substance of the rule. When appropriate, the courts are also attentive to the quality of information and analytical techniques that the agency drew upon when formulating the rule. In the instances when the substance of the rule is being challenged, the court, in its review, must inevitably question the judgment of the officials who wrote the rule. In these circumstances the general posture of the courts toward rulemakers becomes critically important. The extent to which judges defer to the many types of judgments an agency writing a rule must make often determines the outcome of court review.

There are strongly contrasting views of the role courts should assume when considering challenges to agency rulemaking. One, expressed in a series of Supreme Court decisions from the early 1970s to the mid-1980s, argues for a searching and skeptical review by the judges. Perhaps the most frequently cited opinion taking this view is that in *Citizens to Preserve Overton Park v. Volpe*, in which the Court ruled that the "arbitrary, capricious" standard of the APA required review that was "searching and careful." The Court must determine "whether the [agency's] decision was based on a consideration of the relevant factors and whether there had been a clear error in judgement." [52] While offering the general admonition that judges should not routinely substitute their judgment for that of agency experts, the opinion in *Overton Park* is what came to be known as the "hard look" standard of review. It appeared to be reinforced in the Court's decision in *Motor Vehicle Manufacturers Association v. State Farm*. In that opinion the justices stated that a rule should be rejected

> if the agency has relied on factors Congress had not intended it to consider, entirely failed to consider an important aspect of the problem, offered an explanation for its decision that runs counter to the evidence before it or is so implausible that it could not be ascribed to a difference in view or a product of agency expertise.[53]

This would insinuate courts deeply into the details of rulemaking and allow judges considerable freedom to find a rule defective. This general approach to review reveals strong doubts about the ability of agencies to carry out their rulemaking tasks competently and within the bounds set for them by Congress. Under the "hard look" doctrine, the remedy for these expected bureaucratic shortcomings is a vigilant and aggressive judiciary.

There is, however, another view of the proper relationship between courts and the agencies whose rules they review. It is best expressed in two Supreme Court decisions, one dealing with rulemaking procedures and the other with the substance of the decisions that agencies make. In *Vermont Yankee Nuclear Power Corp. v.*

Natural Resources Defense Council the Supreme Court called for a halt to judicial tinkering with the elements of the informal rulemaking process.[54] In the late 1960s and through much of the 1970s judicial decisions were rendered that had the effect of altering rulemaking procedure. In the *Vermont Yankee* case the issue was whether the Nuclear Regulatory Commission had acted properly when it used notice and comment rulemaking or whether a more formal type of process was required. The statute under which the NRC operated for the rulemaking in question did not mandate the use of formal, trial-type procedures. A lower court had agreed with the litigants and ordered the commission to use more elaborate procedures. The Supreme Court found this to be an unacceptable usurpation of agency discretion by the judiciary. The opinion admonished the lower courts to refrain from what it called "Monday morning quarterbacking" and allow agencies to fashion procedures they deemed appropriate to the rulemaking task at hand, within the confines of the statutory direction they had been given by Congress.

The Court took a similar tack in a case involving the exercise of substantive discretion by a rulemaking agency. The now famous *Chevron USA v. NRDC* decision appears to grant latitude to agencies as broad as those that the earlier *State Farm* case appeared to grant to the judiciary. The case involved challenges to EPA rules that define the sources of air pollution. In *Chevron*, the Court stated:

> If the intent of Congress is clear, that is the end of the matter; for the court as well as the agency must give effect to the unambiguously expressed intent of the Congress. If, however, the court determines Congress has not directly addressed the precise question at issue the court does not simply impose its own construction on the statute as would be necessary in the absence of an administrative interpretation. Rather, if the statute is silent or ambiguous with respect to the specific issue, the question for the court is whether the agency's answer is based on a permissible construction of the statute.[55]

Under this model of judicial oversight Congress is expected to be both "direct" and "precise," and when it is not, the agency need only convince a court that its actions are "permissible" or, as the justices state later in the opinion, "reasonable." Unlike the standards outlined in *State Farm*, those in the *Chevron* case would appear to place much discretion in the hands of the agency writing rules under most statutes and would restrict the ability of courts to exercise searching oversight of the rulemaking agencies. In point of fact the apparent dissonance between these two Supreme Court decisions, issued so close in time to one another, is real. While legal scholars have attempted to demonstrate how these disparate judicial philosophies can be interpreted so as not to be hopelessly at odds with each other, from the perspective of judicial oversight of rulemaking it is more important to determine just how influential such doctrines are with the lower-court judges who must apply them in individual cases.

Available evidence strongly suggests that any general policy articulated by the Supreme Court regarding review of rulemaking will be inconsistently interpreted by judges in the lower tribunals. Reaction to the *Chevron* case is instructive. Legal scholars examining its effects on the decisions of lower courts find two distinct patterns. One is consistent with the dominant interpretation of *Chevron* in that some courts in some cases appear to defer to agency decisions when the judges determine that Congress was silent or obscure on the matter under review. Other courts have been no more deferential under *Chevron* than they had been when the "hard look" model of judicial oversight was in full force.[56] This continued aggressiveness is attributable to judges who either interpret *Chevron*'s statements about the substantive content of statutes loosely or interpret its standards for agency use of discretion—"permissible" and "reasonable"—quite rigorously. Like all general doctrines regarding the scope of judicial review, the standards in *Chevron* and *State Farm* are applied in a dizzying array of circumstances presented in thousands of cases before hundreds of different federal judges. As one observer put it, "Like the *Overton Park* decision twenty years earlier, *State Farm* and *Chevron* are likely to continue to provide the framework for the seemingly never-ending dialogue on the shape of the partnership between courts and administrative agencies." [57]

A word is in order on the importance of the *reasonableness* standard to reviewing courts. That term is a constant in review decisions, regardless of their posture toward the role of the courts in the supervision of rulemaking. Hence, it is important to understand how the courts give meaning to this term. The Administrative Conference of the United States devotes considerable time to the evolving relationship between the courts and rulemaking agencies. In their guide to rulemaking issued by the Conference, Mintz and Miller have summarized the judiciary's approach in this manner:

1. A reviewing court normally will not substitute its judgment for that of the agency in making factual conclusions so long as the agency's conclusions have a substantial basis in the record; this is particularly true where the subject matter is technical, on the frontiers of science, or involves a considerable exercise of agency expertise.
2. A reviewing court generally will defer to agency policy judgments, so long as they are "rational" or "reasonable"—concededly vague terms—and they are the product of what has

traditionally been called "reasoned decisionmaking." To demonstrate that reasoned decisionmaking has taken place, an agency must explain in its statement of basis and purpose why it has rejected significant alternative options, why it has departed from past policies, and how its conclusions are derived from the facts in the record.[58]

These paragraphs capture well the types of decisions and forms of support for which agencies will be held accountable. They leave out the important question of how courts will perceive and judge the quality of the analysis and explanations provided by agencies in support of the rules that are challenged. These judicial decisions are framed by the circumstances in each case and by the philosophy and experience of the judge. Ultimately, abstract discussions of the scope of review must give way to the practical implications of the decisions of judges in individual cases. The critical issue that remains is the effect of judicial oversight on rulemaking.

As is the case with White House review, the effect of judicial oversight on rulemaking varies considerably across the agencies of the federal government. Certain agencies conduct a large number of rulemakings each year that are rarely affected by adverse judicial decisions. Notable among these are the Federal Aviation Administration in the Department of Transportation and the Agricultural Marketing Service in the Department of Agriculture. There are many others, as well. Granted, these agencies and others like them issue large numbers of comparatively minor, routine rules, but their relative immunity from judicial supervision is better explained by the behavior of the constituencies affected by the rules they write.

The private sector that is affected rarely sues agencies like these, and without litigious private parties the courts cannot take an active role in overseeing the rulemaking process. The reasons for the absence of numerous lawsuits are many. External constituencies that are most affected by the rules and best situated to litigate if they are unhappy may be intimately involved in the agency's rulemaking process and in general agreement with the overall results. This appears to be the case with both the Agricultural Marketing Service and the Federal Aviation Administration. Further, a few agencies, such as the FAA, deal in highly technical areas, and the interaction between experts in the public and private sectors is both frequent and characterized by substantial amounts of agreement on what needs to be done.

The key variable that triggers the litigation that brings judicial oversight is the magnitude of the negative effects anticipated by parties that have the resources and willingness to sue. One would be hard pressed to find a single rulemaking agency that can always avoid such circumstances. It is safe to say, however, that this type of situation is confronted most often by the major agencies of social regulation, and the reasons are clear enough. Their rules often have enormous effect on certain industries and sectors of the economy. These agencies, such as the EPA, OSHA, the Consumer Product Safety Commission, and the National Highway Transportation Safety Administration, confront multiple private—and sometimes public—constituencies that have opposing views on what rules should contain and whether they should be issued at all. Further, their work spans whole sectors of the economy, affecting well-organized, well-resourced, and litigation-prone individuals, groups, and organizations. Litigation is inevitable. Consequently, judicial oversight is frequent and substantial in its effects.

The frequency of lawsuits that challenge rules in certain agencies is breathtaking. No new health standard issued by the Occupational Safety and Health Administration has escaped lawsuit, and the rules have usually been challenged by both labor and management. One routinely argues that the rules fail to meet the statutory obligation of protecting workers from risk of disease. The other complains that the rules demand levels of worker protection that are excessive and illegal. The Office of General Counsel at the Environmental Protection Agency estimates that 85 percent of the hundreds of nonroutine rules issued by the EPA each year are challenged in court. Agencies of social regulation provide the best opportunity to observe the full range of potential effects that judicial oversight can have on rulemaking. Fortunately, at least one, the EPA, has attracted sufficient scholarly interest that we now have a reasonably firm grip on the many ways judicial supervision can change rulemaking.

Rosemary O'Leary, of Syracuse University, conducted an exhaustive assessment of the effects of federal court decisions on the EPA. Her work is valuable for many reasons, but one is especially pertinent to the topic of this chapter. She places the results of litigation challenging EPA action, many of which were rules and rulemaking, into categories based on the intensity of judicial oversight and the effects on the agency.[59] The categories and the examples she provides for each can easily be extended to other rulemaking agencies. For example, one category consisted of cases in which the decision of the EPA was reviewed and fully upheld by the court. This category held a substantial percentage of the cases she studied, which would support the agency's claim that, although it is frequently sued, it wins in court more often than not.

O'Leary found that sometimes the mere filing of the lawsuit appeared to trigger a change in EPA policy or operation practices. Examples of this type of situation include the agency's decision to study the chemical formaldehyde after a lawsuit was filed in an attempt to force the agency to do so and the agency's change in policy regarding substances that were disposed of in landfills.[60] Her findings confirm a general point made earlier about the power that courts exert by their very presence in our system of government. In these instances the availability of the courts to litigants persuaded the agency and the affected party to reach, in effect, an agreement on a matter in dispute.

Cases in which the courts took action to invalidate all or part of an agency action fell, according to O'Leary's ordering scheme, into three categories. The categories were based on the relative "activism" the judges displayed in their review of the EPA's performance. In the first category were decisions that reflected a relatively passive judicial presence that was "reluctant to intervene . . . but nonetheless issued decisions that affected EPA policy and/or administration." In this category one finds decisions that rejected agreements made between agencies and private companies on testing procedures for toxic substances, required the issuance of certain rules and accelerated the pace of others under the Resource Conservation and Recovery Act, and sent a set of Safe Drinking Water rules back for reconsideration because of "technical uncertainty." Other decisions in this group had the effect of increasing the power of the EPA over the environmental actions of other agencies and opened an entirely new area—the injection of waste into underground wells—for agency rulemaking.[61] Although these decisions cover a wide range of procedure and substance, they are distinguished by the fact that they required change but provided little additional direction.

The second category consisted of decisions in which the judges exercised normal "discretionary powers" to force the agency to make changes.[62] In this group the courts both required change and exercised what is now considered normal levels of supervision. A significant number of cases were in this group, and, again, they cover a wide range of substance and procedure. Examples include mandatory timetables for the completion of certain rules with mandatory semiannual progress reports to the court and mandatory meetings by the agency with all affected parties to develop plans for the completion of rules supervised by the judge. The characteristics that appear to set this group of cases apart from the previous groups are the degree of direction given by judges on the process the agency was to use to develop rules and the role of the judge in supervising the behavior of the agency after the decision was rendered.

The third category in this group included cases in which the judges involved had "gone beyond the normal patterns of judicial behavior" in their oversight of the agency. These cases were not uncommon. They too varied considerably in subject matter. One distinguishing factor in these cases was that the judges involved went beyond process considerations and rejected scientific and technical judgments made by EPA experts. Among the rules affected were those dealing with PCB contamination, radionuclides, and a variety of substances covered by pesticide statutes. Also in this category of decisions were those in which procedural guidance that can only be termed extraordinary was given to the agency. In one case the judge ordered a private interest group, in effect, to oversee the agency's compliance with his decision by filing another lawsuit should compliance lag. In another, the judge doubled the statutorily established notice requirements. One remarkable decision found that a judge, clearly impatient with the pace of agency rulemaking, ordered the EPA to report on "all internal and external agency actions taken to minimize or eliminate all funding and personnel constraints that may serve as barriers to compliance" with his order.[63] In this case the judge was behaving very much like an irate supervisor building a case to terminate an employee with serious performance problems.

For the EPA, at least, this level of judicial interest and activity is not new. In an earlier work, which focuses on the early years of the EPA, R. Shep Melnick found that, soon after the passage of landmark environmental statutes, the agency was in court defending, often unsuccessfully, its performance in several areas of rulemaking. Melnick found judicial decisions that created and completely reoriented whole programs of rulemaking, altered time frames for the production of rules, and altered the process, both by changing patterns of public participation and by rejecting the scientific and technical analyses and judgments underlying regulations.[64]

Although the combination of frequency and intrusiveness of judicial supervision of EPA rulemaking may be unmatched, examples like those in each of O'Leary's categories can be found for most rulemaking agencies. Extrapolating from the experience of this one agency it becomes clear that no area of rulemaking is beyond the reach of the federal judiciary. Our judges are full and active players in the rulemaking process and, in some instances, exert a degree of control that exceeds the reach and grasp of either the Congress or the president. It is ironic, perhaps, that our most passive and least responsive branch of government will, in many instances, be the most aggressive and influential overseer of the rulemaking process.

This chapter has demonstrated, one hopes persuasively, that the enormous volume of rulemaking and its central importance to our system of government has not rendered the constitutionally established branches powerless or irrelevant. Instead, its rise has caused a redirection of effort by members of Congress, occupants of the White

House, and judges. They expend considerable time and effort attempting to learn about the rulemaking activities of the agencies and then to influence the content of the rules that are produced. We have seen that the powers at the disposal of the three branches are quite different but that each is in its own way formidable. Some mechanisms are preemptive and direct; others are indirect and subtle. As we have seen in other dimensions of rulemaking, these mechanisms are not used in all cases. Oversight, like the many legal requirements of rulemaking procedure, becomes a factor most often for rules that are likely to have major effects and generate opposition.

It is also apparent that there is competition, and occasional cooperation, between the branches in the struggle for control of rulemaking. The competition is evident in the sometimes intense conflict between Congress and the White House over the legislative veto and presidential review of proposed and final rules. But Congress has also increased the capacity of presidential oversight by writing the Paperwork Reduction Act with provisions for OMB review and clearance. The White House has returned the favor with its agreements on disclosure of rulemaking-related communications by OMB staff and its quiet acceptance of rulings of the lower courts on the importance of releasing rules in a timely manner so they meet congressional deadlines. The courts have umpired this contest for institutional advantage. The results for the other branches have been mixed, whereas the judiciary's own oversight capacity has been carefully preserved. The courts eliminated the legislative veto but have consistently upheld the supremacy of legislative intent in the rulemaking process. The courts have also been the major force behind the continuing influence of congressional deadlines. Judges have consistently upheld the legitimacy of presidential management of the rulemaking process but have also made it plain that it cannot perform in such a way that either congressional or judicial mandates are ignored or subverted. For itself, pronouncements to the contrary notwithstanding, the judiciary has issued decisions that not only influence the process and content of rulemaking in profound ways but also invite lawsuits in the future. This is a way of ensuring that its inherent passivity will not be an obstacle to effective oversight.

NOTES

1. Matthew McCubbins, Roger Noll, and Barry Weingast, "Administrative Procedures as Instruments of Political Control" (Paper delivered to the Annual Meeting of the Midwest Political Science Association, Chicago, March 1987), p. 53.
2. Theodore Lowi, "Two Roads to Serfdom: Liberalism, Conservatism and

Administrative Power," *American University Law Review* 36 (1987): 317.

3. 42 U.S.C., 6924(d)(1),(2).

4. Benjamin Mintz and Nancy Miller, *A Guide to Federal Agency Rulemaking,* 2d ed. (Washington, D.C.: Administrative Conference of the United States, 1991), p. 15 at n. 54.

5. Rosemary O'Leary, *Environmental Change: Federal Courts and EPA* (Philadelphia: Temple University Press, 1993), p. 171.

6. Christopher Foreman, *Signals from the Hill: Congressional Oversight and the Challenge of Social Regulation* (New Haven: Yale University Press, 1988), pp. 93-94.

7. William Niskanen, *Bureaucracy and Representative Government* (Chicago: Aldine, 1971), pp. 29-30.

8. Barry Mitnick, *The Political Economy of Regulation* (New York: Columbia University Press, 1980).

9. Matthew McCubbins, "Legislative Design of Regulatory Structure," *American Journal of Political Science* 29 (1985): 721-748.

10. Randall Calvert, Matthew McCubbins, and Barry Weingast, "A Theory of Political Control of Agency Discretion," *American Journal of Political Science* 33 (1989): 588-611.

11. Gary Bryner has argued that bureaucrats exercise little or no discretion during rulemaking. See Gary Bryner, *Bureaucratic Discretion: Law and Policy in Federal Regulatory Agencies* (Boston: Little, Brown, 1987).

12. Calvert, McCubbins, and Weingast, "Theory of Political Control," p. 606.

13. Joel Aberbach, *Keeping a Watchful Eye* (Washington, D.C.: Brookings Institution, 1990).

14. Matthew McCubbins and Thomas Schwartz, "Congressional Oversight Overlooked: Police Patrols versus Fire Alarms," *American Journal of Political Science* 28 (1987): 165-179.

15. Foreman, *Signals from the Hill,* pp. 100-101.
    This list includes examples that one can comfortably place in each of the categories established by McCubbins and Schwartz. Foreman notes that they include both "public spirited values and narrower constituency interests." Ibid., p. 100.

16. For example, see General Accounting Office, *The Consumer Product Safety Commission Needs to Issue Safety Standards Faster* (Washington, D.C.: General Accounting Office, 1977).

17. Barbara Craig, *The Legislative Veto: Congressional Control of Regulation* (Boulder, Colo.: Westview Press, 1983), p. 27.

18. Foreman, *Signals from the Hill,* pp. 139-140.

19. Ibid., p. 141.

20. Ibid., pp. 142-144.

21. 462 U.S. 919 (1983).

22. Harold Bruff, "Presidential Management of Agency Rulemaking," *George Washington Law Review* 57, no. 3 (1989): 540.

23. Executive Office of the President, *Regulatory Program of the United States Government* (Washington, D.C., 1991), pp. 636-638, 646.

24. Bruff, "Presidential Management," pp. 568-572.

25. Richard Weyman, "A Better Way to Conduct Regulatory Review," *Washington Lawyer,* November/December 1992, p. 17.

26. Robert Percival, "Checks without Balance: Executive Office Oversight of the Environmental Protection Agency," *Law and Contemporary Problems* 54 (1991): 156-161.

27. Bruff, "Presidential Management," pp. 557-558.
28. Ibid., pp. 560-562.
29. Ibid., p. 561.
30. See *National Grain and Feed Association v. Occupational Safety and Health Administration*, 866 F.2d 717 (5th Cir. 1989), and *Environmental Defense Fund v. Thomas*, 627 F. Supp. 566 (D.D.C. 1986), discussed in Mintz and Miller, *A Guide to Federal Agency Rulemaking*, p. 33.
31. National Academy of Public Administration, *Presidential Management of Rulemaking in Regulatory Agencies* (Washington, D.C.: National Academy of Public Administration, 1987).
32. The controversy over the OMB's role triggered a considerable amount of theorizing about the proper roles of Congress and the president in rulemaking. For a review of these theoretical arguments, see James Bowers, "Looking at OMB's Regulatory Review through a Shared Powers Perspective," *Presidential Studies Quarterly* 23 (Spring 1993): 331-345, and Joseph Cooper and William West, "The Theory and Practice of OMB Review of Agency Rules," *Journal of Politics* 50 (1988): 864-895.
33. George Eads and Michael Fix, *Relief or Reform? Reagan's Regulatory Dilemma* (Washington, D.C.: Urban Institute Press, 1984).
34. Bruff, "Presidential Management," p. 595.
35. For a good review of literature and an in-depth discussion of the use of cost-benefit analysis in rulemaking, see Thomas McGarrity, *Reinventing Rationality: Regulatory Analysis in the Federal Government* (Cambridge: Cambridge University Press, 1991).
36. Howard Ball, *Courts and Politics* (Englewood Cliffs, N.J.: Prentice Hall, 1980), chap. 8.
37. R. Shep Melnick, *Regulation and the Courts* (Washington, D.C.: Brookings Institution, 1983).
38. The discussion of the various levels of courts and functions they perform and the effects of their decisions draws on the analyses found in Lawrence Baum, *American Courts: Process and Policy* (Boston: Houghton Mifflin, 1988), chaps. 2, 7, 8, and Ball, *Courts and Politics*, chaps. 3, 6, 7.
39. Mintz and Miller, *Guide to Federal Agency Rulemaking*, pp. 304-307.
40. The outline of issues and selection of cases related to judicial review closely adheres to analyses that can be found in many administrative law texts. See, for example, Stephen Breyer and Richard Stewart, *Administrative Law and Regulatory Policy* (Boston: Little, Brown, 1985) or Walter Gelhorn, Clark Byre, and Peter Strauss, *Administrative Law: Cases and Comments*, 7th ed. (Mineola, N.Y.: Foundation Press, 1979). For this section I have relied especially heavily on part IV of *A Guide to Federal Agency Rulemaking*, issued in 1991 by the Administrative Conference of the United States. It is both authoritative and accessible to nonlawyers. See Mintz and Miller, *Guide to Federal Agency Rulemaking*, pp. 279-372.
41. *Perkins v. Lukens Steel*, 310 U.S. 113 (1940).
42. *Associated Industries v. Ickes*, 134 F.2d 694 (1943).
43. 5 U.S.C. 702.
44. For example, see 42 U.S.C. A-7604.
45. *U.S. v. SCRAP*, 412 U.S. 669 (1973).
46. *Senior v. Eastern Kentucky Welfare Rights Organization*, 426 U.S. 26 (1976).
47. *Duke Power v. North Carolina Environmental Group*, 438 U.S. 59 (1978).
48. Breyer and Stewart, *Administrative Law*, pp. 1122-1144.
49. 5 U.S.C. 706.

50. Mintz and Miller, *Guide to Federal Agency Rulemaking,* 322-323.
51. See Martin Shapiro, "APA: Past, Present, Future," *Virginia Law Review* 72 (1986): 454. He notes that the plain meaning of these terms would allow agencies to issue rules with any content as long as judges did not find they had "acted like a lunatic."
52. 401 U.S. 402 (1971).
53. 463 U.S. 29 (1983).
54. 435 U.S. 519 (1978).
55. 467 U.S. 637 (1984).
56. Mintz and Miller, *Guide to Federal Agency Rulemaking,* pp. 340-341.
57. Ibid., p. 371.
58. Ibid., p. 333.
59. Rosemary O'Leary, *Environmental Change,* chap. 7.
60. Ibid., p. 154.
61. Ibid., p. 155.
62. Ibid. pp. 155-156.
63. Ibid., p. 37.
64. Melnick, *Regulation and the Courts.*

CHAPTER 7

Rulemaking: Theories and Reform Proposals

Practical, pragmatic readers are no doubt casting a wary eye on the title of this final chapter. They likely value facts, cold-eyed realism, and a problem-solving attitude. For many, "theory" connotes a painfully abstract or irrelevant academic exercise too removed from the problems of the real world to help those who must live with them, or try to solve them. Theorizing, like anything else, can be done badly. But it is folly to dismiss it out of hand. The simple fact is that the construction of a theory of rulemaking is not a luxury; it is an indispensable tool for all students of rulemaking, whether their interests lie in scholarship or practice.

THE VALUE OF THEORY

Theory brings order to a large and otherwise fragmented body of knowledge about rulemaking. It highlights the most important general features of rulemaking and the variations in each. Theory explicitly and clearly defines the relationships between those different characteristics of rulemaking and reveals how such interactions affect its process and results. In this manner it educates scholars about rulemaking and provides the essential foundation for the creation of new knowledge. Theory enables the development of predictions, or hypotheses, about rulemaking, which can then be tested through empirical research. The new knowledge that is created during the course of this research contributes, in turn, to the further development and refinement of theory.

The identification of theory with scholars, however, can divert attention from the important contributions it can make to actual practice. Theory is the servant of practice. It helps those engaged in any aspect of rulemaking to understand how their particular work contributes to the larger whole and how their contributions are affected by others working on other aspects of the process. At any given moment, someone is at work attempting to change rulemaking in order to achieve a higher purpose, fix a recognized problem, or simply serve his or her own interests. These changes are promoted by members of Congress, the president and his staff, judges, the many bureaucracies of the federal government, or interest groups. Whatever the motivation of those who would change the rulemaking process, be it lofty or venal, they should at least be sure that the actions they contemplate are likely to produce the results they desire. Theory, properly tested by solid research on actual rulemaking practice, can give these change agents confidence that the reform they are supporting will be successful or at least not make matters worse.

THE ELEMENTS OF RULEMAKING THEORY

A theory of rulemaking must provide the answers to at least three fundamental questions. First, why does rulemaking occur? The reasons why rulemaking has come to play so crucial a role in making law and establishing policy are many and reveal much about our institutions of government and the nature of our politics. Second, what determines the results of rulemaking? The conduct of rulemaking and the content of rules are influenced by many different forces. Identifying these forces and the means by which they influence rulemaking is critical to understanding how the process works and the factors to be considered when contemplating reform. Third, and most important, what are the implications of rulemaking for our constitutional system? Each of these questions has been raised and dealt with in various ways in the previous chapters. A review of what we know about each of these questions strongly suggests that a comprehensive theory of rulemaking is well within our grasp.

WHY DOES RULEMAKING OCCUR?

The fact that rulemaking has been occurring since the dawn of the Republic means its existence is owed to something quite fundamental in our political system. At the most superficial level, we can argue that rulemaking happens because throughout our long experience as a representative democracy the legislature has always turned to the executive branch or other administrative entities to provide the minor details of programs set in motion by statutes. In this view, while technically a legislative function, rulemaking is not to be confused with the real powers of Congress. The subject matter of rules is too innocuous, trivial, or routine to be considered on a par with statutes.

Congress is simply handing off work that is not worthy of its attention to subordinates who act on its behalf. This type of argument was embraced by the federal judiciary earlier in this century when it rejected arguments that Congress was unconstitutionally delegating powers to agencies. However reassuring this quaint view of rulemaking might be, material presented in earlier chapters make it plain that it is an unsatisfactory explanation for the occurrence of rulemaking. Many rules are inconsequential or minor, but their cumulative weight most certainly is not. The roots of rulemaking are found in the relative capacities of governmental institutions and the preferences of the various actors who together comprise our governmental system.

The growth of the federal government, particularly during this century, was both the cause and the consequence of rulemaking. As members of Congress created ever-greater responsibilities for the federal government, they repeatedly confronted and acknowledged the limitations of their own institution. Unable to provide all the essential elements of virtually every public program they formulated, they turned to agencies for help. Whether the growth of government since the onset of the Great Depression is a result of congressional responsiveness to unprompted constituency demands or due to the discovery of the electoral bullet-proofing provided by pork, the effects on rulemaking are indisputable. Congress has always chosen to cede crucial elements of the design and virtually all implementation of thousands of programs to rulemaking. Overwhelmed by demands from the public or by their own ambition, it was clear to the members of every Congress since the first that they could not provide in statutes all that was needed to define and guide public policy.

To argue, in effect, that rulemaking is both a cause and consequence defies logic. Perhaps it is more accurate to say that a symbiotic relationship exists between the growth of government and the role of rulemaking. Government could not have grown as rapidly as it did unless rulemaking had supplied the specifics of law, policy, and procedure. Rulemaking would not be so prominent if the reach of public policy and law was less ambitious. The habit of relying on rulemaking, once established, has proven impossible to break as successive waves of statutes created ever-larger agendas for rulemaking by agencies. Although it is conceivable that Congress could provide all the necessary operating principles and procedures of every public program it creates, the time taken in assembling the requisite information and resolving the inevitable disputes over these minute details would ensure there would be far fewer programs than there are today. In addition, the enormous technical complexity would stymie the current Congress. An alternative is a vastly larger Congress and attendant staff, a development that would require massive constitutional change and political adjustments. Of course, there is always the option of turning general and vague statutes over to agencies without the authority to write rules. Then, agencies could function entirely free of the channeling and constraining effects of rules and deal with all clients, regulated parties, and applications according to their own discretion. Under our Constitution this would obviously be unacceptable. Some critics argue that even under our present system bureaucratic discretion is too great. Congress sees rulemaking as a tool for maintaining accountability.

The institutional limitations on Congress and the huge legislative capacity rulemaking adds to our governmental system are important factors in explaining the occurrence of rulemaking. But at an even more fundamental level the incidence of rulemaking can be explained by an examination of the preferences of the actors who make up our political system. It was argued in Chapter 1 that rulemaking served the interests of Congress, the president, the courts, agencies, and organized interests. It is useful to review at somewhat greater depth the reasons these actors prefer rulemaking to other means of specifying law and policy.

Any attempt to explain the occurrence of rulemaking must begin with Congress. Fortunately, there is considerable literature devoted to the general question of delegation of legislative authority and even more to questions related to Congress's apparent preference for transferring powers like rulemaking to administrative agencies. Some years ago Morris Fiorina developed the "shift responsibility" model of legislative behavior.[1] In it members of Congress delegate functions like rulemaking to administrative agencies whenever they suspect that the decisions made during the course of these types of actions could stimulate controversy, criticism, and adverse political consequences. Since many, if not most, of the programs initiated since the start of the New Deal carried with them the possibility of alienating one or more powerful interests, Fiorina's model, now accepted by many political scientists, would explain the great profusion of rulemaking. By shifting responsibility and deferring difficult or dangerous decisions to rulemaking, Congress does not necessarily cede control over the content of rules. Congress remains concerned and active with regard to rulemaking through a variety of oversight devices. Kenneth Culp Davis argued twenty-five years ago that by insisting on rulemaking Congress increases its capacity to oversee the administrative process.[2] Rulemaking is easier to track, observe, and intervene in than other forms of bureaucratic action.

Presidents and judges, to the extent that they prefer rulemaking, do so for reasons different from those of Congress. Administrative agencies present both the executive and judicial branches of government with formidable challenges to their constitutional responsibilities and prerogatives. For the president, this vast bureaucracy is a threat to his ability to obtain the policies promised during campaigns. For the judges, administrative agencies are the source of millions of decisions with quite direct and sometimes profound effects on the lives of individuals. The actions that cause these effects must be grounded in the law that judges interpret and apply. The observation and supervision of rulemaking is distinctly advantageous to both the president and the judiciary.

The clearing of all rules through the Office of Management and Budget could have been initiated by any president. Presidents may prefer no rulemaking whatsoever and move to frustrate it, as recent presidents have. But rulemaking is inevitable, so presidents must choose an alternative route to influence it. Rules are a form of administrative action that are peculiarly susceptible to presidential scrutiny. In addition, they establish general policies and procedures that form the basis of the countless actions taken in individual cases by thousands of bureaucrats. This makes rulemaking a tempting target for intervention. Any effort to control other types of administrative actions, such as the granting or denial of government benefits, enforcement actions in regulatory programs, or the direct delivery of services would simply not be feasible because of the sheer volume of these types of actions. Review of rulemaking allows the president to put a policy stamp on significant agency decisions that in turn affect all pertinent aspects of a program's implementation.

The judiciary faces a problem similar to that of the president, with the obvious difference that our judges are not proactively pursuing a partisan political or policy agenda. Davis argued strongly twenty-five years ago that courts should insist that agencies write rules in order to assert their authority over administrators.[3] The enormous number and variety of interactions between agencies and people, all of which are supposed to be based on law, far exceed the limited capacity of the courts to hear cases or the ability of those aggrieved by illegal agency actions to bring them in the first place. Rulemaking alters both of these conditions. While quite numerous to be sure, the volume of significant rules pales in comparison to other forms of administrative action. More important, rules often affect a large number of people, and when these effects are adverse such groups have the incentive and may have the organization and resources to challenge the legality of the proposed governmental action. Their authority thus invoked through litigation, the judges are presented with the opportunity to review and influence rules in a manner analogous to that used by the White House, albeit for very different reasons. In this instance judges who are so inclined are able to impose their view of the law on the development of rules, thus having a broad effect on the programs for which rules provide the architecture. Rulemaking thus provides both the president and the courts, institutions with limited capacities, something that no other common form of administrative action provides: an opportunity to observe and supervise the bureaucracy. We would expect, then, both the chief executive and the judiciary, whatever their attitudes, at least grudgingly to encourage rulemaking because it broadens their oversight powers.

Rulemaking is congenial to interest groups. During the past several decades interest groups have grown in number, diversified, and narrowed their focus. Interest groups are sufficiently sophisticated to understand the benefits and costs that may arise from rules. They have also developed the means for monitoring rulemaking processes and for communicating their views to the rulemakers. They prefer the relative calm and predictability of a process that operates according to fixed procedures, participation in which requires at least a modicum of technical expertise and a certain understanding of bureaucratic decision making. Congressional decision making hinges less often on technical considerations than on politics. While rulemaking may affect large numbers of people, it also tends to deal with narrow, highly specific issues. As rules become increasingly detailed, more specific to an industry or product, and more technical, the rulemaking process grows more susceptible to the strengths of interest groups. In such situations agencies frequently lack some or all of the essential information to formulate the rule and must turn to interest groups or their individual members for the data or analyses that are required. Information becomes influence.

Finally, there are the personnel in the agencies that write the rules. Their preferences for rulemaking are as diverse as the rulemakers themselves. Much has been written about those who populate our federal agencies. The most persistent distinction drawn in the literature is between political appointees and the career civil servants. Of the two, it is apparent that the political appointees are more likely unequivocally to welcome rulemaking. Like that of the president, the ability of appointees to review rules written in the offices and bureaus under their discretion allows them to influence policy within their limited sphere. It also enables these officials to express themselves in the content of rules and in the way they are written. Involvement in rulemaking provides political appointees one of the best ways to leave a mark on an agency that they will probably be with for only a short time.

The posture of career civil servants toward rulemaking is not as clear, because these individuals may be motivated by many different goals. In his classic work *Inside Bureaucracy,* Anthony Downs posits that there are five types of bureaucrats: climbers, conservers, advocates, zealots, and statespersons. Climbers are personally ambitious. Conservers are cautious, even fearful, of any action that might expose them to criticism or disturb the status quo to which they have grown accustomed. Advocates are more pragmatic bureaucratic politicians. They act to protect their particular office's programs. Zealots are true believers, ideologues who are convinced that theirs is the sole legitimate vision for the program in which they work. Statespersons are concerned with the health of their agency and its program, seeking consensus based on reasoned discourse and fair consideration of all positions. Some may consider these caricatures, rather than archetypes. Motives and behavior vary with situations, but Downs's types do capture traits of real-world bureaucrats. Each of these traits has implications for the occurrence of rulemaking.[4]

The climber can enhance his or her reputation by leading a work group responsible for a significant, highly visible rule. The conserver, while generally preferring to do nothing, can take solace in those agencies and situations in which rulemaking is a collective decision-making process with many participants and multiple layers of review and approval. Then, rulemaking is a process in which the individual bureaucrat can easily avoid the sometimes harsh light of recognition. The advocate can participate in rulemaking work groups and protect his or her program. The zealot regards rulemaking as a marvelous opportunity to impose his or her world view on a program, comparable to rewriting the statute. Finally, the statesperson views the collective nature of most significant rulemaking quite differently from the conserver. Work groups and task forces are seen by the statesperson as vehicles for forging consensus. Therefore, rulemaking becomes a way to strengthen the agency and its programs.

The occurrence of rulemaking is thus explained by the convergence of four factors: the volume of demands presented to Congress by the American people, the tendency of Congress to respond positively to those demands, the limitations that prevent Congress from writing laws specific enough to be administered, and the confluence of self-interests among the most important actors in our political system. The first cornerstone of a theory of rulemaking is in place.

WHAT DETERMINES THE CONTENT OF RULES?

Of the fundamental questions that a theory of rulemaking must address, this one is clearly the most complex and difficult. It is also one that is the most intriguing to scholars and practitioners alike. For scholars, the answer to this question reveals much about the underlying dynamics and distribution of power in our contemporary political system. Practitioners should be anxious to learn about the forces that impinge on them and affect what they produce when they function as rulemakers. Those who have struggled through the book to this point have some appreciation for why the answer to this question is neither simple nor easy to construct. As we have seen, rules are enormously varied in content and effect. This ensures variation in the basic forces that are present to a greater or lesser extent in all rulemaking efforts.

GENERAL INFLUENCES.   Considering what has been discussed in the preceding chapters, and the full body of research relevant to rulemaking, it appears that the results of rulemaking, including the contents of rules, are determined by four large and interrelated forces. Some combination of law, information, politics, and management is present in every rulemaking effort. The importance of these factors to rulemaking has been identified by other scholars.

Keith Hawkins and John Thomas have argued that rulemaking is "a complex activity subject to a variety of legal, political and bureaucratic constraints."[5] The effects of each of these factors on rulemaking should now be apparent. Law establishes the substantive goals and procedural requirements for rulemaking; it directs agency efforts and provides the standards against which the agency's final product is judged. Information is the raw material from which rules are formulated in accordance with law. The availability and quality of information largely determine the quality and affect the timeliness of the rule. Politics permeates the rulemaking process, bringing strong pressures to bear on those developing rules. Management can affect both the content and pace of rulemaking. Internal concurrence systems, for example, ensure that the political leadership of agencies have their say during the process, and various kinds of administrative devices can either expedite or impede the flow of rules.

We must acknowledge, however, that it is a serious mistake to consider these forces as mutually exclusive categories or in some instances even easily distinguishable from one another. These dimensions overlap; each exerts some influence over the others. In the interactions of these dimensions the contents of rules are formed. Law sets the goals and objectives of rulemaking. In so doing it determines the type of information agencies must consider, provides parameters within which political forces will contend for influence, and provides management structures in agencies with their rulemaking mission. Information influences the content of law insofar as its availability and quality allows Congress to be specific in the goals and objectives it sets for agencies. Information is the currency of politics as it is practiced in rulemaking. The various parties use technical, scientific, economic, administrative, and attitudinal information strategically to influence the content of rules. The collection and analysis of information dominates rulemaking management systems, from the setting of priorities to the publication of a final rule in the *Federal Register*. Politics determines the content of law in the first instance. It heavily influences the interpretation and significance afforded information developed during the course of rulemaking. Politics affects both the internal and external environments that impinge on agency rulemaking management systems. The management of the rulemaking, including both culture and operating systems, determines the personnel who interpret the law and the means by which information is collected, analyzed, and used. The culture of agencies, consisting of widely held values and customary procedures, determines how internal politics play out and how rulemakers interact with the external forces attempting to influence their work.

Across the range of governmental rulemaking the variation within each of these dimensions is considerable. Law varies in the specificity and scope of goals it sets for agency rulemaking and in the type of information that must be considered during the rulemaking process. There are dramatic differences in the quality and availability of information in individual rulemakings. Political conflict can be widespread and intense or nonexistent. Management of rulemaking in agencies varies as well. In addition to the findings on management systems presented in Chapter 4, there is solid evidence that the rulemaking cultures of agencies can vary widely.

Every major player in the American political system—Congress, the president, the courts, interest groups, and the bureaucracy—is deeply involved in rulemaking and in each of its dimensions. They influence the formation and interpretation of law. Each generates or evaluates information used in the formation of rules. Most are politically active or must deal with the fallout from political conflict. Each is either actively involved in or trying to influence the management of the rulemaking process. But like the dimensions of rulemaking, there is considerable variation within each of these categories of major institutional players. None is monolithic. Congress is highly decentralized, speaking with many voices on any issue of substance. The courts, populated by judges who have varying legal philosophies, have been known to send conflicting messages to agencies. Interest groups come in all sizes, beliefs, policy concerns, and capacities to influence government decision making. The bureaucracy is populated by political and career officials. The political appointees may be faithfully following the president or pursuing their own agendas. There is tremendous variation in the educational backgrounds, professional orientations, and experience of career staff members. Further, they bring to their work different motivations.

It is also important to note that each of these players may focus his or her attention on different dimensions of rulemaking in order to influence the result. Congress is preoccupied with setting goals and objectives through law, but doing so requires attention to information requirements. Congress also exerts political pressure during the rulemaking process and involves itself in management to the extent that statutes or oversight activities set rulemaking priorities, provide budgets for programs requiring rulemaking, and set deadlines for the completion of work. Presidents to date have focused on management, notably the review analyses, and on the political dimension. Interest groups try to influence the content of law, including information requirements. They use the information they have in hand to affect the agency's thinking about the content of rules. They too mobilize political pressure and bring it to bear on agencies. The courts focus on the law, but this leads inexorably to the information on which rules are based. Decisions of courts can bear on management insofar as priorities, budgets, and deadlines are affected. The agencies, by necessity, focus on all four dimensions. They interact with Congress on the formation of statutes. Once rulemaking is under way they become preoccupied with management and information. And individual bureaucratic participants may attempt to mobilize political pressure to achieve their objectives.

Every one of these actors is important, but one, the bureaucracy, deserves special attention. Ultimately, the personnel in the rulemaking agencies are the ones who transmit the final rule to the *Federal Register* for publication. Each dimension of rulemaking is evident in the work of rulemaking agencies. The attention of all the other actors must focus on the agencies if they hope to influence the content of rules or the process by which they are written. What, then, can existing theory tell us about the factors that determine how personnel in agencies reach decisions on the contents of the rules they write? There are, in fact, two theories of agency behavior that offer contrasting ways to structure a study of rulemaking. Neither is adequate, but one provides a point of departure for a more acceptable, albeit complex, theory of how rules are formulated.

THE "BUREAU DOMINANCE" SCHOOL.   Law, information, politics, or management must structure, channel, or otherwise affect the behavior of bureaucrats if it is to influence rulemaking. Who or what controls bureaucracy is one of the central questions in contemporary scholarship devoted to public affairs. In this literature there are pronounced differences between those who have concluded that bureaucracy is the dominant force in our public policy process and others, who view bureaucrats as the servants of external masters. The bureau dominance school has included scholars as disparate as the political scientist Theodore Lowi and the economist William Niskanen. As evidence of bureau autonomy they point to massive delegations of authority, the near monopoly that bureaus enjoy with regard to critical information related to program operations, and the lack, in the other constitutional branches of government, of resources, power, or incentives to monitor and control agencies. Lowi has referred to the bureaucrats who write rules as "patrons" who dole out benefits to the American people, who have been reduced to "serfs." Niskanen focused on the behavior of bureaucrats in attempting to obtain budgets and argued that the congressional committees that reviewed such requests would frequently accede to their "budget maximizing" proposals.[6] According to the bureau dominance perspective, if law, information, or politics plays a role in rulemaking it is largely to the extent that bureaucrats allow.

Let's assume, for the sake of argument, that the bureau dominance school of thought is correct and that agencies are largely free to fashion rules to their liking. What implications does this hold for the content of rules? Existing scholarship on the composition and behavior of bureaucracies indicates that the results of rulemaking are influenced by personal, professional, and structural-cultural factors. The personal level has already been introduced through Downs's bureaucratic types. Just as each may adopt a different posture toward rulemaking per se, each seeks to achieve different results in rulemaking. The goal of conservers is likely to be a rule that represents the least threat to their comfortable status quo or, alternatively, the least potential disruption to their careers. Climbers actively pursue any rulemaking result that might advance their careers. This may mean acting to establish themselves as experts in a new area of law and public policy, thus enhancing career options in the private sector, or simply currying favor with a superior in the agency capable of recommending or granting promotion, a salary increase, or bonus. Zealots seek content in the rule that mirrors their vision for the program, whatever that may be. Advocates promote the views of their particular corner of the bureaucracy and may be every bit as strident as zealots, albeit for different reasons and perhaps with less energy. Statespersons seek results and thus behave as conciliating versions of zealots.

Thus, bureaucracies that write rules are populated with people with different motivations and personal goals. As Downs notes, pure forms of these types are probably not as common as what he calls "mixed motive" bureaucrats who vacillate between behaviors of the various types, depending on the circumstances surrounding the rule and the stage of their careers.[7] What is clear, however, is that when these motivations and behaviors manifest themselves in rulemaking agencies the results of rulemakings are affected.

William West, as we have seen, has identified professional differences among bureaucrats that affect the content of rules, focusing on the importance of training and viewpoint. He properly conceives of rulemaking as a bureaucratic task that routinely requires the involvement of lawyers, scientific and technical experts, policy analysts, and senior agency officials serving as political appointees. He hypothesizes that each of these professional groups brings different perspectives and objectives into the rulemaking enterprise. These arise from their education, training, and allegiance. Attorneys seek rules that are true to the statutes they implement, that are enforceable and capable of surviving judicial review. Scientific and technical personnel seek rules that reflect the state of knowledge in their respective disciplines, whereas policy analysts, at least those trained in cost-benefit analysis, want rules that maximize net benefits. Through a survey of agency personnel West confirmed that the hypothesized differences can be observed in the responses of these various professional groups to questions about various aspects of rulemaking.[8] Like Downs's work, West's analysis established that conflict is likely when different types of bureaucrats are engaged in rulemaking.

Thomas McGarrity has provided important insights into the variations in rulemaking structure and cultures. Based on his observations of the EPA, the National Highway Transportation Safety Administration, and other agencies, he has developed five "structural models for the internal decisionmaking process" for rulemaking. Each emphasizes different agency values and different management approaches to the rulemaking task. The "team model" conducts rulemaking in work groups comprised of representatives from all agency offices "that have an interest in the outcome of the rulemaking process" and are "co-equal partners in pursuit of the common goals of promulgating a rule that will survive internal and external review."[9] We noted that many agencies use teams of some sort. McGarrity notes that team members share a commitment to reaching consensus on important issues. Under the "hierarchical model" of rulemaking "a single office is responsible for all aspects ... except the final determination of whether the rule is consistent with the particular statute involved."[10] It appears that this model is most often used in highly technical issues and in agencies in which the essential expertise is confined to a single office, but it may also be used in other situations when the agency "is under great pressure to accomplish something in a hurry."[11]

Another model, the "outside advisor," combines features of the team and hierarchical models by vesting authority in a single office, the experts in which reach out selectively to others in the agency on an as-needed basis.[12] Obviously, this model seeks to combine the virtues of speed and economy while preserving access to others across the agency, whose expertise or acquiescence may be needed. The "adversary model" is quite different in its approach in that it actually sets up an internal, usually bilateral, trial in which interested officers develop and defend their own positions while challenging those of their adversaries; final decisions are made by senior decision makers.[13] Finally, McGarrity notes a "hybrid" model that was used for a time at the EPA. This model combines, improbably, elements of the team approach with certain features of the adversary model. The agency used an "options selection" process to consider different approaches that might be taken in selected rulemakings.[14] The process at that stage was adversarial, but when an approach was selected, the team model was then followed to develop the rule.

McGarrity's work is important because it describes bureaucratic settings in which these differences in motivation and professional orientation play themselves out. In rulemaking agencies that adopt the hierarchical model, the professional training of the individual(s) in whom decision-making authority is vested is quite important, although, as McGarrity points out, the attorneys also have some say over the final product. Of Downs's types, the zealot, climber, or advocate could be relevant as well. In the team model all professional categories and bureaucratic types could conceivably be present. For team or work-group operations, both the statesperson and the zealot are potentially important. The statesperson is likely to act to smooth differences and seek consensus and thus may serve as a mediator between advocates from various program and nonprogram offices. If the statesperson emerges as a team leader, then a result that has widespread support becomes more likely. The presence of one or more zealots, on the other hand, makes the consensus-building process more difficult, because they are unlikely to yield much if they believe their vision for the program in question is threatened. In the outside-advisor model any professional may be consulted by the office with primary responsibility. Since policy analysts with training in cost-benefit methodologies are often assigned to specialized units, they are likely candidates for consultation. Because the adversary model places a clear premium on advocacy skills, one might assume that the passion Downs's zealots bring to the preparation of their case would make them particularly effective. From West's perspective, attorneys educated in the art of advocacy would appear well positioned to take on a central role.

So, if we accept the bureau dominance theory, it is evident that there are multiple influences and often internal spirited competition for control over the results of rulemaking. The literature devoted to bureaucratic motivation, professional training, and organizational culture and structure all indicate clearly that some level of conflict is likely in significant rulemakings involving multiple personnel or offices in an agency. Even in the hierarchical model, the agency attorney, in making final determinations about the legality of the rule in question, introduces the potential for conflict. In the other models, conflict is either explicitly sought, as in the adversary approach, or an almost certain by-product of throwing together diverse professional perspectives and personal ambitions. These factors have no intrinsic political bias from which one can hypothesize the emergence of a particular type of policy.

Although the bureau dominance theory is sufficiently complex to keep interested students of rulemaking busy for some time, it is far too simplistic. The most important test of the bureau dominance model is how well it explains how rulemaking really works. If the bureau dominance school is correct, we would expect to see those who work in agencies enjoying substantial, although not unbridled, discretion in the writing of rules. This is not what Gary Bryner found in a recent study of the rulemaking processes in four major agencies: OSHA, the EPA, the Consumer Product Safety Commission, and the Food and Drug Administration. He summarized his finding this way: "If we mean by discretion that agencies are free to do as they choose, are free to allocate their resources and can exercise their power unencumbered by external checks then agencies clearly have little discretion." [15] The author went on to cite the "oversupply" of "overseers" as the major influence on rulemakers. From this perspective, attention must shift from inside the agency to these outside forces.

THE "PRINCIPAL-AGENT" SCHOOL.   Those working in agencies are aware of and responsive to institutions and actors outside their walls. Even the literature that deals exclusively with the internal workings of bureaus and bureaucrats hints at strong links to external forces. The concern of attorneys that rules accurately reflect statutes and survive judicial scrutiny suggests identification with Congress and the courts. Downs's climbers may look outside for opportunities to advance. But we need not spend time teasing relationships between agencies and the outside world from this literature because there is now a large body of scholarship that finds the theory of bureau dominance limited and explores the powerful forces in the external environment that influence the course of rulemaking.

The alternative to the bureau dominance model and now a more widely accepted school of thought was aptly described by Wesley Magat, Alan Krupnick, and Winston Harrington as the "external signals model" of rulemaking, which they attribute to the work of economist Roger Noll. [16] This general view of bureaucratic decision making has several variations, including the "interest representation" model of Richard Stewart, and the principal-agent model, identified first by Barry Mitnick.[17] Although there are some differences in emphasis in these various approaches, all stress that rulemaking bureaucracies are focal points of their decisions.

The principal-agent model posits an ongoing relationship between the bureaucratic agent and a principal, often thought to be Congress. The relationship is characterized by goals that motivate each of the parties but may not be compatible, and by bureaucratic operations that lead to results other than what the principal prefers. The principal sets its goals and establishes an agenda that it expects the agent to pursue. The agent, however, may be tempted to shirk and pursue his or her own goals. Even when the agent's goals coincide with those of the principal, bureaus may employ decision-making procedures that lead to perverse results or manage programs in such a way that the desired results are much delayed. The principal-agent model provides a starting point for an examination of the influences on the rulemaking process. But it must be drastically modified to account for the sometimes fierce competition among multiple principals, including the president and the courts, for influence.

Interest groups are never considered principals, but they profoundly influence these other institutions. Their actions stimulate and sometimes motivate those of Congress, the White House, and the courts. When threatened by action or inaction by bureaucrats, interest groups petition Congress and the White House for help. Of course, agencies with strong links to certain interests may respond directly to their entreaties. It is reasonable to suspect this to be especially true of political appointees in agencies.

Consider the information dimension of rulemaking mentioned above. Early in the process agencies may rely on their own resources for the development of a proposed rule or, as we saw in Chapter 5, the agency may reach out immediately to interest groups for necessary information. Whether they provide it early or not, interest groups have ample opportunity to share the information they do have during comment periods or other forums for public participation. Information from the White House during its review may alter the contents of rules, and it is always possible that no matter where the information used by the agency comes from a reviewing court will find it the wrong type or of insufficient quality.

The sources and channels of the political dimension are also richly varied. The internal politics of the agency may exert profound influence over the priority order of rules and determine which office in the agency and which personnel are assigned the task of writing it. But if internal political activity surrounding the rule is intense, it is likely that external parties will take an interest as well. Congress, the White House, and interest groups may be involved at virtually any stage in the process, and it is evident from the research presented in previous chapters that communication is quite common among these actors and between them and the agency personnel writing the rules. The importance of the political dimension and the role of political pressure is influenced by other dimensions, notably law and information. Where the law is subject to alternative interpretations and where information is hard to get, of poor quality, or difficult to interpret, politics, both internal and external, is very important. Where law and information are precise and thus highly directive, politics holds less significance. When politics is important in rulemaking we can also expect to find principals and agents joining in temporary and ever-shifting coalitions to leverage their individual capacities to influence rules. There are as many possible combinations as there are permutations of the players. It is possible to play out many plausible scenarios to demonstrate the conditions under which one or more of the many relevant actors will influence, or even dominate, the results of rulemaking.

ALTERNATIVE RULEMAKING SITUATIONS.   When one attempts to sort out the factors that determine the content of rules, theory confronts enormous complexity. The enormous range of the effects of rules brings even greater variation in the viewpoints of external groups and institutions that take an interest in a particular rulemaking. There are countless scenarios, and exploring a couple of archetypes might be helpful.

Take, for example, the rulemaking that is initiated in accordance with an unambiguous and clear statutory mandate. Authority for development of the rule has been vested within a single program office in the responsible agency. The expertise and information needed to complete the rule is in ample supply in the program office. Those outside the agency who will be affected by the rule have discussed the subject matter with the agency for many years. The agency and external interests have developed a close working relationship, with frequent informal consultations. The agency in question writes this particular type of rule so often that nothing other than the most routine check-in with the office of general counsel is required. The involvement by other offices in the agency is rare or nonexistent. The rule is formally or informally exempted from White House scrutiny because of its routine or noncontroversial nature. Congress takes little interest in the rule because no constituent has pulled a "fire alarm." The entire affair is handled with relatively little effort, internal tension, and external conflict. Hence, no litigation occurs.

We have reviewed rulemaking programs not unlike the one described here. Agricultural marketing orders, airworthiness directives, airspace management rules, adjustment of radio transmission policies, and waterway management rules of the Coast Guard display some if not most of these characteristics. The results of these types of rulemakings are dictated by technical considerations, be it accepted maintenance practices, known relationships between the supply of a given commodity and its market price, or simple judgments regarding the allocation or principles of safe waterway use.

A dizzying variety of alternative situations arise when we consider how each of the key elements in the above example could change. Consider the case of an agency that undertakes to write a rule to deal with a developing or newly discovered problem or situation that it believes to be within its statutory jurisdiction. The congressional delegation of authority to write rules in this particular area, however, is ambiguous, or the statute is altogether silent. The agency may undertake a rulemaking that it infers from the statutory language, but the agency's interpretation is subject to dispute. A struggle will ensue over the legal dimension of rulemaking. Alternatively, the authority to write rules is unambiguous, but the statute is unclear as to the information it expects the agency to consider when writing the rule. The parties will then contend over what information is relevant, making this dimension highly influential, at least temporarily. Responsibility within the agency for writing the rule may not be fixed or, as significant, there may be multiple offices with a legitimate claim of participation in its development. If the statutory authority is unsettled, the office of general counsel will take a keen interest. The rule may affect the jurisdiction of more than one program office, and since it represents a new area of activity, numerous policy options may be open. Visible and potentially controversial, it catches the attention of the political leadership of the agency, as well. The management dimension of rulemaking emerges in these circumstances, and takes on a special significance.

Because the rule is breaking new ground it is likely that working relationships with affected interests will simply not be established or the interactions will immediately be hostile because government is viewed as once again extending its reach. Of course, there may be interests who support this new public initiative. Still, the securing of reliable and complete information is more difficult. There may be a number of affected interests with distinctly different views on what the rule should contain. They may have substantial resources, be sophisticated about the importance of rulemaking, and have strong links to Congress, the White House, or both. They bombard the agency with position papers, requests for meetings, and long written comments when the draft rule is issued. The information dimension again becomes important. The interested parties activate their allies on

Capitol Hill or in the White House to exert pressure on the agency. The political dimension begins to loom large. The bureaucratic types offered by Downs provide a point of departure for considering how the rulemakers in agencies perceive and interact with external principals. "Conservers" may seek to sidestep what they perceive to be dangerous levels of conflict in the external environment by finding a way to avoid involvement in the rulemaking, leaving the decision to more ambitious and less risk-adverse officials. Among these are the "zealots," who are likely to join in an explicit or implicit coalition with those external principals whose views most closely match their own. They will use available information to bolster this position, perhaps on a selective basis. "Climbers" will champion the cause of those who can do them the most personal good. This may mean affiliating themselves with the White House petition, joining in a quiet coalition with principals in Congress, or colluding with an external group. Affiliation and joint action depend entirely on whom they wish to impress. Finally, "statespersons" may express their concern for the agency's overall program by serving as brokers and mediators between the contending external principals. Those at odds with each other may or may not be receptive to agents' playing this type of role.

When the rule is issued, those interests who are unhappy sue in federal court. The legal dimension once again emerges and dominates.

This complex scenario may not be as common as the first example, but many of its features can no longer be characterized as extreme or rare. These are two of the many variations that might occur. Congress might be unambiguous about the delegation of authority to write rules but still unclear about the direction the agency might take in the rule or the criteria it is to employ when determining its contents. Within the agency an outside-advisor model might be used, or the agency might rely on a formal advisory committee to assist it with some aspect of rule development, or it might pursue full-blown regulatory negotiation. Information may be available but contradictory. The agency may have to conduct extensive original research to resolve the contradictions or fill the gaps in what is known. Contractors may be needed to supplement agency personnel in the collection and analysis of this information. External interests may be numerous but unequal in their awareness of the subtleties of rulemaking and the resources at their disposal to influence the process. Consequently, the agency may find itself compensating for this imbalance by fashioning means of outreach in order to ensure that all points of view are represented before a rule is finalized.

The mere bleat from a stuck constituent will not guarantee effective intervention by Congress or the president. Also, members of Congress may receive mixed signals from different groups. And, when they act, rulemakers do not treat all inquiries by Congress equally. Similarly, the White House must weigh the source of the complaint about a rule under development, and it must husband its resources by picking its spots.

In activating Congress or the president, interest groups must think strategically, because a victory due to this type of intervention might be short-lived if it incurs the wrath of the others. Studies of presidential management activities of rulemaking emphasize the great power he or those acting in his behalf can exert when choosing to become involved in rulemaking. But the notion that the White House will confront easy decisions regarding the positions it might take in a controversial rulemaking is certainly open to challenge. Although the most recent presidential administrations have clearly tended to favor business in their review activities, one can hardly argue, given the volume of new rules that were produced during these years, that other interests were wholly unsuccessful. In fact, like Congress, the White House often faces powerful contending interests, and choosing between them is not always an attractive prospect. In such circumstances the presidential staff may take a hands-off attitude, preferring, perhaps insisting, that the agency find a way to accommodate the various positions that have been taken.

Groups possess an incomplete understanding about the positions adopted by their competitors and, more important, the relative quality of the supporting documentation. This is a potentially dangerous situation, especially when competitors are litigious and agents are unhappy with the content of the emerging rule. It may appear curious that a group capable of invoking the White House chooses instead to accept, or even promote, a rule it finds less than fully satisfactory but forestalls challenge by the competition. The main consideration here is litigation. The groups may reason that while they could initially have their way in the rulemaking, they might ultimately lose everything gained in the rule if a lawsuit were successful. We need only refer back to the preceding chapter to note the variation in the results of rulemaking brought about by judicial review. Agencies do not merely win or lose, they win or lose more or less. There are a number of possible results, ranging from a finding that a rule is utterly without merit because it is not authorized by the statute it claims to implement to complete endorsement of the rule by the judge or judges hearing the case. In between these extremes are outcomes that require the agency to undertake revisions of varying degrees and types. The court might find misinterpretation of statutory intent, inadequate or inappropriate rulemaking procedures, insufficient information, or faulty analysis supporting a rule. In effect, the court can order the partial or full repeat of a rulemaking.

THE CENTRAL IMPORTANCE OF NEGOTIATION AND COMPROMISE. Across the dimensions and among the major players in rulemaking, negotiation and compromise are constants. This is especially true for major rules in which the issues are numerous, stakes are high, and conflict intense. Whether it is a statesperson mediating between a zealot and an advocate in an agency, discussions that occur in agency work groups and teams, informal consultations between responsible officials and external interest groups, full-blown regulatory negotiations, or give-and-take between the White House and the rulemaking agency, negotiation and compromise are ubiquitous elements of the process. In this crucial respect, rulemaking resembles our larger political system. However deeply felt a personal ambition or deeply held a belief, and however strong a desire to gain or not to lose, many in the rulemaking process have powerful reasons to negotiate and compromise. The players in rulemaking have incentives to maintain good working relationships with one another. They may have to deal with one another again, whatever the outcome of the rulemaking at hand. Within bureaucracies, McGarrity has shown us that there are structures to promote consensus. Even structures other than the team model of rulemaking ultimately force contending parties to compromise. Several of Downs's bureaucratic types will lean toward compromise and negotiation. The statesperson does it for the public interest, the advocate to protect the interests of his or her office, the climber to curry favor, and the conserver to minimize disruption. External to the agency, we have seen that the White House maintains an active dialogue with agencies during the course of rulemaking review. Congress, at the staff level especially, does the same. In Chapter 5 we observed close communication among interest groups and between interest groups and rulemaking agencies that might not be called negotiation but certainly suggests a common if not pervasive atmosphere of mutual accommodation.

Again the role of the agency deserves special attention. Stewart's interest representation model is one way to look at the agency's role in negotiations. The agency may serve as an explicit or implicit broker among contending interests. Alternatively, it may be one party in a negotiation. Or it could be merely a ratifier of compromises reached by other parties.

Willingness to bargain is not universal, of course, but even when conflict persists and is unresolved during the entire rulemaking process, a compromise is still quite possible. Litigation is always an option when affected parties are unhappy with the results of a rulemaking. We saw that it is not uncommon for a court to issue a decision that forces agencies to rewrite rules to correct errors or other shortcomings first identified by the persons bringing the lawsuit. In some instances the court requires the agency to negotiate and reach agreement with the plaintiffs. In this manner a result based on forced compromise and negotiation can occur after the rulemaking is completed. Again, the foregoing does not suggest any consistent bias in the contents of rules, and we can be reasonably certain that negotiation and compromise, within and between the major institutional players, are common if not ubiquitous elements of the process by which the most important rules are created.

PROSPECTS FOR RIGOROUS ANALYSIS.   From an overall perspective we now understand the great forces that determine the contents of rules. The dimensions—law, information, politics, and management—and the players—Congress, the president, the courts, interest groups, and agencies—are known. The capacities are generally understood. The great challenge for future scholarship is to examine these forces at work at the level of individual rules. We must examine these dimensions and players in a large number of case studies to determine the conditions under which each of these forces becomes particularly important. The research that is needed is enormous in scope, but we have at least one example that suggests the possibility and potential value of rigorous empirical research of this sort to explain the content of rules.

Magat and his colleagues, using a rigorous research design and sophisticated statistical analysis, attempted to explain the varying levels of pollution control mandated in effluent guidelines issued by the Environmental Protection Agency under the provision of the Clean Water Act.[18] These rules determined how much of specified pollutants would be allowed in the waste-water discharges from a large number of industries. They found that the quality of the information had a positive effect on the stringency of standards. Politics, measured by trade association budgets and firm profitability, had negative effects on standards. Written comments filed by affected parties were found to be not very persuasive to the EPA. The authors also noted a similar conclusion in an earlier case study of a similar type of rule. They acknowledge, however, that other types of communication could be occurring, a proposition consistent with yet another set of case studies of effluent guidelines done by the Environmental Law Institute and with findings from the interest group survey reported in Chapter 5 of this book. Although it is not a comprehensive study of all dimensions and players in rulemaking, the study by Magat and his coauthors provides encouragement to those seeking rigorous tests of existing theories. They were able to study the qualitative dimension of a particular type of rule, and they developed and measured a large number of variables, each drawn from existing theory, to explain the level at which a given type of rule regulated the private sector. Magat and his colleagues have shown that rigorous empirical research is feasible and can be repeated in a large number of other rulemaking programs. It is important that such research be conducted, because the last question a theory of rulemaking must answer makes it plain that the stakes are quite high for our democracy.

How Does Rulemaking Affect Our System of Government?

Rulemaking affects every institution and process of government, every participant in policy deliberations, and every person affected by rules. Rulemaking frees Congress from the drudgery and political perils of providing the essential details of every program it sets in motion through statute. The legislature must, however, remain vigilant so that its bureaucratic agents remain true to statutory intent. Rulemaking also increases the opportunities for members of Congress to intervene on behalf of constituents, thus enhancing their prospects for reelection. Presidents are given an unparalleled opportunity to affect the course of public policy through the review of rules. But time and the rush of events limit severely the number of rules they deal with personally. So they must establish elaborate monitoring and review procedures, set criteria for intervention that will be used by their staff, and maintain the political will to withstand the inevitable criticism when their involvement benefits one group to the detriment of another. And we as a people should now be concerned when we cast a vote for president how he or she intends to become involved in rulemaking.

The judicial branch is also given the opportunity to shape law and public policy when presented with a lawsuit by a party aggrieved by a rulemaking. Again, the opportunity for influence is purchased at a cost. Rulemaking litigation represents a workload that competes with a wide variety of disputes for judicial time and attention. It is often complex, hinging on arcane technical and scientific evidence or the nuances of procedure. And it frequently requires supervision after the fact, especially when judges impose deadlines for the completion of rulemaking, or mandate that agencies and successful litigants work together to produce an acceptable rule and present their handiwork for judicial approval. Interest groups and others who seek to achieve public policy objectives must monitor rulemaking closely, determine how best to influence its course, and plan for those occasions that it does not go their way. If the groups surveyed in Chapter 5 are at all correct in their assessments, we have in rulemaking a governmental process that rivals in importance the legislative process in Congress for the production of law and public policy.

And interest groups are responding by devoting resources to the task of influencing rulemaking and by developing sophisticated strategies to get what they want.

No history or explanation of the democratic form of government as it has evolved in this country is complete without the story of rulemaking being fully and accurately told. The will of the people, the concept from which all democratic principles arise, can never be precisely articulated without rules. So the democratic process is never completed until the close of rulemaking. Dislike it as we might, the health of our democracy now hinges in no small part on how well rulemaking works.

THE REFORM OF RULEMAKING

In Chapter 3 we explored issues associated with rulemaking that have been identified by academic and professional observers. Each of these observers suggested a condition for rulemaking that some would prefer to what they perceive to be its current state. If rules are a poor reflection of congressional intent, we want them to be truer to the statutory promises they are supposed to be making a reality. If they are technically inept or otherwise poorly written, we want them instead to incorporate the best quality and most complete information. If there are too many rules, we want fewer. Of course, those of us who think there are too few want more. If it takes too long to issue rules, we want the process to move faster. But if compliance is going to cost us money, we may want to slow it down to a crawl. If we think that the public is not sufficiently involved in the development of rules, the process should encourage more participation. But we may also want participation of a certain type because we wish to make the process more equitable between the rich and the poor, the powerful and the not so powerful. To do this we will have to spend effort and money motivating and empowering those who are not able currently to participate effectively. If the rulemaking process is fraught with conflict, as it most certainly will be if we ensure that all interests are represented, we must find ways to make it more consensual.

There is no shortage of ideas about how to solve the perceived problems with rulemaking. Gary Bryner, a thoughtful and expert observer of rulemaking, has offered a number of specific reforms, including decentralization of policy making, more resources for those who write rules, better statutes, and fewer procedural requirements.[19] The Committee on Rulemaking of the Administrative Conference of the United States agrees with some of these suggestions but adds a number of others. The committee members recommend that White House review of rules be more selective and its standards be more clearly articulated. They want Congress to stop imposing "hybrid" procedures on rulemaking agencies. They would reorient judicial review to give more leeway to agencies on matters of fact and focus instead on procedure and statutory interpretation. They also recommend that agency management be strengthened through a variety of devices, including priority setting and better internal concurrence systems.[20] The Carnegie Commission recently chimed in with ideas of their own, ranging from means to improve public participation and make it more specific, to early, informal communication with the White House.[21]

The National Performance Review, chaired by Vice President Al Gore, also made a number of recommendations designed to improve rulemaking. These include increased use of regulatory negotiation, the use of information technology to improve the quality and frequency of public participation, streamlining internal agency procedures for noncontroversial rules, and faster treatment of petitions for rulemaking.[22]

Agencies are experimenting with more than regulatory negotiation in an effort to improve rulemaking. Two—the Environmental Protection Agency and the Department of Labor—have developed a "tiered" system in which rules are categorized by their significance, usually measured by economic impact whether positive or negative. The internal process used for each of the usually three or four categories or "tiers" varies. The less significant the rule, the less elaborate the process used, the fewer agency offices participate, and concurrences, both horizontal and vertical, are reduced.

Achieving any one of these improvements would alone be a formidable task, but the most serious dilemma these reformers face is that individual reforms are not always compatible with each other. Several potential reforms would inevitably add to the time it takes to issue a rule. In addition to frustrating those who want a quicker process, anything that slows rulemaking, or makes it more expensive, will reduce the number of rules produced as well. Public participation and concerns about leveling the playing field for those who are disadvantaged may even hamper efforts to incorporate the best-quality information into rules if agencies feel the need to respond to the wishes of those expressing their views, even if they are something less than fully informed. Contending goals and objectives are not peculiar to rulemaking; contradictions can be observed at any important stage of the public policy process.

Let us assume for a moment that these inherent contradictions could somehow be resolved. What type of task would we face if we attempted to improve the rulemaking process? Some issues can be dealt with as isolated problems. We could provide more money, both for the basic staff resources to produce rules and for research to produce higher-quality information for rulemakers to work with. We can further open the process of decision making in agencies, Congress, and the White House and revive the experiments of the 1960s and 1970s that promoted more widespread participation. These may result in some change, but fundamental reform must account for other problems that are not really those of rulemaking, although they are clearly reflected there. These problems go to the very core of our political system and the most fundamental characteristics of our basic institutions.

Seeking rules that are more faithful to congressional intent, and thus the will of the people as expressed by their representatives, first requires statutes that are sufficiently specific and unequivocal that the legislative purpose cannot be mistaken. Institutional limitations and political obstacles prevent legislation from preempting rulemaking or rendering it trivial. At an even more fundamental level, however, the American people have developed a habit that is the ultimate cause of rulemaking. To reduce significantly the number of rules written by agencies someone or something must persuade the American people to stop turning to government as a means of achieving their aspirations or solving their problems. The demands made by the American people contribute in some way to each of the problems and contradictions we observe in rulemaking. For example, often agencies are asked to write rules in areas in which human knowledge is developing, incomplete, or nonexistent. Not surprisingly, mistakes are made when information of such quality becomes the basis for law and policy. How we might reduce public demands and expectations, or if we should even want to, is not at all clear.

The conflict that attends the rulemaking process is merely an extension of the differences that divide persons and groups throughout the rest of the political system. Again we are dealing with something quite fundamental, namely the persistent tendency observed in people to pursue their self-interest. The specificity of the subject matter dealt with in rules guarantees a very clear understanding of the implications of rulemaking for their needs and wants and diverse values. It also guarantees that these will be presented clearly by those affected. To the extent that there are differences in needs, wants, and values, there will be conflict.

The shortcomings in public participation in rulemaking go deeper than the openness of the process and the resources available to those who are affected. If we are to avoid a "government by the interested" and a rulemaking process in which those not immediately and significantly affected have no role in the formulation of law, we must reverse the forces that have led to the issue networks and policy subsystems that dominate our political system. We must convince those with little or no direct stake in the outcome of a rulemaking that they too should be concerned about the result. This is a very tough sell when people are able to keep up with only a fraction of the issues that profoundly affect their lives and become involved in only a few of these. In a nation where so many fail to vote, is it reasonable to expect that the rulemaking process will soon be seeing an outpouring of interest from average citizens with comparatively little to win or lose? Perhaps not, but lowering our expectations is dangerous.

Rulemaking in all its aspects is a core governmental function that cannot be understood if considered in isolation or as a secondary or peripheral activity. Contemporary rulemaking is the product of a long evolution and now consists of complex institutional and political forces. To attempt fundamental reform to rulemaking without reform of these larger institutions and forces is futile. Rulemaking is inextricably bound to these forces; it cannot be separated from them. To fix what we think is broken in rulemaking, we must fix the core elements of our political system from which the problem truly arises.

Rulemaking now constitutes a layer of decision making so important that the constitutionally established branches of the national government compete, often consciously and aggressively, for control of its processes and results. Further, it has become a magnet for those interests sophisticated enough to understand where the policy that affects our lives most directly is made, and sufficiently well-organized and in command of enough resources to be able to participate effectively in the development of rules. The Constitution's directive that the legislative power will be vested in Congress is not, and never has been, completely true. The functions performed by Congress and the other branches are central to the conduct of government but no more so than the often obscure and homely rulemaking activities conducted in departments, agencies, commissions, and the like.

We are living near the close of a century that has seen momentous events. Nations have risen and fallen while the great theories of government have competed and warred for hegemony. One, democracy, survives and appears at this writing to be widely accepted as the government of choice for the next century. For this reason alone, rulemaking occupies a position of great importance. America is hardly alone among democratic nations in its inability to function without rulemaking. But rulemaking is especially central to the American democratic experience. Our popularly elected representatives have, especially during this century, embraced an ever more expansive view of government. Never mind the incessant complaints issuing from Congress and the White House about government's stranglehold on our lives, its poor performance, mismanagement, and waste. The past century is mute testimony to a faith, however misplaced, that no problem is beyond government's capacity to solve, no aspiration is beyond government's ability to realize. The growth in the scope and volume of rulemaking is a direct consequence of the growing and changing expectations of the American people. Change the political system—our expectations; the characteristics of Congress, the presidency, and the courts; the behavior of interest groups, bureaucrats, and bureaucracies—and rulemaking will inevitably follow.

Anyone concerned with the state of our democracy and the performance of our government must be concerned with the state of rulemaking. We can be no less demanding about this process than we are about any other, and certainly no less aware. We should, for example, be as concerned with the frequency and quality of participation in rulemaking as we are with voter turnout in elections. Because we do not have the opportunity to determine through election who the rulemakers will be, participation in the actual process of developing rules is crucial to maintaining the link between democratic principles and lawmaking. The absence of elections is no small sacrifice of democratic principles, but we have virtually every other means of participating in the development of rules that is available to us when Congress is considering legislation. In fact, we may be in a better position to participate in rulemaking because the issues are usually more specific and their effects on our particular circumstances easier to predict. Rulemaking is a legislative process well designed for an era when both issues and interests are narrowly defined. We should be as demanding about the management of rulemaking by agencies of government as we are about any of the other functions they perform. Is rulemaking less important than personnel systems, budgeting, financial management, or procurement? Most agencies have acknowledged that it is important by establishing management structures that identify rulemaking as a significant function.

One could not know the importance of rulemaking from the curricula of political science, public administration, and public policy programs that educate those who work in agencies. In these, rulemaking rarely, if ever, merits more than a small fraction of a single course. Clearly, this is an area in which the academic community lags behind practitioners. The best way for rulemaking to assume a more prominent place in our teaching is for it to become a more prominent topic for research. It is a subject worthy of the attention of the finest minds in all disciplines. If it does nothing else, this book will be worthwhile if it prods other scholars to examine some phase of rulemaking better than I have done here.

Through the rulemaking process passes the sum and substance of the hopes and fears of this democratic nation. We will understand it, our government, and ourselves better when we treat rulemaking as the most important source of law and policy for the conduct of our daily lives. It will occupy that status unless the improbable occurs and we find some very different way to govern ourselves.

NOTES

1. Morris Fiorina, "Legislative Choice of Regulatory Forms: Legal Process or Administrative Process," *Public Choice* 39 (1982): 33-66.
2. Kenneth Culp Davis, *Discretionary Justice: A Preliminary Inquiry* (Urbana: University of Illinois Press, 1969), p. 15.
3. Ibid., pp. 220-221.
4. Anthony Downs, *Inside Bureaucracy* (Boston: Little, Brown, 1967), chap. 9.
5. Keith Hawkins and John Thomas, "Rulemaking and Discretion: Implications for Regulatory Policy," in *Making Regulatory Policy*, ed. Keith Hawkins and John Thomas (Pittsburgh: University of Pittsburgh Press, 1989), p. 265.
6. Theodore Lowi, "Two Roads to Serfdom: Liberalism, Conservatism and Administrative Power," *American University Law Review* 36 (1987): 321-322; William A. Niskanen, Jr., *Bureaucracy and Representative Government* (New York: Aldine Atherton, 1971).
7. Downs, *Inside Bureaucracy*, pp. 101-103.
8. William West, "The Growth of Internal Conflict in Administrative Regulation," *Public Administration Review*, July/August 1988, pp. 773-782.
9. Thomas McGarrity, "The Internal Structure of EPA Rulemaking," *Law and Contemporary Problems* 54 (1991): 90.
10. Ibid., p. 94.
11. Ibid., p. 95.
12. Ibid., pp. 97-98.
13. Ibid., pp. 99-100.
14. Ibid., pp. 102-103.
15. Gary Bryner, *Bureaucratic Discretion* (New York: Pergamon, 1987), p. 208.
16. Wesley Magat, Alan Krupnick, and Winston Harrington, *Rules in the Making: A Statistical Analysis of Regulatory Agency Behavior* (Washington, D.C.: Resources for the Future, 1986), p. 49.
17. Richard Stewart, "The Reformation of American Administrative Law," *Harvard Law Review* 80 (1975): 1667-1711; Barry Mitnick, *The Political Economy of Regulation* (New York: Columbia University Press, 1980).
18. Magat, Krupnick, and Harrington, *Rules in the Making*, chaps. 6, 7.
19. Bryner, *Bureaucratic Discretion*, chap. 7.
20. Committee on Rulemaking, Administrative Conference of the United States, "Draft Recommendations," Administrative Conference of the United States, Washington, D.C., March 30, 1993.
21. Carnegie Commission on Science, Technology and Government, *Risk and the Environment: Improving Regulatory Decision Making* (Washington, D.C.: Carnegie Commission, 1993), chap. 7.
22. Al Gore, *Creating a Government that Works Better and Costs Less: Report of the National Performance Review* (Washington, D.C.: U.S. Government Printing Office, 1993), pp. 167-168.

APPENDIX A

Titles and Chapters in the Code of Federal Regulations

Title 1—General Provisions
Title 2—[Reserved]
Title 3—The President
Title 4—Accounts
Title 5—Administrative Personnel
Title 6—[Reserved]
Title 7—Agriculture
    Subtitle A—Office of the Secretary of Agriculture (Parts 0-26)
    Subtitle B—Regulations of the Department of Agriculture
Title 8—Aliens and Nationality
Title 9—Animals and Animal Products
Title 10—Energy
Title 11—Federal Elections
Title 12—Banks and Banking
Title 13—Business Credit and Assistance
Title 14—Aeronautics and Space
Title 15—Commerce and Foreign Trade
    Subtitle A—Office of the Secretary of Commerce (Parts 0-29)
    Subtitle B—Regulations Relating to Commerce and Foreign Trade
    Subtitle C—Regulations Relating to Foreign Trade Agreements
    Subtitle D—Regulations Relating to Telecommunications and Information
Title 16—Commercial Practices
Title 17—Commodity and Securities Exchanges
Title 18—Conservation of Power and Water Resources
Title 19—Customs Duties

This list was revised January 1, 1993.

Title 20—Employees' Benefits
Title 21—Food and Drugs
Title 22—Foreign Relations
Title 23—Highways
Title 24—Housing and Urban Development
    Subtitle A—Office of the Secretary, Department of Housing and Urban Development (Parts 0-99)
    Subtitle B—Regulations Relating to the Department of Housing and Urban Development
Title 25—Indians
Title 26—Internal Revenue
Title 27—Alcohol, Tobacco Products and Firearms
Title 28—Judicial Administration
Title 29—Labor
    Subtitle A—Office of the Secretary of Labor (Parts 0-99)
    Subtitle B—Regulations Relating to Labor
Title 30—Mineral Resources
Title 31—Money and Finance: Treasury
    Subtitle A—Office of the Secretary of the Treasury (Parts 0-50)
    Subtitle B—Regulations Relating to Money and Finance
Title 32—National Defense
    Subtitle A—Department of Defense
    Subtitle B—Other Regulations Relating to Defense
Title 33—Navigation and Navigable Waters
Title 34—Education
    Subtitle A—Office of the Secretary, Department of Education (Parts 1-99)
    Subtitle B—Regulations of the Offices of the Department of Education
Title 35—Panama Canal
Title 36—Parks, Forests, and Public Property
Title 37—Patents, Trademarks, and Copyrights
Title 38—Pensions, Bonuses, and Veterans' Relief
Title 39—Postal Service
Title 40—Protection of Environment
Title 41—Public Contracts and Property Management
    Subtitle B—Other Provisions Relating to Public Contracts
    Subtitle C—Federal Property Management Regulations System
    Subtitle D—Other Provisions Relating to Property Management [Reserved]
    Subtitle E—Federal Information Resources Management Regulations System
    Subtitle F—Federal Travel Regulation System

Title 42—Public Health
Title 43—Public Lands: Interior
    Subtitle A—Office of the Secretary of the Interior (Parts 1-199)
    Subtitle B—Regulations Relating to Public Lands
Title 44—Emergency Management and Assistance
Title 45—Public Welfare
    Subtitle A—Department of Health and Human Services, General Administration (Parts 1-199)
    Subtitle B—Regulations Relating to Public Welfare
Title 46—Shipping
Title 47—Telecommunications
Title 48—Federal Acquisition Regulations System
Title 49—Transportation
    Subtitle A—Office of the Secretary of Transportation (Parts 1-99)
    Subtitle B—Other Regulations Relating to Transportation
Title 50—Wildlife and Fisheries

APPENDIX B

Agency Documents Consulted

Department of Agriculture. Departmental Regulation—DR 1512-1. September 7, 1990. (Provides guidance to agencies in the development and clearance of USDA regulatory actions.)

Department of Agriculture, Farmers Home Administration. "Managing and Processing National Office Directives." FmHA Instruction 2006-D. October 9, 1985.

Department of Agriculture, Farmers Home Administration. "Processing Non-Major FmHA Regulatory Documents." Diagram, FmHA. February 1990.

Department of Agriculture, Food Safety and Inspection Service. "Docket Management Procedures." FSIS Directive 1232.1. March 14, 1985.

Department of Commerce, National Marine Fisheries Service. "An Evaluation of the Implementation of the Magnuson Fishery Conservation and Management Act." Draft discussion paper produced by the Council/NOAA Task Group. December 1985. (Discusses management issues related to rulemaking in NMFS.)

Department of Education. Departmental Directive OGC: 1-100: Regulations. March 3, 1988.

Department of Housing and Urban Development. *Operating Plan for Development of HUD Regulations.* Washington, D.C., n.d.

Department of the Interior. "Administrative Procedure," June 30, 1982.

Part 318, Federal Register Documents. In *Departmental Manual.*

Department of the Interior, Bureau of Land Management. "Proposing Regulations." Section 1761 of the *BLM Manual.* Washington, D.C., 1972.

Department of Labor. "Departmental Regulatory Review Procedures." In *DLMS 3-2 Handbook.* Washington, D.C., 1987.

Department of Labor. "Example of Options Memorandum" and "Example of Discussion Memorandum." January 1985.

Department of Transportation, Federal Highway Administration. "The Regulatory Process." N.d. (Provides overview of rulemaking.)

Department of Transportation, Maritime Administration. *Maritime Administration Regulations Manual.* Washington, D.C., 1990. (A comprehensive guidance document on rulemaking.)

Department of Transportation, Maritime Administration. "Regulations of the Maritime Administration, the Maritime Subsidy Board and the National Shipping Authority." Maritime Administrative Order 200-2. January 31, 1990.

Department of Transportation, National Highway Traffic Safety Administration. "Illustrative Format for Project Plan Description," attachment 2, exhibit 1. NHTSA Order 800-1. February 2, 1977.

Department of Transportation, National Highway Traffic Administration. "Rulemaking Procedures: Motor Vehicle Standards." NHTSA Order 800-1. February 2, 1977.

Department of Transportation, U.S. Coast Guard. "Initiating Regulatory Projects," chap. 2. N.d. (Provides guidance on the development of rules in the Coast Guard.)

Department of Transportation, U.S. Coast Guard. "Procedures Guide for Operations of the Marine Safety Council." September 30, 1988. (A procedures guide for use by everyone involved in the Coast Guard rulemaking process.)

Environmental Protection Agency, Regulation and Information Management Division, Office of Standards and Regulations. "A Decision System for Regulatory Development." Regulation Management Series. June 1984.

APPENDIX C

Agencies Surveyed

Department of Agriculture
  Farmers Home Administration
  Food Safety and Inspection Service
  Animal and Plant Health Inspection Service
  Food and Nutrition Service
  Agricultural Stabilization and Conservation Service

Department of Commerce
  International Trade Administration
  National Marine Fisheries Service

Department of Health and Human Services
  Social Security Administration
  Health Resources and Services Administration
  Health Care Financing Administration
  Federal Drug Administration
  Family Support Administration
  Public Health Service

Department of Housing and Urban Development
  Department of Education
  Department of Energy
  Federal Trade Commission
  General Services Administration

Department of the Interior
  Office of Surface Mining
  Minerals Management Service
  Bureau of Land Management

Department of Labor
  Employment Standards Administration
  Pension Welfare Benefits Administration
  Employment Training Administration
  Occupational Safety and Health Administration
  Mine Safety and Health Administration

Department of Transportation
  Federal Highway Administration
  Federal Railroad Administration
  National Highway Traffic Safety Administration
  Coast Guard
  Federal Aviation Administration
  Maritime Administration

Environmental Protection Agency (Uniform Agency-wide System)
  Office of Air and Radiation
  Office of Water
  Office of Solid Waste and Emergency Response
  Office of Pesticides and Toxic Substances

APPENDIX D

Questions Asked in Survey of Agencies

1. Is there a process for establishing the priority order of rulemaking in the agency? If so, how is the priority list established?

2. Must those who wish to start a rule obtain permission from higher authorities before they can begin work? If so, is this permission obtained through a formal "request process," or is it obtained informally?

3. Is there a system for senior management to provide technical and/or policy direction to those writing rules at the outset of the rulemaking process?

4. Do those writing rules have to prepare a planning document that outlines the issues in the rulemaking and how they will resolve them?

5. Is there a schedule for each rulemaking? Is the schedule the same for every rule or does each rule get its own?

6. Is there a budget set for each (or any) rulemaking? Are the rules developed in work groups or by individuals?

7. Is there a formal horizontal concurrence process? If so, who gets to sign off on the rule?

8. Who has the authority to determine the form that public participation will take? Who evaluates the results of public participation and incorporates it into the final rule?

9. Who drafts the actual language of the rule that will appear in the *Federal Register?* Is there a central office that does the drafting?

10. How often are contractors used to support the rulemakings in the agency? What tasks do they perform?

11. Who conducts the paperwork analysis? Who handles liaison with the Office of Management and Budget on paperwork issues that arise in the course of rulemaking?

12. Who conducts regulatory impact analysis when it is required?

13. Who maintains liaison with OMB for review of draft and proposed rules?

14. Is there contact maintained with the Congress during the rulemaking process? If so, does Congress review rules before they are issued?

Index

ABA (American Bar Association), 46-49, 247-248
Aberbach, Joel, 224-229
Acceptable risk levels, 231
Accountability, 54-57, 215-216. *See also* Oversight
  Congress and, 71, 216-229, 274
  to courts, 250-267
  litigation and, 252, 255, 260, 263-265
  mechanisms, 70-71
  to president, 70-71, 229-249
    objectives, 230-231
    OMB and agencies, 245-249
    OMB delays, 242-245
    OMB review record, 231-242
ACTION, 233, 236
Adjudication, 50-51
Administrative Conference of the United States, 180, 189, 247-248, 262, 293-294
Administrative law judges, 55
Administrative Procedure Act (APA), 3, 5-6, 21-22, 49-51, 184
  changes in model, 71-72, 258
  exemptions, 73
  information requirements, 64-66
  notification requirements, 172, 193-194
  participation provisions, 53-54, 169-170, 172
  rulemaking provisions, 51-52
  scope of review, 256-259
  standing provisions, 254-255

Administrative Procedures in Government Agencies, 49
Administrative Rulemaking (O'Reilly), 77
Advance notice, 173, 174-175, 178
Adversary model of rulemaking, 283-284
Adversary process, 116
Advertising industry, 192-193
Advisory committees, 67-68, 166
Advocates, 277, 281, 283, 290
African Development Foundation, 233, 236
Agencies, 3-5, 29
  authority, 257-259
  culture of, 279
  information considered by, 57-63
  information provided to public, 63-65
  negotiation role, 290
  OMB relations, 14, 245-249
  preference for rulemaking, 276-277, 279-280
Agency-level management, 127-146
  budgeting, 133-137
  concurrence systems, 139-141
  conduct of required analyses, 143-144
  contractors, 142-143
  draft rules, 144-145
  elements, 128-137
  initiating rules, 130-131
  participation in, 141-142
  planning documents, 132-133

priority setting, 128-130
rule writing responsibility, 137-139
schedules, 133
senior officials' input, 131-132
Agendas, 175
Agricultural Marketing Service, 44, 148, 176-177, 188, 196, 206-207, 263, 286-287
Agricultural Stabilization and Conservation Service, 142
Agriculture Department, 23, 263
    exemptions, 73
    marketing orders, 44, 148, 176-177, 188, 196, 206-207, 263, 286-287
    OMB review record, 232, 234-235, 237, 240
    OMB review time, 243-244
    participation and, 167, 176-177
    rule conflicts, 109, 230
Aid to Families with Dependent Children, 177
Air bags, 226
Air Canada, 207
Air pollution, 261
Airworthiness directives, 27, 29-30, 101, 148
Alcohol, Tobacco and Firearms, Bureau of, 115
Alcohol testing, 112
American Banker's Association, 166
American Bar Association (ABA), 46-49, 247-248
American Railway Association, 165
Animal and Plant Health Inspection Service (APHIS), 115
APA. See Administrative Procedure Act
APHIS (Animal and Plant Health Inspection Service), 115
Appointments to judiciary branch, 251
ARAC (Aviation Rulemaking Advisory Committee), 190
Architectural and Transportation Barriers Compliance Board, 233, 236
Asbestos, 239-240
Association of Official Agricultural Chemists, 164

Attorney General's Committee on Administrative Procedure, 11, 46, 49, 164
Authorization, 78-79, 257-259
Authorizing statutes, 57-59, 66-67
Automobile passenger safety, 226
Aviation Rulemaking Advisory Committee (ARAC), 190

Benzene, 106, 107-108, 113, 190
Berry, Jeffrey, 182
Biological Survey, Bureau of, 165
Bituminous Coal Act, 167
Bituminous Coal Board, 168
BLM (Bureau of Land Management), 131, 142
Breyer, Stephen, 47, 102, 148
Brownlow Committee, 11
Bruff, Harold, 239, 245-246, 249
Bryner, Gary, 284, 293
Budgeting, 111-113, 127, 133-137, 219-220
Bureaucracy
    capacity of, 27-30
    preference for rulemaking, 279-280
Bureaucratic discretion, 117
Bureaucrats
    self-interest in rulemaking, 34-35
    types, 277, 288, 290
Bureau dominance theory, 280-284
Bureau of Alcohol, Tobacco and Firearms, 115
Bureau of Biological Survey, 165
Bureau of Land Management (BLM), 131, 142
Bureau of Marine Inspection and Navigation, 12, 166
Bush, George, 16, 78, 111, 125-126, 184-185, 195, 251
Business interests, 22-24, 195-199, 206-208, 210

Cable television, 95
Calvert, Randall, 221
Career civil servants, 276-277
Carnegie Foundation, 294
Carter, Jimmy
    participation and, 46, 165, 174-182, 197
    reforms, 62, 122-127, 174-175, 230, 231

Carter v. Carter Coal Co., 47
Case studies, 206-208, 222-223, 226-229
CFR. *See Code of Federal Regulations*
Cheit, Ross, 193, 196, 207, 208
Chevron USA v. NRDC, 261-262
Children's Bureau, 164
Cigarette warning labels, 192-193, 207-208
Citizen lawsuits, 255
Citizen organizations, 196, 197-198, 210
Citizen participation. *See* Participation
Citizens to Preserve Overton Park v. Volpe, 260, 262
Civilian Conservation Corps, 13
Civil Rights Act, 21
Civil servants, 276-277
Clayton Act, 9
Clean Air Act, 1-2, 19, 139, 146, 184
Clean Air Act Amendments of 1990, 78
Clean Water Act, 172, 173, 291
Climbers, 277, 281, 283, 284, 288, 290
Clinton, Bill, 78, 126-127, 248-249, 251
Coalition formation, 200
Coast Guard, 101, 143, 287
Code of Federal Regulations (CFR), 10, 13, 19, 20-21, 26. *See also Federal Register*
  titles and chapters, 299-301
Codes, 10
Colleague networks, 200
Collective bargaining, 185-186
Commerce Department, 64, 232, 234-235, 237, 243-244
Commission on Civil Rights, 233, 236
Communications strategy, 81
Compliance, 55, 73, 74, 78, 95
Compromise, importance of, 290-291
Concurrence systems, 139-141, 146
Conference approach to participation, 66, 166
Congress
  accountability, 71, 216-229, 274
  early rulemaking, 45-46
  early sessions, 8
  limits of, 27-30
  OMB relations, 247

participation promotion, 171, 173
  preference for rulemaking, 32, 274, 279-280
  regulatory impact analyses, 144
Congressional Record, 247
Congruency, 97-99
Consensus, 92-93, 154, 189
Conservers, 277, 281, 288, 290
Constitutionality, 257-260
Consultation, 165-166, 169
Consumer groups, 196-198
Consumer Product Safety Act, 172, 173
Consumer Product Safety Commission, 207, 264, 284
Contacts, 200
Contractors, 142-143
Controversy, effects on timeliness, 108-110
Convenors, 189
Corridoring, 194-195
Cost-benefit analysis, 62, 125, 249
Cost-effectiveness, 96, 242
Council of Economic Advisers, 123
Council on Competitiveness, 78, 111, 126, 184-185, 242, 248-249
Council on Environmental Quality, 82
Council on Wage and Price Stability, 125
Courts. *See also* Judicial oversight; Judicial review
  accountability, 250-266
  levels, 252-253
  preference for rulemaking, 274-276, 279-280
Courts of appeals, 252-253
Craig, Barbara, 226

Davis, Kenneth Culp, 31, 52, 65, 274, 275
Deadlines, 218-219, 257
Decisionmaking models, 262-263, 282-284
Defense Department, 110, 232, 235, 243-244
Delegation of authority, 4, 117
Department of Agriculture. *See* Agriculture Department
Department of Commerce, 64, 232, 234-235, 237, 243-244

Department of Defense, 110, 232, 235, 243-244
Department of Education. *See* Education Department
Department of Energy, 110
Department of Health, Education and Welfare (HEW). *See* Health, Education and Welfare Department
Department of Health and Human Services. *See* Health and Human Services Department
Department of Housing and Urban Development (HUD). *See* Housing and Urban Development Department
Department of Justice, 232, 234-235, 237, 243-244
Department of Labor. *See* Labor Department
Department of State, 232, 234-235, 237, 243-244
Department of the Environment, 232, 234-235, 237, 243-244
Department of the Interior. *See* Interior Department
Department of the Treasury, 115, 232, 234-235, 237, 243-244
Department of Transportation (DOT). *See* Transportation Department
Disclosure requirements, 172
Discretionary Justice (Davis), 31
District courts, 252
Diver, Colin, 3, 97-99
Dockets, 64, 72
DOT. *See* Transportation Department
Downs, Anthony, 277, 281, 282-283, 284, 288, 290
Draft rules, 80-84, 144-145
Dry cleaning establishments, 1
Dunlop, John, 185, 186

Education Department
  concurrence systems, 140
  Division of Regulation Management (DORM), 129, 139, 140, 149-150
  OMB review record, 232, 234-235, 237, 239
  OMB review time, 243-244
  participation and, 142
  priority setting, 129
  regulatory negotiation, 189
  training programs, 149
  work groups, 139
Effectiveness, 96
Efficiency, 96
Effluent guideline program, 193, 196, 291
EIS (environmental impact statement), 60, 68, 82
Eisenhower, Dwight, 122
Eisner, Neil, 105, 133
Employee Retirement Income Security Act (ERISA), 24
Endangered Species Act, 173
Energy Department, 110
Energy Policy and Conservation Act, 173
Environment, Department of, 232, 234-235, 237, 243-244
Environmental groups, 196-198
Environmental impact statement (EIS), 60, 68, 82
Environmental Law Institute, 291
Environmental programs, 218
Environmental Protection Agency (EPA), 1-2, 19-20, 99, 147, 291-292
  accountability, 264, 266
  budgeting, 127
  communications strategy, 81
  concurrence systems, 140
  deadlines, 218-219
  exemptions, 73
  hammers, 78
  information requirements, 58-59
  initiation of rulemaking, 130
  litigation, 116, 261, 264-265
  notification requirements, 184
  Office of Solid Waste and Emergency Response (OSWER), 93-94
  OMB review record, 232, 234-235, 237, 239-242
  OMB review time, 243-245
  participation and, 179-180, 196, 207
  planning documents, 132
  procedural requirements, 111, 284
  reform efforts, 294
  regulatory negotiation, 190
  rule conflicts, 16, 109, 110
  source performance standards, 148
  staff, 103

steering committee, 130, 139
timeliness, 106, 107
training programs, 149
work groups, 139, 150-151, 152
EPA. *See* Environmental Protection
Agency
Equal Employment Opportunity
Commission, 21, 233, 236
ERISA (Employee Retirement In-
come Security Act), 24
Ethics, 168
Ethylene oxide, 242
Evasions, 72-75
Exceptions, 72-75
Executive Order 12044 (Carter), 62,
123-125, 174
Executive Order 12291 (Reagan), 62,
64, 69, 73, 125, 183
Executive Order 12372 (Reagan), 69
Executive Order 12498 (Reagan), 62,
69
Executive Order 12612 (Reagan), 62,
64
Executive orders, 61-63, 69, 73, 231
Exemptions, 72-75
Explosives and Combustibles Act of
1908, 39
External review, 82-84
External signals model, 284

FAA. *See* Federal Aviation Adminis-
tration
FACA (Federal Advisory Committee
Act), 68, 80, 171
Fair Labor Standards Act, 45, 166-
168, 185, 189
Family impact study, 62-63, 69
Farm workers, 190
FCC (Federal Communications Com-
mission), 27, 95, 97, 164-167
FDA (Food and Drug Administra-
tion), 165, 177-178, 184, 222-223,
226, 284
Federal Acquisition Regulations, 236
Federal Advisory Committee Act
(FACA), 68, 80, 171
Federal Aviation Administration
(FAA), 24, 107
accountability, 263
airworthiness directives, 27, 29-30,
101, 148
draft regulations, 145

exemptions, 73
participation and, 207
priority setting, 129, 130, 137
regulatory negotiation, 190
Regulatory Review Board, 141
rulemaking process, 134-136
schedules, 133
training programs, 149
Federal Communications Commis-
sion (FCC), 27, 95, 97, 164-167
Federal Credit Systems Assistance
Board, 236
Federal Emergency Management
Agency (FEMA), 232, 234-235, 237
Federal Energy Regulatory Commis-
sion (FERC), 26, 78, 107, 110
Federal Highway Administration,
139
Federal Home Loan Bank Board, 236
Federal Insecticide, Fungicide and
Rodenticide Act (FIFRA), 59
Federalism assessment, 62-63, 69
Federal judges. *See* Judges
Federal Mediation and Conciliation
Service, 233, 236
Federal Power Commission, 167
Federal Railroad Administration,
142
Federal Register, 10, 21, 83-84. *See also*
Code of Federal Regulations
analysis of rules from, 16-19, 192
as information provider, 63-64
for monitoring, 200
participation reports, 197, 199-200
Federal Reserve Board, 164, 166
Federal Reserve System, 9, 164
Federal Trade Commission Act, 63-
64
Federal Trade Commission (FTC), 5,
9, 12, 15, 67
accountability, 226
information sources, 148-149
participation and, 193
rule conflicts, 230
Federal Trade Commission Improvements Act of 1980, 172, 173
Federal Water Power Act, 9
FEMA (Federal Emergency Management Agency), 232, 234-235, 237
FERC (Federal Energy Regulatory
Commission), 26, 78, 107, 110
Field staff, 103-105

FIFRA (Federal Insecticide, Fungicide and Rodenticide Act), 59
Finality, 256
Fiorina, Morris, 274
Fire alarm oversight, 222-226
Fire extinguishers, 207
Fish and Wildlife Agency, 165
Fishing industry, 46
Food, Drug and Cosmetic Act, 167-168
    Medical Device Amendments, 173
Food and Drug Administration (FDA), 165, 177-178, 184, 222-223, 226, 284
Food and Nutrition Service, 144
Food labels, 23, 178, 230
Food Safety and Inspection Service (FSIS), 130-131, 137, 140-141
Food Standards Committee, 165
Ford, Gerald R., 62, 122, 125
Foreman, Christopher, 222, 226-229
Formaldehyde, 265
Formal rulemaking, 167-168
Freedom of Information Act, 26, 171, 185
Fritschler, A. Lee, 192, 196
FSIS (Food Safety and Inspection Service), 130-131, 137, 140-141
FTC. See Federal Trade Commission
Funding. See Budgeting
Funeral homes, 226
Furlong, Scott, 208
Future effect, 7

GAO (General Accounting Office), 28, 106, 143, 223
Gas Appliance Manufacturers Association, 207
Gazell, Jaime, 228
General Accounting Office (GAO), 28, 106, 143, 223
General Services Administration, 144, 232, 234-235, 237, 241
Georgetown Law Journal, 185
Georgetown Law School, 255
Glendale Law Review, 228
Gore, Albert, 127, 294
Government
    effects of rulemaking, 292-293
    expectations for, 295
    growth of, 8-10, 273
    rules for, 26-27

rules for approaching, 25-26
Government in the Sunshine Act, 171
Grain elevator safety, 207
Grass-roots mobilization, 200
Great Society programs, 171
Guidelines, 74, 258

Hammers, 75-78, 218-219
Handgun control, 115
Hard look standard of review, 260-262
Harrington, Winston, 284
Harter, Phillip, 116, 161-162, 185-188, 205
Harvard Law Review, 205
Harvard University, 122
Hawkins, Keith, 278
Hazardous and Solid Waste Amendments (HSWAs), 93
Hazardous materials regulation, 41-42, 93-95, 108, 115
Hazardous Materials Regulations (HMRs), 39-40
Hazardous materials transport, 43-44, 106
Health, Education and Welfare Department (HEW), 106, 124, 177-178. See also Health and Human Services Department
Health and Human Services Department, 23, 106
    OMB review record, 232, 234-235, 237, 239-240
    OMB review time, 243-244
    participation and, 177
Health Care Financing Administration, 106, 138, 145
Health Resources and Services Administration, 138
Hearings, 67, 167, 173
Hepburn Act, 9
HEW. See Health, Education and Welfare Department
Hierarchical model of rulemaking, 282-284
HMRs (Hazardous Materials Regulations), 39-40
Holmes, Oliver Wendell, 3
Horizontal review, 82
Housing and Urban Development Department (HUD), 129

concurrence systems, 140-141
OMB review record, 232, 234-235, 237, 239-240
OMB review time, 243-244
participation and, 142
planning memoranda, 132
Regulations Division, 139, 142
senior officials, 131
work groups, 139
HSWAs (Hazardous and Solid Waste Amendments), 93
HUD. *See* Housing and Urban Development Department
Hydroelectric power licensing, 100, 107

ICC (Interstate Commerce Commission), 9, 12, 112, 165, 167, 255
Immigration and Naturalization Service, 233, 236
Immigration and Naturalization Service v. Chadha, 229
Impact statements, 60, 62-63, 68-69, 82, 122, 171-172
Implementation, 5-6, 28, 94-96
Importation, 8
Industry
    as information source, 102
    participation of, 196
Inertia, 113-114
Inflation impact statement, 122
Informal contacts, 200
Informal rulemaking, 52
Information, 52-53
    agency consideration of, 57-63
    APA requirements, 64-66
    influence on rulemaking, 278-279, 287-288
    legal requirements, 57-65
    limitations of, 101-105
    management of, 146-150
    OMB requirements, 69
    in principal-agent model, 285-286
    provided by agencies to public, 63-65
    resources and, 181
    sources, 102, 148-149
    types, 147-148
Information Agency, U.S., 233, 235
Information rules, 25
Information statutes, 59-61

In-house research offices, as information source, 102
Inside Bureaucracy (Downs), 277
Institutional capacity, 90-94
Inter-American Foundation, 236
Interest groups, 102, 183, 292-293
    accountability, 248-249
    defined, 164
    participation patterns, 191-210
    preference for rulemaking, 34, 276, 280
    in principal-agent model, 285-286
Interest representation model, 205, 209-210, 284, 290
Interior Department, 11-13, 46, 109
    Bureau of Biological Survey, 165
    OMB review record, 232, 234-235, 237, 240
    OMB review time, 243-244
    participation and, 178-179
Internal Revenue Service (IRS), 99, 255-256
Internal review, 82
Internal Review Service, 64
International Association of State Game, Fish and Conservation Commissioners, 165
International Development Corp. Agency, U.S., 232, 236
Interpretation, 5-7, 28, 74
Interpretive rules, 21-22, 28
Interstate Commerce Commission (ICC), 9, 12, 112, 165, 167, 255
Investigation, 165
IRS (Internal Revenue Service), 99, 255-256

Jackson, Robert, 11
Johnson, Lyndon, 122, 171
Judges, 55
    accountability, 71, 250-267
    preference for rulemaking, 274-276
Judicial appointments, 71, 251
Judicial oversight, 250-267
    effects on rulemaking, 263-267
    scope of, 259-262
Judicial review, 54-55, 67, 69-70, 219
Justice Department, 232, 234-235, 237, 243-244

Keeping a Watchful Eye (Aberbach), 224-226
Kennedy, John, 122
Krupnic, Alan, 284

Labor Department, 100
  OMB review record, 232, 234-235, 237, 239-240
  OMB review time, 243-245
  participation and, 179
  reform efforts, 294
  Wage and Hour Division, 45, 66
Labor unions, 196, 197, 210
Landfills, 265
Landis, James, 29
Land Management, Bureau of (BLM), 131, 142
Law
  influence on rulemaking, 5-6, 21, 278-279, 288
  in principal-agent model, 286
  as subject matter of rules, 5
Lawsuits. *See* Litigation
Leadership, 151-154
Legal information, 147, 148
Legal interests, 254
Legal requirements
  evasions, 72-75
  exceptions, 72-75
  exemptions, 72-75
  for information, 57-65
  for participation, 65-70
Legislation
  relationship with rulemaking, 8
  as source of rulemaking, 91-92
Legislative hearings, 67, 167, 173
Legislative rules, 21
Legislative veto, 225-229, 248, 257
Legislative Veto, The (Craig), 226
Legislature, limits of, 27-30
Litigation, 289, 292
  accountability and, 252, 255, 261, 263-265
  participation and, 116
Lobbying, 194
Local governments, 34
Love Canal, 93
Lowi, Theodore, 182, 194, 218, 220, 281

Macromanagement, 230
Magat, Wesley, 207, 284, 291-292

Magnuson-Moss Warranty--Federal Trade Commission Improvement Act, 173
Management, 121. *See also* Agency-level management
  elements, 128-137
  of individual rules, 146-158
    information requirements, 146-150
    work group roles, 150-158
  influence on rulemaking, 278-279
  obstacles to timeliness, 112-113
  of participation, 141-142
  by presidents, 122-127
Managerial information, 148
Marine Inspection and Navigation, Bureau of, 12, 166
Maritime Administration, 138
Maritime Commission, 164
Marketing orders, 44, 148, 176-177, 188, 196, 206-207, 263, 286-287
McCubbins, Matthew, 217, 221, 222
McGarrity, Thomas, 180, 282-283, 290
Medicaid, 100, 106, 177
Medical Device Amendments, 173
Medicare, 177
Melnick, R. Shep, 266
Miller, Nancy, 219, 262
Mine Safety and Health Administration, 132, 142
Mintz, Benjamin, 219, 262
Mitnick, Barry, 285
Model Cities Program, 171
Money. *See* Budgeting
Monitoring, 199-205
Motor Carrier Act, 12
Motor Vehicle Manufacturers Association v. State Farm 260-262

NASA (National Aeronautics and Space Administration), 232, 234-235, 237
National Academy of Public Administration, 247-248
National Academy of Sciences, 196
National Aeronautics and Space Administration (NASA), 232, 234-235, 237
National Archives and Records Administration, 232, 234-235, 237

National Endowment for the Arts, 233, 236

National Endowment for the Humanities, 233, 236

National Environmental Policy Act (NEPA), 14, 60-61, 171-172, 259
compliance, 78
exemptions, 73
hydroelectric power licensing, 107
scoping requirements, 68, 177

National Highway Transportation Safety Administration, 144, 264

National Highway Transportation Safety Agency, 226

National Highway Transportation Safety Board, 137

National Industrial Recovery Act (NIRA), 10, 47-48

National Labor Relations Board (NLRB), 12, 15

National Marine Fisheries Service (NMFS), 138, 141

National Performance Review, 294

National Rifle Association, 115

National Science Foundation, 233, 236

National Youth Administration, 13

Nation's Hazardous Waste Management Program at a Crossroads, The, 93-94, 95

Negotiated Rulemaking Act of 1990, 68, 189

Negotiation, 166-167, 185-191, 290-291

NEPA. *See* National Environmental Policy Act

Net benefit rule, 125, 126

Networks, 200

New Deal, 8-13, 46-50, 122, 164-169, 169

NIRA (National Industrial Recovery Act), 10, 47-48

Niskanen, William, 220, 281

Nixon, Richard, 61-62, 122, 125, 230

NLRB (National Labor Relations Board), 12, 15

NMFS (National Marine Fisheries Service), 138, 141

Noll, Roger, 217, 284

Northwest Airlines, 24

Notice and comment, 52

Notification requirements, 172-175, 178, 184, 193-194

NRC (Nuclear Regulatory Commission), 81, 131, 133, 189-190, 261

Nuclear power plants, 255-256

Nuclear Regulatory Commission (NRC), 81, 131, 133, 189-190, 261

Occupational Safety and Health Act, 6, 57-59, 92, 173

Occupational Safety and Health Administration (OSHA), 6, 92, 98-99, 184
accountability, 264
benzene rules, 106, 107-108, 113, 190
contractors, 143
litigation, 116, 264
OMB review record, 242
participation and, 142, 179, 207
rule conflicts, 16, 230
rulemaking process, 284
sunset review, 124

Office of General Counsel, 138, 142, 252

Office of Government Ethics, 236

Office of Information and Regulatory Affairs (OIRA), 183, 245-247

Office of Management and Budget (OMB), 16-17, 40. *See also* Presidents
agency relations, 14, 245-249
Carter reforms, 174-175
congressional relations, 247
delays in rulemaking, 242-245
Executive Order 12044 and, 123-124
external review, 82-84
information requirements, 69
mandatory review, 125-126, 182-184
review record, 231-242
review time, 242-245

Office of Personnel Management, 232, 234-235, 237, 241

Office of Solid Waste and Emergency Response (OSWER), 93-94

Office of Special Counsel, U.S., 236

Office of Surface Mining, 139, 143

OIRA (Office of Information and Regulatory Affairs), 183, 245-247

O'Leary, Rosemary, 264-266

Olson, Mancur, 177
OMB. *See* Office of Management and Budget
OMB Watch, 248
Open discovery, 71-72
Oral communications, 165-166
Orders, 7
O'Reilly, James, 72, 75, 77, 85
OSHA. *See* Occupational Safety and Health Administration
Ostriches, 115
OSWER (Office of Solid Waste and Emergency Response), 93-94
Outside experts, as information source, 102
Outsider-advisor model of rulemaking, 282-283
Oversight, 28-29, 215-216, 221-229. *See also* Accountability
Overspecificity, 99

Panama Canal Commission, 236
Panama Refining Co. v. Ryan, 47
Panels, 252
Paperwork Reduction Act (PRA), 60-61, 64, 68-69, 73, 82, 123, 144, 247, 259, 267
Participation, 30, 83-84, 114-117, 161, 295-296
  in agency-level management, 141-142
  APA provisions, 53-54, 169-170, 172
  conference approach, 66, 166
  effects of, 205-210
  history of, 163-191
    congressional promotion, 171, 173
    early inattention, 163-164
    at end of New Deal, 164-169
    expansion of scope, 171-173
    Participation Revolution, 170-171
    presidential participation, 174-185
    regulatory negotiation, 185-191
    rise of social regulation, 170-171
    turn of century, 164
  legal requirements, 65-70
  litigation and, 116
  management of, 141-142
  patterns, 191-205
  in planning stage, 80
  purposes, 162-163
Participation Revolution, 170-171
Peace Corps, 233, 236
Pennsylvania Avenue Development Corp., 233
Pension Benefits Guarantee Corp., 233, 236
Pension Welfare Benefits Administration, 139
Perchloroethylene, 1
Pesticides, 190
Petitions, 78, 85
Plain English, 123-124
Planning documents, 132-133
Police patrol oversight, 222-226
Policy, 5-6, 21
Policy information, 147, 148-149
Policy statements, 258
Political appointees, preference for rulemaking, 276
Political information, 147-149
Politics
  influence on rulemaking, 278-279, 288
  in principal-agent model, 286
  of rulemaking process, 46-52
Portney, Kent, 182
Post-rulemaking revisions, 84-85
PRA (Paperwork Reduction Act), 60-61, 64, 68-69, 73, 82, 123, 144, 247, 259, 267
Preambles, 63-64, 81, 100, 124, 192, 206
Presidents. *See also* Office of Management and Budget
  accountability to, 70-71, 229-249
  management by, 122-127
  participation and, 174-185
  preference for rulemaking, 32-33, 274-276, 279-280
Principal-agent model, 220-221, 284-286
Priority setting, 128-130, 137
Privacy Act, 26, 171
Private attorneys general, 254
Private behavior rules, 22-25
Procedural rules, 21-22, 26-27
Procedure, importance of, 217-218
Public Citizen, 248
Public participation. *See* Participation

Public policy, 5-6, 21
Pugh, Darrell, 228

Quality of life review, 122
Quality standards, 96-105
Quayle, James Danforth, 126, 184-185, 242

Radioactive isotopes, 189-190
Railroad Retirement Board, 232, 234-235, 237
RARG (Regulatory Analysis Review Group), 123, 126, 174
RCRA (Resource Conservation and Recovery Act), 93-94, 95, 218-219, 265
Reagan, Ronald, 111, 147, 239
    judicial appointments, 71, 251
    participation and, 182-185, 195
    reforms, 16, 33, 62-63, 125-157, 231
Reasonableness standard, 261-263
Reasoned decisionmaking, 263
Records, 64, 72
Reform, 293-298
Regulated industries, participation of, 196
Regulation drafting, 80-84, 144-145
Regulation Quality Manual, 140
Regulatory agenda program, 175
Regulatory analysis, 124-126
Regulatory Analysis Review Group (RARG), 123, 126, 174
Regulatory Council, 123, 125, 126
Regulatory Flexibility Act (RFA), 60-61, 64, 82, 259
Regulatory impact analyses, 62, 69, 73-74, 143-144
Regulatory negotiation, 166-167, 185-191
Regulatory Program of the President, 1990-1991, 128
Reilly, William, 147
Research, 291-292
Resolution Trust Corp., 236
Resource Conservation and Recovery Act (RCRA), 93-94, 95, 218-219, 265
Resources. See also Budgeting
    information and, 181
    shortages, 111-112, 113
Resources for the Future, 207
Reviews, 82-84

Review scope, 256-259
Review time, 242-245
RFA (Regulatory Flexibility Act), 60-61, 64, 82, 259
Right to sue, 254-256
Ripeness for review, 256
Risk assessment, 59, 113, 231
Roosevelt, Franklin Delano, 10, 11, 48-49, 122, 169
Rosenbloom, David, 46
Rosovsky, Henry, 122
Rulemakers
    limitations of, 102-105
    limiting discretion of, 217-220
Rulemaking, 1-2
    alternative situations, 286-289
    analysis, 291-292
    for containing administrative discretion, 30-32
    contradictions, 117-118
    defined, 3-7
    dissatisfaction with, 89-90
    effect on government, 292-293
    growth, 14-19
    history, 7-20
    implementation, 94-96
    influence of law, 5-6, 21, 278-279, 288
    influences on, 278-280
    management influence, 278-279
    models, 283-284
    process, 39-52
    reasons for, 27-35, 272-277
    sources, 91-92
    stages, 75-86
    volume of, 90-96
Rules
    for approaching government, 25-26
    categories, 20-27
    complexity, 107-108
    content, 277-292
    effects, 6, 22-27
    functions, 21-22
    for government, 26-27
    implementation aspect, 5-6, 28
    influence on, 199-205
    initiation of, 130-131
    interpretation aspect, 5-6, 28
    origins, 75-78
    to prescribe, 5-6, 21, 28
    for private behavior, 22-25

range of influence, 5-6
subject matter of, 5
substance of, 43-52
writing, 137-139

Saccharin, 226-229
Safe Drinking Water Act, 59, 68, 173, 265
Schechter Poultry Corporation v. United States, 47
Schedules, 133
Schwartz, Thomas, 222
Scope of review, 256-258
SCRAP (Students Challenging Regulatory Agency Procedures), 255
Seatbelt rules, 226
Securities and Exchange Commission, 165
Selective Service System, 233, 236
Self-interest, 32-35
Senior officials
    input by, 131-132
    role in work groups, 156-157
Shapiro, Martin, 50
Shift responsibility model of legislative behavior, 274
Signals from the Hill (Foreman), 222-223
Simplicity, 97, 99-101
Small Business Administration, 82, 232, 234-235, 237
Small businesses, 100
Smoking and Politics (Fritschler), 192-193
Social regulation, 91-92, 102, 170-171, 239, 264
Social Security Administration (SSA), 12-13, 131, 145
Space heater safety, 207-208
SSA (Social Security Administration), 12-13, 131, 145
Standing, 254-256
State Department, 232, 234-235, 237, 243-244
State governments, 34, 62
Statespersons, 277, 281, 283, 288, 290
Statute law, 8
Statutory controls, limiting discretion through, 217-220
Stewart, Richard, 47, 110, 205, 209, 284, 290

Students Challenging Regulatory Agency Procedures (SCRAP), 255
Substantive rules, 21
Sunset reviews, 123-124
Supreme Court of the United States, 252-253, 260-262
Surveys, 128, 192, 194, 208-209

Task Force on Regulatory Relief, 78, 125-126, 184. *See also* Council on Competitiveness
Task forces. *See* Work groups
Team model of rulemaking, 82, 138, 282-283
Technical information, 147, 150
Technical manuals, 74, 81, 258
Tennessee Valley Authority, 233
Test rules, 58
Theory
    elements, 272-293
        contents of rules, 277-292
        reasons for rulemaking, 272-277
        rulemaking effects on government, 292-293
    value of, 271-272
Thomas, John, 278
Thomson, Ken, 182
Threshold analysis, 131, 140
Timeliness, 105-114
    effects of controversy, 108-110
    effects of inertia, 113-114
    effects of procedural requirements, 111
    effects of resource shortages, 111-112, 113
    management obstacles, 112-113
Tobacco industry, 192-193
Toxic Substances Control Act (TSCA), 58-59, 173
Toxic waste. *See* Hazardous materials regulation
Trade associations, 196, 197-199, 208, 210
Trade Representative, U.S., 236
Training programs, 132-133, 149-150
Transparency, 97-98
Transportation Department (DOT), 40, 105-106, 108, 109
    accountability, 263
    OMB review record, 232, 234-235, 237, 240
    OMB review time, 243-244

resource shortages, 112
sunset review, 124
Treasury Department, 115, 232, 234-235, 237, 243-244
Truman, Harry, 122
TSCA (Toxic Substances Control Act), 58-59, 173

Underground wells, 265
Uniform Guidelines on Employee Selection, 21, 23
Unions, 196, 197, 210
Used-car rules, 226

Vermont Yankee Nuclear Power Corp. v. Natural Resources Defense Council, 260-261
Vertical review, 82
Veterans Administration, 232, 234-235, 237, 243-244
Veterans' affairs, 12
Veto, 225-229, 248, 257
Vice President's Task Force on Regulatory Relief, 78, 125-126, 184. *See also* Council on Competitiveness

Wage and Hour Division, 45, 66
Walter-Logan Bill of 1940, 49, 169
Washington, George, 45
Washington Post, 1, 30
Water pollution rules, 207-208
Webster's New Collegiate Dictionary, 55
Weingast, Barry, 217, 221
West, William, 108, 193, 282, 283
Wilson, James Q., 177, 195
Woll, Peter, 49
Woodstove safety, 207
Work groups, 138-139, 140
leadership, 151-154
membership, 155-156
role in rule management, 150-158
role of senior officials, 156-157
Work plans, 132-133
Works Progress Administration, 13
Writer-editors, 137-139, 145
Written communications, 165-166

Zealots, 277, 281, 283, 288